T0381507

GROWING UP
Grandpa

Order this book online at www.trafford.com
or email orders@trafford.com

Most Trafford titles are also available at major online book retailers.

Print information available on the last page.

ISBN: 978-1-4269-0675-6 (sc)

Trafford rev. 08/22/2020

www.trafford.com
North America & international
toll-free: 844-688-6899 (USA & Canada)
fax: 812 355 4082

Growing Up Grandpa

Desmond E. Berghofer

If you find your task is hard,
　　Try, try, try again;
Time will bring you your reward.
　　Try, try, try again.

All that other people do,
Why, with patience, should not you?
Only keep this rule in view,
　　"Try, try, try again."

Author Unknown

For All My Grandchildren

In honour of times too important to be forgotten
and memories too precious to be lost

Benjamin	Jamie
William	Haley
Julya	Geoffrey
Layla	Chantelle
Dylan	Justin
Victoria	

And any who are yet to come

Whene'er a task is set to you
Don't idly sit and view it:
Nor be content, *to wish* it done,
Begin at once, and *do* it.

Author Unknown

Contents

Part 3: City School Years 217

Maps and Photos

A Note about the Quotations

The quotations appearing throughout the book were taken from the Queensland School Readers that were in use in Queensland schools in the 1940s. Like many of the stories and poems in the Readers, these quotations from named and anonymous sources were intended to inspire values of perseverance, courage, compassion, friendship, responsibility and humility. Those admonitions remain firm in mind all these many years later.

A Note about Spelling

The spelling of words in the text follows the English tradition in use in Australia at the time of the events described. Specifically, it follows *The Concise Oxford Dictionary of Current English*, edited by H.W. Fowler and F.G. Fowler, based on *The Oxford Dictionary*, Fourth Edition (1951).

A Note from Grandpa

Please Read This First

Hello. The boy in this story is me, 60 plus years ago. It's a story told by a child, and one thing you surely know is that children are notorious for stretching the truth. So, is this a completely accurate account of my boyhood? No, not exactly, and, indeed, how could it be?

However, because I was there, I can assure you about one thing, the places mentioned and described are all real, just as they were in the 1940s in this small slice of rural and urban Australia. As for the characters and events, well this is where the child's selective memory and active imagination are most at work. If you happen to encounter yourself in the story, please don't chastise the child if he has tried to make the story more interesting by embellishing the details. And who can say in human encounters whose memory is the more accurate?

The story set down here was written mainly for those who were not there, and in particular for those with family connections to me, who were born long after these years of what might seem to be a simple uncomplicated time. But, of course, it wasn't, as no time is for those who wind their way through it. What I have sought to do in allowing this child's voice to come through is to ensure that the magic of growing up in this particular place at that particular time is not lost to future generations, whose own lives can be enhanced, and perhaps enlightened, by the knowing.

So please, sit back, suspend judgment, enter this child's world, and enjoy.

Climbing

Never look behind, boys,
  When you're on the way;
Time enough for that, boys,
  On some future day.
  . . . .
Success is at the top, boys,
  Waiting there until
Patient, plodding, plucky boys
  Have mounted up the hill.

Author Unknown

Acknowledgments

When I set out to write the story of my early life, I had the challenge of bridging a time gap of more than 60 years and a distance gap of over 10,000 miles. It is now 2010 and the events in this story took place between 1942 and 1951. I wrote the story in Vancouver, Canada, but the setting was in Queensland, Australia.

To bridge the gaps of time and distance I received help from numerous sources. My sister, Gloria, who lives in Dinmore, Queensland, helped prompt and correct my memory on many details. She also supplied some of the old photographs included with the text. My oldest friend, Grant Williams (Willy), who lives in Cleveland, Queensland, filled in some facts about our exploits together as young boys. Conversations I had with others by phone and in person prompted me to make a number of changes to the original manuscript. Thank you all.

Two print resources of great value in fleshing out details of my life as a pupil at Athol School were the "Athol School" chapter in *Bunker's Hill State School Centenary: 100 Years of Memories* (1999) and Harold Newton's lovingly researched *Accent on Athol* (1998). Harold also kindly gave me permission to include the sketch of Athol School from his book in mine. I also had the opportunity to look at the one remaining copy of the History of Buranda School, which helped to confirm my memories of the years I spent there as a pupil. I should also thank the anonymous contributors to the store of knowledge on the Internet that allows one to travel through time and space and revisit the haunts of childhood. I could sit in Vancouver and check out the details of Redcliffe, Caloundra, and even how to get to Milmerran across the Condamine River. The Internet is truly a great tool for research.

On the production side, I must express my thanks to Pat Dobie, who typed the manuscript with incredible speed and accuracy. Pat was also an enthusiastic first reader. It encouraged me to continue writing knowing that someone so far removed from any of the events of the story could find the life of this young boy an interesting read. My three daughters, Sarah, Katie and Charlotte, also encouraged me with their interest. Sarah, in particular was most enthusiastic for her children to know the story of how their Grandpa grew up. That is how her sons, Ben and Will, come to appear on the covers and in the Prologue.

Another old friend, Earle Cross, with whom I have only recently reconnected, was also an enthusiastic reader of the manuscript and was kind enough to give me a testimonial for the cover. Thank you, Earle.

Lastly, as always, I must acknowledge how much the infectious enthusiasm of my wife, Geraldine Schwartz (Gerri), inspired me to persist. She grew up as a young girl on the streets of Montreal in Canada, a world so far removed from the farm at Athol that they could be on different planets. Yet Gerri was continually prompting me to write the next piece and read it to her as she followed the story with great interest, even when she didn't fully understand the Aussie slang or quirky sense of humour. (At her suggestion I have included the Glossary in order to explain the meaning of many of the words, expressions and terms used in the text for readers who might not be familiar with them). Her infectious laugh-out-loud enjoyment of my exploits as a young boy she never knew gave me many precious moments in the weeks and months it took to set the story down. Thank you, Gerri, very much for your love and encouragement.

Desmond Berghofer
December 2010
Vancouver

Foreword

Inside every adult is the child we were at 4, at 6, at 10, or the awkward adolescent we were at 12 or 13, but rarely on a life's journey are these children inside us called to attention. In Desmond Berghofer's "Grandpa," the young voice is so strong and authentic that our own inner children tumble into the road unbidden to witness the unfolding episodes heart first.

Interestingly, for a girl growing up in the big city streets of Montreal in Canada, the Australian farm, bush and seaside settings are strange exotic places; but the human childhood experiences of family, friends, imaginary playmate, and school teachers, and the fun of first experiences and adventures are so universal that the emotional context is immediately recognizable.

Once, visiting a museum in the city of Tralee in Ireland, I went to see the "Geraldine Experience." Sitting in open carts that moved along a track in the pitch black darkness, the audience learned the history of the Fitzgerald's and the Desmond's, travelling through a series of three dimensional dioramas as a disembodied voice narrated episode after episode, lit up large in front of our eyes as we passed.

In Berghofer's "Grandpa" the reader, like the audience described above, experiences episode after episode of growing up in an Australian farm family, then follows the farm boy to a big city school. But here the stories are alive, enhanced by the sound of Aussie voices and the songs of bush birds; by the texture, colours and smells of the farm, the school and the city; and especially by the dimension of a small boy's feelings and his commentary on what others must be feeling. The images and voice are so crystal clear that your own mind floods with old memories of your childhood self as you become a participant, rather than a spectator, in the unfolding drama.

The questions of childhood tumble out. Where do people babies come from? Who is God? Why do we have war? What is going to happen to me? How can I be a success?

The story's images are so vivid, and the child's narrative is so rich with detail that you can taste the hot pies, the cold sweet ice-cream, the milk and cakes offered as treats by various aunties, and the squashed watermelon on a hot summer's day. Your nose tingles with the farm smells of fresh cut hay, warm milk and cow dung.

The descriptions of firsts are entrancing, like riding your own horse to school and sitting in the classroom for the very first time. The childhood memories are alive with the magic of Christmas holiday celebrations on the farm, where the tables are laden with good food, and the company of special people adds greater warmth to the already hot summer day. The reader is entranced, charmed and fully engaged by the episode at Helidon Spa, the train ride to Aunty Joy's, the holidays at Redcliffe and Caloundra, the first try at steering the tractor in a freshly ploughed paddock, and the unforgettable story of the bees.

Even better is the evocation of the school experience, first in the one teacher school at Athol and later at Buranda Boys' School in Brisbane. For most of us the stories from the books of our childhood fuse together as a kind of mush of narrative and character. However, to read about the effect of the stories and poems in the Queensland School Readers on the mind of a young and growing child is to reawaken the wonder we had forgotten in those stories from our own childhood, and to understand, perhaps for the first time, the origins of the values and principles we express in our lives.

If this were all, then this book would be feast enough, but the best parts are the laugh-out-loud moments, like the episode in the textile store where the money and the bill are placed in a kind of internal shuttle that zings along a system of wires to a fellow like God in an upper window, who returns a chocolate frog to a mesmerized small boy; or the school composition written in a Don Quixote style about the head teacher who sets off with his companion on borrowed bikes to fight the monster tram.

In "Grandpa" the life and experiences of the Berghofers simply told reveal layer over layer of the feeling of this warm and decent family until you know them almost better than your own.

Even more important to the story is the underlying theme of the power of friendship in a boy's life. From this we recognize the intense desire, the respect, the value, and, yes, the love of the one special friend whose presence enriches every experience and makes life fun. In this book the powerful effect of friendship and relationship so openly narrated from such a young and tender heart transcends everything else. In "Grandpa" the descriptions of the adventures with friends touches the very soul.

If the intended purpose of this book is to illuminate the life of a child growing up on a farm on the Darling Downs in Queensland in the 1940s and early 1950s, it does so admirably. But the book transcends this purpose to reveal the tenderness and the eagerness for life, for love, for adventure and for learning about the life of the universal child in all of us.

This book feels like a series of books for children, a graphic novel, a television series, or a film. It deserves a wide audience of readers of every age. If this book is in your hands, you are in for a treat. Savour it.

Geraldine Schwartz

Prologue

How It Began

The Power of Kind Words

So, as up life's hill we journey,
    Let us scatter all the way
Kindly words, to be as sunshine
    In the dark and cloudy day.
Grudge no loving word, my brother,
    As along through life you go,
To the ones who journey with you;
    If you love them, tell them so.

Author Unknown

"Grandpa! Grandpa!" the bright cheery little boy voices greet me as I come in the door. It's only the voices at first, for the active bodies that belong to them are one floor above. They have been waiting for the "beep, beep, beep" of the alarm system as I let myself in with my own key. It's Grandpa Day, almost time for Daddy's cheesy egg breakfast, and Grandpa is here to join in.

Clump, clatter, bang! They are coming down the hardwood stairs, one of them dragging a truck or train engine in tow. As I take off my shoes, Ben's sunshine face full of light and laughter appears around the corner of the landing. "Grandpa!" he shouts again and catapults down the last few steps into my warm hug.

Close behind, twinkle-eyed mischief named Will appears, train engine clattering to the floor as he leaps off the last step into my arms. "Grandpa!" his enthusiasm is not to be outdone by Ben's. "Grandpa! Grandpa! Grandpa!" the chorus continues in cheerful falsetto. There is no question that Grandpa has arrived and been well greeted.

"Good morning, boys," I say. "What's on today?"

"Cheesy egg!" shouts Ben.

"Cheesy egg!" echoes Will.

"Well, let's go to it," I say, taking one small hand in each of mine as we squeeze three abreast up the narrow staircase. "Ouch!" I step on the discarded train engine.

"Why'd you say ouch, Grandpa?" asks Will.

"I stepped on Thomas."

"That's not Thomas, it's Gordon," Ben corrects me.

"Either way it hurts to step on him."

"I pick him up," says Will.

"Good boy. Now let's find Daddy."

At the top of the stairs we navigate a path through more toys and books strewn around the living room floor. Then up three more steps into the kitchen breakfast room. Ben has flown ahead. Will is dragging up the rear.

"Daddy, Grandpa is here for breakfast," cries Ben.

"Good morning, Grandpa," says Daddy who is busy ladling cheesy egg onto toast. Bibs on we breast up to the table, Will in his handcrafted wooden high chair made by Grampy, Ben on his booster seat. At two and four years of age the boys are the energy systems of the house.

"Umm! Daddy makes good cheesy egg," I say, tucking into my generous serving. "Is Mummy out running?"

"Yes, she's coaching," says Ben,

"Mummy's coaching," repeats Will.

"Well, it's nice to see everyone up early and busy. That's the way it was on the farm when I was your age."

"Did you live on a farm, Grandpa?" asks Ben.

"Yes, In Australia—a long, long way from here."

"We live in Canada, in Vancouver," says Ben.

"That's right. You're very smart to know that. Do you know what we did on the farm?"

"I dunno," Ben says. "Tell us."

"Well, we had a lot of animals. Can you guess what kind of animals, Will?"

Will screws up his face and thinks about that.

"I know, I know," says Ben.

"Let Will answer, Ben," says Daddy, listening in the background.

"One says moo," I suggest.

"A cow!" Will shouts.

"Yes lots of cows. What else do you think, Ben?"

"Horses and pigs."

"Yes, all of those."

"Elephants," suggests Will.

"No elephants."

"Elephants are in zoos, Will," says Ben, "not on a farm."

"Well, elephants live in the country in Africa," I say. "But that's another story. On our farm my Daddy and brother milked the cows and I made the butter."

"You made the butter?" Ben's face was on open mask of surprise and curiosity. "How did you do that?"

"Well, my Mummy put the cream into this round metal tub called a butter churn, and then you put the churn onto a stand with a handle and you turn the handle really fast to make the churn spin round and round. Vroom! Vroom! Vroom!" I demonstrate.

"Vroom! Vroom! Vroom!" the boys shout, turning their own make believe handles as hard as they can go.

"Faster than that," I say, turning harder, and the boys crank up their speed.

"Then all of a sudden," I say, slowing down, "the cream turns to butter and it goes slosh, slosh, slosh inside the butter churn. That's how you do it."

"Wow, let's do it again," Ben shouts.

"Maybe later, first we've got to finish our cheesy egg, or Daddy will be mad at us."

After breakfast when I am alone with the boys, Will brings me a book about farm animals off the bookshelf in the living room.

"Here's a cow," he says, opening it up. Ben crowds in to look.

"Yes, and here are all the other animals, too," I say, flipping the pages. "And here's the farmer on his tractor. My Daddy drove the tractor on our farm."

"Where's the butter churn?" asks Ben.

"I don't see a butter churn," I say.

"Well, can we do it again?" asks Ben. "Make the butter, I mean."

"All right, let's put in the cream. Put the churn on the stand. And turn the handle."

"Vroom! Vroom! Vroom!"

We have our imaginary butter churn going full speed when Mummy walks in the door.

"Well now, what are you guys up to with Grandpa?" she laughs.

"Mummy, Mummy," shouts Ben. "Grandpa is showing us how he made butter on the farm in Australia when he was a little boy."

"Yes, your Grandpa grew up on a farm," says Mummy. "I'm sure he can tell you lots of stories about that. Would you like to hear them?"

"Yes, please," they shout together.

"There you are, Grandpa," says Mummy, "you've got an audience. Now it's up to you."

I think about that for a moment.

"Well, maybe I could. There sure are a lot of things I could tell you. It's hard for you boys to imagine that I was once a little boy like you and I had to grow up to become a Grandpa. It's a long story."

"We don't have to hear it all at once, Grandpa," says Ben. "We have to have time to go out and play."

"Yes, Ben, you're right as ever," I say. "We'll take our time, but I promise to tell you about 'Growing Up Grandpa.'"

*****

And I have kept my promise.

Happy the man, and happy he alone,
He who can call today his own:
He who, secure within, can say,
Tomorrow do thy worst, for I have lived today

Author Unknown

Part I
The Early Years

He who loses wealth loses much; he who loses a friend loses more; but he who loses his courage loses all.

Cervantes

To improve the golden moment of opportunity, and catch the good that is within our reach, is the great art of life.

Author Unknown

Grandfather and the Cheese Factory

Grandfather was dead in his coffin. I saw him. He wore a white shirt and his big beard spread out all over it. His eyes were closed like he was asleep. But everyone said he was dead. I knew that dead was like a bird that my brother had shot, first warm and soft then later cold and stiff. But it didn't seem like that with Grandfather. It looked like he was asleep.

I remember seeing him only one other time. We were driving to the cheese factory in Dad's 1936 Chev utility with a load of milk in cans. Dad let me ride with him sometimes, not often, but sometimes. I don't know why Grandfather was there. He never came before. He didn't live with us. He had an old house just across from the school about a mile and a half away. I didn't know what a mile and a half was, but that's what everyone said. I had never been in Grandfather's house, but I saw it from the school when I went there for the picnic day when my brother and sister ran in the school races. I was too small to run much and sometimes I had asthma and couldn't breathe too good.

This day when Grandfather came to the cheese factory I stood in the middle of the seat with the gear lever sticking up out of the floor in front of me. Dad was a big man, and he squeezed in behind the steering wheel, smelling of cows and fresh milk from the morning's milking. Grandfather was old and breathing heavily as he climbed in next to me on the other side. Mum had dressed me in my blue overalls and combed my long curly hair, before she sent me up from the house to the cow bails to go to the cheese factory with Dad and Grandfather.

Grandfather looked at me through his round wet eyes above his long shaggy grey beard and said to Dad, "Is it a boy or a girl?"

I don't ever remember Grandfather Berghofer saying anything else in my life. Now he was dead in his coffin, and he seemed to be asleep. It was hot and stuffy in that room where he was, and there were a lot of other people there, mostly my aunts and uncles. Dad told me there were fourteen children in his family. That's more than ten, so it's a big number. He was number seven, I think. Grandfather must have had a lot of grandchildren, so maybe that was why he didn't know who I was, and whether I was a boy or a girl.

I liked going to the cheese factory. There were always a few other farmers there unloading their milk cans, and pouring the frothy white milk into the big vat inside, then getting their cans back and filling some of them with smelly whitish green whey for their pigs. I would get out of the ute and watch everything going on. The other farmers were always cheerful at that time in the morning. They grinned at me out of sunburnt faces, and sometimes poked me and ruffled my curly hair with their rough hands. I was usually the only kid around. I suppose all the others had gone to school, like my brother, Gordon, and sister, Gloria—except for my younger sister, Val, who was too small and stayed home with Mum.

I would wander around inside the factory. I didn't really know how things worked. There were big paddles moving the milk around, and somehow white lumps of curds would collect in another big vat. I suppose it was something like the way we made butter at home. That was my job.

Mum would pour fresh cream into the butter churn. Dad had skimmed the cream off the top of the milk in the milk cans that morning from last night's milking. The butter churn was round and silver coloured and made of steel like a space ship. There was a paddle inside for the cream to slosh against as the churn went round and round. I would put the churn onto its stand where there was a handle that I could turn and make the churn spin round and round. I would pretend it was a spaceship taking off from Earth and travelling through space. I could make it go faster and faster the harder I turned, and we would whiz crazily past the moon and all the stars in the sky until my arms were about to fall off from the turning. Then suddenly would come the slosh, slosh, slosh of the lumps of butter that had somehow come out of the cream and left behind the thin watery butter milk. That was the end of the space travel, and I would take the churn inside to Mum, who would put the butter into a bowl and squeeze all of the butter milk out of it with a wooden spoon.

I suppose it was something like that for the cheese, too, except they must have done something different to get cheese curds instead of lumps of butter. And they didn't have any spinning churns that I remember. That would really have been something to see—a giant spinning churn like a real space ship. But that wasn't how they did it. The man who knew all the secrets was the manager of the factory. He was a big friendly man with a cheerful face and not much hair. Dad called him Jock. I called him Mr. Rosenberger. He told me they squeezed all the milk and stuff out of the cheese curds and let it go hard inside round moulds. Then they would take it out of the moulds and set it in blocks of different sizes on racks in the cheese room. All the blocks were covered in red rind and stamped with a special stamp that said Rockview Cheese Factory. We always had a lot of it at home. I didn't like it much, but Dad said it was the best cheese you could get.

The cheese room was cool and dark with all those big blocks of cheese on the racks. I think it would have been a better place for Grandfather to be lying in his coffin than that other stuffy place. I suppose it would have been a surprise for Mr. Rosenberger to come in and find him there. But it would have been better for Grandfather. Much more peaceful and cool for him to rest.

I think there was what people called a funeral later on, and after that they took Grandfather in his coffin away somewhere, and we all went and had some sandwiches. I remember a lot of my aunties crying and looking very sad.

"Where do people go when they die?" I asked Mum.

"If they have been good they go to Heaven," she said.

"Is everyone asleep in Heaven?" I asked.

"What makes you ask that?" said Mum.

"Because Grandfather looked like he was asleep," I said.

One of my aunties was listening, and she knelt down to look at me. She was very pretty and smelled nice. She took my hand.

"You're right, Desie," she said. "Your Grandfather is at rest." She smiled, but then started to cry, and I didn't know what to do, so I started to cry, too. After that we all had some sandwiches, and I had a glass of cold lime cordial. I still didn't know about Heaven, and I had it a bit mixed up in my head with the cheese room at Rockview Cheese Factory. Whenever I went there after that, I always looked to see if Grandfather was there, but I never found him.

In with the Pigs

When we went back home from the cheese factory we always brought some whey for our pigs. It was a long drive. I don't know how many miles, but I think Dad said it was five or six. There was a long hill going down on the way back, and Dad would turn the engine off and let the ute run down hill on its own. It was quiet and we whistled along like the wind. Dad said he was saving petrol because of the war, and you couldn't always get what you needed.

The pigs lived in yards up behind the cow bails. I think you called them sties, but I don't know why. There was a big vat, and Dad would lift the heavy cans of whey up and pour them into the vat. I don't know how he could do that. He was very strong. I couldn't even move the cans they were so heavy.

All the time Dad was unloading the whey the pigs would be squealing like mad, because they knew their breakfast was coming. I would wander around looking at them over the top of the wood fence. There were three or four long pens with pigs of different sizes in them. My favourite was the one with the big mother pig—I think you called her a sow—and all her little pigs, maybe ten or more. Next to her was a pen with the big father pig in it. He was called a boar, and he was huge and would push his big nose against the wood fence between them and grunt and snort and rattle the fence. Sometimes Dad would let him in with the mother pig when there weren't any little pigs. And then after that there would be more little pigs, and the father pig would be put back in his own pen.

All the pens had a long trough made out of a hollowed out tree with the ends blocked up. Dad would carry the whey in buckets from the vat and slosh it into the troughs, and the pigs would snuffle and snort and squeal and grunt and push each other and get their noses down into the trough to drink the whey. After a while, they would raise their heads with the white whey dribbling out of their mouths, and look at me with their piggy eyes, then put their heads down again for more food. Dad would mix some grain in with the whey, and sometimes there were other slops, and it would be a great feast, and all the pigs would have such good fun.

The little pigs with their mother were just learning how to drink from the trough. Before that they got their milk from their mother, when she would lie in the shade in the shed at the back of the pen, and they would crawl all over her, pushing and shoving to get one of her big juicy tits. I would have liked to get a closer look, but Dad told me I wasn't to go into the pen, because the mother might knock me over and bite me.

But this morning the little pigs were bigger and starting to feed from the trough for themselves, except for the smallest one, who didn't seem to know quite what to do. He tried to drink from his mother, but she just kicked him out of the way while she tucked in for her own breakfast with the other little pigs. So this smallest one was running around in circles and didn't know what to do. I decided to help.

I wasn't supposed to get into the pen, but I had to help the poor little pig. So I climbed over the fence. The mother pig just looked at me out of one eye and kept on feeding. I circled around behind her and tried to grab the little pig, who was over by the fence where the big boar was snorting and banging against the boards from the other side. I could see his big eye staring at me through the fence, but I knew he couldn't get me, so I grabbed the little pig to take him over to the trough to show him what to do.

It was really muddy in the pig pen, because it had been raining overnight. The pigs love to play around in the mud, and they had it all churned up into a thick gooey mess. I sank over the tops of my shoes into the mud, and fell over a few times, so I think I was pretty dirty by the time I caught the pig. He squealed a lot when I caught him, and his little legs were kicking like mad as he tried to get away. But I told him it was all right and I was just trying to help, and I carried him over to the end of the trough and dipped his nose into the whey and scooped some of it up with my hand into his mouth. He sputtered and choked a bit, but then he started to drink on his own and stopped squirming, so I could let him go.

All at once it felt very peaceful and quiet in the pig pen. Well, maybe not quiet, because there was still a lot of snorting and squealing, but I felt really good, and knew the pigs were my friends, and we all shared something. I don't mean the food, because I wouldn't want to share that, but there was just this feeling of us all belonging together. The old mother pig came over on the other side of the trough. She looked at me with both big eyes, and shoved her nose into the trough to help the little one drink and let me pat her on her nose. It was wet and warm and very hairy, but it felt good to touch. That was when Dad saw where I was.

"Desmond, what the bloody hell are you doing?" he yelled.

With one big bound he came over the fence and picked me up in his big hand by the back of the overalls. He practically threw me over the fence out of the pig pen.

"You silly little bugger," he yelled some more. "I told you never to go into the pig pen."

"But I was just helping the little one," I said. "He didn't know how to drink and I showed him."

Dad quieted down a bit, but I knew he was still mad at me. "Look at you," he said, "You're covered in mud. Get back down to the house. Your mother will skin you alive when she sees you."

I ran away down to the house. Mum met me at the door before I could go inside. (I looked to see if she had a knife to skin me alive, but she didn't). She just took one look and whisked me into the shower room under the water tank, where there was a big tin dish that Dad used to wash up in before he came into the house after working. Mum stripped off my overalls, and dunked me into the cold rain water from the tank to clean me up. As she rubbed me dry she said, "Now, tell me all about it." And I did, and it felt good. Mum just smiled and took me into the house and dressed me in clean overalls, and gave me a nice breakfast of corn flakes and sausages. It had been a really good morning.

The Cats and My Imaginary Friend

There were a lot of other animals on the farm, and I tried to make friends with all of them. My favourite friends were the cats. We had a lot of them. They lived in the barn, where their job was to catch the mice that would chew holes in Dad's bags of grain. I think they did a good job, because we didn't see many mice, but the cats always looked skinny and hungry, so whenever I could I would take scraps of food from the house to feed them. They liked that and would follow me around. My brother would make fun of me for always having a string of cats following me around. But I didn't care. Sometimes I would sit down and play with them for a long time, and they would crawl all over me, making this loud purring sound, and going backwards and forwards for me to rub them from the tops of their heads to the tips of their tails.

I had one special cat. She was a mother and had a lot of little kittens, who grew up to join all the other cats in the barn. But the mother cat stayed near the house, and would usually be waiting for me when I came out. I always tried to have some pieces of meat or cheese in my pocket to give her. But I never had enough, so I would try to think of other ways to feed her. I knew she liked grasshoppers, and in summertime we usually had a lot of grasshoppers jumping around, so I would lead her over to the grass paddock near the house, and together we would crawl through the long yellow grass looking for grasshoppers.

She was a browny-black colour with patches of yellow, so I called her Caramel, like the toffee that's very sweet and sticks to your teeth. As soon as we got into the grass, the grasshoppers would jump out of our way, and Caramel would crouch down watching very carefully, then quick as a flash, she would pounce and catch a grasshopper, and I could hear it crunch up in her mouth as she ate it. I didn't really like killing things, but Dad said the grasshoppers were pests like the mice, so I thought it was all right to help Caramel catch them. While she was catching one on her own, I would crawl along in the grass, watch where one landed, then grab it with my hand. Caramel would come over right away, and I would give it to her, and she would crunch it up. I don't think it could have hurt the grasshopper very much, because she ate it so quickly, usually head first so the long back legs would be sticking out of her mouth, then she would swallow it down.

We would do this over and over, until I thought Caramel had eaten enough grasshoppers, then I would lie down on my back with the long grass waving over my face. I would just lie there very still in the warm sun, looking up at the blue sky. Caramel would cuddle in beside me, purring loudly, and I would stroke her and lie there listening to the wind in the grass and the birds in the trees not far away. I thought this was a very nice place to be.

After a while, I would feel that there was someone else there with me, not just Caramel, but a friend I couldn't see. I called him Triloaf. I don't know how I knew his name. Maybe he told me, because I know I could hear his voice in my head. But anyway I knew his name was Triloaf, and he was always with me, even if I couldn't see him. Maybe he was an angel. I had heard about angels, but I know that Triloaf didn't have wings or anything like that. He was just a friend, who was always there, and I could talk to him when there was no one else around.

Triloaf would go with me on adventures. There was a pile of old boards at the back of the house. Dad said they were from the old house we used to live in before our new house was built. It's funny I don't remember the old house, but I do remember the carpenters working on building the new house. Mum had a picture of me sitting on the verandah of the old house, so I must have been there, but I just don't remember it.

Anyway, the pile of old boards was a great place for adventures, and Triloaf and I would go crawling under it, pretending we were in a cave looking for treasure, then over it, balancing on the long planks like pirates out on the ocean. I had never seen the ocean, but I knew about it from stories I heard on the radio, and from books that my brother had. I couldn't read the stories, but I could look at the pictures and the ones about pirates were among my favourites.

One day I was running along the pile of boards, chasing after pirates with a little sword I had made from a broken axe handle and a piece of rag, when I took a big leap over a gap in the boards, slipped and tumbled off the boards down on the ground with a thump. I think I hit my head, because I could feel blood all over my face. I was really frightened, and I knew I would get into trouble with Dad, because he told me not to play on the boards. But right away Triloaf was there, and he told me not to worry, because he would take care of me. Suddenly it didn't seem so bad, and I could get up and run to the shower room and wash the blood away. I had to tell Mum that I had an accident, but she said it didn't look so bad and that I must have someone looking after me. I never told her about Triloaf, but I know she was right.

The Chooks and the Goanna

Another one of my jobs was to feed the chooks. I couldn't do it on my own so my sister, Gloria, helped me. Actually, I suppose, I was helping her, because she was two years older than me. Before I was old enough I think she helped my brother, Gordon, but then he went on to do more important things, like help Dad with the milking, and Gloria and I fed the chooks.

We carried two slop buckets of scraps from the kitchen and dumped them in the chook yard. The yard was fenced all round with wire netting, so that the foxes couldn't get in to grab the chooks while they were asleep on the roosts under the tin roof at one end of the yard. During the day, we let the chooks out to run around wherever they liked, but at night they went in to roost, and we would close the gate to keep them in.

As we carried the buckets of slops to feed them, the chooks would come running from everywhere. They knew it was meal time. There were some big old hens, mostly red and black, but some white, too. There were also some smaller ones. I think you called them bantams, and one big rooster, red and black striped with a big red cone on the top of his head, and long tail feathers almost dragging on the ground at the back. He was always bossing the others around, especially one or two smaller roosters, but the hens, too. He had an evil eye, flicking open and shut, open and shut, while his head darted from side to side. Then he would rush in to attack and all the others would scurry out of his way.

But he didn't scare me, even though he was as tall as my waist, and I expect his beak could really hurt if he got you. I would just get in amongst all of them while they picked at the food, and Gloria went off to get some grain. If the rooster got too bossy, I would stare him down, and he always backed off. He might have been the boss of the chooks, but he wasn't the boss of me. Actually, after a while everything was usually pretty quiet, with the chooks feeding and me standing in the middle of them.

One day when Gloria came back with the grain, I said to her: "I think the chooks think I'm one of their family."

"Well, you're silly enough," she replied.

I didn't know what she meant by that.

"It's just like the pigs and the cats," I said. "They all like me, because I like them. We're all good friends."

"Yes, well I'd watch that rooster if I was you," Gloria said.

I turned around and saw the rooster taking a run at me.

"Cock-a-doodle-doo!" I shouted at him and stamped my foot. He darted away, and I'm sure I heard all the chooks cackling. They really liked me.

The other part of that job was gathering the eggs. Dad had made boxes under the roosts with straw in them for the hens to climb in and lay their eggs. Some would do that, but others liked to make their nests in different places—under the tank stand, in the machinery shed, in the grass—and we would have to go and find them. I usually knew where to look. Maybe the chooks sent me messages in my head, because I was their friend.

One day when I was out looking for eggs there was a big—commotion, I think is the word—in the grass at the far end of the chook pen, and a couple of hens came flapping out of the grass. I went in to take a look, and just as I got there, a great big goanna as long as a broom stick rushed out of the grass with an egg in his mouth, and darted up one of the tall fence posts, and stopped out of my reach at the top, looking at me while he munched the egg.

"That's all right, Goey," I said. "You can have that one, but don't get greedy." It was lucky for him that my Dad or brother wasn't there with a gun, or that would have been the end of him. I never told them, and I don't remember that the goanna ever came back.

Up in the Cow Bails

We had only one dog on the farm. His name was Jim. He was black with a few brown patches on his face and feet. He was big and strong, and could easily knock me over if I played with him. Dad didn't like us to play too much with Jim, because he was a working dog. He lived in his kennel up by the cow bails, and his job was to round up the cows for milking.

Dad had Jim trained so that no matter how far away the cows were, he would go and get them. Sometimes they were way up in the top paddock, so you could hardly see them. Dad would say, "Jim go get the cows," and off he would go like a flash, running as fast as he could, until he was just a little black dot. Sometimes he would stop, not sure where to go, and Dad would use his big voice to say "Go on" or "Go back," and Jim would set off again. He had to be sure not to miss any of the cows, and not to bring them in too fast, or that would shake up their milk or something. Sometimes a cranky cow would go charging at Jim, but he would just duck out of the way, then chase her in with the rest. He was a really good cow dog.

When he got all the cows into the cow yard, my job was to close the big wooden gate, so they couldn't get out again. Then Jim would jump all over me, because he was very pleased with himself. We would go round to the milking shed where Dad and my brother Gordon were setting up, and Dad would give Jim a big feed of milk in an upside down lid from a milk can.

I didn't always help with the milking because I was too small, but when I did, it was always in the afternoon. Gordon would come home from school, and after he had a feed he would go and start setting things up for milking. Dad would come in from wherever he was working, and send Jim for the cows. That's the way it was every day. Then they had to do it again in the morning, while I was still asleep, and before Gordon went to school. Both Dad and Gordon said it was a pain in the neck, but the milking had to be done.

On the days that I helped, my job was to keep the cows moving up to the front, and chase the next one into a bail when Dad or Gordon let one out after milking. Sometimes I would wash the cows' tits with a tit rag and a dish of warm water. You had to make sure to get all the mud or poop off the tits before Dad or Gordon put the milking machines on. These were like four cups hooked up to two rubber hoses. One hose would suck out the milk, and the other would carry it away to the vat in the milk room. We had four bails with two cows in each bail, and Dad and Gordon had to keep switching the milking machines from cow to cow as each one finished.

If one of the cups came loose, it would suck air, and you had to move fast to fix it, or all four cups would fall off, and the cow would stamp all over them, and they would get dirty, and it would be a big mess. I had to rush and shove up the cup if it started to suck air. If I was too slow and the machines fell off, Dad would get mad at me. Sometimes the cow would shit all over the place while it was in the bail, and I had to scrape it out with a scraper with a long handle. If more than one cow shit at the same time I was in a panic. Sometimes I slipped over in the warm smelly stuff, and that wasn't very nice.

And it was always very noisy, because the big engine that did all the sucking was right beside the cow bails, and it was thump, thump, thumping all the time. Sometimes the cows were bellowing, because they were upset about something, or a calf that had been taken away from its mother would be bleating.

And I was rushing around trying to do all my jobs as best I could. I didn't really like it very much, and I would try to get out of it as much as I could.

The best part was when the last cow was let out of the bail, and the engine was turned off, and everything was suddenly quiet. We still had to clean things up to be ready for the morning milking, but at least there was nothing more to worry about going wrong.

Sometimes Dad would let me feed one of the calves that had been taken away from its mother. He would give me a bucket half full of milk, and I could go in the pen with the calf, and try to get it to put its dumb head into the bucket. It would bang the bucket around with its head and almost knock me over. But after a while, I would get it to calm down, and it would slurp up the milk, and I would rub its back and talk to it. I liked that.

The calves were usually born out in the paddock, and would come in with their mothers until they were old enough to be taken away. I remember once, though, the cow was having trouble trying to get the calf to come out from inside her, and Dad had to bring her into the cow yard after milking to help her. He said the calf was turned round the wrong way, and he had to reach up inside her and turn the calf around. The cow was bellowing like crazy, and Dad had her in a pen so she couldn't get away, and Gordon was holding her head, and I was running around bringing water and rags. Then I saw the calf's head coming out, then its body and its legs, all slimy and bloody. But it was alive and could sort of stand up a bit, then fall over. Its mother stopped bellowing, and Dad washed them and left them together in the yard, and gave the mother some hay to eat, and the calf started to suck on its mother's tits. I thought Dad was just about the smartest person in the world that he could make things come out all right like that. I had never seen a calf born before, and I thought it was really special, and most of all because the calf was all right, thanks to Dad.

The Mystery of Babies

I might have known something about how calves and pigs and kittens were born from inside their mothers, but I didn't know much about how a people baby was born. I remember one day hearing that my Aunty Joy was going to have a baby. She lived on a farm a long way away from us, but she was visiting at my Grandfather's and Granny's home in Toowoomba. This was the big town where we used to go every week to shop. This was my other Grandfather, not the one that died. He was Grandfather Grundy, because he was Mum's father. Granny Grundy was Mum's mother. They were very old. Granny always wore a long spotted dress, and Grandfather wore a flannel shirt and smoked a pipe. They lived at 10 Lilley Street in Toowoomba.

Our farm was at Athol. It would take a long time to get to Toowoomba in the ute. Dad said it was fourteen miles. I would always ride in the back of the ute, sometimes on my own, and sometimes with Gordon and Gloria, if they weren't going to school that day. We had to be careful not to fall out of the back of the ute as Dad drove along over the bumpy dirt roads. My little sister, Val, rode inside with Mum.

There were wooden seats on both sides of the back of the ute that we could sit on, but if it was too rough, or if I was on my own, I sat on the wooden floor. It was a pretty rough ride, but usually we had some bags to sit on, so it wasn't too bad. If it was raining, we had to crawl under a big sheet called a tarpaulin. But mostly it was bright and sunny, and we would whiz along enjoying the breeze that blew the flies and all the other bugs away. I wore a big round helmet, and I had to hold it on tight so it wouldn't blow off my head.

I remember this day when we came to Granny and Grandfather's place Aunty Joy was there. I didn't know who she was at first. I had seen her a few times before, and she was always thin and pretty like Mum. But this day she was really fat. I thought it must be something to do with the baby, but no one explained anything to me, so I don't think I said anything, but I was really puzzled. There was no baby around as far as I could see, but everyone was talking about it. I still don't know where the baby was, but I did hear later that it was a boy, and his name was Barry, and he was my cousin.

Grandfather and the Loony

Grandfather had a wonderful vegetable garden in the back yard. The soil in Toowoomba was bright red, not like the dark black soil out on the farm. Grandfather had the soil piled up high in long beds with tracks in between, where you could walk to get at the vegetables. He grew everything—radishes, potatoes, beans, peas, cauliflower, tomatoes, cabbage, lettuce, carrots, beet roots, onions, and a lot of others I can't remember. Whenever we came into town, we would load up a sugar bag full of fresh vegetables to take home, but it never seemed to make any difference to the garden. There was always plenty more.

Grandfather showed me how to plant bean seeds, which were big enough for me to hold in my fingers and push down into the dirt, then water with a watering can. I would look at the seeds with wonder as they were all lined up in their little trench like soldiers, before we covered them over with the red dirt and watered them. I wondered how anything could come out of those brown seeds, but sure enough, when I came back to visit in a week or two, there would be these tiny bean plants poking their heads up through the soil. I thought it was amazing that the plants could come out of those little seeds, and grow into bushes with long green beans on them. I felt lucky to be in a place where bean bushes and kittens and pigs and calves could all come from somewhere, and grow up to be big and strong. I wondered if that was the way it was with people babies, like my cousin Barry, except that I never saw him, and I still didn't know why Aunty Joy was so fat.

Grandfather had a big pile of stinky stuff under a tree near the vegetable garden. There were smelly oranges, and rotten vegetables, and watermelon skins, and all kinds of slop from the kitchen, just like we fed to the chooks on the farm. But Grandfather didn't have any chooks, so he just threw everything onto this smelly pile, and covered it with a bit of dirt. He said that after a while it would turn into soil, and he would put it on the garden. In the meantime the flies sure liked it a lot, as well as the long wriggly worms that you could grab with your fingers and stretch out until they were twice as big. There was always something interesting to see and find in Grandfather's garden.

Sometimes I would stay with Granny and Grandfather for a holiday. I liked that a lot, especially because Aunty Holly lived there, too, and she was always a lot of fun. She was my Mum's youngest sister. She was kind of big and cuddly, and was always smiling and laughing and ready to play games. I got to sleep with her, too, in her big bed, because there were no beds for little kids like me at Granny and Grandfather's.

And there was a big mystery, too, at Granny and Grandfather's place that no one could solve. Grandfather was always complaining that someone would get into his tool shed at night, and move his tools around, and mix everything up. Grandfather called whoever did it "that bloody loony," and said that if he ever caught him he would nail him up on the wall of the shed. I wondered how Grandfather could do that because he was so old, but I could see that he was mad enough to try.

But the problem was no one ever saw the loony. He always came at night, when everyone was asleep. And he didn't come every night, so Grandfather would never know until he went out to the tool shed in the morning to find out. One morning he came in really mad, because the loony had taken an old car tire out of the tool shed, and hung it on the clothes line, then tied a string to it, and fixed the other end of the string to the inside door handle of the shed, so that when you opened the door it pulled the string, and the tire came crashing down off the clothes line onto a box of ripe tomatoes that the loony had put underneath. It was a big red squishy mess, and Grandfather was mad as hell. He said the loony had gone too far this time, and he was going to get him.

Grandfather had this big dingo trap that my Uncle Bill had given him. It had strong steel jaws that opened up when you set it, then snapped shut if anyone stepped into it. Granny and Aunty Holly said he shouldn't set it, because someone might get hurt, and after all, the loony was only having a bit of fun. But Grandfather was too mad to listen, and that night he set the trap on the floor of the tool shed, and left the door a little bit open, so the loony would go inside in the dark and get caught.

When Aunty Holly put me to bed, she said she was really worried about what Grandfather had done, and we could hear Granny and Grandfather arguing about it in their bedroom across the hall. Later that night when it was very dark, I woke up and couldn't get back to sleep. Aunty Holly was snoring a bit, so I knew she was asleep. I crept out of bed in my pyjamas, and decided I would go and take a look to see if anything had happened in the tool shed.

It was really scary as I felt my way along the walls and out to the back door, then down the steps to the back of the house. I could just see the door of the tool shed still a little bit open, but I thought it was wider than how Grandfather had left it. I thought the loony might be inside and about to get caught, and I remembered what Granny had said that it might break his leg, and I was worried. So I grabbed a stick that was leaning against the tool shed, and crept over to the door, and pulled it a bit wider open, and said real loud, "Watch out!"

All of a sudden there was this great commotion, then a loud scream, and two big cats came hurtling out of the door. They knocked the stick out of my hand, and I fell back into some bushes. The next thing I saw was a big shape coming down the side of the house. He came right past me, and I saw that it was Grandfather, and he was carrying a big yard broom. He went up to the door of the tool shed and yelled out, "Who's there?" and shoved the head of the broom in through the door. There was a loud snap, and Grandfather said "Damn!" and staggered backwards waving the broom handle, but I could see it had lost its head. Then everything was quiet, and Grandfather crept back to the tool shed and turned on the light. "Damn," he said again, "It took the head right off!"

I didn't wait to hear any more, but jumped out of the bushes and streaked down the side of the house, and through the back door, and jumped into bed beside Aunty Holly, who was still snoring away. Next morning at breakfast Granny asked Grandfather: "Well, did you catch the loony?"

"No," said Grandfather. "I've decided not to use that trap. It's no good."

I didn't say a word, and I don't think Grandfather ever tried to catch the loony again.

A Present from God

Toowoomba was a very big town with a long main street called Ruthven Street, and a lot of other streets that you could take if you wanted to go to other places, like Granny and Grandfather's house at Number 10 Lilley Street, or to Picnic Point at the top of the Range, where you could look down the scary winding road that went to Brisbane a long way away. I had never been down that road, but Dad said you had to be very careful and drive in second gear, so the ute would not go too fast and crash over the side of the road.

When we went to town, we would go straight to Granny and Grandfather's for lunch. Mum would bring some corned meat, and Grandfather would have lots of vegetables, so we could all have a good meal. Then we would go back to Ruthven Street to do our shopping. There were a lot of big stores on Ruthven Street, like Woolworth's and Penny's and Coles'. Mum called them chain stores. Things there were cheap. Sometimes, if I had sixpence or even a shilling to spend, I could buy lollies and a little toy and a comic book. I couldn't read the words in the comic books, but I could work out the story from the pictures. My favourites were "The Lone Avenger" and "The Phantom." They always wore masks so you couldn't tell who they were, but they always caught the crooks and put them in gaol.

There was a really interesting store called Piggott's, or something like that. They sold clothes and materials for sewing that Mum liked. I would go in there with her, because she didn't want me to get lost in the big town. I didn't think much of the clothes, but I really liked the way you would pay when you bought something. There were these ladies in white blouses and black skirts and frizzy hair behind a counter all around the store. A lady would help Mum find what she wanted, then go to the counter and write it all very carefully on a piece of paper, and tell Mum how much it was. Mum would give the lady some money, and the lady would put the money and the piece of paper in a cup, and fix it on to a long line above her head. These lines ran all over the store like a big spider's web, but they all ended up in the same place, way up high over our heads, where there was a little room with open windows that the lines would go through. I could see someone sitting inside the room, and I wondered if it was Mr. Piggott, or maybe God.

When the serving lady had fixed the cup with Mum's money and the piece of paper inside it to the line, she would pull a cord and let it go with a thwang, and the cup would take off, and go zinging along the line right up inside this little room over our heads. Other ladies in different parts of the store would do the same thing for other customers, so these cups would be whizzing along their lines from all over the store. When they went inside the window at the top, they would stop with a ping, so you could hear whiz-ping, whiz-ping coming from all over the place.

After a while, the cup would come zinging back down the line to the serving lady, who would take it down off the line, open it up, and take out the piece of paper and some money inside. Mum said that was her change. She would smile and say thank you to the lady, and put whatever she had bought into her shopping bag, and we would go outside.

But I could never forget those cups going thwang, zing, ping along those lines. One day I thought I would like to give it a try. Mum had told me to sit down by the door while she went shopping. There was a serving lady standing around with nothing to do, so I went over to her. I only had a penny in my pocket, and I didn't want to buy anything, but I knew you had to put money in the cup to make it work. So I asked the lady if I could put my penny in the cup, and send it up the line.

She smiled at me and took out her little notebook.

"What's your name, dear?" she asked.

"Desmond," I said.

"That's a nice name, Desie," she said, then wrote something in her notebook, and tore off the piece of paper, and put it with my penny in the cup.

"Can I pull the cord?" I asked.

"Certainly, dear," the lady said, so I climbed up onto the counter and pulled as hard as I could on the cord, and let it go with a thwack. But I couldn't have pulled hard enough, because the cup didn't move. It just sat there, and I wondered what was wrong.

"Try again, dear," the lady said.

But it didn't make any difference. The cup just sat there. I almost cried. I heard someone say "Oh dear," and looked around and saw the other ladies in the shop in their white blouses and black skirts and frizzy hair looking at me and smiling.

"Once more and we should do it," the serving lady said to me. This time she held my hand and helped me pull the cord back as far as it would go, and we let it go thwack, and away went the cup, zinging up the line and landing ping in the little room above. All the ladies in the store clapped and said, "Good on you, dear", "That's the shot", and "Good boy."

I felt really pleased with myself, and wanted to see what would happen next. After a while the cup came zinging back down the line, and the serving lady took it down and showed me what was inside. "Oh boy," I said. There was a big chocolate frog wrapped in cellophane with a big shiny penny much brighter than the one I sent up and a piece of paper. The lady took the piece of paper and read it to me.

"Hello, Desie," it said. "This frog will keep you hopping. Good boy!" She read it loud enough so the other serving ladies could hear, and they all clapped again.

I looked up along the line, and saw this nice old man with grey hair smiling down and waving. I waved back at him. I thanked the lady, and jumped down off the counter, and ran to find Mum.

"Mum, Mum," I said when I found her. "Look what I've got. A chocolate frog! It came back down the line with a shiny new penny. And God smiled and waved to me."

I Get My Leg Pulled

The last things we bought before we left town to go home were the meat from the butcher's shop and groceries from the grocery store. They were next to each other, and usually Dad would come into the shops with us, because we were on the way home, and he had nothing else to do. We would buy just enough meat to last us a week, because it was hard to keep it fresh on the farm in our safe that hung from a hook in a cool place. We bought lamb chops and pork chops and some steaks and a roll of roast beef or a leg of mutton for Sunday's dinner. I also liked the big red savs and the skinny frankfurters and the beef sausages that the butcher made in his shop, and that Dad said you wouldn't want to know what he put in them. Sometimes we would get sheep's brains and pigs' trotters for a special treat.

The butcher was a fat man with a round face, and he wore an apron with blood all over it. He had a big chopping block behind the counter and what you called a big meat cleaver that he would use to chop up the meat. I think that's why you called them chops. There was sawdust all over the floor behind the counter to soak up the blood. The butcher would wrap our meat up in white paper first then in newspaper. He was friendly and smiling, and sometimes gave me a piece of sausage to eat.

In the grocery store we would buy bags of flour and sugar and tins of stuff like fruit and jam. The grocer's name was Mr. Wright, and his wife also worked in the store. They were friends of Mum and Dad and would sometimes visit the farm with their kids, who didn't know much about being on a farm. Mr. Wright always wore a white apron that was very clean, not like the butcher's, and smelled of flour. Mum would give him some coupons for the stuff we bought, because there was a war on somewhere, and people said things were rationed. Mr. Wright would put our groceries in a cardboard box, and Dad would carry it out and put it in the back of the ute.

On the way home we would stop at a place called Drayton not far from Toowoomba. We stopped to buy petrol for the ute so we could get home in time for Dad and Gordon to do the milking.

On the day I got my chocolate frog we stopped at Drayton as usual. I was in the back of the ute with the meat and the groceries and some rope and tools and other things Dad had bought, and the other parcels Mum had bought, and the sugar bag of vegetables we got from Grandfather.

Mum and Dad went inside the store with Val, and I watched while this man put petrol in the ute. It was a hot day and he was wearing a Jackie Howe and a pair of shorts and an old beat up hat. He had to pump the petrol up from somewhere by pulling on a long lever on the side of the petrol pump. You could see the reddish brown petrol come up slowly inside the glass top of the pump, where there were marks on the side that told you how many gallons of petrol you had.

While he was pulling slowly on the lever, he looked at me and said, "G'day, mate. Ow yer goin?"

"I'm orright," I said.

"Good on yer," he said, then after a bit, "Wot d'you know?"

"Not much," I said.

"Thas orright," he said, "me neither."

I watched the petrol come slowly up inside the glass top of the pump, until it got to five gallons, then the man stopped pumping. He took the long hose on the side of the pump with a nozzle on the end of it, and put the nozzle inside the hole on the ute where the petrol went. Dad had already unlocked the cap with his car keys, so the man could take it off. He pulled a lever on the petrol pump, and the petrol started to drain down into the petrol tank of the ute, which was under the floor boards where I was standing.

"Where does the petrol come from?" I asked the man.

"Outa the ground," he said.

"How does it get there?"

"I dunno. There's this great big ocean of petrol sloshin' around under the ground, and we just pump it out."

"If there's an ocean of petrol, why does Dad say he can't always get what he wants, and he turns the engine off while we coast down the hill on the way back from the cheese factory?"

"Well, that's becos the Japs and the Germans are stealin' it from us. They're pumpin' it all away, and we have to fight 'em to stop 'em."

"Is that what the war is?"

"Yeah, somethin' like that."

The man finished filling the petrol tank and put the cap back on. Then he came over closer, and looked at what I had in my hand in the back of the ute.

"Watcha got there?" he asked.

"A chocolate frog," I said. "God gave it to me."

"Is that so?" said the man. "Yer wanna trade?"

"Wot for?" I asked.

"I'll give yer a snake's skin," he said.

"Where'd cha get it?"

"I found it back of the shed over there. It's a big black one. They're the most poisonous y'know. He musta slipped right out of his skin when he was tryin' to get away."

"Na, I don't think so," I said. "We got plenty of snakes on the farm."

"Ow about a wishbone from a crocodile?"

"That's stupid. Crocs don't have wishbones. Only chooks do."

"Yeah, well, wot's this?" the man said and he pulled a great big wishbone out of his pocket. It was a lot bigger than any I had seen from any of the chooks that we killed and ate.

Just then Dad came back to lock the petrol cap. He saw the wishbone.

"That's a big one," Dad said. "Must be from one of those turkeys over there."

I looked over at a pen behind the petrol station where there were a whole lot of big birds with long necks running around. We didn't have any turkeys on the farm, but I knew what they were from picture books.

The man didn't say anything, but he gave me a big wink and walked away.

"He said it was a wishbone from a crocodile," I told Dad.

Dad just laughed and said the man was pulling my leg. Just then Mum arrived back from the store.

"Here, Des," she said. "I bought you a hot pie to eat on the way home."

Oh boy, I said to myself as we drove off. I opened up the paper bag with the hot pie in it and started to eat it. The hot wet gravy dripped all over the place as I buried my face in the pie. My friend Triloaf was there with me sitting on the floor in the back of the ute.

"It's too bad you can't eat pies and chocolate frogs," I said to him. "I would share them with you."

"That's all right," he said. "If you're happy, I'm happy."

And I was happy, even though that fellow had tried to pull my leg. I reached over and felt both my legs. They were all right, and I still had my chocolate frog for later. It had been a very good day in town.

Herbie and the Pitchfork

On the road to Toowoomba we always went past the Farm Home for Boys at a place called Westbrook. I didn't know much about it, but Mum and Dad said it was a place where they sent boys who had been bad. As we drove past it on the way home to our farm, I could see the boys out working with hoes, while some men in khaki shirts and shorts and round hats watched them. Behind them there were trees and some buildings, but you couldn't go there because it wasn't allowed.

One day Dad came back to our farm with this older boy called Max. Dad said he had brought him from the Farm Home to work for us on our farm. Max didn't say much to me. He stayed with us for a while, helping Dad and Gordon do the farm work. He slept on a stretcher in a room we called the office near the bedroom where Gordon and I slept. One morning Dad told us at breakfast that Max was gone. He had left, cleared out overnight, and that the police had found him and taken him back to the Farm Home. So we got another boy. His name was Johnny. Dad said he wasn't as clever as Max, and sometimes when he got excited he would speak with a stutter, like, "C-c-c can I have some br-br-bread, p-please?" He ran away, too, but the police brought him back, and when I asked him where he went he said, "W-W-W-Wallaby Hill." I knew Wallaby Hill was a big hill way over past the school, so that was a long way to go. When I asked him why he ran away he said, "I dun-dun-dun-no." I think these boys from the Farm Home were a bit sad because they didn't have their mother and father to look after them like we did. Mum and Dad were kind to them, but they always seemed sad.

One day Johnny did a very silly thing, so he was taken away, and we never had any more boys from the Farm Home again.

It was a very hot day, and all the men were out bringing in hay from one of the paddocks to put in the hay shed, where it would be kept nice and dry for the cows to eat if they didn't have enough feed in the paddocks. To bring in the hay we used a big heavy wagon with four big wooden wheels. Only one horse on the farm could pull the wagon. He was a big red horse with black mane and a long black tail. We called him Plum. He was called a draught horse.

To help with the hay, we had my cousin Herbie from Toowoomba staying with us. He was a lot older than the rest of us. His mother was my Aunty Jane, who was one of Dad's sisters. Herbie was always kind to me. I liked him a lot.

Dad showed Herbie and Gordon how to put the leather harness on Plum and back him into the shafts of the hay wagon. Then away we went, with Plum pulling the heavy wagon slowly to the hay paddock. There was Gordon and Johnny and me with Herbie driving Plum. Dad had gone off to do some other work. It was a very rough ride in the hay wagon, and every time the wheels hit a rut it would jar my body all the way up to my teeth.

When we got to the hay paddock the other three older boys used pitchforks with long handles and three sharp steel prongs to pitch the hay into the wagon. I was too young to do much, so I just hung around chasing the flies away from Plum, while he stood there quietly waiting for the wagon to be filled. When the hay started to pile up higher than the sides of the wagon, Gordon got on top of the pile to spread it around, while Herbie and Johnny pitched the hay up to him as fast as they could. Sometimes Johnny would hit Gordon with a fork full of hay, which would make Gordon mad because the hay was very itchy if it got down inside your shirt and shorts. But Johnnie would just laugh and say, "S-s-s sorry."

When Herbie decided the pile of hay on the wagon was high enough, we all climbed up on top of it to ride back to the hayshed near the house. The ride back was much smoother because you could bounce around on the hay when the wagon wheels hit a bump. We had a couple of billies of cold water, which we drank and splashed over one another as we rode back. Herbie sang and yodelled and told us funny stories.

When we got to the hay shed, Herbie backed Plum up to the open doors. The shed was already half full of hay, so it was hard work to pitch the hay up from the wagon to the top of the stack, and it got harder as the hay got lower in the wagon. Herbie and Johnny were the strongest, so they pitched the hay up to Gordon, who spread it around. Towards the end Herbie told Johnny to climb up the ladder to the top of the stack to help Gordon, while Herbie pitched the last few forkfuls up. I couldn't help much, but I had a pitchfork with a broken handle that was just long enough for me to manage, so I got in the wagon with Herbie, who let me scrape the last bit of hay into a pile so he could pitch it up to the others.

At last Herbie called out to the others that the job was all done, and they could come down from the top of the stack, and we would all go down to the house for smoko. That doesn't mean to have a smoke, because no one smoked, but Mum would have a pot of tea and biscuits ready for the men and cordial for me. I heard Johnny give a loud "Yippee" from the top of the stack, because he was happy the work was finished. Then he did something very stupid. He threw his pitchfork down from the top of the stack into the wagon. But Herbie was still in the wagon with his back turned away from the stack, and I looked up just in time to see Johnny's pitchfork come sailing down and hit Herbie with the sharp prongs in his shoulder.

It was really terrible. Herbie let out a cry and fell to his knees. I screamed at the top of my voice for Gordon and Dad to come and help, because Herbie was hurt. I'm not sure what happened next. Gordon came down from the stack, Dad appeared from somewhere, and I ran down to the house to get Mum. Dad must have pulled the prongs out of Herbie's back and tore off his shirt. Mum had some bandages to stop the bleeding, but there was blood all over the wagon floor. Herbie could kind of half walk, and Dad brought the ute over to the wagon and got Herbie into the front seat, and they took off right away in a cloud of dust to get to the hospital in Toowoomba.

Johnny never came down from the top of the stack. I could hear him up there crying and saying he was sorry. Gordon and Mum and I had to figure out how to get Plum unhooked from the wagon, and take off his heavy harness, and put him in the horse yard with some water and hay. Mum called out to Johnny to come down, that no one would hurt him because it was an accident, but he wouldn't come down. So we went down to the house. I never saw Johnny again. He must have run away and this time no one brought him back.

Later on I helped Mum and Gordon do the milking, while we waited for Dad to come home. Gloria looked after Val down in the house. After a few hours it got dark, and then we saw the headlights of the ute coming up the driveway from the road. It was Dad on his own. He said that Herbie was all right. The doctors had put some stitches in his back, and Dad had taken him home to Aunty Jane to recover.

Not long afterwards Herbie came back again. I asked him how he was, and he said he was all right, but his shoulder was a bit sore. I told him how scared I was when it happened, and that I was really pleased he could come back. He said not to worry and put his arm around my shoulder. I really liked him a lot.

My First Picture Show

We did not see Aunty Jane very often, but sometimes Gloria and I would stay with her for a holiday in Toowoomba, when Herbie and his brother Kenny were helping Dad on the farm. Auntie Jane and Uncle Ernie lived in a nice house with a white fence. There was a wide gate where two red car tracks made of cement ran up the side of the house. Uncle Ernie drove a car, not a ute like us, because he lived in the town, and that's what town people drove.

Aunty Jane was a happy person with a crackling kind of laugh. She was one of Dad's sisters. He had a lot of sisters, and they all were very pretty and looked alike, and had the same crackling voice. I didn't see most of them very often, except for Aunty Milly who lived with Uncle Ralph near us on the farm. It was fun to stay with Aunty Jane. She had a piano that she would play very loud and sing along. She said she couldn't read music and played by ear. I didn't quite know what she meant by that, because she played with her hands. She said she could only play on the black keys, which seemed silly to me because there were a lot more white keys on the piano than black ones. But we would have fun singing with Aunty Jane. Gloria said she would like to learn to play the piano one day. I wanted to play the guitar and sing like Tex Morton and Buddy Williams. I would listen to them on the wireless on 4GR Toowoomba on the Hilly Billy Half Hour at 12 o'clock when I was having dinner on the farm.

Aunty Jane gave us money, like a sixpence or a shilling to buy things at the shop down the street. We didn't have anything like that on the farm, and that's why it was such fun to stay with her in town. You could buy a little bucket of Peter's Ice-Cream for threepence that you could eat with a wooden spoon, or get it in a cone and make sure you made it last until the end of the cone had some melted ice cream in it that you could have as the last bite.

One of the most special things we ever did with Aunty Jane was to go to the pictures to see "Snow White and the Seven Dwarfs." The picture show was down town on Ruthven Street. I had never been to the pictures before. It was a big building with rows of soft seats and a lot of fancy stuff on the walls and ceiling. In front of us was a big curtain, and when the picture show started it would shine on the curtain, then the curtain would go whirring back, and there was what you call a screen behind it for the moving pictures to shine on. I had never seen anything like that, real pictures like in my comic books, but with big people on the screen moving and talking and music playing really loud.

There was what you call a newsreel with a lot of stories about the war. It looked really terrible with guns firing and soldiers in helmets wading up to their waists through water in the jungle. Then "Snow White and the Seven Dwarfs" came on. It was amazing. I knew the story a little bit from a picture book we had, and from what Mum had told me. But it was nothing like seeing it on the big screen. Everything came alive, not like the black and white pictures of the soldiers in the jungle, but these were drawings in colour moving on the screen with Snow White talking and singing too. Her wicked stepmother was looking in the mirror saying, "Mirror, mirror on the wall, who is the fairest one of all?" When the mirror said "Snow White," the stepmother got really angry and Snow White had to run away into the forest.

She found this little house where the dwarfs lived, but they weren't home, and she went to sleep across a few of the seven beds. Then all of a sudden you could see the dwarfs come marching home singing, "Heigh Ho, Heigh Ho, It's home from work we go!" They were all so funny with Grumpy and Sneezy and Happy and all the others and especially Dopey, who couldn't talk but smiled a lot. At first they were afraid of Snow White, because she was so big, but they all grew to love her, even Grumpy, and they had such fun singing and dancing.

Then the stepmother turned herself into an ugly old witch, and found Snow White when she was all alone because the dwarfs had gone to work in the mines. The witch gave Snow White a poisoned apple, and all the kids in the picture show called out to her not to eat it because it was poisoned. But she did, and she fell down fast asleep, like I remember my Grandfather, when he was dead. And there was this terrible storm, and the witch was struck by lightning and fell over the cliff and was killed, which was good, because she was a bad person.

When the dwarfs found Snow White was asleep and they couldn't wake her up, it was very sad. Gloria and I were crying, and I think Aunty Jane was, too. They took Snow White into the forest and covered her with flowers and all the animals and birds were crying, too. Then, suddenly along came the prince on his great big white horse and kissed her, and she woke up, and he carried her away on his horse to the castle, where they got married and were happy, and so were the dwarfs and all the animals and birds in the forest, and all of us in the picture show, and we clapped and cheered, and the lights came on, and it was what you call intermission.

Aunty Jane bought us some ice-cream and lollies, and then we went back to our seats for the second picture show. This was called the main attraction. It was a new show that had never been to Toowoomba before called "Yankee Doodle Dandy." There was a lot of singing and dancing and fast talking. I didn't know what it was about, so I went to sleep. Aunty Jane said it was a really good show, but all I can remember is Snow White and how beautiful it all was, except for the witch, who was scary. It was my very first picture show, and it was wonderful.

Life in Our Farm House

Even though I liked to go on holidays to stay with Aunty Jane or Granny and Grandfather and Aunty Holly in Toowoomba, I was always pleased to come home to the farm. We were lucky because Dad worked so hard that he had built this new house for us to live in. I think we had the nicest house in Athol. I know because when I went to visit other kids' homes they didn't have all the things we had.

Most especially, we had electric lights. Dad said it was a twelve volt system. I'm not sure what that means, but I know it worked best when we had the engine running up in the cow bails, because that made the thing called the generator go. The electricity was stored in rows of heavy black batteries on the wall behind the engine, and it ran down some wires on poles to the house. When you turned on the switch the light hanging from a cord in the middle of the ceiling would come on. We had lights in every room, but Dad would get mad if we had too many on at once, because he said it drained the batteries. So I was always careful to turn off the light whenever I left the room (if no one else was there). The light would not go off right away, but kind of glowed for a bit before it went out. I liked to turn the light on and off to watch it fade in and out, but Dad said that was not a good thing to do either, so I didn't do it very often. I think some other homes in Athol may have had lights like ours, but most just had kerosene lamps that you had to carry from room to room.

We had a lot of rooms in our house, so it was good you didn't have to carry lamps around. You could creep around in the dark and feel for the light switch on the wall, then turn it on so you could see what you were doing. The light switches were a bit high for me to reach, but I could just do it if I tried hard.

My favourite room was the kitchen, especially in the winter, when everywhere else would be really cold, but the kitchen was always warm, because it had this nice wood stove that Mum always kept clean and shiny. There was a water fountain on the side of the stove, so we always had hot water for washing our hands and the dishes. The cold water came out of taps over the kitchen sink, and in the bathroom and laundry, too. The water came from the tanks that stood on tank stands outside the house. The water ran into the tanks off the roof of the house. If we got a lot of rain the tanks would overflow, and the water would run in a little drain down to the orchard. But mostly it didn't rain a lot, so we had to be careful with the water, just like with the electricity.

We used to wash our face and hands in a dish in one of the tubs in the laundry. You would have to carry the hot water from the fountain in the kitchen in a dipper. I had to stand on a stool to reach the dish in the tub. When I had finished washing my face and hands, I would put the dish on the floor and sit on the stool and wash my feet and wipe them dry on the towel. Once a week on Thursday night we would all have a bath in the big tub in the bathroom. You would run some cold water from the tap into the tub, then carry dippers and kettles of hot water from the kitchen, until you had enough water in the tub to sit in so your bum was a bit covered, and you could splash the water over your tummy. Mum would come in after a while and wash my back and around my ears with a washer. When one of us was finished our bath, the next person would add some more hot water and have their bath. The biggest people went last, so they had more water. When everyone was finished, we would let the water out of the tub, and it would drain away down to the orchard.

The dunny was outside near the great big peperina tree, so we had to go outside to poop. The girls went there to pee, too, but boys didn't have to do that, because we could stand up and pee anywhere, but not too close to the house, or in the garden, and not in the same place all the time. When we had to go outside to poop or pee at night, we had a torch near the back door, so we could take it and see where we were going. You always had to check the seat on the dunny to make sure there were no redback spiders hiding there, because if one of them bit you on the bum, it would make you very sick. That never happened to anyone, but once Gordon was bitten by a redback that was on a stretcher we had brought inside from the shed for him to sleep on, because one of my friends was staying with us and sleeping in his bed. Gordon got very sick and we were very sorry about that, but after a while he was all right again.

Everything in our house worked really well. At the back we had a gauze door with a spring on it, so it closed whenever you went in and out, and that's what kept the flies out of the house. Of course, you had to brush them off your clothes first, then duck quickly through the door. The door always closed with a bang, so you would know whenever someone was coming in or going out. The windows all had gauze on them, too, to keep the flies and other bugs out. The windows opened easily by going up and down on a cord. Some flies would always get in, but not many, and you would find them dead on the window sills where they were trying to get out, but couldn't because of the gauze.

The breakfast room was next to the kitchen, and that's where we had all our meals, though we would have snacks around the table in the middle of the kitchen. In the breakfast room there was a really long table, and Dad would sit at the far end. Along the wall where the windows were we had a long wooden stool. Gordon would sit on the end next to Dad, and I would sit at the other end, and Gloria would sit in the middle, though sometimes she sat in her own chair on the other side of the table. Mum would sit close to the kitchen, because she was always coming and going with the food. Gloria would help with that. Val sat next to Mum in her high chair. Val couldn't talk, but she made very loud noises. The meals were always good times. Dad would talk about what was happening on the farm, and what was going on in the war. Gordon and Gloria would talk about school, though Gordon didn't like school much and preferred to work on the farm. I would tell everyone about all the fun things I did during the day. Mum would not say much, but she was always interested in what we said.

The best meal of the week was Sunday dinner, when Dad would try to be there instead of out working. We would have either roast beef or a leg of mutton that Mum had cooked all morning in the oven, with baked potatoes and pumpkin cooked in the same pan, so that the meat and everything tasted of delicious gravy. We would also have beans or peas and sometimes cabbage that I didn't like very much. Another nice thing was that we could have the leftover meat cold in sandwiches for tea at night with tomato sauce or pickles. The next day we would mince it up in the mincer, which we screwed to the kitchen table, and have it as shepherd's pie baked in the oven with a thick crust of potatoes on the top. And there would always be a steam pudding, or something like that, with syrup or treacle and covered with thick yellow custard.

We also had a dining room, but we never ate in there. I think the table and sideboard with its nice dishes were just for show. The main thing in the dining room was the great big wireless that worked with two batteries. One was called an A battery that Dad could charge up on the generator. The other was called a B battery that was in its own cardboard box and would last a long time. The wireless was wonderful, because it had a dial with all the stations marked on it, and you could turn on whatever you wanted to listen to. At night after we had done the washing up in the kitchen sink, we would all go into the dining room to listen to the wireless.

The washing up was usually done by Gloria and me. Sometimes she would wash and I would dry, but sometimes we did it the other way round, and sometimes we argued about who would do what. Mum was always there to smooth things over, and Dad never put up with much nonsense from us kids, so usually it worked out all right.

We had a wonderful sofa in the dining room in a little nook by the wireless. This was Dad's favourite spot, where he would lie down and stretch out after his hard day's work. We all had our favourite shows to listen to. Dad liked to listen to the ABC News and to a show where there was a really funny man called Mo McCackie, and to the Bob Dyer show with a lot of different people talking and singing. Gloria and Mum liked "When a Girl Marries." That was about this father who had seven daughters. Everyone liked "The Amateur Hour" where singers would get a chance to be the best and go on to become famous. On Sunday night Lux Radio Theatre was always good, though I didn't always understand what was going on.

My favourite show was "The Search for the Golden Boomerang," which was on every afternoon before tea. It was about this family who travelled around in a caravan with an Aborigine boy and had a lot of adventures. I think they found pieces of the boomerang but most of the time there was nothing at all in the story about a boomerang.

Mum gave me a book with the same name, "The Search for the Golden Boomerang." It had all the people I listened to on the wireless in it. They didn't look quite the same as I thought they would look, but it was good to have the book. I couldn't read the words, but I pretended to, looking along the lines from left to right as I saw Gloria and Gordon do. They said I couldn't really read, but I said I could. So they asked me what I was reading, and I made up something from what I heard on the wireless, but they just laughed and said that wasn't what the words said at all. I got mad, and said that one day I would prove that I was right, when I went to school and learned how to read properly.

Asthma and Tonsillitis

Another one of my favourite rooms in the house was the sun room at the front. It was next to the dining room and you could also come into it through the front door, which we hardly ever used. I liked the sun room because that's where

I would sit in one of the cane chairs in the warm morning sun after I had an asthma attack during the night. My chest would be very sore because of the wheezing. Mum would do everything she could to help me. I had some black awful tasting medicine and some little white pills, but nothing helped much, at least not right away. Mum would come into the room where I was sleeping with Gordon, and sit on my bed, and hold me and rub my chest and back with Vicks Vapour Rub. It didn't help with the wheezing, but it felt so good for my aching chest. In the morning I couldn't do much, and Mum would prop me up in the chair in the sun room with cushions and a blanket and a cup of hot milky cocoa. I would just sit there in my pyjamas with the warm sun on my face and try to get better.

I don't know why I had asthma. I was the only one in the family who had it, and sometimes I felt very sorry for myself. I wondered if I would ever be able to grow up big and strong like Dad and Herbie and Gordon, and be able to work on the farm.

Mum and Dad did everything they could to help me. After I had a bad attack they would take me to Dr. Furness in Toowoomba. He was what you call an ears, nose and throat specialist. He was very kind and would try different things to help me, but nothing made much difference. Once when my head was all stuffed up and my chest was hurting, the doctor and his nurse put me on a couch in his office with my head hanging down over one end. They put some awful drops up my nose, and hooked the holes in my nose up to two tubes, just like we hooked the milking machine to the cow's tits. There was a bottle beside the couch, and they set the machine going to suck all the snot out of my nose into the bottle. I had to lie there saying, "Ga, ga, ga, ga," over and over, with this terrible smell from the drops, and this machine sucking away and me going, "Ga, ga, ga, ga!" Mum was there holding my hand, otherwise I would have jumped up and run away. When it was all over the bottle was half full, but I didn't feel much better.

Another time the doctor said I had bad tonsils and they should be taken out, as well as something else called adenoids. I think these are things somewhere at the back of your nose and in your throat. This time I had to go into the hospital. I was a bit scared because I had never been in hospital before. They said I would have to sleep there, and I didn't like that very much.

The hospital was called St. Vincent's in Toowoomba. Mum said it was a Catholic hospital, and it was the best. There was a statue at the front of the hospital of Jesus' mother holding the baby Jesus. There were ladies in long black dresses and big hoods called nuns, and others called sisters and nurses in white uniforms. The nurses wore caps and the sisters wore veils and were older. They were all very kind. I had a bed in a room with one other boy. Mum and Aunty Holly were there until I went to sleep, and then the next morning the nurses came and took me to this room for the operation. Dr. Furness was there in a white gown and cap, and another doctor, who said he was going to put me to sleep. He asked me if I could count, and I said I could a little bit. I wasn't feeling very brave. He put a mask over my face and told me to start counting. Then I smelled this really strong smell of something called chloroform, I think, and the doctor said to keep counting. I did my best, but I must have gone to sleep, and when I woke up I was back in my hospital bed, and Mum and Aunty Holly were there. I had a very sore throat. The nurse came in and said that I couldn't have any breakfast, only things to sip, but that I would be able to have ice-cream for dinner, so that didn't seem so bad.

After a few days I left the hospital and went to stay for a while with Granny and Grandfather and Aunty Holly until I felt good enough to go home to the farm. I am not sure what difference losing my tonsils made to my asthma or to my stuffed up nose, but anyway it was an interesting adventure and something different I could tell everyone about, because not everyone gets to go to hospital and have as much ice-cream as you like.

My Christmas Present

Our house was built as a big square. The bedrooms were along the front and down one side, and you got to them from a long hall that ran around the lounge that was right in the middle of the house. It was always dark in the lounge, because it was in the middle. There were windows along the side where the breakfast room was, as well as swinging glass doors from the dining room. Two big soft armchairs and a sofa with dark flowery coverings always looked new, because no one hardly ever went in there. It was a good place to hide in games of hide and seek, and if you were quick you could climb out through the windows and get "home" before anyone found you.

Mum and Dad had a really big bedroom at the front of the house. I used to sleep in there in a cot when I was small, but then I moved to my own bed in a room with Gordon around the corner of the hall. Val slept in the cot, and Gloria had her own room with a big bed in it at the front next to Mum and Dad's bedroom. All the bedrooms had really big wardrobes built into the walls for our clothes with cupboards above them right to the ceiling, where you could store all kinds of stuff. I was too small to get up there, but if I could, it would have been a great place to hide. No one would have ever found me there.

We had a really big house, but when people came to stay at Christmas we all had to move around so that everyone would have a place to sleep. I'm not sure how it all worked. I remember one Christmas, I was back in the cot in Mum and

Dad's room and Granny and Grandfather were sleeping in Mum and Dad's bed. Mum's friends, Carrie and Evelyn, from Brisbane were there too. We called them Aunty Carrie and Aunty Evelyn, even though they weren't really our aunties. They slept in Gloria's big bed, so Gloria must have moved somewhere, probably into the lounge. No, that's not right, because Aunty Holly was there, too. So she slept on the sofa in the lounge, and Gloria slept on the sofa in the dining room. I think Mum and Dad went into the boys' room with Val in a cradle, and Gordon was on a stretcher in the office.

Whenever Aunty Carrie and Aunty Evelyn came to visit we had to turn off the chimes on the chiming clock that was on the sideboard in the dining room, because Aunty Carrie said it kept her awake. It had a short chime when it was quarter past, and a longer one at half past, and a longer one at a quarter to, and a really long one on the hour, as well as a dong for each hour. Aunty Carrie said it drove her crazy. She also complained that everything was too quiet on the farm, with no cars or trams rattling by, like they did in Brisbane. I think they would have been a lot noisier than a clock, but Aunty Carrie was Aunty Evelyn's older sister, so we had to make sure things were right for her. Aunty Carrie and Aunty Evelyn were not married, and they worked at making clothes in Brisbane, so we always got new clothes from them at Christmas. Aunty Evelyn was tall and thin and Aunty Carrie was short and chubby, and they talked and laughed a lot, and were usually a lot of fun.

Christmas was always special. We would get lots of cards from people who wrote on them things like "To Una, Ken and Family from Joy, Bill and Family." The cards usually had pictures on them of snow and Christmas trees like none that I had ever seen. For a Christmas tree we would bring in a twisted old branch off an iron bark tree, and string some ribbons on it. Mum would put her cards everywhere on the sideboard, and on the mantelpiece above the brick fireplace in the dining room. Because it was summer and very hot, we never had a fire going, so it was quite safe for Father Christmas to come down the chimney and bring presents. I never saw him, but there were pictures of him in the snow with his reindeer on some of the cards. It must have been very hot for him in his red suit and white fur when he came to Athol.

We never had Christmas stockings like on some of the cards. Even better, we would hang pillow cases on the ends of our bed to make sure there was plenty of room for Father Christmas to put the toys. The pillow cases were never full, because we didn't get a lot of presents, but I usually got one special thing I wanted. On the Christmas morning when I was back in the cot I woke up really early, and I could see that the pillow case was bulging with a big box. I was sure right away it was what I had told Mum and Dad I really wanted, so I suppose they told Father Christmas. I climbed quietly out of the cot and lifted the pillow case down onto the floor and pulled out this big wooden box with a sliding lid. I knew right away from the picture on the box what it was. It was a great big Meccano Set. I pulled off the lid and saw all these pieces of metal painted red and green with holes in them. The short pieces and long pieces were in different compartments with the big pieces in the middle, and there was a box full of hundreds of tiny bolts and nuts and a shiny silver screwdriver. The picture book inside showed all the different things you could make, like cars and trucks (there were even axles and wheels so you could make them go), and planes with a propeller, and cranes with a string hanging down from a pulley at the top. It was absolutely wonderful, and just what I wanted. I don't know whether or not I made a noise, but when I looked up I saw Granny staring at me from her bed with a big smile on her face. I gave her a kiss and rushed out of the bedroom, carrying the Meccano Set and dragging the pillow case to find Gloria and Gordon to show them what I got.

Christmas on the Farm

Christmas Day on the farm was beaut. We always had a lot of family come to visit, so we needed plenty of food. Everyone brought something, but Mum cooked the chooks. We caught and killed them the day before. That was always a bit of a circus.

Mum knew which ones she wanted, but the chooks didn't know about that. We would trick them into coming over to the woodheap (where the axe was) by spreading grain on the ground. We kids would stand around in a circle so the chooks couldn't get away and Mum would grab the one she wanted. Then one of us would rush in and help her get the head on to the chopping block, and quick as a flash she would chop the head off. Blood would spurt everywhere, and the chook without its head would kick and struggle like it never did before, and Mum had to hold its legs otherwise I'm sure it would have run away. But after a bit it stopped kicking, and Mum tied it upside down by its legs on the clothes line so all the blood would drain out. Then we would catch another one the same way. The chooks never seemed to work out what was going on, but kept on coming back for more grain, until we had three of them strung up on the clothes line.

After that we had to pluck off the feathers. We did that under the peperina tree in a tub of hot water brought in buckets from the kitchen. The hot water loosened up the feathers, and we all plunged in up to our elbows with feathers flying everywhere as we plucked them out and tried to stuff them into a sugar bag. When that was all done, Mum would open up the bottom of the chook with a knife and scoop out the innards into a slop bucket. She kept the heart and other parts called the giblets for cooking. Later on we would feed the slops to the other chooks, who didn't seem to mind eating the insides of their friends and family.

On Christmas morning we had a good breakfast together. Dad and Gordon came in later after milking and taking the milk to the cheese factory and feeding the pigs. All the regular jobs had to be done even though it was Christmas. I would wish all the animals I saw a Happy Christmas, though I don't think they knew it was a special day. After breakfast Mum would cook the chooks along with the potatoes and pumpkin roasted in the oven. She had a lot of help from all the other women and I had time to play with my Meccano Set with Grandfather.

Later in the morning other families would start to arrive. Uncle Ralph and Aunty Milly and my cousin Dawn usually came first. They lived about a mile away on the road to the school. Then Uncle Henry and Aunty Eileen would come up the driveway in their shiny blue Chev ute that was newer than ours. Their farm was down a side road somewhere in the bush not too far away, though I had never been there. Aunty Eileen was one of Mum's sisters. She was a big jolly woman, and Uncle Henry was short and a bit of a wag. Everyone, except us kids, called him Stumpy. They didn't have any kids, so they were always interested in playing with us.

Mum had two brothers, Uncle Gordon and Uncle Alf, who had farms a bit further away near a place called Biddeston, so we didn't see them so often. It was always fun when they did come because then we would play with our other cousins. I don't think they ever came at Christmas, but it would have been fun if they did. Uncle Alf and Aunty Edna had a son, my cousin, Lewis. He was younger than me, and was what you call an only child, so Aunty Edna was always fussing over him. Uncle Gordon and Aunty Elsie had three children: Roy, who was the same age as Gloria, Jan, my age, and Gail who was just little like Val. Gordon (my brother, not my uncle, though they had the same name) and Dawn were the oldest, so the rest of us kind of followed them around.

By the time everyone arrived it was like a big picnic. The weather was hot and sunny so us boys were running around in shorts and shirts. I had a new pair of short pants for Christmas from Aunty Carrie and Aunty Evelyn that were a bit big and flapped around like an empty bag. The girls wore pretty dresses and had ribbons in their hair. The men were wearing their town pants and sports shirts, and all the women had put on light flowery dresses with stockings and a little bit of lipstick. We were all spruced up for Christmas and looked pretty good.

As everyone arrived it was one long morning tea. Dad had set up a table out of planks and carpenters' horses on the lawn outside the house, and Mum spread a big table cloth over it. Every part of the table was covered with plates of good things to eat. They kept on coming out of cake tins that my aunties had brought – buttered scones and jam, rolled oats biscuits, kisses stuck together with raspberry jam, thin slices of dark fruity Christmas cake, date squares, and my favourite of all, Mum's lamingtons covered with chocolate icing rolled in coconut with raspberry jam in the middle. Big pots of tea kept coming for the grown ups and us kids could choose out of three or four different kinds of cordial.

Gordon got an air rifle for Christmas, so he ran over by the machinery shed to try it out. Dad and Uncle Henry and Uncle Ralph went along to supervise and I tagged along, too. The girls weren't very interested in air rifles so they played their own games and pushed Val in the swing under the peperina tree. Dad found some tin cans and put them on the top of the orchard fence posts near the machinery shed. He said they were the targets for Gordon to shoot at.

The way you loaded the air rifle was to break it in the middle by pulling the barrel down. Then you pushed a lead slug into the barrel and closed it up. The gun was then ready to fire, and you had to be careful not to touch the trigger too soon. Dad said it was a really good air rifle made in Germany. I don't think it was new, because I think it used to belong to our cousin Herbie and it was being passed along.

Dad showed Gordon how to sight it, and he took a shot at one of the cans. The rifle went crack, but the can just sat there. He missed. So then he took another shot, and another one, and another one, but the can just sat there. But Gordon said not to worry, he was just getting the hang of it. He took a few more shots, and at last he hit the can and it flew right off the fence post.

"Hooray!" we all shouted. "Good on you, Gordon."

I ran over and put the can back on top of the post. I was just tall enough to do it. Nobody saw that I also picked up a handful of stones and put them in my pocket.

Dad said he would show us how to do it. He loaded the gun, and bang, down went one can, then the next and next, just like that, three in a row!

"Wow!" I said. "Good shooting, Dad."

"Want to have a go?" he asked, smiling at me. "You can have just one shot for Christmas, then you'll have to wait a couple of years. Guns are not toys. You have to be old enough to know how to use them properly. Here, I'll show you. Put up another can, Gordon."

Gordon went over slowly to put up a can. I don't think he really liked me trying out his gun. I was a bit scared, too, because I didn't know what to expect. Dad knelt down beside me, and together we aimed the gun at the can. I squeezed the trigger. Crack! The gun gave me a little kick in the shoulder and the barrel flew up. I looked to see what had happened to the can, and there it was still sitting on the fence post.

"Good try," said Dad, "now, give the gun back to Gordon."

"Thanks for letting me try it out," I said, handing the gun to Gordon.

He nodded and gave me a big brother kind of half smile.

"Yay!" I cried out and rushed over closer to the fence, pulling the handful of stones out of my pocket. I threw them at the can and knocked it right off the fence.

"Silly little bugger," I heard Gordon say, just as Mum called out from the house, "Come on, everyone. It's dinner time."

Christmas Dinner

What a great Christmas dinner! Mum had it set up for us kids to eat at the table outside. All the cakes and biscuits had been cleared away, and the table was set for dinner, with some Christmas decorations that Mum and Gloria had made out of coloured paper. Before we sat down, I crept into the house through the back door to take a look inside. You never saw such a sight.

The whole of the kitchen table was covered with piles of food. The three chooks that Mum had cooked were there with bowls of gravy and stuffing, as well as big dishes of baked potatoes and pumpkin and every other vegetable you can think of. But that was only the half of it, because the aunties had brought lashings of ham and corned beef and plates of minced meat and sausage rolls, even another big bird that I found out later was a duck. Aunty Eileen and Aunty Milly were busy carving everything up, and the uncles had gone into the breakfast room with Dad and Grandfather and were pulling up chairs. Grandfather sat at one end of the table and Dad was at the other end in his usual place, opening up big bottles of beer that foamed up when they were passed around the table and poured into tall glasses. The women were going every which way bringing in plates of food, and the men were tucking in.

I wondered where Granny and Aunty Evelyn and Aunty Carrie were, so I crept back through the kitchen and took a look in the dining room. For the only time I can remember the table was set for eating. Granny was sitting at one end with Aunty Carrie and Aunty Evelyn next to her on either side. The other aunties and Mum were up and moving around with the food.

"It's nice to be waited on," I heard Aunty Carrie say. "We're going to play the toff today, aren't we Evie. What do you say, Granny? Too many cooks in the kitchen can mess things up." Aunty Carrie was drinking red cordial, which may be why she was in such good spirits. I never heard what Granny said, because just then Mum grabbed me by the shirt collar and steered me back outside to where the rest of the kids were.

Dawn was in charge of the kids, but Aunty Holly said she would also help out and sat with us, while Mum and Aunty Eileen were coming backwards and forwards with the food. There were half a dozen farm cats hanging around as well, and every now and then one would spring up on to the table to grab a piece of food then scuttle away. Before we all tucked in, Aunty Holly said we should say a little prayer to be thankful that we could all sit down to such good food when there was a terrible war on overseas. So we all took a moment to think about the soldiers in the jungle like I saw on the newsreel when Aunty Jane took Gloria and me to see "Snow White and the Seven Dwarfs." Those dwarfs never had so much fun with Snow White as we did at Christmas dinner with Aunty Holly and Dawn trying to keep order as we all tucked in.

We were finished our meal long before the grown ups, who seemed to be having a good time, because we could hear the voices through the open windows getting louder and louder. The men were singing songs I had never heard before. To keep us busy Dawn said we should play a game of Red Rover on the lawn. She knew all about such games from school, and I thought it would be good when I could go to school and play like that. "Red Rover, Red Rover, won't you come over." And we would rush from one end of the lawn to the other, and try not to get caught.

What we were all waiting for was the plum pudding. I knew that Mum had made two of them wrapped in cloth. She had lit the fire in the copper in the laundry room, and when the water in the copper was bubbling and boiling the puddings were lowered in and left there to cook. There was a great cheer from the men in the breakfast room, so we all rushed over to the windows to look in, just in time to see Mum and Aunty Eileen come marching out of the laundry, each carrying a steaming plum pudding to shouts of "Good on you, girls" and "That should sink the Jap battleships" from the men, who were all looking red faced and very happy.

Dawn cried out, "Come on kids, back to your places," and we all doubled back to our table to sit down. "There's a special pudding for us," Gloria shouted. "I know, I know," I cried, "It's full of threepences and sixpences."

Just then Mum came out of the house, carrying our pudding and a big bowl of white sauce to spread over it. Aunty Holly was in charge of cutting it up, and we all craned our heads to see if we were going to get some money in our piece.

"Now wait, wait 'til everyone's got some," Aunty Holly shouted over all the noise we were making. "And be careful you don't bite too hard or swallow anything hard."

"Yeah, yeah," said Gordon, "or you'll have to wait until it comes out the other end before you get your sixpence."

"Oh, yuk," we all chirped up, then started to dig in to our slice of pudding. Right away I hit a threepence with my spoon and dug it out and sucked it clean, being careful not to swallow it, like Aunty Holly had said. She watched us carefully to make sure we all ate our piece of pudding, and not just look for the coins. In the end everyone had at least one threepence or sixpence. Aunty Holly said she would look after them for us, so we wouldn't lose them, and we all rushed off to play.

In some ways this was the best part of the day. Of course, Christmas dinner was terrific, but to be able to play afterwards with Dawn and the rest of the family was just beaut. At first we were a bit slow after all the food so we kind of hung around in the shade of the peperina tree. It was really very hot, and it must have been a lot worse inside the house, so one by one the grown ups started to come out and flop down on the lawn in the shade of the house. Uncle Henry and Uncle Ralph didn't seem to be able to walk too good, and they were still talking very loud. Mum and the other women were still inside cleaning up. I couldn't see Granny, and thought she had probably gone somewhere to have a sleep. Aunty Carrie and Aunty Holly seemed to be having a lot of fun talking and laughing with the uncles.

It was then that Gordon got a great idea. He was going to play Tarzan in the peperina tree. He dragged an old tub from the shower room and asked me to help him carry buckets of water to fill it up. Then he got a rope, and he climbed up the tree, and crawled out on a limb to tie the rope. The girls giggled and shouted at him to be careful. When the rope was tied, Gordon came down a bit lower, grabbed the end of the rope, and swung out over the tub of water shouting "Ai-oh-ai-oh-ai!" just like Tarzan did in the comics. The tub of water was a river full of crocodiles, and if he fell in, he would be eaten alive. But he sailed right over the top, and landed safely on the other side, beating his chest and crying "Ai-oh-ai-oh-ai!"

We all clapped and cheered as he swung back again. I shouted out, "Me too! Me too!" but the girls said, "No, you're too small," so I decided to show them. When Gordon was taking a rest and nobody was looking, I grabbed the end of the rope and climbed up onto a low branch of the tree. I could see the tub of water through the leaves and was sure I could swing over it. With the loudest "Ai-oh-ai-oh-ai!" I could yell, I jumped off my branch and hung onto the rope. I had never done anything like that before. Suddenly the rope jerked tight, and I got such a fright that I let go and landed splash right in the middle of the tub.

The other kids roared laughing yelling, "Look out for the crocs! Look out for the crocs! They'll bite your bum!" I splashed around feeling a bit stupid, then said, "Well, at least it's cool in here. Better than the hot sun." With that everyone wanted to get in the tub, not up to their necks like me, but jumping in over their bare legs. I had to scramble to get out or I would have been drowned.

Mum took me inside and helped me change. When we came out again, Dad was standing up with one foot on his chair and everyone was looking at him. He was getting ready to recite a poem. He liked doing that (especially when he had had a few beers), not usually all the way through, but pieces of poems like

"The boy stood on the burning deck, whence all but he had fled." I didn't know what a burning deck was, but I knew the boy was in danger from a fire, and I was afraid for him, because he was all alone.

Anyway, this time Dad started to recite another one I had heard before called "A Bush Christening."

> "On the outer Barcoo where the churches are few,
> And men of religion are scanty."

Before Dad could go any further Uncle Henry called out in a funny wobbly voice, "Good on yer, Dad. That's a good one. About the boy who gets christened with a bottle of whiskey."

"Starve the lizards, Alf. Don't' interrupt me or I'll lose my place," Dad replied.

"Crikey, Dad, I'm sorry," said Uncle Henry. "D'ya want me to help?"

"Gawd struth," said Dad, "will you put a sock in it."

Everyone was laughing and cheering, and even I knew what they were doing. They were pretending they were on the radio in the "Dad and Dave" show that everyone listened to at a quarter to seven. Uncle Henry was pretending to be Alf from Snake Gully, who was a bit simple, and Dad was playing Dad, who always knew what to do.

"Now, where was I?" Dad began again.

"Out on the Barcoo without yer panties." This time it was Uncle Ralph who had chimed in, in another funny voice that I knew was Ted Ramsey from the show.

"Stone the crows," Dad shouted. "If you want to be a comedian, Ted, go and join Mo McCackie."

This made everyone laugh louder, because Mo McCackie was a funny man on another radio show everyone listened to. Finally, Dad got going again on the poem:

> "On a road never cross'd 'cept by folks that are lost,
> One Michael Magee had a shanty."

I don't remember how all the words go, but it's the story of how Michael Magee's son didn't have a name because he had never been christened, because there was no minister to do it. When a minister finally comes, the boy runs away and hides up a hollow log. When Dad got to this part, Uncle Henry interrupted again.

"Hey, Dad, we need a boy for this bit." Then Uncle Henry looked at me. "Come on Desie, you're the right size. Hide under the table and pretend it's a log." Now everyone was egging me on. I looked at Dad, and he just nodded, so I climbed over Aunty Holly and Aunty Eileen, who were sitting on the lawn, and crawled under the table and stuck my head out through the legs of the carpenter's horses. Dad continued with the poem:

"Poke a stick up the log, give the spalpeen a prod
As he rushes out this end I'll name him."

The next thing I knew someone was jabbing a broomstick in my backside (I think it was Gordon), so I gave a yell, and shot out the end of the table, tumbled over Aunty Carrie and ran away to the end of the lawn. Everyone was laughing and clapping as I heard Dad finishing up the poem.

"As the howling young cub ran away to the scrub
Where he knew that pursuit would be risky,
The priest as he fled, flung a flask at his head
That was labeled 'Maginnis's Whiskey'."

That was how the boy came to be christened Maginnis Magee. I didn't quite know what was going on, but when I came back everyone was smiling and calling me a good sport. Dad had a big grin on his face, and Mum gave me a big hug.

"After that it must be time for watermelon," Dad said. "You boys go and get one each," he said to Gordon and me, "and bring them back."

The watermelons were growing in the garden at the top end of the orchard near the machinery shed. There were a lot of them of all sizes on the vines. Gordon knew how to pick a ripe one by tapping on them. He picked a big one for himself and a smaller one for me, and we ran back with them as fast as we could. Gordon was a lot faster than me, so by the time I got there he was already washing his in a dish of water to get the mud off the skin. I came running down the concrete path to the house, and tripped over my own feet, and fell splat right on top of my watermelon, which split wide open so pieces of red juicy fruit went in all directions. I was almost ready to cry, but when I looked up everyone was smiling.

"Good job, Des," said Uncle Ralph, "that saves cutting it up." And he and several others came over to help me up and gather up the pieces of watermelon. Soon we were all spread out around the lawn eating great thick slices.

After that it was time for people to leave, because everyone had to get home in time to milk the cows, and Dad and Gordon had to get ready to milk ours. But it had been a really good Christmas Day. I don't remember ever having such fun, even though I fell in the water tub and dropped my water melon. Somehow I think that just made things more fun for others, and that's not a bad thing to do.

With Dad on the Tractor

Another job I liked to do was to take Dad his dinner when he was working on the tractor in one of the paddocks away from the house. Just like the house, Dad had laid out the farm so everything worked well. There was a long lane up the middle with four paddocks on each side, so to get to any paddock all you had to do was go up the lane. There weren't any trees on this part of the farm, so it was always really hot out there in the summer sun.

One day when Dad was working in one of the middle paddocks Mum packed him a nice dinner of hot roast beef, potatoes, pumpkin and peas. She put it on a plate, then put another plate over the top of it to keep it warm, and tied it all up in a white pudding cloth with a knot at the top, where I could put my fingers through to carry it. She packed some cake and biscuits and fruit in an old school bag that I could carry on my back. This was for Dad for afternoon tea. In my other hand I carried a billy of tea with milk in it and lots of sugar, because Dad liked it sweet. The tea was hot, so I had to be careful not to let the billy touch my bare legs. It was a pretty heavy load, but I could rest along the way.

As I walked up past the machinery shed, Jim the dog came out from under the cart where he had been lying in the cool dust in the shade. He knew where I was going and came along for the walk. When we came to a fence, he would jump through the wires quite easily, but I had to be careful not to get caught on the strand of barbed wire that always ran through as the middle wire in the fence. When we got to the windmill halfway up the lane, Jim jumped in the cows' drinking trough to cool off. I put my load down and splashed the water over my face and hands. The water was nice and cool, and I would have liked to jump in the trough, too, like Jim, but I knew Dad wouldn't like that.

It must have been really hot where he was on the tractor, going round and round the paddock in the hot sun. I could see where he was working, in the next paddock up the lane, with a cloud of dust following him and the tractor around. By the time I got there he was almost finished that paddock, and was working on a strip down the middle, so I had to walk in over the loose soil, which got down inside my shoes. He was working with the scarifier getting the paddock ready for planting, so the soil was soft and pretty dry because we hadn't had any rain for a while, though a few clouds were building up in the west and it looked like we might get a storm.

When I got to the edge of where Dad was working, he was at the far end of the strip, so I had to wait at the corner for him to come around. Jim was half-heartedly chasing a few magpies that were rooting in the loose soil turned up by the scarifier, looking for grubs.

Dad's tractor was not very big as tractors go. He called it a small CASE but it was plenty powerful enough to do the kind of work Dad did. It was also fairly fast, as tractors go, so he got things done faster. I watched him as he came towards me with the small front wheel of the tractor always in the furrow in a steady straight line. The big rubber tires on the back of the tractor bumped along over the rough ground, as he came up to me in a roaring noise of the engine and a cloud of dust.

He stopped the tractor and turned the engine off, so suddenly everything was quiet, except for the squawking of the magpies and peewees as they fought over the worms and grubs in the ploughed ground behind the scarifier. Dad's clothes were covered in dust, and he had a ring of dust around his eyes and nose under his big broad-brimmed hat. He took a rag he carried on the tractor and wiped the dust off his face and hands. He took off his sweaty hat, and sat down in the shade of the big tractor wheel, with his back propped against the big rubber tire.

I gave him the enamel mug out of the school bag. He took the lid off the billy and poured some of the sweet milky tea into the mug, and had a long drink.

"It's probably not very hot," I said, "but I got here as quick as I could."

"Ah, it's just right," Dad said. "Washes away the dust."

He tucked into the plate of roast beef and vegetables.

"Looks like you're almost finished this paddock," I said.

"Yeah, a couple more rounds, then the corners, and it's all done," Dad replied. "Then I want to make a start on the top paddock before milking. You wanta come up for a ride?"

"Oh, yeah, that'd be beaut," I said. I didn't often get to the top paddock, because it was a long way to walk.

Dad continued to eat. He threw a few crusts of bread to Jim who gobbled them up. I poked around a bit, checking out the scarifier, then climbed up on the tractor and pretended to steer it. It soon got too hot up there, so I came down and sat in the shade beside Dad.

"You're gonna be starting school soon," he said as he drank some more tea. "I think we'll have to get a couple of new horses for Gordon and Gloria. Then you can have Blackie to ride."

Oh boy! This meant that Blackie would be my own horse, and I could ride him to school, just like Gordon and Gloria did now, except that I would have him all to myself, and not have to double up like Gordon and Gloria did.

"Would you like that?" Dad asked.

"You bet," I said. "Blackie's a beauty."

"Yeah, well, you'll have to learn how to ride first. But you're old enough. Gordon can teach you."

"Where are we gonna get the other horses?" I asked.

"Aunty Dora has a couple of ponies she wants to sell," said Dad. "We can take a drive up there next week and take a look."

Wow! This was getting better all the time. Aunty Dora was Dad's aunt, so that made her my great aunt. She was a lovely old lady. I had met her a few times, and I knew she had a property at a place called Millmerran that I had heard about but never seen. It would be a great adventure to go there.

"All right, smoko's over," Dad said, getting up. "Climb up on the tractor and we'll finish up here, then go up to the top paddock."

Dad tucked the dinner stuff away in a safe place on the tractor, and I climbed up onto the mudguard over the big back tire on the left hand side, and hung onto a cross bar. Dad had to crank the engine to get it started, and it roared into life right away. He got up behind the steering wheel, held it with one hand, throttled up the engine full bore, then let in the clutch with his other hand, and the tractor jerked forward while I hung on tight.

It was too noisy on the tractor to talk, so I just sat there bumping up and down. The dust was behind us at first, but when we turned the corner the wind blew it right back into our faces. I shut my mouth tight and squinted my eyes. I had to hang onto my hat with one hand and hold onto the crossbar with the other. I saw Dad grinning at me from time to time, as he swung the tractor around to go up and back on each corner strip to get the little bits that had been missed each time he had turned a corner.

At last we were all done. We dropped off the scarifier at the gate, then Dad told me to come down onto the seat behind the steering wheel and have a go at steering the tractor as we went up the lane. Because we had nothing to pull, the tractor could go a lot faster, and Dad throttled it up, while I hung onto the steering wheel, trying to keep us going straight as we bumped over the ruts in the lane. Every time we started to head for a fence, Dad would grab the wheel and bring us back, then I would be on my own again, steering the bouncing tractor up the lane. It was great fun.

When we got to the top paddock, I looked back down the lane and could just see the house away in the distance. Boy, Mum would be surprised if she could see me way up here with Dad. He hooked the tractor up to a plough that was already up here because he was ploughing out an old crop to put in a new one. We set off to do the first round with Dad steering again, while I held on to my perch on the mudguard over the big back tire. Jim trotted along behind.

On the far side of the paddock Dad had left a strip of bush when he cleared the land, because the soil there was full of gravel. The men who worked on the roads had scooped out some of the gravel and made a small dam that filled with water when it rained. When we got round near the dam, Dad stopped the tractor and said I could get off and poke around in the bush where it would be much cooler.

"Keep an eye out for snakes and be careful around the dam," he said. "It's not very deep, but you can't swim, so don't go into the water. Stay near the edge of the bush, so I can keep an eye on you." He then set off again on his round and was soon a long way off, so that I could hardly hear the sound of the tractor.

I always loved to be alone in the bush. Not that I was really alone, because Jim was there, and Triloaf, too.

"Isn't this a great place," I said to Triloaf. He didn't say anything, but I knew he was listening. "I reckon when I grow up I'll be an explorer and find places like this that no one has ever seen before. Did you hear Dad say he was going to teach me to ride? I could ride off on Blackie and find all kinds of places."

"He said Gordon was going to teach you to ride," Triloaf replied.

"Well, that's the same thing," I said. "Gordon's the oldest, so he's the one who gets taught first by Dad. But Dad let me steer the tractor, today."

"Yes, I saw that. You did very well."

"Yes, I did, didn't I? Let's go and throw some sticks in the dam."

The dam was just a few yards into the bush. I had seen it before a couple of times when I had been up here. It wasn't very big, not like the ocean or anything like that, but it was still nice to have it all to yourself. The water was a dirty brown, and it had dried up a bit around the edges, because we hadn't had any rain for a while. The ground was cracked into small cakes that crunched under your feet, until you got to the edge, where it got muddy, and tall grass grew up out of it. I could see dragon flies with their long bodies and silver wings dive bombing out of the grass onto the water, then taking off again.

I picked up a stick and threw it into the water. Before I knew what had happened, Jim went bounding out into the water to fetch it. I wondered who had taught him that trick. Probably Gordon. He didn't really have to swim, because the water wasn't deep enough. He brought the stick back to me, and shook the water off his coat all over me, which felt nice and cool. I threw the stick into the water again, but this time he just looked at it, then ran away to do something else. He probably thought I didn't know how to throw the stick properly.

Further up the bank there was a meat ants' nest. It was a low mound of red dirt that they had piled up from digging their tunnels. The big red ants were running along their tracks back and forwards to the nest. I sat down on my haunches to watch them. They certainly seemed to know what they were doing. I thought it was pretty smart of them to be able to build a nest like a big city where everybody seemed to know what to do without having any farms or machinery or shops. Maybe it would be a bit boring, but I expect if you were an ant, you would think it was all right.

"Do you think ants are happy?" I asked Triloaf.

"Maybe they don't know what happy is," he said.

"But they know what being mad is," I said, "because if I poke the nest with a stick, they will get mad and try to find me and bite me. If they can get mad like that, why couldn't they be happy when everything is all right?"

Before Triloaf could reply something really amazing happened. A small spiny animal came out of the bush right onto the nest, and started to dig with his claws. Well, what a commotion! Ants came from everywhere—up out of the nest, back from the tracks—piles and piles of them, attacking this small animal. I had never seen such a sight. But it didn't seem to bother the animal, because he just squatted there with the ants crawling all over his spines, and flicking his long sticky tongue out eating the ants. He was actually gobbling up the ants! It was amazing. I just sat there staring. Then all of a sudden the animal decided he had had enough, and he got up and wandered back into the bush. Some of the ants chased after him, but they had more important things to do at home, because the top of their nest was now wrecked. But then as I watched, they started rebuilding it. It would take a long time, but I could see they would do it.

"Boy, did you see that?" I asked Triloaf.

"Too right," he said. "That's the way things work in the bush. Happy and mad have got nothing to do with it."

I kind of thought Triloaf was right. He usually was. Then I heard the tractor coming round again. I wanted to run out and tell Dad about the animal and the ants, but I knew that was not a good reason to stop him when he was working, so I just waved to him as he went by. I hung around on the edge of the bush and thought about how wonderful it was that all the animals and birds and insects were there. They seemed to get along all right without us. Maybe they attacked each other from time to time, like that strange animal attacked the ants. But he only took what he needed, and there certainly were plenty of ants left behind. I thought about the war people kept talking about. That was different from the animal and the ants. That was people fighting with people, and that didn't seem to make sense. I don't think ants attack other ants. There are a lot of different kinds of ants in the world, but they don't seem to fight with each other. I sat down in the grass with my back against a log thinking about all this.

I must have gone to sleep because the next thing I knew Dad was there shaking me by the shoulder.

"Come on, Des," he said. "There's a storm coming. We better get back to the house before it breaks." He must have been worried because he left the plough in the middle of the paddock, and we just took off on the tractor full throttle bouncing over the ground. Dad put me on the seat and stood behind me so I wouldn't bounce off. I could see the big black clouds coming up out of the west with flickers of lightning and some rumbles of thunder. Half way down the lane we came to the paddock where the cows were, so Dad stopped the tractor for a minute and sent Jim off to round them up to bring them in for milking. Then we took off again flat out. The lightning flashes were brighter now, and the thunder a lot louder. Just as we got through the last gate, the rain came pouring down in buckets. We were wet through, but Dad got the tractor into the machinery shed. By then the rain was coming down so heavy on the corrugated iron roof of the shed that it sounded ten times worse than the roar of the tractor engine. Dad wrapped me up in a bag to dry off. He looked half drowned. A big bolt of lightning suddenly lit up the whole place, and the crack of thunder shook the shed until it rattled.

"It hit a tree over there," said Dad pointing up past the cow bails. "Don't worry we're safe here."

After a while the rain eased off, but there were sheets of water all over the ground, and streams running everywhere. When the rain slowed down enough, Dad put another bag over my head and we made a run for the house. Mum was at the door looking really worried about what had happened to me. She grabbed me and wrapped me up in a big towel, and changed my clothes.

When we were all having a snack before Dad and Gordon went out to do the milking, I told them about the animal and the ants.

"That's an echidna," said Dad. "There's a few of them around here, but you don't see them too often. You were lucky to see one."

I thought that I was pretty lucky all round. What kid could have had a more exciting afternoon than me? I really wanted to go to school, but I was certainly learning a lot just being on the farm. Even Triloaf agreed with me about that.

A Visit to Aunty Dora's

It was a bright sunny day when we set off to go to Aunty Dora's to see about the horses. It was the school summer holidays, so Gloria and Gordon could come and make their pick. The three of us got in the back of the ute, and Val rode in the front with Mum and Dad. It had been raining a bit the day before, so Dad said we should all throw in our rubber boots, in case we got stuck in the mud.

I had never been to Millmerran before, so the road was all new to me. Soon we were driving through the bush. I could see the road was a bit muddy on the edges, but in the middle it was fine, so there were no worries about the ute getting bogged. The road twisted and turned quite a bit, but Dad was driving slow, so we could stand up and look over the hood to see where we were going. The bush was full of birds singing. I saw the flash of Rosella parrots in the trees and flocks of quarions overhead.

"Hey, look at the 'roos!" Gordon suddenly shouted.

I followed his pointing finger, and saw three or four kangaroos bounding away in front of us on the edge of the road, then they took off into the bush. That was the first time I had seen kangaroos, because we didn't have any around our farm. I knew what they were, though, from picture books. This was getting to be a great adventure.

Dad slowed down a bit, and we all heard a big burst of laughing from some kookaburras. It rang out over and over, and we could see at least six of them in a big gum tree on the edge of the road.

"Silly old jacks," Gloria said. "I wonder what they think they're laughing at."

"They're not really laughing," I said, trying to show I knew a thing or two. "That's just the noise they make."

"Oh, yes, smarty pants," said Gloria. "Well, they might just be laughing at you."

As it turned out they might have been laughing at all of us, because right about then we came down a bit of a hill, and in front of us was this big river, and the road just ran right into the water. Dad stopped the ute and got out to take a look.

"That must be the Condamine," said Gordon.

"What's the Condamine?" I asked.

"It's a river," said Gordon. "We have to cross it to get to Millmerran."

I couldn't see how we were going to do that, because there was no bridge, not like there was over Westbrook Creek on the way to Toowoomba. Dad came round to the back of the ute to get his rubber boots.

"I'm just going to see how deep the water is," he said. "It should be all right. There's hardly been any rain, and the river's barely running."

"What happens if we can't get across?" asked Gloria.

"We'll have to go back and go round the long way," said Dad. "It'll take a lot longer."

"Won't we get to see the horses?" I asked. I was worried that I might miss out on getting Blackie if Gloria and Gordon didn't get their new horses.

"Don't worry," said Dad. "We'll get there."

With that he picked up a big stick from the side of the road and walked into the water in his rubber boots. The water wasn't too deep, but in the middle it came close to the top of the boots. Dad kept prodding around with the stick.

"What's he doing?" I asked.

"Fishing for yabbies," said Gloria with a smile.

"He is not," Gordon said importantly. "He wants to make sure there's no big hole under the water that a wheel might drop into, and we'd get stuck in the middle."

"I knew that," said Gloria.

"Then why didn't you say so?"

"I was being funny."

"Ha! Ha! Ha!" I pretended to laugh. Gloria glared at me.

Dad walked out onto the other side of the river, then turned around and came back, prodding with the stick as he came.

"It looks all right," he said to all of us. "The bottom is sound enough. It's a bit rough in places, but no big holes."

Gordon smiled.

"All right, hold on back there," Dad said to the three of us. He got into the ute, gunned the motor, and into the river we went. The water sprayed up from the wheels on all sides. I ran from side to side in the back of the ute to make sure I wouldn't miss anything. I could hear the water splashing up under the floor boards. I looked off on both sides of the crossing and the river looked wide and deep.

"We wouldn't want to get stuck," I said to no one in particular, and then we all heard the ute's engine cough and splutter. It stopped, and so did we, right in the middle of the river. Everything was suddenly quiet except for the river running around and under the ute.

"Bugger!" I heard Dad say. "The distributor must have got wet." The rest of us were too surprised and a bit scared to say anything. Val was yelling from inside, where she was standing on the seat looking out at the water.

Dad was carefully opening his door. Luckily the water was just up to the top of the running boards, so he could open the door without getting any water inside. He was still wearing his rubber boots, so that was a good thing.

"I'll have to dry the distributor out," said Dad, "but I think we should try to push her out of the water first."

I wasn't sure what a distributor was, but I knew it must be important. I was sure Dad could fix it, but I didn't think I wanted to get out into the water to push.

"Don't worry kids," Dad said. "We're quite safe. Just like Noah's Ark without the animals."

"Noah built a boat for the animals in the Bible," Gloria said to fill me in. I nodded wisely.

"Come on, Mum," said Dad. "You'll have to help push. I'll bring your boots around. You too, Gordon. Get your boots on. Gloria, you stay in the back for now. Des, I want you to climb down through the door and take the steering wheel. You can steer us out, just like you did on the tractor. Here, I'll give you a hand."

Dad lifted me down from the back of the ute and I climbed in through the half open door. I stood on the seat and grabbed the steering wheel like it might fall off. Dad closed the door. Val was standing beside me on the seat, eyes and mouth wide open, making all kinds of strange noises. Mum was holding her and saying quietly that everything was going to be all right. Dad came around to Mum's side with her rubber boots.

"Sorry, Mum," he said. "You might get the bottom of your dress a bit wet."

"That's all right," said Mum and got out into the water and closed her door. Val was really excited now, and scrambled over to Mum's side of the ute, and stuck her head out the window yelling, "Ma! Ma! Ma!"

"All right," I heard Dad say. "One, two, three push!"

The ute rocked a bit, then slowly started to move. I held onto the steering wheel like it was saving me from being washed away. The ute moved some more. I held it straight. Yay, we were coming out! We were escaping from the raging river. Nothing could stop my Mum and Dad. Then suddenly there was a bump out the back, and we stopped again. I could hear a lot of heaving and grunting, but the ute was stuck.

"The back wheel's caught on a rock," I heard Dad say. "We'll never move her now. I'll have to try to work on the engine in the water."

Just then I heard another voice.

"G'day, mates," it said. "Looks like you're in a bit of a pickle."

I looked up and saw a man on a horse in front of us at the edge of the water. Dad came around from the back of the ute. "Yeah," he said. "She conked out in mid stream. Now we're stuck on a rock."

"Not to worry," said the man. "You just need one more horsepower. So happens I've got a bit of rope here. Hook it onto the bumper, and Matilda will pull you out."

Dad tied one end of the rope to the ute's bumper bar, and the man got down off his horse and tied the other end to the big pummel on the front of his saddle. Dad went back around the back again, and gave the word for everyone to heave. I was still hanging onto the steering wheel like it might get away. The horse took up the strain on the rope, and dug its legs in and pulled. The ute rocked a bit, then lurched forward with a bump and slowly rolled up out of the water. I held it as straight as Dad's furrow.

"Hooray!" everyone shouted.

"Good on you, mate," Dad said to the man, whose name turned out to be Bill.

"Not me, mate," said Bill. "Thank old Matilda here. She did all the work."

While Dad worked on fixing the ute, Mum made a bit of a picnic on the river bank, and Bill joined us.

"I saw you steering the old girl," he said to me. "You did a good job." I smiled a bit and fed Matilda a crust of bread. Then the ute's engine roared into life, and soon we were ready to go. We waved good-bye to Bill and Matilda, and set off again for Aunty Dora's.

Not long after that we came out of the bush into open grass country, which looked nice and fresh from yesterday's rain. We came to a gate, and Gordon jumped out to open it. I could see a house among some trees up a long driveway.

"This must be Aunty Dora's place," I said. Then I noticed some grey animals bobbing up and down a little way off along the edge of some trees. "Wow! Look at all the kangaroos," I shouted.

"Not 'roos," said Gordon, as he climbed back up into the ute and we set off up the driveway. "They're wallabies. They're just feeding before it gets too hot. Then they'll go into the shade in the bush and come out again later to feed."

Gordon certainly seemed to know a lot of stuff. That's because he was four years older than me, and he had learned a lot of things. It was good that he was teaching me. I asked him what was the difference between wallabies and kangaroos. "Wallabies are smaller," he said, and that was that.

When we drove up to the house, Aunty Dora and our cousin Alma came out to meet us. Aunty Dora was an old lady like Granny, and she had a sweet kind voice. Alma was a lot older than us, and she was dressed in what she told us were her riding clothes, with a brown shirt and puffy pants that she said were called jodhpurs. She was wearing long leather riding boots and looked really smart.

"Come on in," said Aunty Dora. "We've got a nice lunch ready for you."

After lunch while the others were talking, I wandered around in the yard near the house. I noticed a huge vine growing along the fence, and saw bunches of green grapes hanging off it. Now we had a lot of fruit trees in our orchard, but I had never seen grapes growing before. I grabbed a bunch to eat. They were a bit tangy, but quite nice and juicy. Aunty Dora came out and saw me.

"Do you like grapes, Des?" she asked.

"Oh, yes," I said, "but we don't have them very often."

"Well before you go, we'll pick a few bunches for you to take," she said, "and I've got some jars of lovely grape jam that you can have, too." Aunty Dora was just kind like that.

Then we went to see the horses. They had a lot of horses running around in a paddock near the house, but the most interesting thing of all was the track that went round the edge of the paddock with little low fences set up at different places. Alma said that this was her practice track for when she went riding in the shows. Now, that was something special. I had been to the Toowoomba Show with Mum and Dad and had seen the riders in the show grounds jumping over these fences, but here was my cousin with her own riding track. Later on she showed us all the ribbons and prizes she had won. This was a whole new world for me.

Alma said she would show us how it was done. She caught her horse, saddled her up, and got on, looking really smart, just like the ladies I had seen riding at the Show. We all stood in the shade, while Alma rode around a bit, with her horse doing this fancy sort of high stepping canter. Then she gave the horse a bit of a nudge with her heels, and away they went heading straight for the first fence. The horse just leaped into the air, and Alma went up in the saddle a bit, and they just sailed over the fence.

"Hooray," I shouted and ran out a bit to get a better look. But Alma and her horse were already way off, jumping over the second fence, then the third, until they came prancing back to where I was standing.

"Wow," I said, "that was terrific." The horse was snorting a bit, and its flanks were steaming. I reached up to touch it, and it felt warm and just so full of life. I went round to stroke its nose and it nuzzled my ear, and I could feel its breath all steamy and warm.

"Do you like horses?" Alma asked.

"Oh yes," I said, "I can't ride yet. But after we get some horses from you today, I'm going to have Blackie for myself, and be able to ride to school."

"That's wonderful," Alma said. "Would you like to have a ride now?"

Would I ever! She lifted me up so I could put my foot in the stirrup, then helped me while I swung my other leg over the saddle, and there I was sitting on Alma's wonder horse. It was very high up, and the saddle was way too big for me, and my feet couldn't reach the stirrups, but I didn't care, because I knew that soon I would be able to ride. Alma gave me the reins to hold, then she walked the horse around a bit, while I sat there in the saddle feeling like the king of the world.

After that we all went over to take a closer look at the rest of the horses.

"Are there any girls?" Gloria asked.

"Yes, Patsy is a nice quiet pony," said Alma, pointing to a brown pony with a long golden mane and a white patch on her forehead.

"Can I have her, Dad, please?" asked Gloria.

"Yeah, it might be good to have a mare," said Dad. "We can put the stallion in with her, and then we'll have two for the price of one."

I wasn't sure what he meant by that, but I thought he was talking about his own big horse at home that didn't have a name and was just called the stallion. He was a lot bigger than Patsy, though, so I wondered if he would like her.

"I don't want a mare," said Gordon. "How about that one over there?" He pointed to another pony a bit redder than Patsy. It was doing a pee, so we could see he was a boy.

"That's Larry," said Aunty Dora. "I don't know about him. He can be a bit wild."

"That's the kind I like," said Gordon. "Let's take Larry, Dad."

"What do you think, Ken?" Aunty Dora said to Dad. "He's a good pony, but likes to act up a bit."

"Gordon's a good rider," said Dad. "He'll be able to handle him. We'll take Patsy and Larry. They'll be good company for each other."

"And for Blackie, too," I chimed in.

"Yeah, for Blackie, too," said Dad, smiling at me.

So it was all fixed up. Dad and Aunty Dora talked some more about how the horses were going to be brought over to our place at Athol from Millmerran. It was too far to ride them, so they would have to come in a truck. Gloria went over to pat Patsy, who just stood there quietly swishing her long brown tail, and stamping one foot because a horse fly was bothering her. Gordon tried to catch Larry by the mane, but he threw up his head and snorted and ran away. I just stood there thinking about Blackie.

Soon it was time to go. Dad said we would go home the longer way over the bridge. We certainly didn't want to get stuck in the river again. Aunty Dora took me over to the grape vine, and we picked a few bunches. She put them into a paper bag with a big jar of grape jam, and gave them to me with a nice smile.

"I have something else for all of you," said Alma. She went into the house and came back out carrying a big book." This was one of my favourite books when I was your age," she said. "It's called an Almanac, and it's full of stories and games and smart things to do." We all crowded around looking at the book with a big picture of a horse on the cover. Gloria got to carry it, so we could look at it in the back of the ute on the way home. We drove off waving good-bye to Aunty Dora and Alma. I looked over towards the line of trees and saw the wallabies.

"Look, Gordon," I said. "You were right. The wallabies are coming out to feed."

Gordon didn't say anything, just nodded wisely. Maybe he was thinking about riding Larry to school. I just knew that I had had another wonderful day.

Learning to Ride

The next time we went to Toowoomba Dad bought me a bridle for Blackie. We already had a saddle. Well, it was not quite a proper saddle. It was called a pad. It had stirrups and little leg guards so I could grip the horse properly with my legs, but it sat kind of flat on the back of the horse. Dad said it was best for me while I was small and learning to ride. That's how Gordon and Gloria had learned to ride. Dad already had a saddle and bridle for Gordon to use on Larry, and Gloria could have the old saddle and bridle they were using on Blackie for Patsy. So now we were all set.

Next day I asked Gordon to start to teach me to ride. We went into the grass paddock near the house where Blackie and Dad's big red stallion were feeding. After a bit of chasing around, Gordon caught Blackie and put the bridle on him. I could just reach up high enough to put my arms around his neck. He lowered his head a bit and looked at me with one of his big black eyes.

"You and me are going to be good mates," I said to him. He twitched his ears, so I'm sure he knew what I meant. Gordon showed me how to lead him properly by holding the reins short with one hand, and holding the end of the reins with the other. I led Blackie over to the harness room in the barn where we kept all the saddles. Gordon walked along in front of us.

Gordon put the saddle cloth on Blackie, then threw on my saddle and showed me how to hitch up the girth. Next he showed me how to measure the length of the stirrups against my arm, but I was a bit short to do this properly, so he said he would fix them when I got on. That was the hard part, because even though Blackie was only a pony and not very high, it was still hard for me to get my foot in the stirrup and pull myself up into the saddle, and I had to hold onto the reins at the same time, and keep Blackie's head up. Gordon showed me how I could bounce around a bit to help get off the ground, then he gave me a shove, and up I went into the saddle. The stirrups were still a bit long, so Gordon shortened them for me, and I was all set to go.

"Hold the reins with both hands," Gordon said. "Keep his head up, and just touch him with your heels, and grip him with your knees."

"All right, Blackie," I said. "Let's go."

And away we went, just walking, but I was doing it. I was riding Blackie on my own, while Gordon walked along beside. The first clump of grass we came to Blackie decided he wanted to have a feed, and he put his head down and nearly pulled me up over his neck.

"Don't let him get away with that," said Gordon, "or he'll do it all the time. Pull his head back up."

That was easier said than done, but I kept pulling on the reins, and finally got his head up again.

"You have to show him who's boss," said Gordon. "He knows you're a bit wet behind the ears, and he'll try all kinds of tricks to test you out. Just keep working him with your hands and knees, and he'll soon do what you want."

"Come on, Blackie, old boy," I said, "Let's go. You and I are off to school." This time he set off at a pretty good walk, and we headed down towards the house. Mum must have been watching, because she came out and waved at me.

"Look at me, Mum," I called out. "I'm riding Blackie all by myself."

"I can see that," she called back. "You look really good."

"Come on, Blackie," I said, "let's go a bit faster." I slapped his neck with the end of the reins and gave him a little kick with my heels. Right away he broke into a trot, and every bone in my body started to shake, and I felt my teeth rattling in my mouth.

Gordon must have been running along behind, though I couldn't see him. "Keep a tight rein," I heard him calling, "and work yourself up and down in the stirrups." I tried all that as best I could, but it still felt like someone was shaking the daylights out of me. I tried to sit up straight, but kept flopping forwards. I could see the ground going by below, and I was scared stiff I was going to fall off. If there was any old kookaburra around, he'd sure have something to laugh at now.

"Keep your knees in tight, and pull the bugger up," Gordon's voice was still coming at me, though it sounded a bit further away. I looked up over Blackie's ears and saw the house fence coming up, so I pulled on the reins and tried to steer him straight for it. He ran right up to the fence, and stopped dead. I shot forward right onto his neck. I lost one of my stirrups, but managed to hold onto the other one and stop myself from falling off. Blackie just stood there, waiting to see what I would do next. I straightened up, got my foot back in the stirrup, and pulled his head around, just as Gordon came running up.

"That's one way to stop," he said, laughing at me, "but you don't always have a fence to head for."

I got Blackie walking again, and we went over to where Mum was standing, looking a bit worried, but also trying to smile. She came over and gave my leg a squeeze.

"You did fine," she said. "Soon you'll be a champion."

"Yeah," I said, feeling a bit braver now, "and jump over the fences in the shows just like Alma."

"Not with Blackie, you won't," said Gordon. "He'd be lucky to jump over a log without stumbling. Let's get him back to the barn without any more trotting. I think you've had enough for one day."

And that's exactly what we did, and this time I kept his head up and mine, too. It might have been my first lesson, but I already knew that I would soon be able to ride, and that Blackie and I were going to have some wonderful times together.

The next day Larry and Patsy arrived in the back of a big truck with high sides on it so they couldn't jump out. Dad helped the man driving the truck put up a ramp, then opened up the back of the truck and led the ponies out. Right away Gordon and Gloria wanted to ride them, but the truck driver said that wasn't a good idea.

"I'd give 'em a bit of a spell, if I were you," he said. "They're probably shook up from the trip, and might be a bit skittish. Give 'em a good feed, and some time to rest, and they'll be right as rain."

"Yeah, that's a good idea," Dad said. "Put them in the horse yard with some hay and water, and tomorrow you can have a crack at riding them."

Gordon and Gloria led the ponies over to the horse yard and I followed along behind.

"In the morning I'll catch Blackie," I said, "and bring him over to meet his new friends. I'm sure they'll all be good mates."

Next day Gordon helped me catch Blackie. I tried to put the bridle on him, but he kept clenching his teeth, and spitting out the bit. Gordon laughed.

"He's trying all his tricks on you," he said. "You'll just have to keep trying until he knows he can't get away with it."

Gordon got the bit into Blackie's mouth for me, and I managed to get the rest of the bridle over his ears. Then I walked him over to the horse yard to meet his new friends. Patsy and Larry were just standing around looking out through the rails, and swishing the flies with their tails. They pricked their ears forward when I came up with Blackie, but didn't bother to move. Gloria was already there waiting, and Val had come along as well to watch. Dad was over in the machinery shed, and had left Gordon in charge of us.

"Tie Blackie up to the rails over there for now," Gordon said to me, "while we catch the other two." I did what I was told, then came back and stuck my head through the rails to watch. Gordon and Gloria went into the horse yard with bridles. Patsy stood still and let Gloria put the bridle on her without any fuss, but Larry threw up his head and ran away to the far end of the yard. Gordon just quietly walked towards him very slowly, telling him everything was all right. Larry tossed his head and scratched the ground with a front hoof, but Gordon kept closing in, the bridle in one hand and his other arm stretched out to kind of make himself a bit bigger. Larry backed up a bit, but didn't try to run away again, and Gordon just walked right up to him and put the bridle on. Gordon sure knew how to handle horses. I was learning a lot from him.

Gordon and Gloria saddled their ponies and got on. Right away Larry began to act up, dancing around and throwing up his head. I heard Gordon telling him to take it easy. He had to show Larry who was boss. Gloria had no trouble with Patsy. She was a quiet pony. They started to ride away.

"Hey, what about me and Blackie?" I called out.

"Hang on for a bit," said Gordon. "We'll come back for you. Keep an eye on Val." And they rode off out of sight, around the corner of the barn.

"Come on, Val," I said. "Let's go and talk to Blackie."

We went over to where I had tied Blackie up to the railing fence. It was then I got an idea. I sat Val down on a log and told her to stay there. Then I untied Blackie and got him to stand by the fence. I threw the reins over his neck, and climbed up onto the third rail of the fence so I was just high enough to jump off the fence onto Blackie's bare back. I had seen Gloria and Gordon do this when they were smaller like me.

"Hold on, Blackie," I said, and put my hands on his neck and jumped. He knew what I was doing, and started to move right away, before I could get my right leg properly over his back. So there he was walking away with me kind of half sprawled out across his back.

"Wait, Blackie, wait," I cried, and let go of the rains, and held onto his mane with both hands, while I struggled to get my leg over him. That only made him walk faster. He was a bit fat, too, which made it harder for my short legs. Val must have thought I was going to fall off, because she started to yell. But I hung on, and kept working at it, until I finally got my leg over, and could sit up on Blackie's bare back. He just kept walking to follow after the other horses. I gathered up the reins, and finally felt I was in charge again. Val was running along behind, still yelling at the top of her voice. Just then Dad appeared from out of the machinery shed to see what was going on.

"What the devil do you think you're doing?" he said.

"I'm riding bare back," I replied.

"How did you get on? Where are the others?"

"I climbed up on the fence. They rode off around the barn."

Just then Gloria and Gordon came back. They were sure surprised to see me riding Blackie bare back. Dad was a bit mad at Gordon for riding off and leaving me and Val, but I said it was all right and it was my idea to climb up on the fence to get on. Dad still seemed to be a bit angry, but I don't think he was really, because he kind of smiled and asked me how it felt to ride bare back.

"It's all right," I said, "but a bit hard on the bum."

"Yeah, well don't try it again until you're a better rider. But you look pretty good up there all the same. How about you other two? How are Larry and Patsy?"

"Patsy's real quiet," said Gloria. "I love her."

"Larry's a bit fresh," said Gordon, "but he's a good horse."

"Yeah, well saddle up Blackie and the three of you can ride down to the gate. But don't go out onto the road. Gloria, why don't you put the cushion on and give Val a ride."

We went back to the harness room, and Gordon saddled Blackie for me, while Gloria hooked a cushion on behind her saddle on Patsy's rump. Dad helped me get up on Blackie, then lifted Val up and put her on the cushion behind Gloria. We all set off at a good clip down past the house to the front gate.

"You look good," Dad called after us, and I'm sure he must have been pleased to see the four of us all riding away. Mum came out and waved to us as we went by the house. I knew I still wasn't a very good rider, but I was learning, and it wouldn't be long before I could ride to school with Gordon and Gloria. That would be a whole new adventure, and I could hardly wait.

I Begin to Build My Road

Mum said school would be starting in two weeks. I was really excited about that, but I had something important to do first. Dad also had some ideas of his own about what he wanted me to do. So it turned out to be a busy time.

I was building a long road from the pile of boards behind the woodheap up the hill towards the cow bails. It was hard work, because I had to cut through the tall grass, go around a few prickly pear bushes, and cross over a lot of rocky ground. No one had ever tried to build such a road before. It had to be done, because I needed a good road for the big red truck that Granny and Grandfather had given me for Christmas. I had my Meccano set for building things inside the house, but the truck needed its own road for when I was playing outside. If I didn't get the job finished before school started, how would I ever have time to do it, what with all my other jobs, like making the butter, getting the wood and chips for the kitchen stove, and helping Gloria feed the chooks? I was going to be very busy.

I could, I suppose, have used the track we walked on to get from the house to the cow bails. But that wasn't a proper road for a truck. It needed to have its own road that I could cover with ashes from the wood stove to make it look like a real highway.

I told Dad about my plans, and he said I could use a hoe for chomping out the grass and grading the dirt. But he said that I would have to work on it early in the morning and in the afternoon, while he and Gordon were doing the milking, because in between that he had another job for me and Gordon to do. Wild mint was growing in some of the paddocks, and it needed to be pulled out, because it was a pest and would stop the crop from growing properly, if it wasn't kept under control. That sounded like a really big job, too, so I wasn't sure how I was going to get everything done. And I still needed some time to practice my riding on Blackie.

I lay awake at night thinking about all this, then woke up early in the morning with Dad and Gordon. They had their snack before going off to do the milking, and Mum gave me some breakfast, so I could get started on my construction job.

I took the hoe that Dad had left out for me by the back door, and went over to the pile of boards that would be the start of my road. I put my big red truck on top of the boards, so I could look at it and know why I was doing all this hard work. There was a nice clear space under the boards that could be the home base for the truck, so that's where the road would start. I then looked up across the grass towards the cow bails, where the road was going to go.

"Boy, this is going to be a lot of hard work," I said to Triloaf.

"Do you really want to have the road?" he asked.

"Of course I do," I replied.

"Can you see the road?" he asked.

"No, not yet, silly," I said. "It isn't built."

"Look hard," he said. "Can you see it yet?"

"Well, sort of," I replied, "but it's only in my head."

"That's where it starts," he said. "Now, stop complaining and get on with it."

Triloaf was always right, so I didn't argue any more. I really could see the road in my head, but it was going to be hard to build it. I took a few whacks with the hoe and found out just how hard it was going to be. The ground was hard and the grass was thick.

"You need to have a plan," Triloaf said. "Find the easier way to go and build it there."

That sounded like a good idea, so I set off through the grass and made marks with the hoe as I went. It was interesting how, as I did that, the job didn't seem to be so hard any more. I soon found some softer places, and even where there were rocks sticking out of the ground I could find my way around them. I kept clear of the prickly pear, because I didn't want to get tangled up with those sharp needles. I finally got to a clear patch of ground near a meat ants' nest, and I decided to end the road there. The truck could bring stuff up to the ants, I thought. They should like that.

Now that I had my road marked out, I went back to the beginning to start building it. Just as I got there Gloria came out to see what I was doing.

"I'm building a road for my red truck," I told her. "It goes way up there past the prickly pear bush to the ants' nest."

"Are you going to do that all by yourself?" she asked.

"Sure," I said, and I made a few whacks with the hoe.

"Would you like some help?" she asked.

Now that was nice of her. I thought she might make fun of me, but instead she went and got another hoe and between the two of us we really began to get things done. I whacked out the tufts of grass, and Gloria smoothed out the dirt just like a grader on a real road. By the time Gordon came down from the cow bails after milking, we had got over the first rocky ridge, and were on the way towards the prickly pear bush.

"What are you two up to?" Gordon asked.

"We're building a road for my red truck," I said. "It's going all the way up to the ants' nest by the gate."

He looked around from where we were, then up to the ants' nest. He picked a piece of grass, and started chewing on it, while he thought about what I said.

"That'll take you a month of Sundays," he said.

"How long is that?" I asked.

"Don't take any notice of him," said Gloria. "He's just trying to be funny."

"I'm going to put ashes on it to make it look like a proper road," I said.

"And what will you do when it rains?" he asked.

"I dunno. What d'ya mean?" I asked.

"You'll see," he said, and walked off down to the house. Then he turned around and called back to me, "You better come in soon. Dad wants us to get started on picking the mint after breakfast."

Gosh, I had forgotten all about that.

"We better go in anyway," said Gloria. "You don't want to get blisters on your hands. Let me see." She looked at my hands. They were feeling a bit sore. She rubbed them and it hurt. "I thought so," she said. "Come on, we need to clean them up and rub some lotion into them." We put our hoes over by the red truck on the pile of boards, and she took me by the hand and led me down to the house. Sisters can be very kind and nice.

Picking Mint and Finishing the Road

The mint picking was going to be a really big job. Gordon knew what to do, so he was the boss, and I was his helper. It was a hot day, so we took a billy of cold water to drink, and some Vegemite and tomato sandwiches to eat, and set off. We stopped at the barn, and Gordon got a grain sack for each of us to stuff the mint bushes in as we picked them. We started in the paddock closest to home, just on the other side of the orchard.

"The way you do it," said Gordon, "is to line up with the posts on the other side of the paddock, and work your way across, picking all the mint as you go. You can take the first two panels, and I'll take the next three, and we'll go across together. Can you see the post you're heading for?"

I said I could, but it was a long way across the paddock, so I wasn't exactly sure, but I thought Gordon would keep me straight anyway. The crop was just a few inches out of the ground, and the dark green mint bushes were a bit taller, so they were easy to see. There sure were a lot of them, so I could see why Dad wanted us to pull them out. I started off along the headland by the fence where they were a bit thicker. They pulled out easily, so that was good, but there was a lot of bending to do. As I pulled each bush out, I stuffed it in my sack that I pulled along behind me.

Gordon kept an eye on me at first to make sure I didn't miss any, but after a while he must have been satisfied, and began to get ahead of me. The sun got hotter, and it seemed to be taking a long time to get even halfway across the paddock. Gordon was now way ahead of me, and I began to think I could never keep up.

"You have to make a game out of it," said Triloaf. "Each one of those mint plants is a chocolate bush, and soon you'll have a whole sack full to take home and make into a giant chocolate cake."

"Mint chocolate?" I asked.

"Yes, it's the best kind," he said, "but you have to pick them fast before they melt in the sun."

I hurried along a bit, and then noticed my shadow bending over each time I picked a bush. It was just a short shadow, with a big round head that was my helmet. Triloaf knew what I was thinking, because the next thing he said was, "See, your shadow is here to help you. He knows about chocolate bushes. If you go faster, he'll go faster, too, and you'll soon be finished."

Sure enough, when I went a bit faster at the picking, so did my shadow. I gave a little dance and waved my arms, and he danced and waved back at me. I started to go really fast, and hopped on one foot and then the other, and my shadow just followed along. After a while I looked up and saw that I had almost caught up to Gordon. He was standing there looking at me.

"What are you so happy about?" he asked.

"I'm picking chocolate bushes to take home for Mum to make a chocolate cake," I said, "and my shadow is helping me."

"Well, you could've fooled me," he said, "I thought they were licorice sticks."

"Maybe yours are licorice and mine are chocolate," I said.

"Yeah, and maybe pigs can fly, too," he replied.

I didn't see what flying pigs had to do with anything, though that certainly would be something to see, too. I just kept working flat out, picking bushes and nothing seemed quite as hard anymore, and we both reached the other side of the paddock together. When we turned around to come back, my shadow couldn't help me anymore, because he was behind me now. But every time I turned around he was there, right on my heels, so I had to go just as fast to keep ahead. I kept up with Gordon right across to the other side, then turned around to come back again. This was getting to be fun after all.

When we came back the second time I was feeling hungry.

"Can we stop for lunch?" I asked. "I'm hungry."

"Good idea," Gordon replied. "We can go into the orchard and sit under one of the fruit trees."

We went back to where we had started to get the school bag with our lunch in it and the billy of cold water. Of course, it wasn't cold anymore because the day was so hot, but it was still good to drink. Gordon found a nice shady spot for us to sit under a plum tree.

We had a lot of fruit trees in our orchard. Most of them were orange trees, but they didn't have any fruit on them at this time of year, because they were a winter crop. Dad always said the oranges were sweeter after the first frost. But the plums and apricots were ready, so we could pick as many as we liked to have with our lunch. Sometimes they would have grubs in them, so you would have to open them up first to check and flick the grub out before you ate it. Aunty Carrie and Aunty Evelyn would turn up their noses if they found a grub, and they wouldn't eat the fruit. That's because they lived in the city and didn't know that grubs won't hurt you. Just like the flies. They would fall in the water in the billy, but you would just fish them out. They would crawl all over your sandwiches, too. They especially liked the Vegemite. So you would have to keep brushing them off, and try not to swallow any. They would get up your nose, and in your ears, and in your mouth, so it was a good idea to keep your mouth shut. That wasn't such a bad thing, because Dad said that most people would be a lot smarter if they kept their mouth shut, even when there weren't any flies.

After lunch we went back to picking the mint, and by the time we had to stop for milking we had the whole of the first paddock finished. We each had two big bags full that we dragged back to the barn, where the mint would be left to dry before Dad burned it. Then we went back to the house, where Mum had some cakes and biscuits and a big glass of milk ready for us.

"I picked two big bags of mint," I told Mum, "but I pretended they were chocolate bushes, and that you would make them into a cake."

"Well, because you've worked so hard I will make you a cake right now," Mum said.

"Oh boy, can I lick the wooden spoon and the bowl when you're finished?" I asked.

"Of course you can," she smiled, "but you've been working so hard you should have a nap now. When you wake up the cake will be in the oven and the bowl will be waiting for you."

"But I have to get back to building my road," I said.

"After your nap," Mum said.

"I'll do your other jobs for you," Gloria said, "so you'll have plenty of time to work on your road."

They were all being very nice to me. I liked that, and thought I was very lucky to have such a nice family.

Over the next few days I kept building my road and helping Gordon pick mint in other paddocks. Then Dad said that I had done enough work and could just keep on with my road job. He helped me over some of the hard places and said that I was doing a really good job, and that it would be a great road when it was done.

I was also worried that I hadn't had much time to practice riding Blackie, but Dad said that I needn't worry about that, because I wouldn't be riding Blackie to school at first. He said it would be better if I rode behind Gloria on Patsy, until I was a bit older. I thought that was probably a good idea, because even though I wanted to ride, I was a bit scared about going out on the road with Blackie, and riding such a long way.

Finally, I had the road finished. When I got to the ants' nest, I went around it in a big circle. The ants didn't like me cutting across their tracks, but they would soon find out how lucky they were when I brought them a load of cake crumbs in my truck. They would be the luckiest ants on the whole farm to have their own special delivery service.

Now it was time to put the finishing touch to the road. I got a bucket and a little shovel, and went over to the place where we dumped the ashes from the kitchen stove. I filled the bucket and brought it back to the road. I had to spread the ashes along the road and smooth it out with the hoe.

Gloria came out to see what I was doing.

"That looks pretty good," she said, "but you should wet it a bit and pat it down. I'll get a watering can."

She came back in a bit with a watering can full of water, and sprayed some water on the ashes, and packed it down by walking on it.

"Hey, that looks really good," I said. "Thanks for helping me."

"That's all right," she said. "I'll help you make it the best road ever."

We were working so hard on the road that Gloria forgot that it was time to feed the chooks and make the butter. Mum came out looking for us, and when she saw how hard we were working and what a great road it was, she said not to worry, and that she would do the jobs for us.

So we kept working, and by the time Dad and Gordon came down from the cow bails after the afternoon milking, it was all done. Now everyone stopped to look at the road. It was getting late, but there was still time for me to do my first run with the truck. Mum had brought out a cake tin full of crumbs, and I dumped them into the back of the truck. Val was there to watch, too, but I don't think she knew what I was doing.

"Here we go," I said. "One truck load of crumbs for the ants coming up."

It was a long way up that road, and it took a while for me to push the truck all the way, but everyone waited and watched and cheered me on. It really was a good road, and the truck went along very smoothly, even over the rockiest parts. Finally, I got to the ants' nest. Because it was late in the day, they weren't all that busy. I sure was going to surprise them. I dumped the load of crumbs onto one of their tracks, then spread them around a bit and up onto the nest. Well, what a surprise that was! It was Christmas time for the ants! The first few workers who found the crumbs rushed around telling the others, and soon there were ants swarming everywhere, picking up crumbs, and carrying them down into their tunnels. I bet the old Queen down inside was pleased about that. I wished I could be an ant for a bit and go down and see what was going on inside the nest.

"Well, you're certainly a big hit with the ants," Dad said. "They never had it so good."

Even Gordon said that I had done a great job in building the road. So I was really pleased with myself, as I pushed the truck back down the hill to its base under the pile of boards. Then we all went in for tea.

That night it rained.

I was so tired that I didn't get up too early, and Gordon was back down from the milking having his breakfast, when I came out in my pyjamas.

"It rained," he said. "You better go and take a look at your road."

"Don't worry, dear, it's not so bad," Mum said.

I grabbed my shoes and ran out of the house in my pyjamas. I could see the grass was wet, and when I got to my road, I saw that all the ashes had been washed away. I started to cry, but Mum was there and put her arms around me.

"Don't worry," she said again. "The rain has stopped, and things will soon dry out, and you can start to rebuild the road."

Gordon was there too. "I'll help you," he said. "Dad said that fixing the road was the number one job for the day."

That made me feel a lot better. Maybe my road might get washed out every time it rained, but it could always be fixed. The really important thing was that everyone thought it was a great road. I was very lucky to have such a nice family.

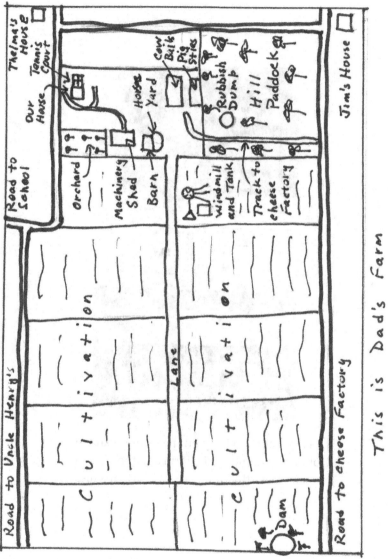

This is Dad's Farm

Here I am as a baby on the front verandah
of the old home on the farm at Athol. I don't
remember this, but everyone says it's me.
(*circa* 1939)

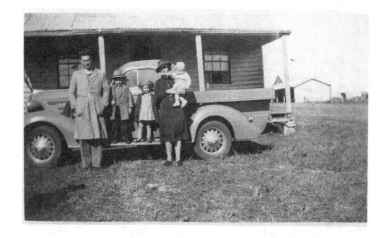

Another one I don't remember, but I am the baby in this
photograph of the Berghofer family with the 1936 Chev
ute in front of the old home on the farm at Athol.
(*circa* 1939)

Here I am again in the middle between Gloria, and Gordon
on the front verandah of the old home on the farm at Athol.
(*circa* 1939)

This is our new home on the farm at Athol.
(*circa* 1942)

That's me with my little wooden horse standing with Gordon
and Gloria outside the shower room, which was under
the water tank of the new home on the farm at Athol.
(*circa* 1942)

That's my Dad, Ken Berghofer.
(*circa* 1942)

Here's my Mum, Una Berghofer.
(*circa* 1942)

This is Dad in the cow bails
on the farm at Athol.
(*circa* 1950)

Here's Dad on the CASE tractor
sowing a crop on the farm at Athol.
(*circa* 1950)

This is where Grandfather and Granny Grundy
lived at 10 Lilley Street in Toowoomba.
(*circa* 1940s)

This is a milk vat and cooler like the ones
used in the Rockview Cheese Factory.

Part 2

Country School Years

The friends thou hast, and their adoption tried, grapple them to thy soul with hooks of steel.

Shakespeare

True wisdom is to know what is best worth knowing, and to do what is best worth doing.

Author Unknown

I Go to Athol School

The big day had arrived. I was going to school for the very first time. I was up early and too excited to eat my breakfast, but Mum said I had to, so I did the best I could to eat some corn flakes, and I smuggled most of the sausage outside in my pocket to give to Caramel. I got dressed in my best khaki shirt and shorts at least three times before I felt I was ready. I must have been running around a lot, because Gloria got a bit mad at me.

"For goodness sake, Eddo" (she often called me Eddo because my middle name was Edward, which was Grandfather Grundy's name), "stop jumping around like you've got ants in your pants."

"But I don't know what to take," I said. "I don't have any books or anything to write on. Isn't that what you do at school?"

"Yes, but you can't read or write anyway," said Gloria.

"I can so, too," I said, "and I'm going to learn more at school."

"You certainly will, dear," Mum said, "but don't worry about books or anything. All you need is at school."

"Well, can I take the book Alma gave us to show the other kids?"

"If you want to carry that big book in your school bag, don't complain to me that it's too heavy," said Gloria.

"I won't, I won't," I said, and I rushed off to find the book. I tucked it into my school bag, along with the nice lunch that Mum had made for me. I put the school bag on my back, grabbed my helmet, and went outside to wait. The cats were all lined up waiting for me, mewing like crazy, just as they always did. I had already given my sausage to Caramel, and didn't have anything else for the rest of them. I suppose that's what they were complaining about.

"I'm sorry boys and girls," I said, "I haven't got anything for you. But you know what, I'm going to school today, and when I come home I'll find something special for you." I don't think they cared much about school, because they kept on mewing and getting under my feet.

"All right, all right," I said. "I'll give you some of my lunch." I took off my school bag, pulled out a sandwich and broke it up into small pieces. I threw them on the ground, and while the cats were fighting over them, I made a rush for the gate.

Gordon was just coming down towards the house leading Larry and Patsy. He had them all saddled and ready to go. He gave me the reins to hold while he went inside to get his school bag. He had put the cushion on behind the saddle on Patsy, and that's where I would ride.

"You're going to have two of us today, old girl," I said to Patsy, "but don't worry, I'll soon be able to ride Blackie, and then you'll just have Gloria to carry."

I looked over to the home paddock, and saw Dad's big stallion and Blackie standing at the fence watching us. Patsy gave a little whinny, and the stallion bobbed his head. I think they liked each other. Blackie just seemed happy to have nothing to do.

Just then Gordon, Gloria, Mum and Val came out of the house, and Gordon tripped over the cats.

"What's wrong with these stupid cats?" he said. "They should be up in the barn. Has someone been feeding them?" He looked right at me.

"They're not stupid," I said. "They're just hungry."

"Yeah, well, they can go and catch some mice like they're supposed to." Gordon pretended to be tough with the animals, but I think he wasn't as tough as he made out to be.

But now it was time to go. Gordon got up on Larry, who did his usual little dance. Gloria got on Patsy, and Mum lifted me up to sit behind her on the cushion. I thought I saw some little tears in Mum's eyes as she said, "Now, you have a wonderful first day of school."

"I will," I said, "and I'll tell you all about it when I come home." I was sorry that Dad wasn't there to see us off, but I knew he was taking the milk to the cheese factory. I couldn't go with him this time, because I was off on my way to school. We waved good-bye to Mum and Val, and set off down towards the road.

At our gate we met up with Thelma on her horse. She lived just down the road from us. Thelma was in the same grade as Gloria. She had an older sister named Bonnie, who used to go to Athol School, but had left by the time I started.

The four of us set off with the three horses going at a fast walk. It was too rough for me sitting on the cushion if we trotted. I was already having trouble not to bump my nose on Gloria's school bag, while I hung onto her waist with both hands. Gordon rode a little bit in front on Larry, who was always ready to take off if Gordon gave him his head. Even early in the morning Gordon's back was black with flies, and all of us had to keep swishing them away as we rode along.

The way to school was a short bit up to a right turn in the road, then down a long straight stretch to a gully and up the hill on the other side. We rode on the tracks in the grass at the side of the road, away from where the cars went along the gravel in the middle. We didn't see any cars on the road.

At the top of the hill was where my cousin, Dawn, lived. She joined us to walk to school, because it wasn't very far from there. The road took a left turn here, and you could see the school at the top of another small hill. We were joined by Rose and Harold on their horses, and Marion and Phyllis riding double. It was Phyllis' first day, too. I'm not sure if they came along the road, or across country, but the whole band of us came chattering along the last stretch of road to school. I was getting excited now. Because it was my first day, all of the older kids made me feel special.

At last we were there. Next to the school was the teacher's house. His name was Mr. Fisher and he had a son, Kenny, who was also in Gloria's grade. Across the road from the school were the tennis courts and Athol Hall, which was built out of corrugated iron—walls and roof and everything. It had a stage and a smooth wooden floor for dancing. But I wasn't interested in the hall or the tennis courts today, because this was my first day of school.

The school was built on high stumps, so that you could get under it to be in the shade to eat your lunch and play simple games. The ground under the school was paved over with bitumen, so you wouldn't want to fall and skin your knees. Running from the road up to the front steps of the school, was an avenue of small bushy trees, where we weren't allowed to play. Part of our job at school was to chip the weeds with hoes to make the avenue look good, but the older kids did that.

There was a small paddock for the horses between the schoolyard and the teacher's house. We rode through the gate up to the school. I jumped off Patsy. My bum and legs felt a bit sore from the long ride, but I didn't mind, because I was so excited to be there. Gordon and Gloria and Thelma and the others took the saddles off the horses, and put them under the school, then led the horses over to their paddock, and took off their bridles, and let them go with a few other horses that were already there. I was feeling a bit shy, because even though I knew some of the kids, it all felt strange and new.

There were three of us starting school that day—me and Phyllis and Margaret. Phyllis was a rough and tumble sort of girl, with a crop of copper coloured hair. Margaret was very pretty. She had short plaits tied with ribbons, and she wore a pink dress with blue butterflies on the pockets. I thought she was special. I'm not sure how she came to school, because she lived in the opposite direction from us. She was the oldest in her family, so she didn't have a brother or sister to ride with. Maybe the Stower boys, Neville and Stanley, picked her up, because they rode that way. We all looked after each other at Athol.

The teacher, Mr. Fisher (Mum and Dad called him Andy, though I don't think that was his name) was already there, and the school was open. Mr. Fisher came down the back steps, looking for the three of us who were starting school today. He looked very important and wore a shirt and tie. He wasn't as big as Dad and was kind of stocky with thin hair. He was very friendly, though, and called out to the three of us, who were sitting quietly together under the school.

"Hello Margaret and Phyllis and Des," he said. "Welcome to school. Come on up with me, and I'll get you settled in."

I looked at Gloria, and she smiled and said quietly, "Go on." So I followed Margaret and Phyllis up the steps onto the back verandah. Mr. Fisher pointed to some pegs on the wall and said, 'You can hang your school bags on those three pegs." He went inside. I took out the big book I had brought before I hung up my bag. Margaret and Phyllis didn't have any books, so I hid mine behind my back and followed them inside.

The school was one big room with three long wooden desks and stools on each side and an aisle down the middle. The teacher's table was in the front, and there were two big blackboards on each side, with the front door in between. I tiptoed in, looking all around trying not to miss anything. Maps and charts with numbers on them hung on the walls, and a big round globe that I knew was the world sat on top of a cupboard. On the back wall were more maps and pictures, and some shelves with books on them. A big picture of the King hung on the wall above the front door. The windows and doors were open, because it was very hot, and I could hear the cries of magpies and the yodelling of butcher birds in the trees outside. But inside it was kind of like a big hush, because this was a very special place, where I was going to learn a lot. It was a bit scary, too, and I was glad that Margaret and Phyllis were there. Of course, Triloaf was right beside me whispering that everything was all right. But I didn't think I could talk to him then, or the others might think I was a bit strange. So I just stood there in the aisle beside Margaret and Phyllis, and waited to see what would happen next.

"This is where the three of you will sit," said Mr. Fisher, pointing to three places in the very front desk near his table. We slipped in and sat together on the long stool. The desk looked like it had been scrubbed very clean, but there were some grooves and a few old blue stains on it. There was a shelf under the desk, so I slipped my book onto it out of sight. I ran my hand over the wood of the desk. It felt smooth and friendly.

"First, we have to get you registered," Mr. Fisher said. I wasn't sure what registered meant, but I knew it must be important, because Mr. Fisher took out a big book with a leather cover on it, and sat down at his table. "Once your name goes down in here, it's there forever," he said. He put on his glasses and opened up the book.

"Let me see," he said. "Ah, Phyllis, your sister Marion was the last one to be registered when she came to Athol last year, so why don't we put you next." Marion was in Gloria's class, but their family had only come to Athol last year, so that must have been why she was the last one in Mr. Fisher's book. He picked up a pen and dipped it in what I knew was an ink well on his desk, and he wrote slowly in his book, while he checked something on a piece of paper.

"Oh, I almost forgot Jeff is starting today, too. I'll put him in next." Jeff was another older boy. Mr. Fisher wrote in his book, then looked down at us over his glasses. "Margaret, next," he said, and wrote some more. Then he looked at me. "Well, Desmond, here you are. Another Berghofer for the book. Do you know how many Berghofers there are in here?"

"No, sir," I said. I knew I was supposed to call him sir.

"Why don't we count them," he said. "Come up here and take a look." He waved for the three of us to come up to his table and look over his shoulder. I knew I was looking at something almost as important as the Bible. The book was filled with beautiful writing, but I didn't know how to read it.

"See, these are the names of all the children who ever came to the school, way back to 1887. That's almost sixty years. See the different handwriting from all of the different teachers. Everyone's handwriting is special to them. You will learn to write like that." I thought that would be great if I could.

"Now, look at all the Berghofers, way back to 1890." He started to count. When he got to 27 he said, "That's your father, Kenneth, 1915," and he kept on counting. He got to 50. "Your sister, Gloria, was number 50," he said. "So you're 51. And your number in the roll is 366. So that's 51 Berghofers out of 366 students." I didn't know what any of the numbers meant, but Mr. Fisher seemed to think it was important. Then he wrote my name saying it aloud. "Number 366, year 1944, name Berghofer, Desmond Edward. That's the only Desmond in the book. It's an Irish name, I think. What do they call you?"

"Usually Des or Desie, though Gloria calls me Eddo."

The girls giggled. "We'll settle for Des," said Mr. Fisher. He picked up a big piece of paper and pressed it over the writing. "See, this is blotting paper to soak up the ink. We can't have any smudges in the school Registry." He closed the book and looked at us.

"So, you've had your first lesson," he said, "counting up to 51 and seeing how to write. But that's not where you start. Sit down again and I'll show you."

We sat down in our places, and he told us to pull out the slates that were in a slot on top of the desk. He gave each of us a slate pencil and showed us how to hold them.

"Now, make an X like this." He made an X with chalk on the blackboard. I pressed my pencil on the slate, and it broke in my hand.

"Rule Number One," said Mr. Fisher, "don't press too hard." We each made the best X we could.

"That's good," he said. "Now put your slates away, and go back down to the others, and we'll all get ready for school."

As I put my slate away, the big book I had put under my desk fell on the floor.

"What have we here?" said Mr. Fisher, picking it up. "Girls and Boys Almanac. Very good. Are you going to read this to us, Des?"

I didn't know what to say, and just looked at the floor.

"Well one day you will," said Mr. Fisher, "but you better put it away until you're a little older. Now off you go the three of you."

Margaret whispered to me as we went out the door, "I bet you'll be a good reader, Des. Maybe we can read it together." I knew then why I liked her so much.

I Learn to Read

When all of the children were sitting in their places at the long desks, Mr. Fisher spoke to all of us:

"Well here we are again at the start of a new school year. A pretty big mob of you, too. Nineteen bodies in the room. I hope you all brought your brains along, too, because you're going to need them. There'll be no time to day-dream about all those things you've been doing on the farm over the holidays. You've got a lot to learn, and there's only one of me to teach all of you spread out over four grades, so I expect you to get on with your school work and do as I tell you. Is that understood? There'll be no nonsense going on in here."

Mr. Fisher looked a bit angry. He had a long thin cane, and he slapped it against his trousers leg as he walked up and down. Then he put the cane down on the desk right in front of where Gordon and the other boys in his class—Dennis, Kerry and Stanley—were sitting across the aisle from me. They all sat up very straight. The two girls in that grade, my cousin, Dawn, and Rose, sat in the desk behind the boys. They were very still and quiet. Behind them in the back desks were the three oldest kids—my cousin, Alma, and Neville and the new boy, Jeff. Gloria and the other kids in her class sat in the two desks behind Margaret, Phyllis and me in the front. There were three boys: my cousin, Jimmy, and Harold and Mr. Fisher's son, Kenny; and four girls: Gloria, Barbara, Thelma and Marion. I think I got all that right.

Now Mr. Fisher smiled as he turned to the three of us in the front. "We've got three little ones starting school today," he said, "so I would like everyone to give a special welcome to Margaret, Phyllis and Des."

All of the other kids clapped their hands. I was too shy to look around, but I'm sure everyone was smiling, and suddenly it didn't seem so scary in the room anymore. Mr. Fisher had work all set out for the other kids to do. He handed out three little books to the three of us and told us to look at them while he got the other kids working. Then he sat down on his chair in front of us.

"Now, you're going to learn to read," he said. "Would you like that?" Oh boy, would I ever! I so much wanted to be able to read.

"These are your Prep 1 Readers," he said.

I opened up my book, and it was like I had stepped into a whole new world. All of the letters that I knew were used to make words were spread out in front of me. It was like they were singing: "Come and play, come and play. We'll make some words today." I looked at Margaret sitting next to me. She was just staring at her book with her hands folded in her lap. I wondered if she could hear the letters singing, too.

Mr. Fisher hung a big chart on the blackboard that had all the same letters and pictures on it that were in my book. It was like a great big page. I thought that was pretty good.

"Now look," said Mr. Fisher, "this is letter 'a' and the picture tells you how to remember what it looks like: a is like an apple on a twig. Let's all say that together."

"a is like an apple on a twig," we all chimed in. This was fun.

"Very good," said Mr. Fisher, "but there's another important thing to know. The letters not only have a name. They also make a sound. This is letter a, but the sound it makes is 'aeh.' Can you say that?"

The three of us grunted "aeh."

"Very good," said Mr. Fisher. "Now we put it all together and it goes like this: a is like an apple on a twig; a says 'aeh.' Let's all say that together a few times."

"a is like an apple on a twig; a says 'aeh,'" we said over and over. I looked around to see what the other kids in school were doing. I wondered if they could see how well we were learning. A few of them were looking at us and smiling.

Mr. Fisher slapped a ruler on the desk in front of me, and I jumped. "Don't worry about anyone else, Des," he said sharply. Then he raised his voice. "And the rest of you keep on with your work." He walked around a bit, and out of the corner of my eye I saw him tweak Stanley's ear and give Gordon a bit of a nudge. I could see that you certainly had to do what you were told in school. Then he came back to us.

"Well, what have we learned so far?" he asked.

"a is like an apple on a twig; a says 'aeh,'" we chirped.

"Good. Now look at the next one. This is letter 'b.' What pictures can you see, Des?"

"It's a cricket bat and ball," I said.

"That's right," said Mr. Fisher. "And you can see that letter b looks like a bat with a ball at the bottom of it. So we say 'b is like a bat and ball.' And b also has its own sound. It says 'buh.' Let's say it all together."

"b is like a bat and ball; b says 'buh,'" we said as one.

And so we went on for some more letters.

"c is like a cake with a bit taken out; c says 'cah.'"

"d drags the drum; d says 'duh.'"

"e is like an empty egg; e says 'eh.'"

"f is like a feather; f says 'fuh.'"

"g is like Grandma's glasses; g says 'guh.'"

"All right," Mr. Fisher said, "now that we know a lot of letters, we can put them together to make words. Watch."

He wrote up on the blackboard: b-e-d. "What do you think that says?" he asked. "Let's sound it out."

"Buh-eh-duh," we said. Then again faster. And again. Then I shouted out, "I know, I know. It's bed." And that's how I learned to read my first word.

"Let's try another one," said Mr. Fisher. He wrote b-a-g on the blackboard. "This one is for you, Margaret. Sound it out. What does it say?"

"Buh-aeh-guh," Margaret said slowly with Phyllis and me softly joining in. "Buh-aeh-guh—bag," Margaret said excitedly.

"Good. One more for Phyllis," said Mr. Fisher. He wrote up d-a-d. I was sure I knew that one without sounding it out, but Phyllis said "duh-aeh -duh" and got "dad" right away.

"Good. Now let's just say the three words together a few more times," said Mr. Fisher, pointing to them one at a time, and mixing them up, while we rattled them off. We were so proud of ourselves.

"Bed, bag, dad, bag, dad, bed, dad, bed, bag."

"Dad went to bed in a bag," I shouted out. The whole school laughed. Mr. Fisher pretended to be angry, but I think he smiled, too.

"All right, that's enough reading for now," said Mr. Fisher. "Soon we'll do some counting, but first Dawn can read you a story while I see what these other people are up to."

Mr. Fisher gave Dawn a story book, and she took the three of us out onto the front verandah to read to us while we heard Mr. Fisher teaching the other children. He certainly was busy, and we were so glad he had taught us how to read.

And that's how the day went. We did some counting and learnt about numbers and drew some pictures. We had a break for snacks and to go to the dunny at the back of the school yard. (The older kids checked it for redback spiders before we went in). We ate our lunch under the school in the shade. Then the older kids set up a game of cricket. We had real stumps that the boys hammered into the ground, then stepped out 22 yards for the pitch, and hammered in the other set of stumps. Neville and Alma were captains and picked their teams. We played it with real bats (small ones for us little kids) and a tennis ball, and bowled from each end to speed things up. Jimmy would run huffing and puffing and bowl over arm really fast at Gordon, who whacked the ball out to the boundary for a four. The girls bowled under arm to us little ones. I tapped the ball with my bat and ran really fast to the other end to score a run. Kerry got caught out, and Dennis clean bowled Dawn for a duck. It was all such fun.

After lunch the older girls helped Margaret, Phyllis and me make up some beds out of cushions and saddle cloths on the back verandah, and we all had a nap. After that we did some colouring and played with plasticine, and then it was time to catch the horses and go home. On the ride home I couldn't stop talking about everything I had learned, until Gloria told me to hush up, or I would get a mouth full of flies. They got in my mouth anyway, but I didn't care, because now I was going to school and learning things. When we got to the house, I jumped off the back of Patsy, and ran inside to find Mum.

"Mum, Mum," I cried. "Guess what? I learned to read 'Dad went to bed in a bag.'" She smiled, gave me a big hug and said, "Now sit down, have a glass of milk and a rolled oats biscuit and tell me all about it."

And that was my first day of school.

The Nest of Snakes

The next big thing that happened about school was when Patsy started to get fat, and Dad said she was going to have a baby. I remembered how my Aunty Joy got fat before she had her baby, and I wondered again about all of that. Patsy started to walk more slowly on the way to school, and Dad said it would be better if she didn't have to carry me as well as Gloria. That meant it was time for me to ride Blackie to school on my own. Oh boy!

I was up early that morning to help Gordon catch and saddle the horses. Blackie was a bit frisky, because he had been having such a good time staying at home with the big stallion with nothing to do. The stallion looked a bit sad when all of the other horses were leaving, especially Patsy.

Just as I was about to get up on Blackie with my school bag on my back and my helmet on my head, I got too close to Patsy's head and she gave me a nasty bite on the arm. It really hurt, and I yelled and cried a bit, but Mum cleaned the bite up with warm water and rubbed some ointment on it. Gordon told me to be careful around Patsy, because she was acting a bit strange, which he said horses would do when they were going to have a baby, which was called a foal. Gloria didn't seem to have any trouble with her. Maybe that's because girls understand each other better.

I still couldn't get on Blackie on my own, so Gordon gave me a leg up, and away we went down to the gate to meet Thelma, who was already there. I felt so proud to be riding Blackie all by myself. I rode up front beside Gordon on Larry, while the girls came along behind. If we got too far ahead because Patsy was slow we would turn around and trot back. I had learned how to work myself up and down in the saddle, so I liked to get Blackie to trot if I could. I thought I was a pretty good rider.

When we arrived at school, Margaret was there and I felt so proud to show her I was riding Blackie all by myself. She stood by me while I unsaddled him, and she walked with me over to the school paddock to let him go.

"Maybe one day soon you can ride Blackie over to visit me," she said, as we walked back together to the school. I thought that was a good idea, except for one problem. I didn't know exactly where she lived, but I didn't want to say so. Instead I said: "Yes, and you can show me all your toys."

"And you can bring that big book of yours and we'll try to read it," she replied. That sounded like a terrific idea to me.

So we had another good day at school. I'm sure all of the kids thought I was getting pretty good at riding. Even Mr. Fisher had something to say about it.

"So now you're riding Gordon's old horse," he said. "You're lucky to have a big brother to teach you how to ride." I thought so, too, but I don't know if Gordon always felt that he was so lucky.

On the way home that afternoon something really exciting happened. We were riding up the hill from the gully with Gordon in front, when suddenly Larry gave a jump and shied off to one side. Gordon held on to him all right, but he called to me right behind him.

"Look out! There's a big black snake," he shouted.

"Where, where?" I cried, trying to see and keep Blackie still because he was starting to fidget, too.

"He ran across the track into a hole in that old stump," Gordon said, pointing to a dried out old tree stump that I could see was hollow in the middle.

"What's going on?" Gloria asked. She and Thelma had caught up with us. All of the horses were crowding together and shaking their heads. They knew something was going on that they didn't like. By now Gordon had edged Larry over closer to the stump, so that he could look down inside.

"Gawd struth," he shouted, "there's a whole nest of them wriggling around down in there."

Now that was something. To see one snake slithering through the grass was one thing. But a whole nest of them. I had never heard of that. Neither had any of the others. We talked about what we were going to do.

"They can't get out," Gordon said. "We can toss rocks on them and kill the lot. Bloody snakes. That big one almost made Larry throw me."

"Dad says snakes are deadly," Thelma said. "We don't want to get bitten, or we can die."

"That's why we should kill them," said Gordon. "We have to come by here every day on the way to school. They could bite the horses on the leg and they would die."

I didn't like the thought of Blackie getting bitten by a snake.

"The black ones are the poisonous ones," Gordon added to make it worse.

"We could get Dad to come back and kill them," Gloria said.

"He's got enough to do," Gordon said. "We can take care of this. If you're too scared, just keep away, and I'll do it."

With that Gordon jumped off Larry and tied him up to the fence. Then he picked up a big rock, and crept along an old white log right up to the hollow stump where the snakes were and threw the rock down inside.

"Bulls eye!" he shouted. "Take that you dirty snakes." Then he ran away to get another rock. I thought that if Gordon could do it I could, too, so I slipped down off Blackie and tied him up to the fence next to Larry. By then Gordon was tossing another rock into the stump. I found a rock, and crept up along the log just like Gordon.

"Des, don't," Gloria cried. "You're too little."

But I was already there. I looked down into the hole. It was a bit dark inside the stump, but I could see the snakes thrashing about. I threw my rock in and jumped back. Gordon was back again and threw in another rock.

"Good job," he shouted. "We'll bury the buggers. Come on girls, give us a hand."

Gloria and Thelma weren't too sure, but Gordon was in charge, so soon all four of us were piling rocks into the stump until all you could see were rocks and no more snakes.

"We did it," Gordon said. "No more snakes to worry about. Let's go home."

We got back on our horses and headed for home. We were all excited and couldn't stop talking about the snakes. Thelma left us at our gate and rode on to her place. When we got to the barn to unsaddle the horses, Dad was there fixing some harness.

"Dad, Dad," I said, "we saw a whole nest of snakes and killed them."

He dropped the harness and looked at us.

"What?" he said. "Snakes, where, what are you talking about?"

I could see that maybe he wasn't so pleased, so I decided to shut up and let Gordon tell the story. When he heard it, Dad looked at the three of us. I could see he was angry now.

"You silly little buggers," he said. "Haven't I told you time and time again to look out for snakes, and keep away from them? You're lucky none of you got bitten. Now I'll have to go and make sure they're all dead. Gordon, go down to the house and get the 22 and we'll go out in the truck. You other two look after the horses."

After a bit Gordon came running back with Dad's 22 rifle and they went off in the ute. We didn't hear anything more about it until that night around the tea table, when Dad gave us another good talking to about snakes. They hadn't found any, so we must have done a good job in killing them, but Dad told us never to do that again.

The next day when we rode past the stump we kept a good eye out for snakes, but we didn't see any. The interesting thing, though, was that there were a couple of kookaburras cackling away in the trees by the stump. Gloria said she had read a story somewhere about how kookaburras kill snakes by grabbing them and dropping them from a tree. Maybe we had saved them the job, and they had found some of our dead snakes to eat.

Anyway we all had a good story to tell at school.

Gloria and I Visit Uncle Henry and Aunty Eileen

Margaret asked me again to come and visit her, and I decided I was going to do it. I knew I couldn't go on my own, so I asked Gloria if she would come with me on Patsy. Gloria wasn't too keen at first, but Mum said we could visit Aunty Eileen on the way, and take her some oranges and marmalade jam. It was winter now, and the oranges were sweet like Dad said, after the first frost. It was Saturday, so we didn't have to go to school. The weather was cold, and that morning there was a big white frost covering the grass. I was wearing gloves and long pants and a thick wool jumper. When I took the horses down to the water trough to have a drink before we left, there was a thin cover of ice on the water. The horses pushed their noses into the ice and broke it up to drink. Steam rose up around their hot breath and the water in the trough. I wondered where the ice came from, and thought that I should ask Mr. Fisher because he would know.

Gloria and I filled up our school bags with oranges and a couple of jars of marmalade jam. I also put in my special book for Margaret and me to read, then we set off on Blackie and Patsy. We started off in the same direction as school, but instead of going down the long hill to the gully, we turned off down a side road that was only two car tracks running through the long dry grass. The top paddocks of Dad's farm were on one side, and my Uncle Peter's on the other side. We rode along the car tracks because that was easier for the horses.

Soon we were riding through bush on each side of the road. I had been along here before in the back of the ute, but it was different on a horse. It felt like we were already a long way from home, because you couldn't see anything except the car tracks and the trees.

I saw a sign nailed up on a tree just inside the fence on the left hand side. It looked very old and rusty and was full of holes, but you could still see some printing on it.

"What does the sign say?" I asked Gloria. We stopped so she could sound out the long words to read it.

"Keep out. T-res-pas-sers will be pros-e-cuted," she said.

I knew what keep out meant, but I had no idea what the rest of it was all about. I asked Gloria.

"I think it means if you go in there you will have your head chopped off," she said.

"Really? Who would do that?"

"I don't know. Maybe the people who own the place."

"I can't see anyone."

"That's because they're hiding behind the trees."

"Really?" I peered as hard as I could, but all I could see were trees and grass. I edged Blackie over to the middle of the road, just to be sure.

In a little while we came to a wooden gate on the right hand side, and Gloria said that was the way to Uncle Henry's and Aunty Eileen's place. I couldn't see any house, just a track winding through the bush. We rode in, and pretty soon came out into the open where there was a house and other buildings. The house looked very old. It had a rusty corrugated iron roof and a wide verandah around all sides.

As we rode up we saw Uncle Henry working at fixing something on his tractor. A couple of dogs started barking, and he looked up and saw us.

"Why, hello, Gloria and Desie. This is a nice surprise," he said.

"Hello, Uncle Henry," I said. "Do they really chop your head off if you go into the bush back there?"

He looked a bit puzzled as he wiped his hands on an old oily rag.

"Haven't heard of anyone losing their head, today," he said. "Mind you, it's still early. Why do you ask?"

"There's a sign, and that's what it says," I replied.

"What does it say?" he asked.

"Go on, Gloria, tell him what the big words say."

"It says, 'Keep out. Trespassers will be executed,'" Gloria said.

"Go on." Uncle Henry looked serious. "Executed, you say?"

"Yes and that means having your head chopped off," I said.

"You mean 'executed' spelled p-r-o-s-e-c-u-t-e-d?" he asked.

"I think so," Gloria said, but suddenly she didn't seem so sure.

Uncle Henry burst out laughing. "That spells 'prosecuted,'" he said. "Not so hard on the neck as executed. It means you might be reported to the police, if they catch you."

"If who catches you?" I asked.

"The silly buggers who put up the sign. That's why it's full of holes."

"What do the holes have to do with it?"

"They're bullet holes. Everyone who goes by with a gun shoots a hole in it."

"Why do they do that?"

"Because stupid signs deserve to be shot at. Mind you, I'm not saying you should do that."

"That's all right," I said. "We don't have a gun. Gordon got an air rifle for Christmas, but I don't have anything."

"How about a shanghai?" Uncle Henry asked. "I could make you one."

"Oh boy! That would be great," I said.

"Gloria, why don't you go and find Aunty Eileen. She's in the house. Desie and me will make a shanghai."

We tied the horses up to the fence, and Gloria went into the house. Uncle Henry broke a branch off a tree and trimmed it down with an axe.

"You call that a fork," he said. "Now we need a bit of rubber."

We went over to his tool shed, and he cut a strip of rubber off an old tube from a car tire. He fixed the ends of the rubber to the arms of the fork.

"A bit rough," he said, "but it should work. Let's try it out."

We went outside and Uncle Henry picked up a few small stones. He put a stone in the rubber and pulled back hard, and looked around for something to shoot at. He peered through the fork at his tractor and let the stone go. Zing! The stone bounced with a bang off the engine.

"There, maybe that'll fix it," he laughed. "Here, have a go, Desie."

He gave me the shanghai and a stone and I pulled back on the rubber as hard as I could. The fork bent over and when I let go the stone just plopped on the ground in front of me.

"Just need a bit of practice," said Uncle Henry. "Here, I'll give you a hand." He knelt down beside me. He smelt good with the dust of his old work clothes. He held my left hand with his, and pulled back hard on the rubber.

"Sight it up by looking through the fork," he said.

Just then an old cow walked by, and I let fly with the stone. It hit her right on the rump, and she kicked up her heels and took off. I was scared Uncle Henry might be mad at me, but he just laughed.

"That's one way to make a milk shake," he said. "But you better be careful and not do that at home, or I'll be in trouble with your Dad. Now put it away and let's go into the house for a cup of tea."

Inside the house it was nice and warm in the kitchen. Aunty Eileen was there and another old lady in a rocking chair. Gloria was sitting at the table having a cup of something and a biscuit.

"Hello, Desie, dear," said Aunty Eileen. "Would you like a cup of hot cocoa and a biscuit?"

"Yes, please," I said.

The old lady spoke to me in a squeaky voice. "You probably don't know who I am, do you? I'm your Uncle Henry's mother, Mrs. Webber."

"Just like my Granny," I said. "We made a shanghai." She nodded and closed her eyes. I don't think she was very interested in shanghais.

"How do you like school?" Aunty Eileen asked.

"It's beaut," I said. "I can read and count to 100."

"I'm sure you're very smart," said Aunty Eileen. "Do you like music? Would you like to play our gramophone?"

I wasn't sure what a gramophone was. Aunty Eileen led us into another room where it was dark and a lot colder than the kitchen. She went over to what looked like a big box and lifted the lid. I looked inside and saw a round black thing and a silver arm. I had never seen anything like it.

"You have to put a needle in the head and wind it up," said Aunty Eileen. I watched while she screwed a thin sharp needle into a slot on the head of the arm. Then she showed me a handle on the side of the box, and told me to turn it until it was tight. It was a bit like the handle on our butter churn, so I knew what to do.

Then Aunty Eileen moved a little catch on the top, and the round black thing began to turn round and round. She moved the silver arm over and put the needle down onto the turning black thing. Right away I heard music coming out of the top of the box.

"That's Bing Crosby," said Aunty Eileen. "Isn't he lovely?"

I thought the music was all right, but what I really wondered was where it was coming from.

"How does it work?" I asked.

"It's a record," said Uncle Henry, who had been watching. "Bing sings into a microphone in America and makes a record, and we play it back here in Athol on our gramophone. Pretty good, don't you think?"

I sure did, but what I really wondered was how it worked. When the record was finished, Aunty Eileen took it off and put on another one. She gave me the first one to look at. I could see it had grooves on it, so I knew the needle must be following the grooves, and that somehow it made the sound of Bing Crosby singing. I thought that we were lucky to live in a world where such amazing things could happen. Just like the electricity that came out of batteries to light our house, and the wireless where you could hear people talking and music playing all the way from Toowoomba. It was amazing, and I thought I would like to learn a lot more about that when I grew up.

Just then the record started to slow down, and the music sounded like a big groan.

"Oops, you have to wind it up again," said Uncle Henry. I turned the handle really fast, and the music sounded good again.

"Do you have any hillbillies?" I asked.

"I think we might," said Uncle Henry. He searched around in a pile of records. "Here's Tex Morton, singing 'Mandrake' about a bucking horse that no one could ride.

"That's one of my favourites," I said. "I want a guitar so I can sing like that."

"Maybe next year you can get your Mum and Dad to take you to the Toowoomba Show and you'll be able to see Tex Morton and his rough riders," said Uncle Henry.

I thought that would be just great.

At Margaret's Place

We stayed with Aunty Eileen and Uncle Henry for lunch, and then set off again for Margaret's place. It was further along the same road where we had seen the sign telling you to keep out or you will be ------. I still couldn't remember the word, but I knew it was bad. At last we came out of the bush to some paddocks of cultivation, and we met up with another road where there was a farm house, and Gloria said that was where Margaret lived.

Right away Margaret came out to meet us. She was full of smiles and helped me tie Blackie up to the fence. She had a small brother named Johnny, who was about three years old, and he was running around waving a stick. I thought I could show him something more interesting than that. I took off my school bag and pulled out the shanghai.

"Look what my Uncle Henry made for me," I said. Margaret kind of stood back, but Johnny right away was trying to grab it. I managed to hold him off so that I could show him how it worked, but he was too small to do it properly. Instead, he grabbed the shanghai and started hitting all of us with the rubber band. Gloria grabbed him and Margaret took the shanghai and gave it back to me.

"You keep it," she said. "He's too wild."

We went inside and met Margaret's mother, who was very nice, and gave us some milk and biscuits. Gloria gave her a jar of Mum's marmalade jam and some oranges. They stayed talking, while Margaret and I went off to play.

Margaret had a lot of toys. Some of them were girl things like dolls that I wasn't very interested in, though I did have a Teddy bear of my own at home. She also had a lot of picture books, and after we looked at them for a bit she asked if I had brought my special book.

"You bet," I said, and I pulled it out of my school bag.

By now at school we were into our Prep 2 Reader so Margaret and I knew a lot of words and could read short stories like the ones about "The Picnic" and

"The Garden." The stories in my book were a lot harder to read because we didn't know all the words, but we sat together at a table in a sunny room and tried our best to figure it out, and what we didn't know we made up. It was nice to have someone my own age, who didn't make fun of me when I pretended to know something I wasn't sure of. I really liked my two sisters, Gloria and Val, but Gloria was a bit bossy at times and Val was too little. But Margaret was just right, and she was happy and sweet and I liked that. I didn't have any boy friends my own age (except Triloaf, but he was just in my head). So it was nice to have Margaret as my friend. I knew girls were different from boys, and you shouldn't be rough with them, or say bad words to them. Margaret talked a lot, and I think she liked that I would sit and listen. So we had a good time together.

In my book as well as stories, it showed you how to make things. I couldn't read what it said, but there were pictures and drawings that you could follow. Mum had already helped me with how to make a paper hat and turn it into a boat. I opened the book at that page and showed it to Margaret. She clapped her hands and said, "Let's do it. Let's make a hat for you and a hat for me."

"We need some paper," I said.

"I've got coloured paper," Margaret said. "We can have pink for me and blue for you." I wasn't sure, but I think Margaret was telling me with the colours one way that girls were different from boys. When she got the paper, I showed her how to follow the pictures in the book to make our hats.

"Will you make a pink one for me?" she asked.

Of course I said I would. I was a bit nervous with her sitting so close and watching me. The hat came out pretty good and I put it on her head. She looked very nice.

"Oh, goody," she said. "Now I'll make the blue one for you." She was much quicker than me, and a lot neater in folding the paper. In no time at all she had made my blue hat, and put it on my head. We ran to find Gloria and Margaret's mother to show them what we had done. They were very pleased, and said we were clever. Johnny was there, too, and he tried to grab Margaret's hat, so I told him I would make one for him, too. Margaret and I made another hat out of white paper and put it on his head. He ran around showing it off.

"Do you know what?" I said. "I can turn your hat into a boat." I could, too, because Mum had shown me how to do it.

"Boat, boat!" Johnny screamed.

"All right, all right," I said, and I fumbled around with his hat and finally turned it into a boat.

"Let's go sail it," said Margaret, and the three of us ran outside, and found an old tub in the garden, and filled it with water, and put Johnny's boat in it. It tipped a bit to one side, but he didn't seem to notice, and he made it go around the tub by pushing it.

"Let's turn our hats into boats, too," said Margaret, so we did and soon had three boats sailing around the tub. Then Johnny picked up a rock and sank his boat to the bottom. Margaret grabbed our two boats before he could do the same to them. She took them inside and said she would keep them together in a special place. I said I would like that.

"Do you know we're Catholic?" she suddenly asked.

"What's Catholic?" I said. I had heard Mum and Dad talk about the Catholic Church on the hill on the way to town, and I had my tonsils out in the Catholic hospital in Toowoomba, but I had never thought much about it.

"We go to church and pray to the Holy Mother," said Margaret.

"What's 'holy' mean?" I asked.

"It's like God. The Holy Mother, Mary, was the mother of Jesus, who is the Son of God."

"Oh, I see," I said. I really didn't see at all, but Margaret looked very serious, so I knew it was important for her.

"I know you're not a Catholic," she said, "but that's all right. We can be good friends." I was certainly glad to hear that, and I told her she was my best friend.

When we were riding home I said to Gloria, "Did you know that Margaret is a Catholic?"

"Of course," she said. "We see their car go past our place every Sunday on the way to church."

"Why aren't we Catholics?" I asked.

"Because, we're not. We're different."

"What are we?"

"We're Protestant."

"Is that like pros-e-cuted?"

"Like what?"

"Like on the sign that says to keep out."

"No, silly. You've got everything mixed up."

"Well, you had it mixed up, too. You thought it meant to get your head chopped off."

"Oh, just forget it."

But I couldn't forget it, and when we came to the sign, I remembered what Uncle Henry said about shooting holes in stupid signs. I told Gloria to stop, and I jumped off Blackie, and took out my shanghai, and picked up some rocks from the road.

"Hold on to Blackie," I told Gloria, as I gave her the reins, and crept over to the fence, and took aim at the sign. I missed it a few times, but finally I hit it with a loud thwang.

"Look out! They might catch you," Gloria called. I got such a fright that I ran back to the road, grabbed the reins, and for the first time got up into the saddle without any help.

"Let's go!" I shouted, and kicked Blackie to make him go. He took off past Patsy into a fast trot, then into a canter, and we didn't stop until we got to the end of the bush. I pulled Blackie up. Gloria and Patsy were way behind, so I waited for them. When she caught up with me, Gloria was laughing her head off.

"One thing's for sure," she said. "You'll never forget that sign, and you'll always keep out of that paddock."

Patsy Has a Foal

Patsy got so big with her foal that Gloria couldn't ride her to school, and we had to double up on Blackie with Gloria in front and me on the cushion again behind. But I didn't mind, because I knew it would only be for a little while, until Patsy had her baby. But it was sure taking its time in coming. Dad said he thought it was almost due, so he put Patsy in the horse yard on her own until it happened. I would go and check every morning and afternoon and give Patsy a handful of oats from the grain shed to help her along. But it didn't seem to make any difference. Mum told me that you just had to let nature take its course. I wasn't sure who "nature" was, because I knew it was Patsy who was going to have the baby. But anyway I was sure Mum was right.

Then one morning when Gloria and I came to the kitchen for breakfast before going to school, Mum said we should go to the horse yard, because Dad had told her there was a surprise there. She said he had stayed up most of the night to make sure Patsy was all right, and now he and Gordon had gone off to do the morning milking.

We darted out of the house and up to the horse yard. There was Patsy looking very pleased with herself, and lying on the ground curled up not far away was a little brown bundle of body and legs. I crawled through the fence rails and crept up to have a look. I had never seen a foal before, and wondered if it would be like a calf. I sure got a surprise when I touched it, because it lifted its head, and I could see right away that it had a long nose and pointy ears like a perfect little horse head.

"Wow! Look at that," I said to Gloria, who was now standing beside me. "Isn't he terrific?"

"Just a little darling," she said.

Patsy came over and gave the little fellow a nudge with her nose. Immediately his long legs started to thrash around, as he struggled to get up. I put my arms around him to help, and he felt warm and soft, and smelled like a saddle cloth.

"Up you go," I said, and he got to his feet and stumbled around with his four legs all trying to go in different directions. But then, almost right away, he got the hang of it, and started prancing around like a kitten on an ants' nest. I laughed and cheered, and that made him dance all the more. Then he went over to Patsy and nuzzled his head under her tummy to find her tits, so he could have some breakfast. Gloria put her arms around Patsy's neck, and told her she was a great little mother. I just stood staring, thinking how wonderful it all was, and probably would have stayed there for ages except that we heard Mum calling us for our breakfast, otherwise we would be late for school. We certainly had something to tell all the kids at school today.

Dad kept Patsy and the foal in the horse yard for a few days, until he thought the little fellow was strong enough to go out into the paddock with Patsy and the other horses. I knew the big stallion was his father, but he didn't seem to pay much mind to his son. Blackie and Larry seemed a bit more interested, and would run around with the foal when he wanted to play. But soon they would get bored with that, and the foal was left to himself to explore all the new places in the paddock. I knew just how he felt, because that was what I liked to do, too; just find out as much as you can about everything around you.

The Dance in Athol Hall

The next exciting thing that happened was the dance in the Athol Hall. It was on a Saturday night. Mum told me in the morning, so I had all day to think about it, because I didn't have to go to school on Saturday. I had been to dances before, but that was when I was small, and I couldn't remember much about them. I was probably asleep, because that was what the little kids did at dances, but Mum said that this time I was to get dressed up and dance with the girls.

"Will Margaret be there?" I asked.

"Yes, I know her family will come," Mum said.

"Will I be able to dance with her?"

"I'm sure you can. But you'll have to ask her."

I wasn't so sure about that, because I didn't really know how to dance. I went out to sit in the swing under the peperina tree to think about it. Triloaf was there, so I decided to ask him.

"Do you think Margaret will want to dance with me?" I asked him.

"Do you want to dance with her?" he asked me.

He was always doing that: asking me a question after I asked him one.

"Why don't you just answer my question?" I said.

"Because the answer is in your answer. Do you want to dance with her?"

"Of course I do."

"Then she'll want to dance with you."

"Really?"

"Too right."

That was that then. I went over to the horse paddock to see what the new foal was up to. He knew me really well now, and would come over when I called. We didn't have a name for him yet, so I just called him Foal.

"Hey, Foal," I shouted, "do you know what? I'm going to the dance tonight."

He came running over to me, so I could tickle his ears and pat his nose. I knew you were supposed to talk to girls while you danced with them, so I could tell Margaret about the foal. Of course, I had already told her about him at school. But that didn't matter. I should be able to think of something new to say.

"I'm going to teach you some tricks so I can tell Margaret about them at the dance," I told him. "I want you to stand still while I back up, then come when I call."

I walked backwards, but he just followed me.

"No!" I said. "You stay there until I call."

I backed up some more, but he just followed me.

"No, no, no!" I shouted. "You stay still."

His mother, Patsy, looked up from where she was feeding on the grass, and looked at me.

"Tell him to stay," I shouted to her, but she went back to feeding. I backed up some more, and the foal followed. Larry came trotting over to see what was going on. I backed up. The foal followed. I gave up, turned around, and walked slap into the barbed wire fence that I didn't know was right behind me.

It was terrible. The top wire scratched my face, the bottom one scraped my legs and the middle one tore my clothes. I could feel blood running down my face, and it was dripping on the ground as I tried to crawl through the fence. But then I really got stuck, and I felt the barbs ripping my shirt and scratching my back. I must have started yelling and crying, because as I got through the fence and stumbled toward the house, Mum and Gloria came running out. I don't remember exactly what happened after that. Mum got me cleaned up, but all I knew was that I was covered in scratches and patched up with sticky bandages right before I was supposed to get dressed up and go to the dance.

Mum helped me put on my best clothes. I wanted to wear long pants to cover up the scratches on my legs, but it was too hot, and I didn't really have any good long pants, just scruffy ones for outdoors and riding in the winter time. I had a nice white shirt with short sleeves, but that just showed up the scratches on my arms, so Mum agreed to let me wear a jacket, even though it was really too hot for that. I also wore a nice red and black striped tie and polished black shoes, so all in all I would have looked pretty sharp, except for the scratches on my face, which no amount of covering up with ointment could do anything to hide.

When we got to the dance hall, it was already dark. There were some cars and trucks there, and more headlights coming along the road. Mum had packed a big basket of sandwiches and cakes for supper, and I helped her carry them into the supper room at the back of the hall. There were some other ladies there fussing around. No one took much notice of me, which was good, except for my Aunty Dolly who took one look at the scratches on my face and legs and asked if I had fallen into a prickly pear patch. I just mumbled something, and ran out into the hall.

There were already some families sitting on the wooden benches along the walls. I saw my Uncle Peter spreading some sawdust and something else on the floor to make it slippery for dancing. A few boys were running up and down and sliding to see how far they could go. It looked like fun, but I was still worried about how I looked, so I hung back in a corner by the stage. My Uncle Ralph and Aunty Milly with my cousin Dawn were setting up to play the music for dancing. Uncle Ralph played the drums. He had a great big drum that he banged with his foot, and two smaller ones on the side that he played with drumsticks, and a set of what you call cymbals that he could clang every now and then. Aunty Milly played the piano off to one side of the stage, and on the other side my cousin, Dawn, played a piano accordion that was almost as big as she was. She sat on a chair, so she could hold it. They were a really musical family, which I thought was pretty terrific, because no one in our family played music. They were just warming up a bit before they started playing for the dancing. I looked up at Dawn, and she smiled and beckoned me to come up on stage.

"Hello, Desie," she said. "Don't you look nice, all dressed up for the dance." I was waiting for her to ask me about the scratches, but she never said a word about that, and neither did Uncle Ralph or Aunty Milly. They just smiled, and let me wander around while they got ready.

There were a lot more people in the hall now, and it was starting to get noisy with all the talking and the kids shouting. Uncle Peter came up on the stage to ask if they were ready to play. Uncle Ralph gave a rat-a-tat-tat on the drums, and a bang on the cymbals. Everyone in the hall went quiet, and Uncle Peter walked to the front of the stage to speak.

"Hello everyone," he shouted out in a big voice. "How are you doing? Good to see you at the dance. We're gonna have fun tonight. Ralph, Milly and Dawn have come all the way from the top of the hill to play for us." Uncle Ralph gave another round on the drums and cymbals, and everyone clapped. Then Uncle Peter continued: "We're also tryin' to raise a bit of money for the school, so the boys and girls will be coming around selling raffle tickets. I know there's a war on and everyone's a bit short, but if you can spare a bob or two for the school, that'd be a bloody good thing to do. Better than pouring it down the drain in the pub." I saw Aunty Dolly glaring at Uncle Peter from the floor of the hall. I think she was afraid he would say something worse. "The old woman's giving me the glass eye, so I better take a pull," Uncle Peter continued, "but you should know that the first prize for the raffle is a big ham donated by my brother, Kenny." That was my Dad. Everyone cheered. "Second prize is what's left of the pig after you make the ham." Everyone groaned. "Just pulling your leg. It's actually a batch of marmalade jam made by Dolly." More cheers and clapping. "Third prize is to sit in school for a day and listen to Andy Fisher." The kids all laughed at that, but the grown ups groaned. I saw Mr. Fisher turn a bit red in the face. "Sounds like they're not too keen about that, Andy, but not to worry, maybe you could go to their place instead and wash the dishes." That got a cheer. "All right, that's enough out of me," Uncle Peter said. "Ladies and gentlemen choose your partners for the Pride of Erin."

"One, two, three," said Uncle Ralph, and they started to play, and soon everyone was dancing.

I stayed up on the stage to one side behind Dawn, watching. I didn't feel like going down to join in. I saw Mum beckoning me, but I pretended not to notice. Everyone looked to be having such a good time, except me. The men already had their jackets off, and were dancing in short sleeves. The ladies looked pretty in their best dresses. In the Pride of Erin you sort of go forward in little steps with the men holding the ladies' hands up behind their heads. Then they twirl around, the men grabbing the ladies around the waist, and holding the other hand up high and sort of leaning towards each other. The men's bums stuck out a bit like they were steering the ladies around, who didn't seem to mind, and were laughing and talking all the time. Some of the younger girls were dancing with each other. I could see Gloria and Barbara having a good time. The older boys and girls were dancing with each other, like Gordon and Rose, but the younger boys were kind of hanging around the edges or pushing and shoving each other at the back of the hall.

When the dance was over, Gloria came up to me on the stage.

"What's up, Eddo?" she asked. "Why are you hiding up here?"

I shuffled my feet, but didn't say anything.

"If it's because of your silly scratches, you shouldn't worry. They make you look cute."

Dawn was listening and joined in.

"Go on, Des," she said. "The next one's a Gypsy Tap. You can dance with Gloria. She'll teach you how to do it."

"Yes, it's real easy," said Gloria, and she started to show me up on the stage. "Just side step, side step, forward and back, then open up and turn around."

"Choose your partners for the Gypsy Tap," Uncle Ralph called out, and they started to play.

I slowly followed Gloria down onto the dance floor. It was already crowded. Mum and Dad were dancing and waved to us. We joined in. I made a few mistakes at first, but soon started to get the hang of it.

"You're right," I said. "It's easy."

When the music stopped and everyone waited for the next number, I saw Phyllis standing on the side looking at us.

"Go on, ask Phyllis to dance," Gloria said.

I had a bit of a lump in my throat, but I went over anyway.

"Hello, Phyllis," I said. "Would you like to dance with me?"

She gave me a big smile and held out her hands. The music started again, and away we went, side stepping and kicking and twirling like a top. Phyllis was pretty good, not as smooth as Gloria, but with a lot of bounce. We had a great time, and after the dance I took her back to where her parents were sitting, like I knew you should.

By now I was all smiles, and even better I saw Margaret just coming into the hall with her parents and brother, Johnny.

"Choose your partners for the Canadian Barn Dance," Uncle Ralph called, and away they went again. Now I had a big problem. I wanted to dance with Margaret before anyone else asked her, but I had never heard of the Canadian Barn Dance. I knew that Canada was a country on the other side of the world, where they must dance in barns, but that didn't help me much with how to do it. Gloria had gone off to dance with Harold. Mum said she would teach me, but I didn't want Margaret to see me learning how to dance from Mum. So I just stood in the corner and watched. It didn't look so hard and was really fast, but I didn't want to mess up the first dance with Margaret, so I hung back. I could see her down the hall sitting and watching, too. I didn't know if she had seen me. The two Johnnies came sliding around the room and kind of leered at me, but I didn't take any notice.

While the dance went on I thought up a plan, and when it was over, I went up to Dawn on stage.

"Could we do another Gypsy Tap?" I asked.

Aunty Milly heard me and said, "We don't usually like to repeat dances too soon."

"But it's the only one I know," I said, "and I want to ask Margaret to dance."

"In that case," said Uncle Ralph, "you've got it." He gave a roll of the drums. "We've got a special request from Desie Berghofer for another Gypsy Tap," he said in a real loud voice. "Choose your partners." Then to me he said softly, "Go for it, Des."

Quick as a flash I was down off the stage and over to Margaret, just as the music was starting. "Hello Margaret," I said. "Can I have this dance?" She smiled really sweetly, but was a bit shy. Her mother was smiling and gave her a little push.

"I'd love to dance with you, Des," said Margaret, "but I'm not sure I know how."

"I'll teach you," I said proudly, and she got up and took my hands.

Away we went. Margaret was a very good dancer and very light on her feet. I was already learning how different girls felt different when you danced with them. Margaret especially just seemed to float along. I didn't need to teach her anything. I guessed she probably already knew all the dances and could teach me, but I didn't say so. Instead I said during a break in the music, "If you're wondering how I got all these scratches, I walked into a barbed wire fence while I was trying to teach Patsy's new foal some tricks."

"That was a funny trick to teach him," she giggled. I wasn't sure if she was making fun of me, but I laughed anyway and said, "You're right about that. It was pretty dumb, actually." We both laughed a lot at that and went whirling by Jim and Thelma, who were also having a great time.

Actually everyone seemed to have a great time at the Athol dance. As the night went on things got livelier and livelier. The men had a few bottles of beer out the back, and whenever they came in after having a drink they danced harder than ever. Uncle Ralph had a bottle up on the stage beside his drums to keep him going. I'm not sure what the ladies were drinking, but there was no stopping them, either. Just before we broke for supper it was a Ladies Choice, and the ladies were off their marks faster than the men. I saw Mum pick Uncle Peter, who was really talking up a storm by this time, and Aunty Dolly chose Dad. I was really pleased that Margaret came over to me, but when we started dancing we saw that Phyllis didn't have a partner, so the three of us danced together. Then the ladies brought in the supper, and we had sandwiches and cakes and cordial all round. After that we danced the Hokey Pokey, and when everyone jumped into the middle at the end, the old hall shook like it was going to fall down. Then it was time to go. We cheered for Uncle Ralph, Aunty Milly and Dawn for playing all night. Uncle Henry won the ham in the raffle. I'm not sure if Mr. Fisher had to wash anyone's dishes, but I saw him and Mrs. Fisher helping with the clean up. A few of us boys ran up and down the hall with brooms to sweep the floor and get in a few more slides. Then we were riding home in the back of the ute, with a bright full moon in the sky and a cool breeze blowing. I think that was the best time I ever had at a dance.

My Birthday Party, the School Picnic and the Christmas Dance

There were three more special events that happened in my first year of school: my sixth birthday, the school picnic, and a Christmas party and dance. They didn't all have a lot to do with school—except the picnic, of course—but I remember them as part of that whole wonderful year for me.

My birthday is on the 28th of October, and it is always hot, so we had the party outside in the shade of the old peperina tree. We had it on a Saturday, so everyone could come. I'm not sure if the party was on my actual birthday, but it was close enough. I didn't have a lot of friends to invite, because there weren't many kids my age in Athol, especially boys. I of course invited my two classmates, Margaret and Phyllis, and because Gloria and Val were coming, we invited other kids their age, especially my cousins Jimmy, Johnny and Joan. Margaret's brother, the other Johnny, came, too.

We set up a table under the peperina tree for the food, but before that we played games like hide and seek and pin the tail on the donkey and blind man's bluff. We had sandwiches and small cakes and biscuits with cordial for the party. This, of course, brought out all the cats, who were mewing and purring and rubbing against our legs and the table legs and any other legs they could find. I told the kids it was all right to feed them, but not to tell Gordon—who didn't come to the party anyway, because it was only for small kids.

When Mum brought out the birthday cake it had six candles on it, set in the thick white icing around a big brown horseshoe that Mum had made out of icing for decoration. Mum lit the candles, and I blew them out with one big puff, and made a wish that every day could be as good as this one. Then I cut it up and gave a big piece to everyone.

All of the kids had brought a present—a book or a small toy plane or car. But the presents weren't the main thing. Just having everyone come to my birthday was the best of all. Margaret gave me a story book and she smiled so sweetly when she gave it to me that I would have liked to kiss her, but I was too shy. She was wearing the pink dress with blue butterflies on the pockets that I liked so much. I was especially glad that she was there.

While my birthday is a special memory, my first school picnic was also a lot of fun. I shouldn't say it was my first picnic, because I had been there before with Gordon and Gloria, who started school before me. But this was the first time since I was going to school myself, which meant that I was going to get a book for a prize. I wondered what it would be. I had seen the books that Gloria and Gordon had got at other school picnics, and they were terrific, so I was sure I would get a great one, too.

But before that there were a lot of fun things to do. The picnic was held on the last Friday of school not long before Christmas. It was the end of my first year of school, and Margaret, Phyllis and I had finished Prep 1 and Prep 2. Next year we would do Prep 3 and Prep 4, and after that we would be in Grade One. We rode our horses to school as usual for the morning, which was a kind of fun day, when we put on a school play that the older kids had made up with parts for all of us. I don't remember the story, but I think I was a little baby Joey hopping along with my kangaroo mother, Dawn, to escape from a bush fire.

In the middle of the day most of the parents arrived, bringing a special picnic lunch that was set up under the school, with covers over the food to keep the flies off. It was good food that we all shared, though we didn't want to eat too much, because we knew there were going to be races. The track was set up to run from the front gate to the school. We brought down the stools from the desks and set them up on both sides of the track for the parents and other small kids to sit on. A couple of us held a long skipping rope as the finish line, and Mr. Fisher was the starter at the other end of the track down by the gate. There were all kinds of races with boys against boys, and girls against girls, then mixed up, with us younger ones and the slower ones given a head start by Mr. Fisher to make it more even. After that we had the special races—the egg and spoon race, the three-legged race, and the sack race.

The three-legged race was a bit of a problem for me because you had to have a partner, but there were three of us in my class, and I didn't want to see either Margaret or Phyllis left out, so I said they should race together, and I would stay out.

"But I'll still be part of our team," I said. "I'll tie your legs together and run beside you to make you go faster."

"Oh, yes, please, Des," said Margaret. "You can be our coach."

I wasn't too sure about what a coach was, but it sounded important, so I said all right, and went over to Mum to get a couple of her old stockings to tie the girls' legs together. I wasn't very good at knots, but I did a pretty good job, I thought, and when the girls did a trial run, and fell over with lots of screams and legs and arms going every which way, and the knots didn't come undone, then I knew they would be fine for the race.

We went over to line up. This was an everyone-in hundred yard dash. Mostly, boys paired up with boys and girls with girls. Mr. Fisher started all the big boys at the back, like Gordon and Kerry, then the next older ones like Jimmy and Kenny, and all the girls were in front of them. Gloria was running with Barbara. But I was the only coach.

Mr. Fisher took Margaret and Phyllis half way up the track to give them a good head start, and I was right there beside them.

"Come on, girls, you've gotta stop laughing," I said to them. "We can win this, but you've got to concentrate." I thought "concentrate" was a pretty good word, but it didn't help much, because the girls just kept laughing, and when Mr. Fisher shouted "Go!" they almost fell over, and I had to jump up and down to get them moving. I was sure finding out what this coaching business was all about.

What a race it was! You never saw such a mess! Half the girls in the front fell down, and the boys at the back crashed into them and tumbled over. All the parents were splitting their sides laughing. Margaret and Phyllis were way out in front because of their head start, but they couldn't get the action right.

"Come on, girls," I yelled. "Step with your middle leg, now both outside together. Together—it's got to be together! Oh, crikey! Come on, try again. Middle step. Outside step. Middle step. Outside step. Now you're getting it. Look out! Here comes Gordon and Kerry. Come on, come on, you're almost there. Oh no! We almost won."

What had happened was that Gordon and Kerry had come over the top of the pile up in the middle, and raced for the finish line. Margaret and Phyllis were almost there, but with five yards to go they tripped over themselves and crashed, and Gordon and Kerry whizzed past. Margaret and Phyllis didn't seem to mind. They were laughing too much to care. I went over to help them up, and the three of us stumbled to the finish line well behind most of the others.

The next race was the sack race, and I was on my own for this one. Dad had brought a potato sack from home, and when I stepped inside it I almost disappeared. It came almost up to my neck. All of us were jumping and stumbling around trying to get into position to start. Mr. Fisher looked at me and laughed and told me to go half way up the track. Just then Margaret's father came over to me.

"You did a great job coaching the girls," he said. "Now I'll give you a tip on how to run in the sack. All those big boys are gonna bounce along like kangaroos, but they'll wear themselves out before they're half way. The way to do it is to wriggle your feet into each corner of the sack, then just run with short steps and you'll beat them all."

I did what he said, and gripped the top of the sack around my chest. When Mr. Fisher said "Go!" I just took off, waddling like a duck. I had plenty of room in the sack to work my feet, and I knew if I could stop from falling over I had a good chance. I could hear all the huffing and puffing and thumping behind me as the older boys tried to catch up, but I just put my head down and went waddle-waddle down the track as fast as I could. I was almost there. I could see Margaret and her Dad cheering me on, and my own Mum and Dad, too. Then I hit the skipping rope that marked the end, and I knew I was the winner!

"Not fair, not fair, he had too much start," I heard someone complaining, but I didn't care, because I knew I had won using the special tip from Margaret's Dad. Mrs. Fisher was handing out the prize money, and I got a bright two shilling piece. Boy, I was rich.

There was one race left, the egg and spoon. You had to run the whole way carrying a hard boiled egg in a tablespoon. If the egg fell out, you had to stop until you got the egg back in the spoon. Of course, there was no problem with the eggs breaking, because they were hard boiled. At least, that was supposed to be the way it was, but some larrikin had got to the basket of eggs, and switched all of the hardboiled ones with fresh ones. Well, you can imagine what happened. As soon as the race started, someone dropped an egg, and it went splat all over the place, then another one, and another one. Everyone was roaring laughing and kids were getting egg all over them, then someone threw an egg at someone else and a real ding-dong battle was on. No one made it to the end of the race without breaking their egg, so everyone was disqualified. Mr. Fisher was pretty mad, and he made us clean up the mess. We never did find out who switched the eggs, which was just as well for him, because I heard Mr. Fisher say he should be skinned alive, and his hide nailed up on the school door as a warning to others. I wasn't too sure about that, because I thought it was a pretty funny joke, actually.

After the races it was time to eat some more sandwiches and cakes, and as a special treat we all got a little bucket of ice-cream that you ate with a wooden spoon. The ice-cream was pretty soft because of the hot day, even though it had been brought from town in a special cold box by one of the parents.

Now it was time for the book prizes. They were all set out on a table under the school. Mr. Fisher gave a bit of a speech about how hard we had all worked, though some could have worked harder. Then he gave out the books, beginning with us little ones. I got my very first school book prize. It was called *The Adventures of Algernon the Ant,* and it was all about this little ant called Algie, whose mother warned him to be careful when he went out. She especially told him to be careful of the lawn mower, but he got things mixed up and called it the corn blower. I took my book over to Mum and showed her how I could read it, and I couldn't wait to take it home, and read it all the way through. It had a special sticker in the front of it that said, "Athol State School. Presented to Desmond Berghofer (my name was in the teacher's handwriting). C.W. Fisher, Head Teacher. Christmas, 1944."

It was a special way to end a very special day and begin the school Christmas holidays.

After the school picnic, it seemed that Christmas was coming pretty fast this year. I already had my Christmas book gift from the school, and the next day we all went to a Christmas party and dance. This wasn't in Athol, but at a place called Biddeston that was a long way away, past the school and up over Wallaby Hill, and a long way after that. It was Saturday, and after Dad and Gordon had done the milking and the rest of us had finished our jobs and had our tea, we all set off in the ute for the Christmas party and dance at Biddeston.

Gordon, Gloria and I rode in the back of the ute on a cool dark night under a sky full of stars. The road was nice and smooth, because Dad drove in the car tracks cut into the black soil on the edge of the rough gravel strip that ran down the middle. When it was dry, the black soil tracks were just as smooth as bitumen to drive on, but if it was raining, look out, because cars could be bogged down to their axles pretty quick in the black mud. However, on this night the weather was fine and clear, and the ute sailed along making no more than a whisper in the wind.

I couldn't remember going to a Christmas party before, so I wondered what it would be like. Mum said that our cousins Roy, Jan and Gail would be there, because her brother, Uncle Gordon, and Aunty Elsie lived down that way. I was really looking forward to seeing Jan again to tell her about my first year of school.

When we got to Biddeston there wasn't much to see. I don't think there would have been much to see, even if it wasn't dark—just a store on the corner, a couple of houses, and the hall lit up across the road. It wasn't brightly lit, because there was a war on, and the rule was you couldn't show much light at night. Even the car headlights were half blackened out so the light didn't spread out as much. I think this was supposed to protect us from bombers, like the ones I had seen on the newsreel at the pictures, but I didn't really know how any bombers would find us way out in Athol and Biddeston.

When we got inside, it was bright enough and a bit stuffy because the weather was hot. I thought the hall was bigger than ours in Athol, but otherwise much the same. But the big thing that was different on this night was the gigantic Christmas tree up on the stage. It was just like the ones I had seen on the Christmas cards we got every year, but I didn't think those trees could be real, because you never saw any like that out in the bush. But here was one on the stage, all dressed up with ribbons and little ornaments hanging from the branches, and with a great big silver star on the top. Under the tree was a pile of packages, all wrapped up in coloured paper, which I knew must be gifts for all the girls and boys, because that was what Christmas was about.

Jan was there as I had expected, and we had a great time together talking about all the things we had been doing and learning since we had last seen each other. I didn't really know any of the other kids there, so I mostly hung around with Jan. We had a couple of dances together so I could show off how good I was, and then it was time for the Christmas party. All of us kids sat on the floor in front of the stage. They had this play about how Jesus was born in a manger and kids were dressed up as shepherds and animals, and at the end this special angel appeared from behind the Christmas tree and said "Peace to the World!" The girl dressed up as the angel was the prettiest girl I had ever seen. She had long dark hair and beautiful white skin, and her silver costume sparkled just like her eyes as she moved her wings up and down with her arms, and stood there smiling at us and saying "Peace to the World."

"Wow!" I said to Jan. "She is so beautiful she looks like a real angel." Not that I knew what a real angel looked like. I didn't even know if there really were any angels, but I was sure if there were they would look just like that.

"Her name is Lynette," said Jan.

I thought it would be nice to meet her, but I was too shy to ask, and anyway I lived so far away at Athol that I would never see her again, but it was a nice memory.

Then a lady began playing very loud on the piano on the stage, and everyone started singing Christmas carols. I knew some of the words, but not all of the way through, because I had never really learned them and just heard them mainly on the wireless. But it was nice to sit there in the hall and hear everyone singing, and I thought about what Lynette, the angel, had said about "Peace to the World," and I wondered why the soldiers were away at the war fighting. I wanted to ask someone about that, but I couldn't do it with everyone singing, and before I could think much more about that there was a loud "Ho! Ho! Ho!" from the back of the hall. We all turned around, and there was Father Christmas in his red suit and black boots and long red hat with white fur around the edges. He was really fat and came waddling down the hall, and walked right in amongst us kids on the floor, with a bell in one hand that he rang, waving at us. With his other hand he held onto a big white bag that he carried on his back, all the while saying over and over in a very deep voice, "Ho! Ho! Ho! Merry Christmas everyone!"

As he came by me, I could see he was very hot, because the sweat was running down his face into his long white beard. I knew he lived somewhere on the other side of the world, where it was very cold, so that must be why he was wearing such a hot suit. He went right up onto the stage and sat in a chair that someone had put in front of the Christmas tree.

Some ladies were up there helping him, handing him presents from under the Christmas tree. Each present had a name on it, and when Father Christmas called out the name, we each went up to get our present. When he called out my name, I ran up on stage as fast as I could.

"Here you are, Desie," he said, "Merry Christmas." His voice sounded a bit like my Uncle Alf, which I thought was rather strange. He gave me a big wink and patted me on the back. I ran back to Mum to show her my present. It was wrapped up in fancy red paper with small white bells all over it. It was tied up with string and Mum helped me unwrap it carefully, so we would be able to use the paper and string again for other presents. Inside was a toy racing car, which was exactly what I wanted.

"Boy, that was smart of Father Christmas to know just what I wanted," I said. "Did you know he sounded just like Uncle Alf, Mum?"

"That's nice," she said, which I thought was a strange answer. I looked around for Uncle Alf to tell him that Father Christmas sounded just like him, but I couldn't see Uncle Alf anywhere. Aunty Edna was there with my little cousin, Lewis, who was too small to go up on stage to get a present, so one of the ladies handed it down to Aunty Edna to give to him. If he had been older, I would have told him that Father Christmas sounded just like his own father, but he was too little, so I told Aunty Edna instead, who just said the same thing as Mum, "That's nice." It's funny sometimes the way grown ups talk.

After all the presents were given out, the ladies brought out some plates of sandwiches and cakes, and we each got a small Christmas chocolate that was soft and melting because it was so hot. So we had to unwrap it and lick it off the silver paper. Most of the kids had chocolate all over their faces, which looked pretty funny. Then Father Christmas left, waving and saying "Merry Christmas" over and over. He still sounded like Uncle Alf. Some of us wanted to follow him outside to see where he went, but the grown ups wouldn't let us. A little bit later I saw Uncle Alf and I told him that Father Christmas sounded just like him.

"You mean like Ho! Ho! Ho! Merry Christmas," he said.

"Yes, yes," I shouted, "Just like that!"

"That's nice," he said and patted me on the head, and walked away smiling. Grown ups certainly are strange.

When the Christmas party was over, the dancing started again, but most of the little kids were getting sleepy, so their parents made beds for them on the floor. Mum put Val down there, but I didn't want to sleep, so I played around with Jan and the other kids, showing off our presents.

When it was finally time to leave, I was starting to feel pretty sleepy, so I climbed into the back of the ute, and Mum made a bed for me on the floor. Gordon and Gloria sat on the seats in the back, and Mum took Val, who was fast asleep, into the front with her and Dad. As the ute sailed along smoothly on the black soil road, I looked up at the stars and wondered about Father Christmas, who I knew was supposed to fly through the sky on a sleigh pulled by reindeer. I thought it must be pretty nice to fly around among the stars and bring presents to children. I closed my eyes and tried to imagine what the world must look like from up there in the sky, and whether Father Christmas could see the headlights of our ute driving back to Athol. When I woke up, I was in my bed at home, and the sun was shining, and I saw my nice new racing car sitting on the table beside my bed.

I Almost Drown at Helidon Spa

Everyone knew that Toowoomba was on top of the "Range," and that it was dangerous to drive down the steep road called the "Tollbar" to the country below. I had often heard Dad talk about it to my uncles.

"It's very steep," he would say. "You have to put her in second gear, and maybe first. Otherwise she could get away on you."

The "she" was the ute, and the gears were what you used to slow her down on a steep hill. We didn't have any steep hills around Athol. There was Wallaby Hill, but that didn't amount to much, and Bunkers Hill, but there was no road up there; so I didn't know much about driving on steep roads.

"The old Tollbar was worse," my Uncle Henry would say. "You could meet yourself coming back on some of those bends."

"Yeah, real widow maker," Uncle Ralph would add. "I remember when a truck went over the edge. Took them a month to get it out."

"But the new road is safe enough," Dad would say, "so long as you're careful and use your gears."

The last time they had this conversation was at Christmas, then Dad surprised us all by making a suggestion.

"Why don't we all have a day out on New Year's Day, and go down the Range to Helidon Spa," he said.

"Crikey," replied Uncle Henry, "do you think we could get back in time to milk?"

"Yeah, if we get crackin' early enough," said Dad. "The women can pack a lunch, and we'll have a bite to eat at Picnic Point on top of the Range. Then it'll only take half an hour to get down the Range to the Spa. We could have a swim and afternoon tea down there, and be home in plenty of time to milk."

I was listening to all this open mouthed, not too sure if I wanted to go or not. It sounded like a great adventure, but going "over the edge," as Uncle Ralph said, didn't sound too good. The men all decided it was a good idea, and when they put it to Mum and my aunties they all agreed.

As Uncle Ralph got up to leave, I grabbed him by the sleeve.

"What happened to the driver?" I asked.

"What driver?" he asked back.

"The one driving the truck that went over the edge," I said.

He thought for a moment, then said, "I dunno. I don't think they ever found him." Then he winked at me. "But I wouldn't worry about it. Your Dad's a good driver, and there's a new road now, so she'll be all right."

So on New Year's Day we all drove in from Athol to Toowoomba, and went straight up to Picnic Point for lunch. Our family went in our ute, Uncle Henry and Aunty Eileen in theirs, and Uncle Ralph, Aunty Milly and Dawn in theirs. On the way through town we picked up Cousin Herbie to join us.

Up at Picnic Point there was this place called the Lookout, where you could go up to the edge and look down over the Range. Away in the distance was a mountain with a flat top called Table Top. Gloria said it was an old volcano, but I wasn't sure what that was.

"How did it get its flat top?" I asked.

"It blew off when it was a volcano," Gloria said.

"Gosh, when did that happen?" I asked.

"Day before yesterday," said Gordon, who was listening.

I gulped trying to imagine what that would be like, and getting scared about going anywhere near a mountain that blows its top off. But Gloria and Gordon just laughed, and Mum told them not to tease me.

"Don't worry, dear," Mum said. "Nothing's going to blow up today. Come and have some sandwiches."

While we were eating, I sat next to Herbie and asked him to tell me again where we were going.

"To Helidon Spa," he said.

"Where is it?" I asked.

"Oh, down the Range, over there towards Table Top," he said.

That didn't make me feel much better.

"What is it?" I asked.

"What's what?" he said.

"What's Helidon Spa?"

"Oh, it's a big pool of water where people go to swim. The water bubbles up out of the ground, and the funny thing is the water is fizzy, and if you catch it and put it into cordial it makes it bubbly, like a soft drink."

"You mean you swim among all the bubbles?" I asked, thinking of Mum's copper in the laundry at home, where she boiled Dad's work clothes to get them clean. I didn't like the idea much of swimming in boiling water.

"Isn't it too hot?" I asked. "The water, I mean?"

"Oh, no," said Herbie. "It's just full of gas when it comes out of the ground. But it's not hot, and after a while all the bubbles disappear, and it's just like a swimming pool. But people say there are special minerals in the water that are good for you, and some people go there for a holiday to sooth away their aches and pains."

This was getting to be more mysterious all the time.

"Where does the gas come from?" I asked.

"Out of the ground," said Herbie. "It's probably because there used to be volcanoes around there."

"You mean the gas might just blow up and blow everything away," I said, remembering what Gordon had said about the volcano.

"No, no, nothing like that." Herbie laughed. "The gas just bubbles up quietly with the water out of a spout. You'll see. You'll think it's great fun."

I still wasn't too sure, but I didn't think Herbie would tell me a fib, so I decided to wait and see.

After lunch Uncle Ralph said he didn't want to drive down the Range.

"We don't need three trucks to go down," he said. "Milly can ride in front with Eileen and Henry, and Dawn and me will get in the back. Herbie, you can ride in the back of Ken's ute with the kids."

I wondered if Uncle Ralph's plan had anything to do with the truck he said went "over the edge." But I decided not to ask.

So off we went, Dad going first, and Uncle Henry following. Gordon, Gloria and I were in the back of the ute with Herbie. Val rode in front with Mum and Dad. After a bit we came to a turn that Herbie said was the top of the Range, and Dad turned the ute down the hill.

Everything seemed pretty much the same at first, just going down hill into the bush, but not too steep. Then all of a sudden the road seemed to drop away, and we were going around sharp bends. The ute gave a bit of a bump.

"Your Dad's changed down into second," said Herbie, "that'll slow her down."

I was sitting on the seat up close to the hood of the ute and I held on tight to the edge. Then all of a sudden I looked out, and all I could see was the edge of the road, and some white posts, and then nothing else, because the ground had disappeared.

"Oh my gosh," I cried, "we might go over the edge."

Herbie came over, and sat beside me, and put his arm around me.

"Don't look over the edge," he said. "Look straight ahead. See there's the road winding down the hill. It's not so bad."

Gordon was standing up looking over the hood and yodelling into the wind. He wasn't scared at all. Gloria sat quietly, but she was smiling, too. So I thought I was silly to be afraid.

Then my ears clogged up. I put my hands on my ears and shouted, "Something's wrong with my ears, I can't hear properly. Oh, oh, it hurts!"

"That's just a change in air pressure," Herbie said. He dug in his pocket and gave me a lolly. "Here, suck on this, and you'll feel your ears pop and you'll be all right again."

By this time I wasn't too sure about anything, but I gave it a try and sure enough after a bit my ears went pop and I could hear properly again.

"Wow, look at that poor bugger," Gordon suddenly shouted.

He was pointing over to the other side of the road, away from the edge towards the steep cliff going straight up above us. Then I saw what he meant. There was a truck pulled up in a bit of a wider spot against the cliff, and as we went slowly past, I could see big clouds of steam coming out of his engine.

"Radiator's boiling," said Herbie. "It's hard work for a truck coming up the Range. He'll just have to wait there until the engine cools down."

"Look, there's another one, and another one," Gordon shouted, and I could see other cars and trucks pulled up, some with their bonnets up and steam gushing out, while the men and some women and kids stood around staring at us, as we went past them going down hill. A couple of the kids waved and I waved back. Then I had a thought.

"Is that going to happen to us on the way back?" I asked. "What if there's nowhere to pull over?"

"I wouldn't worry," said Herbie. "Your Dad will check the radiator at the bottom and make sure it's full of water."

"Not the fizzy water," I said, "otherwise it might blow up."

"No, not the fizzy water," Herbie smiled at me.

We were still grinding along in second gear, when suddenly a yahoo in a black two door car came out of nowhere behind us, and got in between us and Uncle Henry. Then he blew his horn, and went roaring past.

"Silly bugger," I heard Herbie mutter. "Left his brains behind in his hat. I hope we don't have to scrape him off the road further down."

I tried to imagine what that would be like, but I didn't like the picture, so I went back to looking over the edge, which was still a bit scary, but not as bad as before.

"Home, home on the Range
Where the deer and the antelope play."

Herbie had started to sing. We all knew the words, so we all joined in.

"Where seldom is heard a discouraging word
And the skies are not cloudy all day."

As we sang the second verse I looked back at Uncle Henry's ute behind us. I could see Uncle Ralph and Dawn standing up in the back, looking over the hood and waving at us. We all waved back and sang as loud as we could, and thought we could hear them singing, too, even though the rush of the wind was really too loud to tell. And then I noticed that the steep edge had gone, and Dad had changed back into top gear, and we were whistling along the road at the bottom of the Range.

The country down there looked different from Athol. It was mostly bush with some open grassy spaces, but not rich black soil paddocks full of cultivation like I knew. Occasionally we saw cattle feeding on the grass, but I didn't see any real farms with cow bails and machinery sheds and things like that.

It wasn't long before we came to this place that looked like a store on the side of the road, with a high wooden fence behind it, and a big sign that I could read as "Helidon Spa." Dad and Uncle Henry pulled over and bought some tickets at the store, then drove in through the gates. Right away I saw a great big pool of water, bigger than any dam I had ever seen. I could see people swimming and splashing in the water, and it looked like a lot of fun, though I really didn't know for sure, because I didn't know how to swim.

We pulled up in a parking lot where there were a lot of cars and a few utes like ours. Right away I saw the same black car that had raced past us on the road down the Range. Dad pulled in beside it, and I saw a man in red swim shorts with his girl friend in a blue ladies swim suit sitting at a picnic table.

"Look, here are the boys from the bush," I heard the man say to the girl. "Maybe it's the Kelly Gang just out of gaol."

The girl laughed, but shut up right away when Herbie walked over to the man and said, "You've got a bit of a loose lip, mate. Better watch out or you might trip over it."

"It's a free country, mate," the man replied.

"Yeah, that's right," said Herbie. "Some people just don't know how to handle that."

The man in the red shorts stood up and glared at Herbie, who just stood there with his thumbs hooked in his belt. The girl in the blue swim suit grabbed the man and pulled him away. "Come on, Billy," she said, "let's go for a swim." They left, and Herbie came back to join us.

We went into a shed to change into our swim suits, men and boys in one place, and girls and women in another. Mum had bought us all new swim suits, because we didn't have any before, and she thought we would be able to use them again. Mine was black and with straps over the shoulders. It was a bit loose and floppy, but Mum said I would grow into it.

When we came to the pool, we found a small one that wasn't too deep, where the water was coming in, just like Herbie had said from a big spout. You could splash around under it, and though the water was pretty cold at first, you soon got used to it. I caught some of the water in a glass and saw that it was fizzy, just like Herbie had said. It tasted a bit strange on its own, but Gloria had some orange cordial in a bottle, and when we filled it up with the water and shook it, we had a fizzy soft drink. Now, that was really something.

The water from our pool overflowed into the bigger one, where most of the adults and older kids were swimming. Dad took Gordon down there, but the rest of us stayed up in the small pool, where I could stand up and the water was up to my chest. This was one of the most exciting things I had ever done. The water sparkled and danced in the hot sunshine, and when you jumped in the air it just flowed off you in little rivers and showers that splashed back into the water. All of the kids were having such fun splashing and shouting. I pretended to show Mum what a good swimmer I was, but I didn't really know what to do, and just sank like a stone. The water got in my eyes and mouth and up my nose, and I was pretty scared at first, but then Herbie showed me how I could float on my back and look up at the sky and kick my legs, and I didn't sink as long as he was holding me. This was the most fun I had ever had, and I was sure glad that Dad had brought us down the Range to Helidon Spa.

We had been in the water for a while and I was getting a bit tired, so I was playing quietly with Val and Gloria in the shallower part. Herbie was over at the far end swimming with Mum, while Aunty Eileen and Aunty Milly were sitting under an umbrella on the bank. Suddenly, there was a great big splash right beside me, and I saw it was the man in the red swim shorts who had jumped in beside me.

He said something like, "Come on bush boy, let's see you swim," and he picked me up, and ducked me under the water. I thought it was a game at first, but instead of letting me come up, he was holding me under the water. I didn't know you were supposed to hold your breath when you were under the water, so I started to choke and splutter, and suddenly I was so frightened, like I had never been before in my life. It was much worse than the worst asthma attack that I had ever had. I could see all around me with the sun shining into the clear water, but I couldn't get up into the air because the man had his hand on me holding me down. I think I was trying to scream under water but that only made things worse, and I felt like I was going to die.

Then suddenly it was all over. The man took his hand away, and I came back to the surface, and crawled up on the steps beside Gloria and Val, who were screaming their heads off for Mum and Dad. I was pretty groggy, but I could hear and see enough to know what happened next.

Herbie was there, and he grabbed the man in the red shorts and pushed him under the water and held him there while the man's girl friend in the blue swim suit danced around on the bank screaming, "Stop, stop, he can't swim! You're drowning him!"

Then Herbie pulled the man up out of the water, and threw him up on the bank where Dad had just arrived. Dad picked the man up by the seat of his pants and by a fistful of hair and threw him through the air to land at the feet of his girlfriend.

"You get to hell out of here," I heard Dad say, "and if you're still around next time I look, I'll knock your bloody head off."

The man struggled to his feet and his girlfriend helped him stumble away towards the change shed. By this time Mum and everyone were crowding around me and helping me cough up the water and take big gulps of air. I just held onto Mum as tight as I could and cried and cried. I knew I was too big to cry, but I was just so scared I couldn't help myself.

Somehow through all of my tears I remember hearing some men talking to Dad and Herbie.

"Good on yer, mates," they said. "We don't need scum like that around here. Don't worry, we'll get rid of him."

I didn't feel like swimming much more after that, so I just stayed up on the bank in the shade of a big tree. Pretty soon everyone else came out of the water, and we all had some nice afternoon tea of cakes and biscuits that we had brought with us. Gloria filled up a few bottles of cordial with spa water to take with us. Then we all got dressed and went back to the utes. I saw right away that the black car was gone.

On the way back up the Range, I just lay on a blanket and looked up at sky and the tall cliffs beside the road. Dad went along slowly, and the ute got to the top all right without the radiator boiling.

When we dropped Herbie off at his place, Aunty Jane came out and they told her the story of what happened to me. Right way she put her arms around me, and gave me a nice shiny sixpence, to help make me feel better, she said.

Herbie ruffled my hair and said, "You're a good sport, Des. You'll be all right now."

I thought he was a pretty good sport, too. So was everyone in my family, and even though I wished that the terrible thing with that bad man had never happened, I felt really happy about my day at Helidon Spa with the best family you could ever want to have.

The Possum and the Almost Bush Fire

Now that I was in my second year at school I enjoyed reading from my Prep 3 School Reader. What I liked most was that I was learning to read new words that all had the same sound like "room" and "roof." The new words were all part of a story like "The Nest," that told about how birds build their nests in a tree where the little ones were born. I often saw birds' nests on the farm, and sometimes climbed the tree to look inside, and once saw some blue speckled tiny eggs. I don't know what kind of bird it was, because I think the mother was hiding somewhere, hoping I wouldn't steal the eggs, but I knew better than that. So it was good to read about things like that at school that talk about what we saw on the farm.

My favourite story in my Prep 3 Reader was "The Bush-Fire." It was about a possum that lived in a tree and was nearly killed when a bush fire came and burnt up most of the trees except for a big gum tree that stood all by itself in an old church-yard. The big gum tree waved with its branches to the possum who ran over to it just in time to escape the fire. The tree used to be lonely standing by itself, but now it wasn't lonely any more because the possum made his new home there.

We had a possum just like that. It lived in a big box tree up by the cow bails. You hardly ever see a possum because they only come out at night, but Dad said the possum was there, and one night he took us kids up to see it. Dad had a big long silver torch that you put at least six batteries in, and it would shine a long strong beam of light. We all gathered under the tall box tree and waited quietly. Suddenly Dad said he heard a rustling sound, and he shone the torch up into the branches of the tree, and there we saw these two bright eyes shining in the torch light. It was the possum. He quickly turned his head and scurried away and disappeared. Dad said he lived in a hollow branch in the tree. So it was just like the story in my reading book, except that it was a box tree and not a gum tree, and there was no bush fire.

I was glad there was no bush fire, because that would be scary. I had never seen a bush fire, but you heard about them on the wireless. We didn't have much bush on the farm, except in the hill paddock, so maybe that's why we never had a bush fire. But Dad said you had to be careful with fire, or it could get away. Sometimes he used to burn the dry stalks in the paddock that were left after the crop had been harvested. The way he did this was to light a fire in some grass and straw in the set of harrows that he pulled behind the tractor, and as he raced around the paddock dragging the fire behind him, all of the other dry stalks would catch on fire and burn. He never did this if there was a wind blowing, because he said that was how the fire could get away.

Gordon and I had a special job when Dad was doing a burn like this. We had to run along the headlands on the sides of the paddock, where there was dry grass that could catch fire and burn the fence posts. We each had a big wet bag, and we would beat out any flames that got into the grass. I was pretty small, so I wasn't nearly as good at it as Gordon was. Once the fire did get away on us, and started burning the fence posts. I was pretty scared, but luckily our cousin Herbie was helping out that day, and he came running over with his wet bag and thump, thump, thumped the fire until he beat it out. The fence posts got pretty blackened, though, and whenever I went past them after that, I always remembered the fire that nearly got away.

The most excitement came another time, when Dad did a burn after the afternoon milking in a paddock close to the house. There was a lot of straw, so he dragged most of it into the middle before he lit it, and it blazed up into a really big fire. Because it was getting dark, the fire looked pretty spectacular as it lit up everything around. Because it was in the middle of the paddock, and there was hardly any wind blowing, we didn't have much to do along the headlands, so we were mostly standing around watching the flames leap into the air, when suddenly a truck came roaring up to the fence where we were standing and a whole lot of men jumped out.

Dad had just pulled up on the tractor, and one of the men yelled out to him.

"Gawd almighty, Ken, what are you up to? You can see that bloody fire for miles. We thought your house was burning down, so we came to see what we could do."

I think the man was Mr. Newton so they must have come a long way, because his farm was way over by the creek, down past the Catholic Church on the hill.

"No, everything's all right here," Dad said. "We're keeping a good eye on it. But it's really nice of you fellows to come over. I'm sorry to drag you out like that."

"Ah, no worry," another one of the men said. "A bit of excitement at the end of the day is just the ticket."

"Well, so long as you're here," Dad said, "we might as well have a drink on it. Gordon and Des, you cut down to the house and bring back as many bottles of beer as you can carry."

As we raced off, he yelled after us, "And don't forget the opener."

Dad kept the beer in the coolest place we had under the tank stand covered over with wet bags. They were big bottles, so I could only carry two, but Gordon managed two in each hand.

When we got back, the men were all sitting around with their backs propped up against the wheels of the truck and the fence posts. Some were having a smoke, and their faces lit up in the dark when they took a drag on their cigarettes. No one in our family smoked, so I thought it was interesting to watch them. Dad took the beer bottles and the opener and gave a bottle each to everyone.

One of the men looked at me and said, "Geez, kid, you should take a look at yourself. Yer as black as a Pickaninny."

"Must be soot," I said. "I've been beating out the fire with my bag."

"Good on yer, mate," he said, then called out to Dad. "Hey, Ken, you've got some good helpers here. Can we give 'em a swig of beer?"

"One mouthful," Dad said, "then they can go and get some ginger beer."

The man gave me his bottle. It was so big I had to hold it with two hands. I tipped it up to my mouth. I had never tasted beer before, and when I got a mouthful of the bitter frothy stuff I nearly choked and spluttered everywhere. The men all laughed. Gordon got his mouthful down, but I don't think he liked it because he screwed up his face.

"Good lads," someone said. "You should be proud of these boys, Ken. They'll soon be young men."

That made me feel pretty good, being in the circle of men, knowing that I was doing a good job and growing up to be a good help to Dad. I sat down on the edge of the circle and listened to them talk, and watched the fire out in the paddock gradually burn itself out.

The School Inspector

One day at school I was given what Mr. Fisher said was a special assignment. I didn't quite know what that was, but I knew it was important. It was the day when Mr. Fisher was expecting someone he called "the Inspector." As it happened, I was the only one in my class at school that day, because both Margaret and Phyllis were away.

After he got all of the other kids working, Mr. Fisher took me out onto the verandah and said, "Des, I've got a special assignment for you. That's like a job. I want you to take your reading book, and sit out by the front gate reading your book, and keep an eye out for the Inspector. As soon as you see him, run back here and tell me. Have you got that?"

"Yes, sir," I said.

"Good boy," said Mr. Fisher. "Now off you go, and don't forget to run back and tell me as soon as you see the Inspector."

As I walked down to the gate, I thought for the first time that I didn't know what the Inspector looked like. I wasn't even sure what an Inspector was, but I didn't want to go back and ask, because everyone would think I was silly. So I sat down in the shade of a tree by the front gate of the school, and started reading my book.

I think I must have dozed off, because I suddenly looked up and saw a big black car pulled up at the gate. A tall man in a black suit got out. He was carrying a small leather port with shiny gold clips on it. He came over to where I was sitting, and spoke to me over the fence.

"Hello, sonny," he said. "Do you go to school here?"

"Yes, sir," I said.

I could see now that he was wearing a vest under his suit coat all buttoned up, which must have been hot. In the top pocket of his vest I could see the shiny top of what I knew must be a fountain pen. Only important men had a fountain pen, so I knew he must be someone special. He had a friendly round face, and he had put his felt hat sort of on the back of his head, so that he looked like he was ready to have a good laugh.

"I see you've got your reading book," he said. "Do you like to read?"

"Oh yes," I said. "It's my favourite part of school, and my favourite story is "The Bush-Fire."

The man put down his bag and leaned on the fence post.

"Would you read that one to me?" he asked.

"Yes, sir," I said, and I read him the story of the possum who was saved from the bush fire by the big gum tree.

"That's very good," he said. "Are you the only one in your class?"

"No, there's Margaret and Phyllis, but they're away today. That's why the teacher sent me out by myself, to keep an eye out for the Inspector."

"Oh, I see," the man said. "Kind of like a lookout, would you say?"

"I suppose so," I said, "except I don't know what the Inspector looks like."

"That makes things difficult," he said. "I tell you what. I'll sit down here with you, and you can tell me all about your school, and we'll both keep an eye out for the Inspector."

"That sounds good," I said.

The man climbed through the fence, which wasn't too difficult even in his suit, because there was no barbed wire to get caught on. He sat down on his little port with his back against the tree.

"May I ask your name?" he said.

"Desmond, but everyone calls me Des."

"Well, Des, tell me about school. Do you like it here?"

"Oh, yes. It's a lot of fun to learn to read and count, and we even do addition and subtraction."

"Is that so? Tell me, does your Dad have a milking herd?"

"You mean, do we have cows to milk?"

"Yes, that's what I mean."

"Of course. Everyone has cows."

"And do you know how many cows your Dad milks?"

"I think it's 31, because it used to be 29, then two fresh cows came in to make it 31."

"That's good addition. Now, tell me, does your Dad sometimes sell cows at the cattle yards in Toowoomba?"

I thought this was a really good conversation we were having.

"Oh, yes," I said. "He drives them in on his stallion."

"Well, what if he sold four cows at the cattle yards, how many cows would he have then?"

I thought for a moment, then said, "27."

"Top marks for subtraction," the man said. "Tell me more about your school. How many children come here?"

"About 15, I think, because some left last year. Mr. Fisher keeps us all working hard, but complains sometimes that we sit on our brains. He has a cane, but doesn't use it much. He likes to keep things tidy, and gets mad at us if we make a mess. We learn new things every day, and we all play together at cricket or rounders at lunch hour, and sometimes we go over and play tennis, but I'm still a bit too small for that, though soon I will get my own tennis racquet, and learn to play like my brother, Gordon, and cousin, Jimmy."

The man was smiling at me as he got up and said, "Thank you very much, Des, for telling me all that. Now, would you take me in to meet Mr. Fisher."

"I can't go in, because I have to wait here to look for the Inspector."

"Oh, yes. Well, I'll tell you what. If you take me in to meet your teacher, I'm sure he'll say that you don't have to worry about the Inspector any more."

I still wasn't too sure, but I went with him anyway, and together we went up the steps into the school. As we entered the room, I saw that Mr. Fisher was writing on the blackboard with his back to us. The other kids saw us right away, and sat up real straight. I was standing a bit behind the man in the suit, when he spoke in a loud voice: "Good morning, Mr. Fisher. Good morning boys and girls."

All of the kids replied, "Good morning, sir," and Mr. Fisher turned to look at us. I think he dropped his chalk. The man walked to the front of the room, and I slipped into my seat. Mr. Fisher stared at me. The man in the suit continued speaking: "I've been having a good chat with young Desmond here, who has been telling me what a wonderful school this is. He said he was looking for the Inspector, but I told him he needn't worry about that any more. Isn't that right, Mr. Fisher?"

Mr. Fisher kind of half smiled and nodded. I thought I heard some of the girls giggle, but I didn't really know what was going on. The man continued: "Desmond showed me that he is an excellent reader, so now I would like to hear everyone else read. Would you all take out your Queensland School Readers and turn to the last story you were reading."

The man sat down in a chair at the front. Mr. Fisher went over and sat at his table. I thought it was fun to have two teachers. The man pointed to different kids and asked them their names and what grade they were in, then asked them to read. Sometimes he asked other kids questions about the story. This was fun, because we didn't often all work together like this. He even asked me a question about a story Gloria read, and I could answer it, too. After that he gave all the older kids some sums to do in their writing pads, and he asked me to draw a picture of my favourite thing on the farm. I drew a picture of Dad driving the tractor, with me sitting beside him. The man said it was very good.

When we went outside for our 11 o'clock break all the kids were talking about the Inspector.

"How come you didn't come back and tell Mr. Fisher the Inspector was here?" Gloria asked me.

"Is that man the Inspector?" I asked.

"Of course he is, silly," Gloria said, and the other kids laughed.

"Well, I don't care," I said. "He's a nice man, and he says I'm good at school."

By lunch time I think the Inspector thought we were all pretty good, because he said he had enjoyed his visit, and that Athol was a very nice school. Mr. Fisher was smiling, so I don't think he was mad at me for not being a good lookout.

After we ate our lunch, the older boys decided to go over to the tennis courts to have a game. I went over to watch, and be a ball boy. I saw that the black car was still there on the road in front of the school. We thought that the inspector must have gone over to Mr. Fisher's house for lunch. Not long after, I saw the two of them coming towards the Inspector's car, but instead of driving away, he opened up the boot, and took out a brown paper bag, and came over to the tennis courts.

"If I can borrow a racquet, I'd like to have a hit," he said.

"You can have mine," said Kerry, and the Inspector sat down on the bench, and took a pair of tennis shoes out of the brown paper bag. Then he took off his coat, and hung it on the net post.

"All right, who wants a hit?" he said, and walked down to one end of the court. The boys all looked at each other, then Gordon and Jimmy went down to the other end of the court.

The rest of us were standing around watching, and Mr. Fisher joined us. "He used to be Queensland Champion when he went to school," Mr. Fisher said.

"Wow!" we all said, and skinned our eyes to watch. I ran down to the end of the court to be ball boy for the Inspector. He picked up two balls, and threw a third one to me with a smile, and said, "Here you go, son."

He hit a ball up to Gordon and Jimmy, and I could see right away that he was a champion. The ball whizzed over the net low and fast. Gordon tried to hit it back, but it went into the net. The Inspector hit another one to Jimmy, but his return went way out of court. I threw the third ball to the inspector, and ran to pick up the other two.

"Don't worry boys," the Inspector called out to Gordon and Jimmy. "Just take your time, and make your shots." After a while they started to do pretty good, and they had a few good rallies. Then the Inspector thanked them for the game, and said he had to go. Then he turned to me.

"Now what about you, young Desie," he said. "You should get a junior sized racquet and start to play. Here, I'll show you how to hold it."

He gave me the racquet, which was much too heavy and fat around the handle for me. But he showed me how to shake hands with it, and do a swing. "I can see you'll be a good player," he said. "Just remember that it takes a lot of practice."

After that he took off his tennis shoes, put on his coat, and drove off. We all waved good-bye. Mr. Fisher turned to me and said, "You're not much of a lookout, Des, but you're a good ambassador." I had no idea what an ambassador was, but I could tell Mr. Fisher was pleased so I thought whatever it was, it was all right.

The Atomic Bomb

We didn't learn much about the war at school. Sometimes, though, Mr. Fisher would talk to the older kids about it, and I would listen in. He talked about how a couple of years ago, when I was too young to remember, the Japanese planes bombed Darwin, which I think is a town way up north. Then there was a big battle in the Coral Sea between the Japanese on one side, and the Americans and Australians on the other side. Mr. Fisher said that stopped the Japanese from invading Australia, which would have been a very bad thing for all of us.

Mr. Fisher said our soldiers were fighting in the jungles. I knew about that from the newsreel I had seen at the pictures when we went to see "Snow White and the Seven Dwarfs." I also remember reading a Bluey and Curly comic, where Bluey and Curly were Australian soldiers fighting in the jungle, and they would fire their tommy guns up into a tree, and a Japanese soldier would fall out. I didn't really know what it was all about, but I remember Mr. Fisher saying there was another war with the Germans, but that it was over now, and there was a lot of cheering in London, where the King and Queen and the young princesses, Elizabeth and Margaret, lived. He said he thought the war with the Japanese would soon be over, because we were winning, and our soldiers would be able to come home.

Then, just before the August holidays, there was some big news about the war. Everyone was talking about it. Mum and Dad said the Americans had dropped an atomic bomb on the Japanese. It was on the news on the wireless, and then I saw a photograph of it in the newspaper. I had never seen anything like that before. It was like a tall cloud of smoke going way up into the sky, then opening out like an umbrella. On the wireless they called it a mushroom cloud, and that it was the first time a bomb like that had ever been dropped, and that it had destroyed a whole city in one go. It was really terrible, and thousands of people were killed, and Dad said that because it was so terrible, the Japanese would have to give in, and the war would be over.

But I don't think the Japanese did give in, because we heard that another bomb had been dropped, and it was just as terrible as the first. We were talking about it at school, because the second bomb was dropped at around 11 o'clock in the morning, when the children were out playing at their 11 o'clock break, just like we did, and they were all burned to death by the heat from the bomb.

Everyone was saying that this was such a terrible thing. Some said the Japanese deserved it, because they started the war, but I was thinking about the children burned at school, and I didn't think that was right, because the children didn't start the war. I was afraid that someone would drop a bomb on our school, but Mum said that wouldn't happen, because we were safe in Australia.

Then we heard that the war was over, because the Japanese had at last given up. But everyone was talking about the bomb. Some said it was right to drop it, because it made the war end quickly, but others said it was wrong, because so many ordinary people were killed. I kept thinking about the children, and I wondered why there had to be war at all. It just didn't seem right to me, and I hoped now that it was over we wouldn't hear any more talk about war. But I couldn't stop thinking about the children, who were killed while they were playing at school. Surely that wasn't right. It just made me so sad to think about that. They were just little children like me and all my friends and relatives at school. Surely there must be a better way. But I didn't know what I could do about it. And I just felt so sad.

Gloria and I Go to Karara

For the August holidays Gloria and I were invited to go and stay with Aunty Joy and Uncle Bill on their farm at a place called Karara. It was a long way away, even further than Aunty Dora's place at Millmerran. To get there Mum said we would have to go by train to Warwick, and then by rail motor to Karara. Boy, was this going to be an adventure! I had never been on a train before, and I wasn't even sure what a rail motor was. To make sure we wouldn't get lost along the way, Aunty Holly was going to come with us from Toowoomba.

Because it was winter time Mum packed a lot of warm clothes for us in our ports. Mine was so heavy I couldn't carry it by myself. I made sure my Teddy Bear was packed, because I wanted him to come along on the adventure. I knew I was getting a bit old for Teddy Bears, but he had been my friend for a long time, so it was right that he should come. Of course Triloaf was coming, too. He and I had a good talk about it before we left.

"Did you know that Gloria and I are going to visit Aunty Joy at Karara?" I asked him.

"Of course," he said, "I know everything."

"Well, if you're so smart," I said, "tell me how we are going to get there."

"By train and rail motor," he replied.

"What's a rail motor?" I asked.

"It's like a small train, but it has a motor like a car instead of a steam engine."

"That's what Mum said. I'm glad you're coming, too, so I will always have company."

"I will always be with you."

And I was glad about that.

Mum and Dad took us into Toowoomba. We picked Aunty Holly up at Grandfather's house, and then we all went down to the railway station. It was all new for me. Dad carried the ports, and Mum bought the tickets at the ticket office. She said she also bought what she called two platform tickets, so she and Dad could come and wave good-bye. The place where the train comes in is called a platform. When we got there I saw the train. I couldn't believe how long it was. I could see the steam engine way up ahead, and behind it were all the carriages, and right at the far end a funny looking carriage that Dad said was called the guard house.

"What's a guard house?" I asked.

"It's where the guard or conductor rides," he said.

"What's a conductor?" I asked.

"He's the man who makes sure everyone is safely on the train, then tells the engine driver to go."

"But his house is right at the back of the train," I said. "How does he tell the engine driver to go?"

"He waves a flag, then jumps on board before the train starts to move. Look, there he is now, watching everyone get on the train."

I looked and saw this man in a uniform standing and watching us. Then he came over. He smiled and bent down to talk to me. He had a round friendly red face, and smelled a bit like smoke.

"So where are you off to today, young man?" he asked.

"I'm going to my Aunty Joy's in Karara," I said.

"We don't go that far," he said. "You'll have to catch the rail motor in Warwick."

"Yes, I know," I said. "Aunty Holly is coming with us to make sure we don't get lost."

"That's a good thing," he said, standing up. "We wouldn't want you wandering around the station lost, or getting on the wrong train. You could end up in Timbuktu."

Mum and Dad laughed.

"Where's Timbuktu?" I asked.

"Don't worry," Mum said. "You're not going there. Aunty Holly will look after you."

The conductor walked away, and we found our carriage. It was the third from the front. I wanted to run up and look at the engine, but Dad said we didn't have time. He helped Aunty Holly with the ports, which had to go in a rack above our heads. It was a bit of a tight squish getting onto the train. We were in a small room with a long seat facing one way and another one facing the other way. There were already three other people sitting in their seats—a man in a big coat sitting by the window, and two old ladies snuggled up under a blanket. I went over to the window seat, so I could wave good-bye to Mum and Dad. Gloria crowded in, too, so we could both look out the window. Mum looked a bit sad to see us go, and Dad stood big and tall beside her.

Then all of a sudden the train began to move. It was so smooth you could hardly tell it was moving.

"Takes off just like a boat," I heard the man opposite say.

I leaned out the window waving as hard as I could. As I looked back, I could see Mum and Dad getting smaller and smaller on the platform, until I couldn't see them any more. For the first time I thought I had never been away from them before (except when I went to hospital to get my tonsils out, but that was different). Now I was going far far away, and I felt the tears coming into my eyes. I leaned further out the window to see if I could see them, but I couldn't.

"You better pull your head in, son," the man sitting opposite said, "or you'll get an eyeful of soot."

I looked at him, rubbing my eyes, so he wouldn't see I was crying. "What kind of soot?" I asked.

"From the smoke," he said. "It blows back down along the train, and tiny pieces of coal can get in your eyes. Is this your first train ride?"

I nodded.

"Where are you going?" he asked.

"He thinks he's going to Timbuktu," Gloria piped up.

"I do not," I said. "We're going to our Aunty Joy's at Karara."

"I almost went to Timbuktu," the man said. "But you have to go by ship. Can't get there by train, at least not from here."

"You were on a ship?" I asked.

"Yeah, I was a sailor in the war," he said.

Gosh. I had never even met a soldier, never mind a sailor.

"Bad business, war," he said. "I'm glad it's over."

That made me think again of the atomic bomb, and the children who were killed, and suddenly I felt sad.

"I don't like war," I said, "especially when children get killed."

"You're right," he said. "It's a bad business all round. But, cheer up. Here you are in Australia. The best bloody country in the world."

"Don't swear in front of the children," one of the ladies said.

"Sorry Mum," the man said.

"Don't be rude. I'm not your Mum."

"Yeah, just as well."

The lady made a sound like a cow snorting, and turned away. The man looked out the window.

"Hey, look," he said, "we're already out of the city."

I knelt on the seat so I could see better and watched all the farms flashing by. The train was rocking along, and going clackety-clack over the rails. When we came to a corner, it would lurch one way, then as we came to another, it would lurch the other way. On the bends I could see the engine up ahead chuffing out thick black smoke. The ladies had made us put up the windows when we left the station, because they said it was too cold, so I couldn't lean out even though I wanted to.

After a while we left the farms behind, and started going through the bush. The engine blew its whistle, and the train slowed down as it went through a cutting. Suddenly I saw a lot of men outside standing by the tracks, waving at us and yelling something I couldn't understand. The man opposite opened his window, and yelled out at the men: "G'day, mates."

They kept yelling something that sounded like "Paaaaay – Perr." I opened my window to hear better, and the cold wind blew in with some smoke. Both ladies opposite snorted real loud.

"What are they saying?" I asked the man.

"They're yelling 'paper,'" the man said. "They want you to throw them a newspaper to read, or anything else you've got."

"I only have an orange," I said.

"That'll do," he replied. "Toss it out."

I pulled out one of the oranges from our orchard that I had in my pocket, and I threw it as hard as I could. One of the men caught it like a cricket ball, then waved his hat at me. I waved back.

"Would you two lunatics please close the window," the snorty lady said. "It's freezing in here." She glared at Aunty Holly, who got up to come over to help me close the window. The train lurched, and Aunty Holly fell on the man in the coat.

"Good timing, love," he said, as Aunty Holly tried to get up. "That's a C.O.D. corner—come over dear."

Gloria burst out laughing, and Aunty Holly's face went red, as she got up to help me close the window.

"Now don't open it again, Des," she said. "And try to be good."

I didn't' think I was being bad to give my orange to the man working on the railroad tracks, but I didn't say anything.

Just then the door opened, and the conductor I had seen on the platform came in. "Tickets, please," he said. Aunty Holly dug into her purse looking for our tickets, and the conductor looked at me. "Hello, sonny," he said. "Are you enjoying the ride?"

"Oh yes," I said. "It's a lot of fun."

"It may be fun for you, but not for us," the snorty lady said. "Conductor, are there other seats in the carriage? We would like to move."

"Yeah, next door's almost empty. Help yourself," the conductor said.

The ladies stood up, and fell all over the place. The conductor grabbed them, and helped them out the door.

"We need our bags," one of them said.

"It's all right, I'll get 'em," said the man in the coat, as he got up and pulled the ladies' ports down off the rack. "Bloody good riddance," I heard him mutter, as he followed the ladies and the conductor out the door.

When they came back the conductor asked, "What was that all about?"

"Ar, just a couple of old crabs," the man in the coat said. "All shell and no meat. If you cracked them open they'd be full of salt water and grit. We're better off without them. Come over here, love, and sit with me," he said to Aunty Holly, "and let the young ones spread out." Aunty Holly moved over, and I could see she was smiling, but was still red in the face.

"Well, enjoy the rest of your trip," the conductor said. "I'm off to the next carriage."

"How can you do that?" I asked. "Won't you fall off the train?"

"No, the carriages are joined. Want to come and see? It's all right, missus," he said to Aunty Holly. "I'll look after him."

I got up, and he put his hands on my shoulders, and guided me along the narrow passage outside, until we came to a door that he pushed open, and suddenly we were standing on a little bridge between the two carriages. I could see the ground rushing past along the tracks underneath, and there was a big blast of cold air, and all the noise of the clanging and clacking of the train, and the bridge wobbling, and the two carriages bumping against each other. It was the most exciting thing I had ever seen.

After a bit the conductor pulled me back inside the door of our carriage, and I ran back to join the others.

"Wow!" I told them. "You've never seen such a thing. The carriages are joined by a bridge, and all the world is rushing past so fast that it makes you giddy to look."

"You learn something new every day if you keep your eyes and ears open," the man in the coat said. "You're a smart lad. Now I think it's time for some tucker. I bet this lovely lady here has got some nice lunch. I've got a bag of sausage rolls. Let's have a picnic."

Soon we had food spread out all over the seats and on a little table by the window, and we had a wonderful feed as the trees and open country rushed by outside. I thought that travelling by train was just the absolute best way to go. I had already seen and done so much, and I was excited to think about what would come next.

Before we got to Warwick I got so tired that I had to have a nap. I didn't want to miss anything, but I just couldn't keep my eyes open. When I woke up, we were pulling into the station in Warwick.

The man in the coat helped carry our ports while Aunty Holly went to buy tickets for the rail motor. It was very busy at the station, so I was glad we had someone to help us. Aunty Holly came back, and said we had to go to another platform. The man came along to help with the ports. When we got there, we saw what looked like a bus on a railway track. There was a place to put the ports in the back, and the man loaded them in while we found some seats.

"Well, so long mates," the man said, standing on the platform. "You should be right now. Have a good trip."

"Good-bye, and thanks for helping," we all said, waving to him as he walked off.

"He was a nice man," I said to Aunty Holly. "Much better than those two old crabs."

"Hush, Des," Aunty Holly said. "You shouldn't repeat things like that." But I could see she was smiling.

There were just a few other people on the rail motor, and they didn't take much notice of us. Then the driver got on, wearing a uniform and a cap. He asked where everyone was going.

"Karara," I said, "to my Aunty Joy's."

"Oh yes, Mrs. Hunter," he said. "She told me to look out for you. Well here we go."

He started up the motor, which was pretty loud and we set off with a jerk, not nearly as smooth as the train. Soon we were whizzing along through the bush. We passed a few more men waving at us and yelling "paaaay-perr," but I didn't have any more oranges, so I just waved back. Then we came out into some open country, and I saw an amazing sight.

"Wow! Look at the kangaroos," I yelled.

Bounding along beside the tracks, and going almost as fast as the rail motor, was a mob of kangaroos. They were much bigger than the wallabies we had seen at Aunty Dora's. Right out in front was this big red one, making great long jumps with his big hind feet, and thumping his long tail on the ground. He was leaning a bit forward into the jump, and his head and ears were up, and his whole body rippled with power. He was the most beautiful animal I had ever seen.

"Wow, look at him go!" I yelled. "What a beauty!"

He kept pace with the rail motor for a while, then all of a sudden veered off, and the other roos went with him. I craned my neck out the window, but soon they were out of sight.

"That was a bit of luck," the driver yelled over the noise of the motor. "Don't often see a mob like that. I think the big fellow was tryin' to take us on. He could bloody well beat this old rattletrap, if he put his mind to it."

I didn't know kangaroos could go so fast. This was sure turning out to be the big adventure I hoped it would be.

Not long afterwards we pulled up at a small building beside the railway tracks.

"This is it, Karara," the driver said. "Watch your step as you get out. I'll get your things."

It sure was different from Toowoomba and Warwick. There was hardly any platform, and just the one building with a few seats in it. The other thing I saw was a big tank on a high stand with a long spout on it.

"What's that?" I asked the driver.

"Water tank for the trains," he said. "They pump the water up from the creek. There's a weir down there to make sure there's always a good supply of water."

I didn't have time to ask what a weir was, because just then I saw Aunty Joy and Uncle Bill coming through a gate onto the platform. We had big hugs all round, and Uncle Bill picked up our ports and threw them into the back of his ute. The rail motor rattled off, as Gloria and I climbed into the back of the ute. We didn't have far to go, and in no time at all we were at the house.

It was a nice house, older than ours and not as big, and it had a big garden out the back. Aunty Joy had a girl working for her to help with the house, and to look after the children. Her name was Marlene, and I think she was about 16 or 17 years old. She had red hair, and I thought she was very pretty and nice. She came out to meet us when we arrived, holding my cousin, Barry, (who was three) by the hand and carrying the baby, Ian. I hadn't seen Barry since he was a baby, like his little brother was now. He seemed a bit shy, but I was sure we could play together. He watched us as Uncle Bill brought our ports up onto the back verandah, then he said to me, "Want to see Joey?"

I didn't know who Joey was. Maybe he had another brother, or a pet kitten. I said yes, and he ran off inside. I followed him into a big room, where there was a warm fire burning in the fireplace. It was already getting dark, and I couldn't see too good at first, because there wasn't any electric light, just a kerosene lamp sitting on the table. Barry beckoned me to come over closer to the fire, and then I saw Joey. He was a baby kangaroo, not much bigger than a cat, but with big back legs and a long tail. He was sitting in a box filled with rags for a bed by the fire. When I came over to look, he stood up tall and twitched his nose at me.

I could hardly believe my eyes. A baby kangaroo, and right after I had just seen the big one and all the others bounding along beside the railway tracks. This was getting better all the time. I held out my hand to Joey and he nibbled my fingers and flicked his short pointy ears. I knelt down to pat him, and he climbed out of his box, and cuddled up to me, and grabbed my coat with his tiny hands.

"He likes you," Barry said.

"Oh, what a sweetheart!" said Gloria, who had come in behind me, and was kneeling down and petting him.

"Where's his mother?" I asked.

"Don't know. Dead," said Barry.

Uncle Bill had come in, and sat down in a chair.

"We found him in the bush," he said. "I think we shot his mother by mistake. So we brought him home to look after him, until he's big enough to go back to the bush."

"What's he eat?" I asked.

"We just give him warm milk in a bottle for now," said Uncle Bill. Aunty Joy brought in a small bottle with a tit on the top.

"Now, Des, see if you can feed him," she said.

I took the bottle and held it up to Joey's mouth. He knew what to do right away, and I could feel him sucking on it.

"He thinks you're his mother," Gloria said, and everyone laughed.

I didn't care if anyone laughed. I felt very special, because this was the first animal, except the cats at our farm, that had cuddled up to me. Well, of course, there was Patsy's foal, too, and maybe some of the calves, but Joey was special, because he was a wild animal from the bush, and it made me think that all animals could be our friends.

"Why did you shoot his mother?" I asked.

"Well, we try not to kill mothers if we can help it, but you can't always tell," said Uncle Bill.

"But why do you have to shoot any of them?" I asked, remembering how wonderful the ones looked that I had seen from the rail motor.

"We have to keep the numbers down," said Uncle Bill. "Otherwise there won't be enough feed for the sheep."

I thought about that, and I suppose he was right, but I still felt sorry for the kangaroos.

The First Day at Karara

My first day at Aunty Joy's began very early. My bed was on the front verandah, which was closed in, but still very cold. I wore nice warm pyjamas and thick woolly socks to bed, but it was still very cold, and I snuggled down under a pile of blankets. When I woke up, it was still half dark, but I could hear some noise out in the kitchen. So I got up, and wrapped myself in a blanket, and went to look. I checked out Joey's box as I went through the room with the fireplace, but he wasn't there. The fire was out, and it was really cold, so I went out into the kitchen at the back of the house.

Uncle Bill was there, and he had a nice fire going in the wood stove just like ours at home.

"Well, good morning, soldier," he said to me. "Come over here with Joey and warm up."

Right away I saw that Joey was standing up in front of the stove, sort of stretching out his little arms and hands to get them warm. I crept over and wrapped my blanket around him and we cuddled up in front of the stove.

"I've got some warm milk here," said Uncle Bill. "Would you like a cup of cocoa?"

"Yes, please," I said. "Can I feed Joey, too?"

"You bet," said Uncle Bill. "Us lads have got to get our strength up for the day's work. Do you want to come and help milk Bessie, when you've had your cocoa?"

Bessie turned out to be their one cow. I was kind of surprised that on the farm they only had one cow, but Uncle Bill said they had hundreds of sheep, and they needed only one cow just for milk and butter and cream for the house. I went and got my warmest clothes out of my port, and I got dressed in the kitchen, which was really warm now from the stove. We left Joey in there when we went outside.

The sun was just coming up, and all the grass as far as you could see was covered in a thick white frost. Where the sun touched the ground, the frost danced and sparkled like it was alive. As we walked over the grass it crunched under our feet, and our breath steamed up around our ears, like we were walking in a little cloud. I had seen frost before many times at home, but never anything as beautiful as this.

Uncle Bill picked up a milk bucket and a bucket of grain from a little shed, and we went down to the end of the house yard, where Bessie was already waiting for us. She gave a little low moo when she saw us coming.

"Right you are, old girl," said Uncle Bill. "Are you ready for breakfast?"

He put her in a little pen so she would stand still, and he poured the bucket of grain into a feed box, where she tucked in. He sat down on a little stool, and wiped her tits and udder with a warm rag that he had brought from the house, then put the bucket between his knees, and started to milk her. The milk came out in strong white streams that steamed in the cold air, and pinged loudly against the sides of the steel bucket. I rubbed my hands all over Bessie's hide, which was nice and warm.

Soon the milk was frothing up in the bucket, when Uncle Bill said, "Do you wanta have a go?"

"You bet," I said, because this was something I knew how to do, though we didn't milk by hand very much on Dad's farm, where we used milking machines. I wasn't strong enough to get the big stream of milk that Uncle Bill got, but I did all right. Then Uncle Bill took over again and finished off.

By the time we let Bessie out of the pen and brought the bucket of milk into the house, Aunty Joy was in the kitchen cooking up a breakfast of fried eggs and lamb chops.

"You men must be cold and hungry," she said. "Come over to the stove, Des, and warm up. You can make the toast if you like."

This was another thing I knew how to do. Aunty Joy raked some hot coals to the front of the fire box, and I held the white bread on a long toasting fork until it was nicely browned on both sides. Joey looked on, very interested. Aunty Joy smothered the warm brown toast with plenty of butter, and Uncle Bill and I tucked into our breakfast. I thought this was a pretty good start to the first day of my holiday. By the time we were finishing, Gloria came in sleepily rubbing her eyes, then Marlene, Barry and the baby. Aunty Holly was having a sleep in.

"Well, I've got some things to do," Uncle Bill said, as he finished his breakfast. "Des, you can help Mum separate the milk, then Marlene can take you all down to the creek for a walk. Be careful not to go too near the water, and keep your eye out for snakes, especially death adders."

"What's a death adder?" I asked, suddenly feeling a bit scared at the sound of it.

"It's like a lizard," he said, "but it lies very still in the grass, like a stick. It won't bother you, unless you walk on it, or pick it up by mistake. Its bite is deadly and can kill you, but there's nothing to worry about as long as you're careful."

Gosh, I thought, maybe the bush here isn't so friendly after all. I knew about snakes and spiders, but this death adder was something new.

After breakfast Aunty Joy took me out into a side room and showed me the separator. This was something new, because we didn't have one on our farm.

"What does it do?" I asked.

"It separates the cream from the milk," said Aunty Joy. She showed me by pouring the milk into a tub on the machine, then started turning a handle. She let me have a go, and together we worked away at it, until suddenly thick white cream started coming out of a spout into a bowl, and the left over milk came out another spout into a bucket.

"Wow!" I said. "It really works. We get our cream by skimming it off the top of the milk cans, but it's not as smooth and white as this."

"This works best for us," Aunty Joy said, "because you can use some of the cream to make butter and for puddings, and you still have the milk to drink."

This was another new thing I learned. After we were finished, I helped Aunty Joy pull the separator apart, and wash all the different parts. By then Marlene had a nice fire going in the fireplace. I noticed that they had lumps of black stuff as well as wood burning in the fire.

"What's that?" I asked.

"It's coal," Marlene said. "You pick it up beside the railway tracks where it falls off the trains. We can go and look afterwards."

Boy, another new thing. I wondered what else might be coming. We sat around in front of the fire for a while reading books and playing with Joey, until it was warm enough outside to go for a walk down to the creek.

Marlene was in charge, but Barry ran on ahead, because he knew the way. Gloria and I followed along, and Aunty Joy stayed in the house with the baby. It wasn't a long walk. Most of the frost was gone by now, except in the shady places. I was glad I had been up early enough to see it like a big white blanket.

When we came to the creek, I was surprised to see how wide it was, and it also looked very deep. Most creeks I had seen were just trickles of water.

"It's because of the weir," Marlene said. "The railway built the weir a bit further down to get water for the trains. We can go and look afterwards."

I remembered then what the driver on the rail motor had said about the weir. I still wasn't sure what it was, but I thought it must be something to block the water.

"Let's throw some stones and sticks in the water," Gloria said. We all thought that was a good idea. Barry was really excited, and he ran around picking up sticks and throwing them as hard as he could into the water. I was watching him as he bent to pick up another stick, when he suddenly stopped dead, with his hand in the air above the stick.

"Oh, big nake!" he cried.

"What?" Marlene shouted, and we all ran over to look. At first it just looked like a stick to me, but then as I looked closer, I could see that it had a body and a head and a short tail. It wasn't a stick at all.

"It's a death adder," Marlene said. "Stand back, don't touch it. Oh, Barry, you almost picked it up."

"It's a big nake! It's a big nake," Barry kept saying, over and over.

"We better go and get your mother," Marlene said, and we all ran as fast as we could back to the house. When we told Aunty Joy, she told Marlene to stay behind with the baby, and she grabbed a hoe from out of the garden, and told us to show her what we had seen. As we got closer to the spot, Gloria and I crept along quietly, and Aunty Joy held Barry by the hand. It was a bit hard to tell where the exact spot was, and we looked and looked, until we were sure we had the right place, but the death adder was gone, and you could just see the place in the grass where it had been lying. We crept around very quietly, looking and looking, but we couldn't see it anywhere.

"Looks like it's gone," said Aunty Joy. Then she put her arms around Barry, and told him what a good boy he was to be so careful. We were all pretty scared, and I thought that even though Barry was only three, he certainly knew how to be careful in the bush, and was really smart. After that, we decided we had had enough excitement for the morning, and we went back to the house.

After lunch Marlene told us she would take us down to the weir. Barry stayed home to have his nap. Gloria and I followed Marlene in a different direction from the way we had gone this morning. We kept our eyes skinned for death adders and snakes, and anything else that crept or crawled in the bush. But we didn't see anything, and soon came to the creek, which was much shallower here. and looked more like the creeks I was used to.

"That's because we're below the weir," said Marlene. "You'll see what I mean in a minute."

We walked along the creek bank for a little way, then sure enough, we came to a place where a big concrete wall taller than me was built across the creek. Water was trickling over it from the other side.

"That's the weir," said Marlene. "See how it keeps the water back, so it's very deep on the other side, but only a trickle over here. When it rains a lot, the water comes rushing over the weir like a waterfall. It's really something to see."

Right below the weir was a big outcrop of rock, and Marlene climbed out on it and beckoned us to follow her. There were a lot of grooves and strange shapes in the rock under our feet.

"See here," said Marlene, "what do you think that is?"

She was pointing at a shape in the rock where she was standing. Gloria and I stared at it.

"It looks like a footprint," said Gloria.

"You're right," said Marlene. "It's a blackfella's foot print."

"A what?" I asked.

"A blackfella, you know, an Aborigine. It's his footprint."

I had heard about Aborigines in my favourite serial on the wireless, "The Search for the Golden Boomerang." But I had never seen one, neither an Aborigine nor a boomerang.

"Is he still here?" I asked.

"No, it happened a long time ago."

"But how did he get his foot stuck in the rock?"

"I dunno. Maybe the rock was soft then, and it got hard afterwards."

"Are you sure it's a footprint?" Gloria asked. "Maybe the water carved it out, like all these other strange shapes in the rock."

"And maybe they were all footprints once," said Marlene," and the water has washed them all away, except for this one. They could have had a Corroboree here."

"A what?" I asked.

"A Corroboree, you know, a meeting place and dance. Don't you know anything about Aborigines?"

"Not much," I said, "but they must be pretty big, because that's an awfully big footprint." It was, too, because I could put both my feet in it, and there was still a bit left over.

"Well there you are," said Marlene. "You better watch out, because they might be out in the bush looking at you."

I looked around, but I couldn't see anything. Then Marlene laughed, and Gloria said she was only pulling my leg.

"Come on, I'll show you something else," said Marlene, and she crossed the creek, and climbed up the steep bank on the other side. Soon we came to a fence, and on the other side of it I could see the railway tracks.

"See down along the tracks, there are lumps of coal, just like I told you this morning," said Marlene. "We can pick up a few each, and take them back for the fire."

We crawled through the fence, and we were picking up the coal, when I heard a whistle blow, and I could hear rattling on the tracks.

"Look out. Stand well back," Marlene called. "Here comes the rail motor."

I looked and saw the rail motor rattling towards us. As it came past, I dropped my coal and waved my arms like mad and yelled out "Paay-per," as loud as I could. Right away someone tossed a package out the window, and I ran over to pick it up. It was a bag full of ripe bananas.

"Where did you learn how to do that?" Marlene asked, with a strange look on her face.

"Oh, you learn a thing or two if you keep your eyes and ears open," I said smugly, and I tucked the bag of bananas under my arm, and picked up a few pieces of coal, and set off back to the house.

A Day with Uncle Bill

The first day of our holiday had been full of surprises. But there were a lot more to come. A few days later, Uncle Bill said he had to go and check on the sheep in the back paddock. He said that Barry and I could come along. Gloria stayed behind to hang around with Marlene. Aunty Joy made us a nice lunch, and off we went.

Barry and I rode in the front of the ute with Uncle Bill, with Barry in the middle, just like I used to do when I was a little kid like him. Two of Uncle Bill's sheep dogs jumped in the back, barking and whining, because they knew they were going to do something exciting.

We hadn't gone far when Uncle Bill stopped down by the creek. "Here, I want to show you something," he said. We got out, and he led us over to a great big rock.

"Look at that, biggest rock on the property," he said. "We call it Wallaby Rock."

It was really huge, way taller than me, and as big as a bull. It was tucked into the bank on the other side of the creek. The water was low here, and I could get over and climb up on the rock. Uncle Bill carried Barry and sat him down beside me. We were two Kings of the Castle. I wished I had a rock like that back on Dad's farm. I thought I would have to bring Gloria here and show her.

We got back in the ute and started off again. We went over rough bush tracks, and through wire gates that Uncle Bill always closed behind him. We went for miles and miles through the bush.

"Gosh, does all this land belong to you, Uncle Bill?" I asked.

"Yeah, well it's rough country," he said. "Not like your Dad's place. We couldn't grow a stalk of wheat here, but it's good for sheep and cattle."

"And for kangaroos, too," I said.

"You're pretty sharp, aren't you," he said. "Yeah, the roos like it all right, but we can't let them have the run of the place."

I was thinking about what he had told me the first night, about having to shoot the kangaroos, because they would eat the grass that the sheep needed. I was thinking, too, of all of the skins I had seen nailed up on the shed back at the house. Uncle Bill said they did that to dry them out before they sold them to the tannery, which is a place where they make skins into rugs. Aunty Joy had a lot of them on the floor in the house. They were soft and fluffy. The ones nailed up on the shed were a bit gross, because they still had streaks of blood on them, and sometimes you could see the hole where the bullet went in that killed the roo. One of them was probably Joey's mother. I didn't really like thinking about that.

We came through a gate into a paddock where there was a lot of clear ground, and not so many trees, and a lot of grass.

"The sheep should be around here somewhere," said Uncle Bill.

"I don't see any," I said.

"You will soon enough," he said. "The dogs will find them." He slowed down, but without stopping he banged his hand on the roof of the ute, and yelled out to the dogs, "Go find 'em boys." I twisted around, and saw the dogs leap out of the back of the ute, and take off towards a line of trees at the far end of the paddock. Uncle Bill pulled the ute up, and we got out. He pointed to a little hill, and told me to run over to it to see if I could spot the sheep. He stayed back at the ute with Barry.

I didn't see anything at first, but then I heard them bleating, and right away I spotted a big flock of sheep coming towards us. It was like a big white blanket, and the dogs were running around, not barking or anything, but chasing after any sheep that tried to run away, so that they kept them all together.

"I can see them! I can see them!" I yelled out to Uncle Bill.

"Just stay there and keep looking," he called back.

Soon the sheep were getting really close, and coming straight towards me. I had never seen such a thing, just a great big white wooly wave coming right at me.

"They're getting close," I yelled out. "What'll I do? What'll I do?"

"Just stay there," Uncle Bill called back, "and you'll see something amazing."

Then, all at once, the sheep were everywhere around me. They weren't really running fast, and when they saw me, they split apart, and went around me, then joined up on the other side, so that I was standing right in the middle of them. I turned around and around, but all I could see were sheep. I was just a little bit taller than they were, so I was kind of looking over their woolly backs, like I was standing on a rock in the middle of a river. I was a bit scared at first, but none of the sheep bumped into me, and I knew Uncle Bill wouldn't let anything bad happen. I could just see him and Barry and the ute over the bumpy white backs. There was a lot of noise with the sheep baaing, and with their hundreds of feet scuffing on the ground. Away at the back, I could see the dogs running around, keeping all the sheep together in a big circle, with me in the middle.

I started to do a little dance, because I suddenly felt so excited. "Ho! Ya! Hi! Yippee!" I yelled. "Come on sheep, you don't scare me!"

"Good boy, Des," I heard Uncle Bill yell. "What do you think?"

"It's terrific," I yelled back. "This must be all the sheep in the world. Wait till I tell Gloria about this."

Then I saw Uncle Bill wave at the dogs and whistle, and all at once the sheep were all going in one direction, and going past me, and I was suddenly all by myself again on the hill. I ran back to the ute.

"Wow! That was the most amazing thing," I said. "Thanks, Uncle Bill, for showing me your sheep."

"I thought you'd enjoy that," he said. "Now jump in the ute. I've got some more things to show you."

The dogs jumped into the back of the ute again, and we drove off along tracks, through gates, along roads, until we suddenly came to a tall wire netting fence.

"That's the rabbit fence," said Uncle Bill.

"What's the rabbit fence?" I asked.

"It's a fence the government built to keep all the rabbits on the other side. It goes down into the ground so that they can't burrow under. Rabbits are a big nuisance in this country. They're not native. They were brought here from England, and now they're out of control. If it wasn't for the fence, you'd have rabbits hopping all over the place on your Dad's farm, destroying the crops."

Wow, this was another thing I didn't know about. I had never seen a rabbit. We had hares on the farm, but not many, and they didn't do any damage that I knew of.

"All right, time for smoko," Uncle Bill said. "Let's boil the billy and have our tucker."

He made a little fire out of sticks, and propped some longer ones in a criss-cross over the top. Then he got a black billy out of the ute. He put some water into it out of a water bag, and hung the billy on the cross sticks over the fire. Pretty soon the water was boiling, and he threw a handful of tea leaves into it, and stirred it with a stick, then took it off the fire. He poured the tea into a mug for himself, and got some milk for Barry and me, and we all sat on a log eating our lunch.

"It's a pretty good life boys, don't you think?" said Uncle Bill.

"Yeah," I said. "Pretty good." Barry bobbed his head up and down, while he munched on a sandwich.

After that Uncle Bill took us to the shearing sheds, where he showed us how they sheared the sheep. He showed us the old fashioned hand shears, and the new power ones that looked like the hair clippers Dad used to cut my hair. He showed us where they put the wool to press it into a bale. I thought that I would like to come back one day at shearing time. I reckoned that that would be something to see.

When we got back to the house, I couldn't wait to tell Gloria and Aunty Holly all about the day.

"We went to Wallaby Rock that's the biggest rock you ever saw. It's down by the creek not far from here. I can show you tomorrow. Then we drove for miles and miles through the bush, until we found the sheep, and the dogs rounded them up, and I was right in the middle with thousands and thousands of sheep all around me."

"Bill, you didn't do that, did you?" asked Aunty Joy.

"Yeah, I reckoned he could handle it," said Uncle Bill. "And he did, just like a trooper; didn't spook him a bit."

"Then we went to the rabbit fence that runs all around Australia, to keep the rabbits from eating all the crops. And Uncle Bill boiled his billy and we had smoko on a log. Then we went to the shearing shed, and one day I want to come back and have a crack at that."

"That would be really nice," said Aunty Joy. "Now why don't you men get yourselves cleaned up and come in for tea."

I reckoned that was pretty good, being treated like a man. I was learning so much. This was the best holiday ever.

We Begin to Build the Tennis Court

We were sorry when our holiday at Karara was over. Of course, I was pleased to be home again with Mum and Dad, but I certainly wanted to go back again. It was hard to say good-bye to Joey, because I knew I would never see him again. Maybe after Uncle Bill let him go he would grow up to be a big red, like the one I saw from the rail motor, and he wouldn't be shot, but would hide far away in the bush.

Back at school, I really got interested in tennis, but because I didn't have a racquet of my own, I couldn't really learn how to play properly. I talked to Dad about it. He was a good tennis player and was treasurer, I think, of the Athol Tennis Club, where the men would dress up in their white shirts and trousers or shorts, and the ladies in their white tennis dresses, and play on Sundays. I would go along, but mostly to watch or play games with the other kids. But now I wanted a racquet of my own, so I could learn to play properly; so I talked to Dad about it.

"You know, I've been thinking about that," he said. "Because all of us like to play tennis, I thought it might be a good idea if I built our own tennis court here at home. Then we could play whenever we had time."

"Oh boy! That's a terrific idea, Dad," I said. Gordon, who was listening to the conversation, chimed in and also said it was a great idea.

"It'll take a lot of work," said Dad. "And once you build it you've got to look after it—make sure it's watered and rolled, and kept clean of weeds. That'll be a job for the two of you."

"You bet, no problem," we said.

"Well, maybe we can get it built by your birthday, Des, and then I'll buy you a racquet."

Oh boy! I had just wanted a racquet, and now I was going to get a tennis court as well.

Dad got to work right away. He measured up some ground right beside the house in the horse paddock, and ploughed it up with the tractor and plough. Then we had to pick up all the rocks. That was a big job for Gordon and me. We would load them up in the horse cart, and old Plum would haul them away, and we'd dump then in a good place away from the house. Then Dad would come along with the tractor and plough, and root up another whole pile for us to pick up. It seemed it would never end, until finally Dad was satisfied that all the big rocks were gone.

Next he levelled it out by building it up a bit at one end. Then it had to be flattened out and packed down tight. To do that, we had to water and roll it. We had the water, because Dad had just had a new bore put in up on the hill by the cow bails. I used to go up and watch while they were doing the work. The work crew had a big machine that dug the bore by thump, thump, thumping a heavy weight into the ground. It banged its way through soil and all kinds of rock, and they would bring the dirt and crushed rock mixed with water back up to the top, and spread it out all over the place. It took a long time, but Dad said they finally found a good flow of water at over a hundred feet deep. Then they had to put in the casing for the bore, and Dad brought in another crew to build the windmill, and put up the tank, and lay pipes into the cow bails and down to the house. The water was not good for drinking, but we could use it for watering the lawn, and now for wetting the tennis court.

That was the water part. The rolling was something else. Dad built a great big heavy roller by filling a metal casing with concrete, and running a strong metal rod through the middle of it. He built a handle to attach to the rod to pull the roller, but it was way too heavy for any of us to pull it, so we hooked old Plum up to it, and even he had to struggle as he went up and down, over and over, until we had the ground packed down tight. We were just about finished, when the accident happened.

Because we had to build the ground up at one end to make the court level, there was a little hill at that end, and we had to be careful not to let the roller go over the end of the court, or it could go all the way down the hill to the road. Well sure enough, just as we were about finished with this part of the job, that's exactly what happened. Dad and Herbie were both there working with Plum, backing him up to get the roller in the right position, when the roller got too close to the edge, and started rolling backwards down the hill.

"Look out!" yelled Herbie. "It's gonna get away."

"Come on, Plum, you can hold it," yelled Dad. "Everyone grab hold and give Plum a hand."

Well, we all grabbed the handle and tried to hold the roller, but it was just too heavy, and poor old Plum was being pulled backwards as the roller started going down the hill.

"Cut him loose! Cut him loose!" Dad yelled.

Herbie fumbled with the chains connecting the yoke to the roller, and all the while Plum was going backwards, until finally the yoke dropped to the ground and we all jumped clear and the roller took off down the hill, bumping over rocks and everything else in its path, picking up speed, until it was going full tilt towards the fence along the road.

Our neighbour, Ms. Carrington, was working on his tractor in his paddock on the other side of the road.

"Gawd struth!" said Dad, "I hope it doesn't jump the road and hit Roy or the tractor."

We all watched and held our breath. I don't think Mr. Carrington saw it at first, which is probably just as well, because there was nothing he could do anyway. Luckily, when the roller got to the fence it hit a strong strainer post. The post snapped like a twig, but it slowed the roller down enough so that it didn't make it over the ditch onto the road. By this time we were all running down the hill chasing the roller, leaving old Plum behind to catch his breath.

"Thank God for the fence," said Dad.

"Yeah, especially the strainer post," said Herbie. "He's certainly seen better days."

By the time we scrambled over the broken fence and got to the roller, Mr. Carrington had stopped his tractor to look at us.

"What the hell are you boys playing at?" he called out across the road.

"It's a new game," said Dad, "called chase the bloody roller. Hope we didn't scare you."

"Naw, I was laughing too much. You shoulda seen yourselves, like a bunch of jack rabbits coming down the hill."

Then we all looked at each other, and Herbie started to laugh, until we were all splitting our sides. The roller wasn't too much the worse for wear, just a few dents in the metal casing from the rocks. We shut down work for the day. Herbie went to fetch Plum, who was wandering around the paddock in full harness, and Dad went to get the tractor to pull the roller back up the hill. I think we all learned a good lesson, that you can never be too careful when you're doing something that's a bit tricky or dangerous. No one told Mum or Gloria. This was our big secret, at least until the next time Gloria saw Thelma, who said that her Dad was still laughing when he came in off the tractor. So much for that.

The Tennis Court is Opened

The next part of building the tennis court was to lay down a surface of ant bed. Dad said this came from the nests of termites, and it had to be brought in by truck from a long way away. It was a reddish brown colour and would be very hard when it was packed down. We spread it evenly over the court and levelled it out, and packed it down with the roller (being careful not to let it go down the hill again).

Now it was really starting to look like a tennis court, and much more fresh and smart than the courts over by the school. Everyone would want to come and play here. But there was still a lot more work to be done. We had to put up the fence posts and wire netting to stop the balls. Dad had cut the posts out of small trees from our hill paddock. They weren't exactly smooth and straight, but they were pretty good. Herbie and Dad dug the post holes, and Gordon and I worked on painting the posts white before the men put them up. They were really high, so that most balls wouldn't go over the top. Herbie and Dad bolted them together with long boards on the top, so they would always stand straight. Then they stretched rolls of wire netting all the way around. Herbie built three places to put gates for getting in and out of the court, and the gates were also made out of wire netting. The last thing was to put up two strong posts on either side in the middle of the court for the net. Dad and Herbie measured up carefully where the lines were to go on the court, and drove long metal bolts into the court to mark the corners.

We didn't have any fancy machine to make the lines. Dad took a big old enamel teapot, and tied a piece of rag to hang down from the end of the spout. He made a white mixture from wood ashes and water, and poured it into the teapot. Then Gordon and I held each end of a string stretched between the bolt heads to mark the end of the line, and Dad walked along crouched over pouring the white mixture out of the spout of the teapot, with the piece of rag dragging along to sort of smooth out the line. I wouldn't say it was perfect, but it wasn't too bad, and when we were finished you could certainly see the markings of a tennis court.

Dad had bought a brand new tennis net, which we stretched between the two net posts and tightened up to the right height (of one tennis racquet and a head) by turning a screw handle on one end of the posts.

And there we were with a brand new tennis court right beside the house, and all finished before my seventh birthday.

The next thing was to give the court what Dad called a proper opening ceremony. He picked a Sunday a couple of weeks after my birthday. I already had my racquet. It was a beauty—a junior Dunlop strung with cat gut and just the right weight. Dad took me out onto the court on my birthday to try it out, and to give me a few pointers. He showed me how to swing for a forehand, and how to get my feet in the proper position for a backhand. He made me drop the ball and try to hit it over the net. At first I couldn't do it to save my life, but he made me hit ball after ball, until I finally got one over, then another and another. Then he made me move further up the court, and do it all over again, until I could finally get one over from the backline. Then he hit some balls at me from the other side of the net, and I was supposed to hit them back. Well, of course, I missed most of them, and hit a lot of the others into the net, but every now and then I hit one back to him, and he would tell me "good shot" and to keep trying.

The other way I could practice was by hitting the ball against the side of the house, but after I hit the gauze on the windows a few times, and made a dent in it, Mum sent me off to practise against the barn door, which I did every chance I got, so I would be able to play at what was now being called the grand opening of the tennis court.

Finally, the big day arrived. Dad had invited the whole Athol Tennis Club, so instead of playing at the Athol courts that day they came to our place. Gordon and I had to get the court ready. Dad had bought a new roller much lighter than the big old one, which was now parked to remain forever outside the netting at the end where it rolled down the hill. It was propped up with a few big rocks to make sure that wouldn't happen again, but whenever we saw it, we would all remember that day.

Gordon and I pulled the new roller up and down the court, until Dad was satisfied that it was ready for play. Then we did the lines and put up the net, and everything was ready.

After lunch people started to arrive. Mum said we should have a proper opening ceremony, so she strung a ribbon across the gate into the court. Dad said we had to toast it, so he brought out a few bottles of beer and filled the glasses for the men, and made shandies with lemonade and ginger ale for the women, and cordial for us kids. Then he gave me a pair of scissors and said as my birthday present I could cut the ribbon. Everyone raised their glasses, and with cries of "Here's to the new court" and "Good on yer, mate" (and something about "hitting your balls" that made everyone laugh) I cut the ribbon.

Everyone had a great time. We played all afternoon, until people had to leave to get home for milking. They played short sets so everyone would get a chance to play—men's doubles and ladies' doubles and mixed doubles, then some of the older kids played, and finally I had a chance to hit a few balls to show what I could do. Margaret was there, and she told me how good I was, even though I still didn't know how to serve, so I couldn't play a proper game.

But it was a beginning, and a good memory, and I reckon that's what's important, because even though I was only seven, I knew that remembering the good times was the best part of life—and I was already building up a lot of good memories.

Wacky the Small Boy

At the end of the school year I had finished Prep 4, and next year I would be going into Grade 1 with Margaret and Phyllis. Mr. Fisher must have thought I was a good reader, because he gave me a very long book as my school prize for Christmas 1945. It was called *Wacky the Small Boy* and was about a small boy whose real name was Wilberforce Wallaby Jr., which seemed to be a long name for a small boy, so he changed it to Wacky, when his father called him that one day.

I don't know if Mr. Fisher read the book before he gave it to me, or whether he thought I was a bit wacky like the boy in the book, but it certainly made me think. I had to work hard at reading it over the holidays. It was 85 pages long, but that was not the hardest part. What was different was that Wacky lived in a big city and he hung out with a mob of boys his own age, who were all bigger than him. I didn't know any boys my own age, and I didn't live in a city, so it was all a bit strange to me.

I asked Triloaf about it.

"Do you know what it's like to live in a city?" I asked him.

"No, never done that," he said.

"What about hanging out with a mob of boys?" I asked.

"Never done that, either," he said. "You're the only friend I've got."

"Well, you're my best friend, too," I said, "but how am I supposed to know these things if you can't tell me?"

"Read the book," he said, unhelpfully.

"That's what I'm trying to do," I said.

"Tell me about it," he said. "Does Wacky like being a small boy?"

"Not really. But he's smart enough to convince all the tall boys that being small is best, so they all walk along crouched over. Then one day along comes Benny who is smaller than Wacky, so all the other boys think he is the best. So Wacky tries to feed Benny to make him grow."

"Sounds like Wacky thinks more about himself than anyone else," said Triloaf.

"That's very clever of you to figure that out," I said. "He wants to be the boss, and when he doesn't get his own way, he gets sulky and does mean things."

"What happens in the end?" asked Triloaf.

"I dunno. I haven't finished it yet," I said.

"Well, you better go and finish," he said.

So I did, but I didn't really understand the ending at first. Wacky gets very sick and everyone is nice to him. Then he starts to get better and dreams up the idea of forming a Secret Club with himself as President, which I think means the boss, and all the other boys would have to follow him. But when he gets well, and tells the other boys about it, he names one of the other boys, Beppo, as President, and gives everyone except himself an important position. When they ask him what he is going to be, he gulps a bit and says he will be "the member."

"What's it mean to be the member of a club?" I asked Mum.

"Well, there's usually more than one member," she said. "Like the Tennis Club, it has a lot of members."

"But there's also a President and a Secretary and Treasurer," I said.

"That's right, but where did you learn that?"

"In my school prize book about Wacky the small boy. He forms this Secret Club, and he gives everyone an important job to do except himself."

"Well, that was nice of him," said Mum.

I thought about that and went to tell Triloaf.

"I figured it out," I said.

"What did you figure out?"

"Because Wacky was small he tried to be too smart for his own good. All the other boys got tired of him because he wanted to be the boss of everything. Then he formed this Club and made everyone else more important than himself."

"And what happened?"

"I dunno. That's where the book ends."

"Well, what do you think happens?"

"I think Wacky learns to be a good friend, rather than trying to be the boss."

"That sounds like a good thing. You should remember that," said Triloaf.

"But I don't have any friends my own age," I said.

"You will one day. Maybe you'll live in a city, too."

"Not likely. I'm a farm boy."

And that was the end of that. I was glad Mr. Fisher had given me the book, because it made me think, which is what you have to do as you grow up and go into Grade 1.

The Family Goes to Redcliffe

During the school holidays in January, Dad surprised everybody by saying that he had arranged for us to spend two weeks at the seaside. Now this would be something new and different. None of us had ever been to the seaside before. Dad arranged for Herbie to look after the farm and the milking while we were away. He also said that Aunty Dora and Alma were going to come with us, too, which would be good, because Aunty Dora was such a nice, kind old lady, and Alma would be good company. I think Dad wanted to give Aunty Dora a holiday, too, because she was his favourite Aunty.

The place we were going to was called Redcliffe, and it was a very long way away—at least a hundred miles, Dad said. Aunty Dora and Alma came over to stay the night with us before we left, so that we could get an early start. Dad and Gordon and Herbie loaded all of our luggage and the other things we would need into the back of the ute. The four of us kids and Alma climbed into the back ready for the long journey. It was a nice warm day, and we had a big tarpaulin in case it rained. Mum, Dad and Aunty Dora rode in the front.

To get to Redcliffe you had to go through Toowoomba, and down the Range to Brisbane. Mum said we would stop at Aunty Carrie and Aunty Evelyn's house in Brisbane before going on to Redcliffe. I wasn't sure how we were going to do all this in one day, but Dad said it would be no problem. So we set off.

"Have a good holiday," said Herbie, waving goodbye.

This time I wasn't scared going down the Range. It's funny how once you know about something, it doesn't scare you any more—like riding a horse, or going to school, or taking the train. I was still a bit scared of going in the water to swim, and I remembered as we went by Helidon Spa the terrible experience I had, when that bad man held me under the water. I hoped there wouldn't be anything like that at Redcliffe.

After Helidon Spa we kept driving and driving through all kinds of interesting country. We stopped for lunch at a hot pie shop by the side of the road. Then we came to a big town like Toowoomba called Ipswich, and Dad called out to us that it wouldn't be long before we got to Brisbane. Boy, what a surprise that was! I had never seen so many houses and cars and busses and even trams going down railway tracks in the middle of the road. I was sure hoping that Dad wouldn't get lost, but he seemed to know the way. People would kind of stare at us four kids and Alma riding in the back of the ute, but we would just wave to them, and the harder they stared the more we waved, and eventually they would smile and wave back at us. It was fun when we stopped beside a tram and you could almost reach out and touch the people riding on the tram.

"Where you goin', kids?" one man called out to us.

"We're going to Redcliffe for a holiday," I called back.

"Keep an eye out for the sharks," he said.

"What?" I yelled. "Are there sharks at Redcliffe?"

But Dad drove off before he could answer me.

"I think he was just pulling your leg," said Gordon, but I don't think he was too sure.

Then we came to this place where there were roads and cars and trams all going in ten different directions, with a policeman in the middle waving his arms to direct the traffic. You never saw such a thing. I learned afterwards that it was called the Five Ways at Wooloongabba. Someone sure made a big mistake when they made all the roads come together at this one place. Dad was a bit slow in starting off when it was his turn, and the policemen waved at him and blew his whistle and yelled, "Come on, mate, get the lead out." I could have yelled something back at him, but I knew it wasn't a good idea to do that to a policeman.

After that we crossed the river on a big bridge, and then we were really in the thick of it, with shops and tall buildings, and hundreds of people on the footpath, and some trying to cross the road and dodging the cars and trams. Our eyes were popping out of our heads as we rode slowly through all this in the back of the ute. I was amazed that Dad knew where he was going. Whoever would want to live in a place like this? I was sure glad I was a farm boy and didn't live in the city. The noise was terrible—car horns honking, trucks and buses roaring along, trams rattling down the tracks. Val was terrified and crawled under the tarpaulin to hide. I felt like doing the same, but I didn't want to miss anything.

Dad kept on driving, and eventually we got out of the worst of the traffic. Then he turned off onto a side street, and suddenly things were a lot quieter. I saw this great big tank, a hundred times bigger than any water tank we had on the farm. And there was a funny smell in the air, a bit like rotten eggs, but a bit sweeter.

We pulled up outside a small old house with high steps at the front, and rusty corrugated iron on the roof. Aunty Carrie and Aunty Evelyn came down the steps. It was sure good to see someone you knew in all this mess.

"Hello dears."

"Look at you."

"Have you had a good trip?"

Everyone was talking at once.

"What's the rotten smell?" I asked.

"Don't you like our city perfume?" laughed Aunty Carrie. "It's the Brisbane Gas. That big tank over there is a gas tank. There's always a smell of gas in the air around here."

"What's it for?" I asked.

"We use it to cook with and make a cup of tea," said Aunty Evelyn. "Come on in, everyone, I'm sure you're all dying for a cuppa."

Inside in the kitchen they had what Aunty Evelyn called a gas ring by the wood stove. She struck a match, turned a knob, and suddenly the whole ring burst into a blue flame. Wow! I had never seen anything like that before. She put on the kettle, and soon we were all sitting around the kitchen table having afternoon tea.

"It's so nice to see you," Mum said to Aunty Carrie and Aunty Evelyn, "but we can't stay long. We have to get to Redcliffe before dark."

"Yes, and the clouds are building up a bit," said Dad. "We might get a storm."

"Well, you'll have to come back here for a holiday some time," said Aunty Carrie.

Not likely, I thought to myself. Brisbane is no place for a holiday. You could go deaf from the noise, or get run over by a car, or choke to death on the gas. No thanks.

Soon we were on our way again. Dad was right about the clouds. It looked like a storm was coming. But soon we were out of the city and driving through the country again. I knew we were going to the seaside, but it was taking forever, and just as I thought we'd never get there Gordon called out, "Look, look, there it is—the sea."

He was pointing over the hood of the ute, and there we could see in front of us the wide blue sea. There was a story in my Prep 4 Reader called "The Sea Shell" so I thought I knew from the pictures what the sea would be like, but I never thought it would be so big. It just stretched away as far as you could see.

"Is this Redcliffe?" I asked, now very excited.

"No, I think this is Sandgate," said Alma. "You have to go over a long bridge to get to Redcliffe."

I was all eyes and ears now. This was much better than noisy, smelly Brisbane. The breeze was cool, blowing in off the sea, and there was a tangy smell in the air that Gloria said was from the salt water. We drove along beside the sea for a while, past houses and campgrounds with tents and caravans and children playing, and then we came to the most amazing sight.

I learned afterwards that the road we were on was called the Hornibrook Highway, and all of a sudden it turned into a bridge that seemed to be just floating on the water. We were driving right out over the sea, and you could look down and see all these blue blobs of jelly in the water.

"Look at that, look at that!" I cried. "What are they?"

"Jelly fish," said Gordon. "If you see them in the water when you're swimming, don't touch them, because they can sting."

Yuk! So not everything about the seaside was so nice. And the man on the tram had said to watch out for sharks. I was going to be careful.

"Just look at this bridge," Alma said. She was standing up looking over the hood of the ute. I joined her to look, too, and as far as you could see the bridge was going out over the water. We were in our lane going one way and a few cars were in the other lane coming towards us. It sure looked pretty narrow, and I hoped that Dad could see all right. We wouldn't want to have an accident on the bridge. And then there was a big flash of lightning, and the roar of thunder, and the rain started coming down in buckets.

We all ducked under the tarpaulin as fast as we could, but we were pretty wet before we got under cover. I could hear the rain pounding down on the canvas, and I peeked out to see what I could see, and it wasn't much. I was looking back the way we had come, and I could hardly see the bridge at all for the driving rain. The cars behind us all had their lights on, and everything had slowed to a crawl. Poor Dad had to drive through this in the middle of this narrow bridge going on forever. A strong wind had come up with the storm, and I could see that the waves on the sea were getting bigger and rolling in under the bridge. And all the time the lightning was flashing, followed by great claps of thunder. This was sure a spectacular way to arrive at Redcliffe.

But Dad kept going, and at last we were off the bridge, and the rain was easing up. In no time at all the sun came out again to welcome us to Redcliffe. We drove on a bit further, and Dad had to stop for a couple of times to ask directions. It was now getting dark, so we couldn't see much, but eventually we found the house that Dad had rented. The keys were in the mailbox, and soon we had everything unloaded, and Mum was cooking up a meal in our new kitchen. I couldn't wait for tomorrow, to go exploring at the seaside.

I Try My Hand at Fishing

Gordon and I slept on the verandah, and next morning we were up at sunrise, and found Dad in the kitchen making a cup of tea.

"No cows to milk this morning boys," he said. "Let's go to the beach."

It was already hot, so we put on our swimming togs and grabbed a towel and headed out. It was just a short walk to the beach, but we couldn't really see it until we got past a high hedge, and suddenly there it was, a wide sandy beach, running away in both directions as far as you could see, with small waves rolling in, and flopping on the sand, and running up on the beach, then running back out again. I thought it was one of the most wonderful sights I had ever seen.

"The tide must be in," Dad said. "The beach will be even wider when it goes out."

I had heard about tides, but I didn't really know how they worked. Anyway, it didn't matter, because the beach was already wide enough, and I ran over it right into a small wave that swirled around my knees. It felt a bit cold at first, but not for long. Then Gordon went tearing along on the edge of the sea, splashing water everywhere as he went, and I took off after him as fast as I could go, until I tripped and went headfirst into a wave. That's when I found out what Gloria meant by salt water. My mouth was full of it, and it stung my eyes. This was the strangest thing—a whole ocean full of salt water.

Dad called out to us to come back and look at the crabs. They were just little fellows scurrying along sideways or burrowing into the sand or hiding under a shell. I had never seen so many shells, thousands of them all shapes and colours, and they were sharp to walk on, too, in your bare feet.

"Come on boys, let's have a dip," said Dad, and he took us each by the hand, and we headed into the water. Pretty soon I was up to my waist, and a wave would have knocked me over, if Dad wasn't holding me.

"Turn sideways and jump," Dad said. That worked for a while, but then a big wave went right over my head, and I had another mouthful of salt water. I could also feel the water rushing backwards over the sand around my toes.

"That's the undertow," Dad said. "It can be dangerous when you have big waves in the ocean. But it's safe enough here in the bay."

"I thought this was the ocean," I said.

"No, this is Moreton Bay. Look way out there. Can you see that land across the water?" He picked me up and pointed out to sea. I thought I could see something, but it was really too far to be sure. "That's Moreton Island," Dad continued. "On the other side of that you have the ocean. That's where you see the big waves. Maybe we'll go over there one day for you to see it."

"How will we get across the water?" I asked.

"There's a boat you can catch. It's called a ferry. You want to make sure you go on a nice calm day like today. Otherwise, it can get pretty rough out there, and you could get seasick."

I was amazed that Dad knew so much about all this seaside stuff, because we lived so far away from here on the farm. But Dad knows a lot of things, so it was good that he could take time off from his work and show us all this.

Gordon had been splashing around in the waves, when suddenly he stood up and pointed. "What's that over there?" he asked.

"It's the jetty," said Dad.

"What's the jetty?" I asked.

"The jetty is built to go out into the water so that you have deep enough water for the boats, even when the tide is out. If you've had enough swimming for a while, we can walk out on it."

We grabbed our shoes and towels and walked out on the jetty. It was built out of long poles that went down into the water. When I remembered how hard it was to put up the long poles on our tennis court, I wondered how you could do that, when you had to dig down into the water with all of the waves sloshing about. But it felt very strong, so the men who did it must have known what they were doing.

There weren't many other people around this early in the morning, but when we got to the end of the jetty there was a man and a boy out there fishing. The man had his line on the end of a stick, which I later found out was called a rod. The boy was dangling his line in his hand down in the water.

"Wotcha doin'?" I asked.

"Fishin,'" he said.

"I've never been fishing," I said.

"Go on," he said, "everyone goes fishin.'"

"Not where I live."

"Where's that?"

"On our farm at Athol. I have my own horse called Blackie, and I ride to school."

He kind of screwed up his face at me, and smiled a bit.

"That's pretty good," he said. "I have a bike to ride to school. You want to hold the line?"

"You bet. What do I do?"

"Just jiggle it around a bit. If you feel a bite, give it a jerk."

He gave me the line to hold, and I could feel a bit of a weight on the end of it.

"I can already feel something," I said.

"No, that's just the sinkers. You'll know if you get a bite."

"Have you caught any?"

"Yeah, here in the bucket."

He showed me a bucket with two small fish in it.

"They're not very big," I said.

"They're whiting. That's as big as they get."

Just then I felt a jerk on the line.

"Hey, I got one," I called.

"Pull him in. Pull him in. But don't get the line tangled."

I pulled the line up, hand over hand, and looking over the edge of the jetty. Suddenly the end of the line came out of the water, and there was a small fish bouncing around on the end of it.

"Hey, Dad, look. I caught one," I yelled.

We pulled him up onto the jetty, where he flopped around a bit while the boy got the hook out of his mouth, then dropped him in the bucket. He then took a long worm out of a tin, and threaded it onto the hook, and dropped the line back into the water.

The man with the fishing rod had been watching all this. "He's doing better than me," he said to Dad.

"Beginner's luck," said Gordon.

"Yeah, well it deserves its reward," said the man. "You fellas take those fish and cook 'em up for breakfast."

"Are you sure?" said Dad.

"Yeah, there's plenty more where they came from," said the man. "Johnny, wrap the fish up in this newspaper and give 'em to these fellas."

"That was really nice of them to give us their fish," I said to Dad, as we walked back along the jetty.

"Yeah, most people are decent if you treat them right. That man took a shine to you, because you showed them you were interested in something new that they could teach you. People are like that."

"Even if it was beginner's luck," I said to Gordon, as I walked back happily carrying the fish. I couldn't wait to show them to Mum for her to cook for breakfast.

We Go to Moreton Island and I Lose My Toy Soldier

Our days at Redcliffe were just one wonderful adventure after another. We spent a lot of time on the beach, splashing in the water, building sand castles, and collecting shells. Dad bought a couple of fishing lines for me and Gordon, and we spent a lot of time on the jetty fishing. We didn't catch many fish, but enough for a few meals. Dad showed us how to scale the fish and slice them. Mum cooked them up in a frying pan, and we ate them neat just like that, with a bit of salt and vinegar. We loved fish. Other days we would go to the fish and chips shop, and each one of us would get our own package of fish and chips wrapped up in newspaper. We would make a hole in the end, and find a good place to sit watching the waves and the boats, and pull out pieces of fish and a few chips until the whole thing was gone, and all you had left was the salt and the oil on your fingers, and the wonderful taste of the whole meal in your memory.

The biggest adventure was the day we went over on the ferry to Moreton Island. I had never been on a boat before. There were a lot of other people, so we scrambled to get good seats up the front where we could see everything. Dad sat up there with us kids and Alma, while Mum and Aunty Dora sat in the covered part in the shade. Soon we were out on the water, with nothing around us but the wide blue sea, with the ferry boat rocking and rolling a bit in the waves, and the wind blowing all the time, so that I had to hold onto my helmet, or it would blow away.

I was sitting in the front watching the boat cut through the water in a white frothy slice, when suddenly right there in front of the boat a large fish leapt out of the water, then another, and another, until there were at least six, racing ahead of the boat, and leaping in and out of the water, like children playing in the ocean.

"Dad, Gordon, Gloria, Alma, Val, everyone, look, look at this!" I yelled. "Great big fish jumping out of the water. Come and see! Come and see!"

Everyone crowded around to look.

"Porpoises," a man said, "they're not fish, they're porpoises. They like to play like that, run ahead of the boat and show off."

I was right at the front, looking over the edge of the boat, and one of the porpoises came up out of the water and looked me right in the eye, and I could have sworn he smiled at me, before he plunged back in, then leapt up again ahead of the boat. It was the most amazing thing I had ever seen. They stayed there for quite a while, leading the boat, then suddenly, as quickly as they had come, they were gone, and the jetty at Moreton Island was right in front of us.

There wasn't much at the end of the jetty, just a few buildings and a shop selling ice-cream and hot dogs. Dad bought each of us what we wanted, then pointed to a rickety old bus, and told us to climb on board to go across the island to the other side. The bus was all open air, no windows and hard wooden seats. Mum had cushions for her and Aunty Dora, but the rest of us scrambled on, along with all the other people, and the bus took off with a jerk along a bumpy winding track into the bush.

There wasn't much to see along the way, but when we stopped on the other side, we saw in front of us a great white mountain of sand.

"Sand dunes," said the driver. "Those of you who are game can get out and scramble to the top, and then you'll see the ocean. The rest of you stay on the bus and we'll go a bit further."

Dad got out with me and Gordon and a few others, and we started up the sand dune, sinking and scrambling in the fine white sand, which seemed like it was a mile high and long. Finally, we got to the top, and in front of us were a few smaller sand dunes, and beyond that the wide blue open ocean, with great big waves rolling in and crashing on the beach, which stretched away forever in both directions.

"There it is boys, the Pacific Ocean," said Dad. "You're right on the edge of Australia. Nowhere further to go in that direction unless you're a fish or a boat."

I remembered the map we had of Australia on the wall at school, and that Mr. Fisher had said it was the biggest island in the world with ocean all around it. And here I was looking at the ocean. I couldn't wait to get down to the beach.

We scrambled along a bit of a track over the other dunes, and through some small bushes, until we hit the beach at a run. I ran right down to the water, then stopped dead as a great big wave crashed down in front of me, and sent a surge of water up onto the sand where I was standing, right up to my knees and my shoes filled with water. Then I felt it sucking at my legs, and I remembered what Dad had said about the undertow. It was so strong that it started to pull me over, and I saw another big wave crashing down just as Dad grabbed me by the shoulders, and pulled me back up the beach.

"Not too close, Des," he said. "That's a big surf. You don't want to get caught in that."

"Yeah, or it would take you all the way to China," said Gordon, which didn't sound like a very good idea to me, so I happily stayed well clear of the water after that. We hung out on the beach for a while exploring, but mostly watching and listening to the waves crashing on the beach. Part of me thought how great it would be to be one of those porpoises that could leap around and ride on the waves, but another part said that as wonderful as all this was, the best place of all was back on the farm, where I felt most at home. After that we found our way back to the bus, where Mum and Aunty Dora and the girls were waiting, and we rode back on the bumpy road to the ferry.

On the way back on the ferry Aunty Dora asked me to sit beside her, and tell her what I was learning at school. I was glad to sit with her, and talk quietly after all the excitement of the morning.

"Your mother tells me you like to read," she said.

"Yes, it's my favourite thing to do in school," I replied. "I'm learning a lot of new words, but what I like best are stories. I like to read stories, and I also like to make up my own."

"That's very clever," Aunty Dora said. "Tell me one of your stories."

"All right," I said, "but first I have to show you something."

I fished around in my pocket and pulled out one of my favourite little toys. It was a tiny lead soldier, with a brown cap, a red coat, and blue pants. He carried a rifle on his shoulder, and he could stand up all on his own. I stood him on the railing of the ferry to show Aunty Dora.

"Oh, how smart he looks," she said. "Where did you get him?"

"In my Christmas stocking. I saw him with a lot of others in a shop in Toowoomba. I told Mum that I would like to have them to play with, but she said I shouldn't be greedy to want so many, but that if I picked one out maybe Father Christmas would bring it to me for Christmas. So I picked this one, and on Christmas Day there he was in my stocking."

"And have you made up a story about him?" Aunty Dora asked.

"Yes, well you see," I said, "all of his friends, the other soldiers, had to go off to war, but he was too sick to go because he had asthma and he was very sad about that. But his friends said, 'Cheer up, don't be sad, we need someone brave and strong to stand guard while we are away. You have to make sure all of the people in the town, and especially the boys and girls, are safe.' So that's what he does, and because he's all on his own, it's a big responsibility. It's his special assignment. (These are big words I learnt from Mr. Fisher at school). No one can get past him, no matter how hard they try. He will stand guard until the war is over, and all of the other soldiers come home."

"That's a wonderful story," said Aunty Dora. "He had his own special job to do, didn't he?"

"Yes, and it was important," I said, "and look how he stands up tall and strong."

But just then something terrible happened. The ferry gave a lurch, and the toy soldier fell over and slid along the railing. I made a wild grab to save him, but I was too late, and he fell with a tiny splash into the water. I saw him sink out of sight. The tears welled up in my eyes. My toy soldier was gone forever. This was not part of my story. I started to cry, and great big sobs shook my whole body. I felt Aunty Dora put her arms around me, and hold me tight.

"There, there, dear," I heard her saying. "I know you feel terrible. But, you know, there's another wonderful story about a toy soldier. It's in one of your Queensland Readers. You'll read it yourself one day, but I can tell it to you now. It's about a toy soldier who fell out the window of his home, when the little boy who owned him put him there."

"Did he fall in the water, too?" I asked between my sobs.

"Well it was raining very hard where he fell into the street, and the rainwater was rushing down the gutters. Then two boys came along and saw him, and thought it would be fun to make a paper boat and put the toy soldier in it and send him sailing down the gutter."

"I can make a paper boat," I said. "I learnt how to do it from that book you and Alma gave us when we came to see the horses."

"Well, there you are. Isn't it wonderful how things happen? So the toy soldier sailed off in the boat, standing up bravely just like yours. The water in the gutter ran out and into a creek, and the little boat sailed on down the creek, until it joined a river and the boat with the soldier standing up in it sailed on down the river, until the river joined the sea. Away the boat went out to sea, until a wave came along and tipped it over, and the soldier fell out and sank into the water."

"Just like mine," I said.

"Yes, but that's not the end of the story, because along came a big fish, and thinking that the soldier was something good to eat, the fish gobbled him up."

"Gosh," I said, "I know there are big fish like that. We saw them on the way over, remember? They're called porpoises."

"Yes, well, I don't think this one was a porpoise, because a fisherman caught it and sold it to the fish market, and guess what: the mother of the boy who owned the little soldier bought the fish, and when she took it home and opened it up, there was the toy soldier. He was back home again after all his adventures."

"Wow! What a story!" I wasn't crying any more. "Do you think a big fish will swallow my soldier, and we'll be able to find him again?"

"Well, I'm not sure it will happen just like that again," Aunty Dora said, smiling at me, "but it's a nice thought isn't it?"

"Yes, it makes me feel better," I said. I thought about it for a bit, then I said, "You know what I think? I think God was looking after the toy soldier in your story, and He's looking after my toy soldier, too."

"Why, that's a very nice thought dear," said Aunty Dora. "I think you're right about that. Do you learn about God at school?"

"Not really, but there's a prayer in my Prep 4 Reader about thanking God for everything. And there's a story about Jesus, who was the son of God."

"What story is that?"

"It's called 'Our Best Friend,' and it's about how the mothers wanted their children to be blessed by Jesus, but his friends said he was too busy. But then Jesus said, 'Suffer the little children to come unto me and forbid them not.' It's a funny way of speaking, but Jesus picked the children up in his arms and blessed them. And there's a picture in the book showing Jesus with the children all around him."

"Well, thank you, dear, for telling me about that," said Aunty Dora. "Now we both feel better, don't you think?"

"I suppose so," I said. "I'm sorry about my soldier, and I'll miss him. I don't really think I'll find him again in a fish, but that was a good story. Maybe one day I'll write a story like that, and I'll remember you told it to me."

I snuggled up to Aunty Dora, and we rode all the way back together in the ferry to Redcliffe.

The Toowomba Show

After our holiday at Redcliffe it was soon time to go back to school for the start of my Grade One year. Margaret, Phyllis and I were no longer the youngest kids in the school, because now other younger brothers and sisters were showing up. My cousin, Johnny, (Jimmy's brother), Margaret's brother (the other Johnny), Phyllis's brother, Colin, and Harold's sister, Dawn, all started in Prep 1. It was fun to be able to show all these young kids what to do at school and help them out when they made mistakes. Gloria was now in Grade 3, and Gordon's class of Grade 5 were among the oldest in the school. So we were all growing up.

In my class we were soon learning a lot of new things at school: how to write in our copy books instead of just on our slates, memorizing our tables for adding and subtracting, and especially reading all of the new stories in our Grade 1 School Reader. This was a much bigger book than our old Prep readers and most of the stories were teaching us a lesson. Mr. Fisher would ask us to tell him the moral of the story after we finished reading it.

There was the story about a silly mouse that didn't listen to her mother, and went to play with Tabby and her kittens, and ended up getting killed. And another one like that about a fox, who boasted to a cat that he knew a lot of tricks, but the cat only knew one—how to climb a tree. But when the hounds came, that one trick saved the cat's life, while the fox, for all of his boasting, was killed by the hounds. The one I especially liked was about Tommy and the crow. Tommy didn't like going to school, and he decided to lie down in the grass and sleep instead. But then he had a conversation with a crow, who showed Tommy how smart a bird he was, while Tommy was only a boy who needed to go to school to learn how to do things, and he was not even smart enough to do that, but wanted to lie around in the grass all day. Then the crow and all his friends started cawing: "Go to school, Go to school, Go to school." So Tommy ran off to school, and he never forgot the lesson he learned from the wise old crow. The way the story was written was clever, because you couldn't be sure if Tommy really talked to the crow, or if it was just a dream he had while lying in the grass. I think these are the best kinds of stories, because they make you think.

I would come home and tell Mum about all the things I was learning at school, and she would say how pleased she was that I was growing up. This made me feel good, but as well it was part of a plan I had to get her to talk to Dad about taking us all to the Toowoomba Show this year. I had heard some of the kids talking at school about how this was going to be a really big Show, because now that the war was over all the good sideshows would be back, like Tex Morton's Rodeo and Wild West Show and Buddy Williams, the Yodelling Jackaroo. I remembered that Uncle Henry had told me about them, and I really wanted to see them.

"Do you think I might be old and smart enough to go with you and Dad and the rest of the family to the Toowoomba Show this year?" I asked. "I can help look after Val."

"Well, I could talk to Dad about it," Mum said.

I thought that was a good start, but I decided to help her think it through a bit.

"All the best sideshows will be back after the war," I said. "And I'm sure Dad would like to see the buckjumping and the sheep dog trials and the trots and all those things in the ring."

"You certainly know a lot about it, don't you?" Mum said.

"Well, I am growing up, you know," I said.

She smiled and said, "We'll see about it," and I reckoned we were at least half way there.

I talked with Gordon and Gloria about it, and we all decided it would be a good idea to work on Dad. We left it for a few days, and then we brought it up when we were all sitting down at tea time.

"I hear that the Toowoomba Show is going to be really good this year," said Gordon. "It would be great to see all the prize cattle and pigs."

"I think the displays of fruit and cakes and dress making would be good, too," said Gloria.

"The buckjumping and campdrafting and sheep dog trials in the ring would be best," I said.

No one said anything for a bit, then Dad spoke up: "What about the sideshows? Doesn't anyone like them?"

"You bet," I said right away. "Tex Morton's Wild West Show and Buddy Williams, the Yodelling Jackeroo, are going to be there, and it will be special, because during the war they couldn't put on their shows, and Buddy Williams even went to war and got shot, but now he's better and will sing all his hillbilly songs. It's going to be the best show ever."

"You seem to know a lot about it," Dad said. "It's funny, your mother and I were just talking about this the other day, but we didn't think you'd be so keen on going and getting mixed up in all those crowds of people."

"Dad, don't tease them," said Mum.

"No, you meet a lot of interesting people," said Gloria.

"And that's the only way you can get to see Tex Morton and Buddy Williams," I said.

"What do you think, Mum?" Dad asked. "Would you like to go to the Show?"

"It would be nice," Mum said.

"And I would help to look after Val," I said. Little Val was sitting quietly through all of this. She didn't really know what we were talking about, but I knew she would like to go, too.

"Well, as a matter of fact, I'm interested in the Show myself this year," Dad said. "I'm thinking of bringing in a stud herd for the dairy, and this will be a good way to check things out."

I don't think any of us knew what a stud herd was, though maybe Gordon did, but we all told Dad it was a terrific idea.

The Toowoomba Show was on for a week, I think. We took a day off school during the week to go, so the crowds wouldn't be so bad. The Show went on after dark, but we couldn't stay, because we had to be home for milking. The Show Grounds were not far from Grandfather's place, so we went there first for morning tea, then we all went off to the Show. Dad gave us each five shillings to spend so we felt really rich.

When you go to the Show it's like a whole day out. There are just so many things to see and do, with all kinds of food to eat, like hot pies, sausage rolls, hot dogs, fish and chips, fairy floss, toffee apples and ice-cream. If you push some ice-cream down into a bottle of lemonade, you can shake it up and clamp your mouth over the top of the bottle, and let all of the froth bubble into your mouth and ooze out around the corner of your lips.

We all stuck together at first, and went through this big building where all kinds of fruit and vegetables were put together in different shapes, like a great big map of Queensland outlined in oranges, and filled in with all of the other things that grow here. There was a big potato at the bottom with TOOWOOMBA printed on a card stuck into it. Gloria said if the potato was Toowoomba, then the little brown Queensland nut beside it must be Athol. Everyone laughed, but I didn't see the joke.

Tables covered with cakes spilled over into other tables piled high with jars of honey and jam. Fancy little dresses hung on racks, and dolls with glass eyes that rolled back in their heads were decked out in brightly coloured baby clothes, lying under a roof of tablecloths and tea towels, all stretched out higgledy piggledy every which way, so that you had to crick your neck to look at them as you worked your way through the crowds of women ooing and aahing at how beautiful they were, and how you'd have to have more time than Methuselah to do all that. Different coloured ribbons saying First Prize, Second Prize, Third Prize and Show Champion were pinned onto different things, which made the ladies argue and say the judge must be blind in one eye to give a prize to that, or else she was a "relly," or had been given something under the table.

After that we went over to the Show Ring, and sat on the benches and ate our hot pies and hot dogs, while we watched men lead great big bulls past a man standing on a stool and wearing a white hat, who also had a pile of ribbons that he eventually hung around the necks of the winning bulls, while everyone clapped. After that there was campdrafting, where a man on a horse has to work a couple of rambunctious steers through gates, and around small trees, to get them to go where he wants them to go. Then sheep dogs did the same thing with sheep, while the trainer stood in the middle of the ring giving directions with his arms, while the crowd clapped or groaned when the stupid sheep went the wrong way. Every now and then there would be a race of trotters pulling sulkies with big bicycle wheels, driven by little men wearing bright colours and caps. This was very exciting, as the horses went thundering around the Ring on the tracks a couple of times past where we were sitting. The drivers would try to cut each other off to get to the front. The worst thing a horse could do was to break out of a trot into a gallop, which seemed to me a bit silly, because that way they could go faster, but that was against the rules.

Later on Dad took Gordon and me down to the stock yards, where we could take a closer look at the cattle, and where Dad could find out what he wanted to know about a stud herd. While Dad was talking, I played around with the calves, and made friends with a couple of boys, who had their prize calf in for judging. It was all interesting enough, but what I really wanted to do was go over to the sideshows before it was too late, and we'd have to leave to get home for milking.

Finally, Dad was finished talking, and he said, "All right boys, let's go and look at the sideshows."

Sideshow Alley, as they called it, was a wonderful world of tents and ropes, and flashy signs, where the strangest looking men with gravelly voices would yell right in your ear to "'Ave a go" at knocking down whatever you could throw a ball at, or hit with a dart, or shoot with a rifle. Fat ladies in swim suits, and midgets in top hats, sat around outside their tent, while the barker would invite you to spend a bob to come inside to see the real thing. If there was the biggest, smallest, scariest, ugliest, creepiest in the world, it was there in Sideshow Alley. My eyes must have been as wide as saucers as I tried to take it all in.

Then we heard a big drum beating, and Dad took us over to have a look. The sign on the tent said "Jimmy Sharman Boxing Troupe," and big life-size pictures of boxers in trunks and gloves hung down outside the entrance. Up on a platform a man was beating a big drum, and standing beside him were four black men in different coloured dressing gowns, with big boxing gloves on their hands, which they kept hitting against each other in time to the drum, as they danced and shuffled around on the platform. A man in a red coat, who I think was Jimmy Sharman, strutted up and down on the platform beside the boxers.

"Come on mates," he was yelling out to the crowd gathered around, "who wants to take a glove and mix it up in the ring with one of my boys here. There's good money to be made, if you can stay the distance. Mind you, they might knock your block off, but what's that to a red-blooded Aussie? Now who wants to step up and put on the gloves? Tom here" (and he raised the arm of one of his fighters) "has got a punch like a kick from a young heifer in heat, and Dick" (he raised another boxer's arm) "has got the whack of a horseshoe in his glove. But that's the thrill of it, boys. Mixing it up with the best of the best. Who knows, the next Welterweight Champion of Australia might be standing right here in front of me, and you'll never know if you don't give it a go."

I was standing there wide-eyed and open-mouthed taking it all in. Dad stood between me and Gordon with a hand on our shoulders. The man in the red coat looked at Dad. "Come on, mate. Show your boys what you're made of by going a round with one of these lads. It should be a pushover. You're twice their size."

"Yeah, but not twice as stupid," said Dad. "I need to go home in one piece to do the milking."

"I'll give it a go," another man standing near us in the crowd suddenly shouted. I think he was being egged on by some of his cobbers. The man in the red coat helped him up on to the platform.

"Righto, here we go," he said. "Anyone else? Go over there with the boys, mate, and let's take a look at you."

The man from the crowd was a lot bigger than the boxers, and they pretended to back off scared, as he gave a few mock punches.

"Look at that, ladies and gentlemen," yelled the man in the red coat, while the drum beat louder and faster. "A real scrapper. This is going to be good. Now get your tickets. The show starts inside in a few minutes."

"Can we go in, Dad?" I asked.

"No, you're too young for that kind of stuff," said Dad. "Anyway I thought you wanted to see Tex Morton."

"Yeah, that too, but I'd sure like to see if that fellow wins."

"He won't," said Dad. "Those other fellows are professionals. They'll take him apart in the ring. You won't want to see that."

I suppose Dad was right, but it was hard to walk away. But only for a minute, because almost right away we came to Tex Morton's Wild West Show. It was by far the biggest tent on the grounds, and already people were streaming inside, because the show was about to begin. Dad got us some tickets, and in we went.

I had never been inside a big tent like this before. We climbed up onto some wooden seats around a great big ring marked out with high posts and ropes all the way round.

"What's that for?" I asked Dad.

"To stop the buckjumpers from getting into the crowd," he said.

"Boy, are we going to see buckjumpers up real close?" I asked.

"Yeah, that and a lot more," Gordon put in. "See over there, on the other side, that's where they bring 'em into that chute where the riders get on."

A couple of clowns were running around in the ring doing funny things that made us all laugh. Then all of a sudden, right next to us, the side of the tent opened, and in came some men and girls dressed like cowboys and cowgirls, riding their horses at a canter around and around the ring criss-crossing without ever bumping into each other. Then they lined up in two lines, and down the middle Tex Morton rode in on a big stallion, wearing his fancy cowboy outfit with a big hat that he took off and waved to the crowd, as he rode round and round the ring, while everyone cheered and whistled and clapped.

Then he got off his horse in the middle of the ring, while the others rode out and a clown brought out a microphone and his guitar, and he talked to us for a bit and thanked us for coming to the show, then sang a few of his hillbilly songs that I used to listen to on the wireless. Then he said he better get out of the way, because the real show was going to start. He climbed up onto a platform outside the ring and said, "Bring him in boys," and a couple of men led this wild horse into what Gordon called the chute, and a rider climbed down over the rails into the saddle. Then they opened up the chute, and out came the horse as mad as a hornet, and he bucked and twisted and turned like you've never seen, The rider hung on for all he was worth, until suddenly he just flew up into the air, then crashed on the ground, while the horse just kept bucking and snorting, and two other riders rode in and collared him and led him out,, while the rider who was thrown got up and staggered around, and the crowd cheered and clapped. Then they did it all over again, and in between Tex Morton sang his song about his famous buckjumper called Mandrake:

> "Screw down the saddle, make it good and tight,
> Back from the ropes, please. Ask him if he's right.
> Pick up your mate, lads, he's had a nasty fall.
> They're all the same to Mandrake, champions and all."

The song says Mandrake got his name because he was a wizard at the way he bucked. I don't know if Mandrake was one of the horses that day, but they all seemed like wizards to me, and none of the riders could hang on for very long. After that there was trick riding, and stock whip cracking, and clowns juggling, and I don't know what else, until too soon it was all over, and we were in the crowd pushing our way out of the tent.

"That was great, Dad," I said. "Thanks for taking us."

"Yeah, it was quite a show," he said. "Now we better find the girls and be getting home."

"But what about Buddy Williams?" I asked.

"We don't have time to see another show," said Dad. "But we can walk down by his tent if you like."

When we got there, I saw a man up on a platform with a guitar. He was dressed like a cowboy, but not as flashy as Tex Morton.

"Look, I think that's Buddy Williams himself," said Dad.

We pushed over. There were a lot of people crowding around, and he was signing autographs.

"Hello, Buddy," I called out. "I listen to your songs on the wireless." But I don't think he heard me, and that was as close as I got, because then he went inside the tent, and we had to keep moving. But I didn't really mind, because I'd had a wonderful day at the Show. On the way home we couldn't stop talking about it. Everyone had found something special to keep in our memories so we could have it forever—and that's a very good thing, I think.

Dad's Farm Auction

When Dad held the sale of all his cows it was almost like we had a show on our own farm. I don't mean we had buckjumpers or sideshows or anything like that, but we had all these people pouring in from everywhere, and a whole lot of coming and going with the cattle and the trucks and everything. Dad even put up a tent where we served cups of tea and sandwiches and cordial and cupcakes. I thought we should have had hot pies and hot dogs, too, but Mum said that would be too much trouble.

Dad had been working on this for weeks. The deal was this. To get his new stud herd Dad had to sell all of his cows, and the way he was going to do it was at this big sale called an auction. Now, I didn't quite know what an auction was. Dad didn't want to talk about it too much, and Mum explained to us kids that it was a really big move for him. It was like selling all your old toys so you could get some new ones. I certainly wouldn't like to see all my toys taken away by someone else, so I knew Dad must be feeling a bit sad, even though he said he was doing it to get a better herd of cows.

Mum said that at the auction this man called an auctioneer would sell the cows by trying to get the people to bid on them. This meant yelling out how much they would pay, and the auctioneer would try to get someone else to yell out more. It sounded like a lot of fun. Of course, you had to get people to come, but that was the auctioneer's job. I think they put ads in the paper and sent notices out to people in the mail. I saw one of the notices. It said:

HIGH CLASS DAIRY HERD FOR AUCTION
On the Property, Athol, Westbrook
MONDAY, 3RD SEPTEMBER
At 11 a.m.

It said that K. Berghofer, Esq. was selling his high class dairy herd, because he had decided to establish an A.I.S. stud.

"Why do they call Dad K. Berghofer, Esq.?" I asked. "What does E-s-q spell? There's no such word."

"It's an abbreviation," said Gloria.

"A-breve-ee-what?" I asked.

"An abbreviation," she said again.

"What's an ab-breve-ee-a-shun?" I asked, trying to get my tongue around it.

"It's when you shorten a word like M-r. for Mister. E-s-q. is short for Esquire."

"Well, that's a lot of help," I said. "What does 'Esquire' mean?"

"It's a fancy way of saying Dad is an important person. It comes from the word 'squire.' In England a squire is an important man who owns property in the country."

"Oh la-te-da," I said. "K. Berghofer, Esq. on his property at Athol, Westbrook is selling his high class dairy herd."

"Sounds pretty good, doesn't it," said Gordon, who had been listening. "K. Berghofer, Esq. is going to establish an A.I.S. stud."

"What's an A.I.S. stud?" I asked.

"A.I.S. means Australian Illawarra Shorthorn. It's a special breed of dairy cattle in Australia that gives good milk production."

"Why do they call it a stud?" I asked again.

"I dunno," said Gordon. "It's another one of those fancy words that sounds important."

I was beginning to understand that the job of the auctioneer was to make Dad sound important, and it certainly worked, because on the day of the sale people came pouring in from everywhere in their utes and cars and trucks. The sale was held on the first Monday in September, when we were supposed to go back to school after the August holidays, but Dad said we would have to miss school that day because he needed all of us to help with the auction. My job at first was to show people where to park. That worked all right for the first few cars, but then they started coming in so fast that they either didn't see me waving my arms, or didn't care, and started parking all over the place.

Soon we had all these men (and a few women and young kids) walking around looking at everything. The men came in all shapes and sizes in their broad-brimmed felt hats and big boots and suntanned faces and arms, with sleeves rolled up and big hands swinging at their sides, or scratching their heads, or stroking their chins, as they called out to each other saying things like, "Ow yer goin', Shorty? Watcha doin' 'ere? Lookin' fer a steal, I'll bet;" or "G'day, Tom, 'ow's the missus and kids?" — and a lot of talk like that.

Luckily Herbie was around to help keep things sorted out. He could see I was almost ready to cry, because no one was taking any notice of me when I tried to get them to park where they were supposed to.

"Don't worry, Des," he said. "If they box themselves in, they'll have to sort it out. Most of these blokes are all right, so they won't do any damage. There's always a few who are a bit nosey, or light fingered, but I'll keep my eye on them. Why don't you go and help your Mum and Gloria with the lunch."

That sounded like a good idea to me, because the lunch tent was up at the cow bails where the auction was going to happen, and I wanted to get a good look. The auctioneers had arrived a long time ago in their truck with their names painted on the side of it, and they had gone up to the cow bails with Dad to set up. Gordon was up there, too, helping to herd the cows together. So I wanted to get in on the action as well.

I checked in with Mum, but she said things were pretty quiet in the lunch tent for the time being, so I could go and watch the auction. It was almost 11 o'clock, so things would soon be starting.

Dad and Gordon had herded all of our cows together, and that was a lot more than I had ever seen before, because they were usually separated into milking cows, dry cows, springers and heifers. There must have been about a hundred all together, and they were all crowded in, pushing and shoving and bellowing, so it was quite a how'd ya do. Added to that were all the men who were there pushing and poking around among the cows to get a look at what they might buy, or sitting on the top rail of the cow yard so they could see better. The regular cow yard wasn't big enough to hold all the cattle, so they overflowed into a holding area that Dad had set up from where they would be brought in one by one to be sold.

There were three or four men from the auction company, and they had set up in the cow yard with a box for one of them to stand on, and a table for another to write on. The others were there to bring the cows in, and show them off, and tag them when they were sold, and move them into the other yard for holding, until they were picked up.

So when the whole show got going, there was so much coming and going, and yelling and bellowing, and dust in the air, and flies up your nose that I couldn't really make much sense of it. The auctioneer on the box in his broad-brimmed hat and red striped shirt never seemed to stop shouting, and when he ran out of steam his mate took over, so that it was one never ending hullabaloo.

"Now here's a beauty boys. 'Ave ya ever seen an udder like that? Give 'er a squeeze, Tom. Wot d'ya say boys? Who'll start me off?" And then he would go into a long stream of words that I couldn't make out, all the while looking around at the crowd, pointing with a stick to different men, who I think were yelling out prices, and each time the auctioneer would give a little jump saying something like, "Hup, hup, hup," and "Do I hear" this, and "Do I hear" that, and "Yer breakin' me 'eart," and "That's more like it," and "Give me a break," and "My old woman'd cry," and "Never say die," and "Any advance on," and "Goin' once, goin' twice, sold."

I looked around for Dad, and I saw him down among the cows, keeping them sorted out, and talking to the auctioneers. Gordon was down at the gate, ready to bring in a new batch when he was told. It was all too much for me, so I decided to keep out of the way, and go back to help Mum and Gloria at the lunch tent. They were starting to get a steady stream of customers now among the men who had bought their cows, and were loading them into their trucks before taking off.

One of the men talking to Mum and eating a sandwich looked at me and said, "Who's this then, another one of the brood?"

"I'm D. Berghofer, Esq.," I said importantly, "son of K. Berghofer Esq. of Athol Westbrook."

The man looked at me with his mouth full of bread and cheese and nearly choked laughing. Then he shook my hand and said, "Pleased to meet you, sir," and went off still laughing. I knew he and everyone else thought it was a joke, but I was pleased to know that I was part of our family, and that my Dad was an important man, selling all of these cattle so he could set up a stud. I still wasn't sure exactly what a stud was, but that didn't matter, because if Dad was going to do it, it must be right.

I Get A New Friend and Learn to Ride His Bike

After all of the excitement of the auction, it felt like a bit of a break to go back to school and sit quietly in class. Of course, I had plenty of things to talk about, especially the auction, and what I had learned about how to get the best price by getting people to bid against each other. But after a few days no one wanted to hear any more about that, so it was back to regular school work, while I waited for the next exciting thing to happen.

I didn't have long to wait. We were all sitting quietly in school one morning when there was a loud knock on the back door. The door wasn't closed, and we all looked around to see a big man standing there. Mr. Fisher went over to speak to him.

"I've brought my son to start school," the man said. I looked a bit harder, and I could just make out that there was a boy about my age standing on the verandah behind the man. Mr. Fisher told them to come in, and he took out the big school register where I knew the names of all the kids who ever came to Athol School were written down. The boy stood at the front of the room looking a bit scared, while Mr. Fisher got the information he needed from the father. I caught the boy's eye, and smiled at him, and he smiled back.

Then Mr. Fisher stood up and spoke to all of us. "Children," he said, "we have a new pupil. His name is James, Jim for short, and he will be in Grade 1 with Des, Margaret and Phyllis."

"Hooray!" I said to myself. Now I was going to have a new friend, a boy my own age. I moved up on the bench to make room for Jim to sit beside me. I showed him what we were working on in school, but it wasn't until the 11 o'clock break that I had a chance to talk to him properly.

"Where do you live?" I asked.

"Two miles away," he said. "about half way from here to Umbiram. I could have gone to Umbiram School, but Dad decided to bring me here to Athol."

"Gosh, I know where you mean," I said excitedly. "That's where Alison and Graham lived. They came to school here for a few months, but they left in August. You live just across the road at the back of my Dad's farm."

"Do you live in the big house with the red tile roof and the tennis court?" he asked.

"Yes, you have to come right past it on the way to school," I said. "We can come to school together. Do you have a horse?"

"No, I ride a bike," Jim said.

"A bike!" I could hardly believe my ears. "Nobody around here rides a bike."

"Well, I do. It's a bit rough on the gravel, but you can really zip along on the black soil."

"Wow! I've never ridden a bike," I said. "I don't even know how."

"That's all right," said Jim. "I'll teach you."

"You will? Well, I'll teach you to ride Blackie. He's my horse."

"Great," said Jim. "I always wanted a horse, but a bike's a lot easier."

"We're going to be good friends," I said. "Where is your bike?"

"I didn't bring it today. Dad brought me in his ute. He's gonna pick me up after school. But I can meet you at your front gate in the morning."

Sure enough, there he was next morning waiting at our front gate as we rode out. He had this smashing red bike with a bell on the handle bars. He rode along beside Blackie, standing up on the pedals to push as we went up the hill to the corner, but zipping along flat out when we went down the hill to the gully, so that I had to put Blackie into a canter to keep up. But then the long hill on the other side of the gully was too much for him, and he had to get off and push the bike. I could see that riding a bike also had some problems, but it still looked like a lot of fun. When we got to the school yard, all the kids crowded around. Everyone wanted to try it out. Jim let them have a go, but hardly anyone could do it. Jim had to hold on to the seat while they wobbled all over the place. I decided I would wait until I went to Jim's place on Saturday before I would have my first shot at it.

The quickest way to get to Jim's place was to go up past our cow bails and across the hill paddock, which was all bush and grass. On Saturday morning I took off right after breakfast on foot, and I was there in no time at all. It was great to have a new friend living so close.

Jim's Mum and Dad were really nice people, and they said they were pleased to see me. He also had a younger sister, Margaret, who would be starting school next year. I could hardly believe that she, too, had a bike—just a small pink one for girls, and she was riding around all over the place outside the house when I arrived. I felt a bit stupid, not knowing how to ride, when this little girl could do it so easily.

Jim brought his bike out for me to have a go.

"All you have to do is get going, and keep your balance."

Sure thing, I thought, that's all you have to do!

"I think I'll start over by the fence," I said, "so that I've got something to hold on to."

I got up onto the seat, and held onto the fence post with my feet on the pedals.

"Now what do I do?" I asked.

"Just push on the pedals to make yourself go," said Jim.

"Yeah, but I'll fall over if I leave the fence," I said.

"I'll hang onto the seat," said Jim. "All you have to do is get up some speed, and get your balance."

I gave a bit of a push, but the front wheel wobbled all over the place.

"I can't steer it," I shouted and grabbed for the fence, and held on for dear life.

Luckily at that point Jim's Dad came over.

"You've got to learn to do three things at once," he said. "Push, balance, and steer. I'll help you with the balance and steering—you just concentrate on pushing. But you have to let go of the fence."

He put one big hand on the handlebars and another on the seat, and pulled me away from the fence, and got me moving. I felt the pedals start to come around under my feet, and then figured out I could push on them, too.

"Hey, I'm doing it!" I shouted.

"That's the way," said Jim's Dad, as we wobbled along, "but you have to go faster or you'll fall over."

I gave it a bit more of a push, and we started to take off. Jim's Dad was running beside me, still holding onto the seat and the handlebars. I didn't know where Jim was, but I hoped he wasn't too far away.

"One down and two to go," said Jim's Dad. "Now try steering while you keep pushing."

He took his hand off the handlebars. I held on like grim death as the wheel wobbled, but then it straightened up.

"Hey, I'm steering," I shouted.

"Two down, one to go," I heard Jim's Dad say from somewhere behind me. "But I'm bloody winded, you stay with him Jim, and don't let go."

By now I was picking up speed and feeling pretty good. The bike wasn't wobbling as much as I kept pedalling as hard as I could.

"I can't keep up. You're going too fast." It was Jim's voice, but he sounded too far back, and I suddenly realized I was all on my own, and no one had told me how to stop. I saw the front fence coming up fast, so I did the only thing I could, and turned the wheel away from the fence. The next thing I knew I was on the ground, and the bike was on top of me with the front wheel still spinning beside my ear.

Right away Jim and his Dad were there helping me up, and out of the corner of my eye I saw Jim's Mum and Margaret running from the house.

"Are you all right?" asked Jim's Dad.

"Yeah, I'm all right," I said. "The grass made a soft landing."

"That was terrific," he said. "You got it in one go. But just a bit too much speed for your own good."

"How do you stop it?" I asked, "without falling off, I mean."

"There's a brake on the handlebar," said Jim, pointing to a lever. "I didn't think you'd need to use it right away."

"Is the bike all right?" I asked. "I didn't break it, did I?"

"Not to worry," said Jim's Dad. "It's as right as rain. Ready for your next go whenever you are."

"Why don't we all have a break," said Jim's Mum, who had now arrived and was checking me over for scratches. "Come into the house for some milk and biscuits."

"Good idea," said Jim's Dad, "then we'll try again. You should be riding on your own by the end of the morning."

And you know what? He was right. I was sure lucky that Jim and his family had come into my life. It was going to be a lot of fun.

Discovery at the Rubbish Dump

Over the next few weeks Jim and I went back and forwards to each other's house as often as we could. He showed me the books and games that he had, and I showed him all my special treasures. It was like we had been friends all of our lives. When I was alone I talked to Triloaf about Jim.

"It's wonderful to have a new friend to play with," I said.

"I'm happy for you," he replied.

"Of course, you're still my friend, too," I said.

"We've had some good talks," he said, "but a real friend you can play with is better."

"We can still talk whenever we want to," I said.

"Yes, I know, but don't worry if you don't feel like it. I understand."

Triloaf seemed a little sad. I didn't quite know what to say to him. And we left it at that.

Next morning was a Saturday, and Jim came down to our place, and brought Margaret along to play with Val. We had been having a bit of rain over the past few days, but this morning the sun was out, and the day was warming up fast. Gloria came in from feeding the chooks and said she had seen some mushrooms up by the chook house. That meant there would be a lot out in the grass paddocks. We often used to go and pick them, and bring them home for Mum to cook.

"Why don't we all go mushroom picking," I said.

"Dad says you have to be careful about mushrooms," said Jim. "They can be poisonous."

"Don't worry about that," I said. "We know which ones are good. The ones with the pink underbelly are the good ones. The white toad stools and the puff balls are the poisonous ones. You don't want to touch them."

Gloria said she would come with us, so Val and Margaret came along as well, and the five of us set off carrying a couple of billies to put the mushrooms in. We went up to the chook house to get the few Gloria had seen there, then set off by the horse yard and out across the open ground, where the cows came into the cow bails. Soon we started to find plenty of mushrooms among the cow dung, just popping fresh up out of the ground, and we worked our way up along the ridge towards the hill paddock. We went through the gate at the car tracks where Dad took the milk to the factory. Now we were in amongst the trees, but we were still finding clumps of mushrooms, though not quite as many as before.

We decided to split up. Gloria took Val and Margaret along the car tracks, and Jim and I headed off into the bush. We hadn't gone far when Jim said, "What's that over there?"

He was pointing down into a bit of a hollow, where you could see some old milk cans and other kinds of rubbish.

"That's our rubbish dump," I said. "Dad brings all the old stuff that we don't use any more and dumps it here."

"Can we have a look?" Jim asked.

"If you like," I said, "but it's only rubbish. I've never bothered to look at it much."

We went down to the dump, and sure enough it was mostly a pile of old cans, corrugated iron, barbed wire, and what have you.

"Let's poke around," said Jim, "we might find something interesting."

"All right," I said, "but we better keep an eye out for snakes. That's just the place where they like to hide. And be careful you don't walk on any rusty nails, or you could get tetanus."

"What's tetanus?" asked Jim.

"It's a horrible disease," I said. "It makes you swell up, go into convulsions and die."

"That don't sound too good," said Jim. "We better be careful all right."

We grabbed a couple of long sticks lying on the ground under an old ironbark tree, and started poking around in the rubbish dump. It really wasn't very interesting, until I lifted a rusty old sheet of corrugated iron, and saw something shiny and red poking out among some tin cans and old paint tins.

"Look, Jim," I said. "What's that?"

"Dunno," he replied. "Looks like a toy truck or tractor."

We forgot all about snakes and tetanus, and went to work with sticks and hands until we uncovered a pile of old toys. Now these were toys like I had never seen before: airplanes with pilots sitting in the cockpit; cars and trucks with keys to wind them up; tin drums and bugles; cap guns and toy rifles; even a battleship with cannons on the deck. They were all broken and twisted and obviously didn't work properly, but I could only imagine what they must have been like when new.

"Wow!" said Jim. "Where did they come from?"

"I dunno," I replied. "I wonder how they got into our rubbish dump."

Just then we heard Gloria calling to us.

"Des, Jim, where are you?"

"Over here at the rubbish dump," I called back. "Come and see what we found."

"What are you two larrikins up to?" Gloria asked, as she came down to the dump followed by Val and Margaret.

"Look at what we found in the dump," I said. "All these beaut old toys. Where did they come from?"

"They were probably Gordon's," Gloria said. "I was very young, but I remember he had a lot of toys like that."

"He did? But I've never seen toys like this," I said.

"Me neither," said Jim.

"Let me see," said Gloria. She picked up the plane with the broken wing and turned it over. "I thought so. Look, it says 'Made in Japan.' When Gordon was little there were a lot of toys from Japan."

"But I thought we were fighting Japan in the war."

"That was before the war. We were friends then."

"That doesn't make sense," I said. "Why would we go and fight with Japan if they could make beaut toys like this? I'm going to take them home and ask Dad."

"Do what you like," said Gloria, "but don't forget we came here to pick mushrooms. My billy is already full, and there's a whole lot more just over there."

My billy was also nearly full, so I grabbed one of the old paint cans from the dump and we went with Gloria to pick some more mushrooms. We soon had the paint can full, and decided that was enough. Jim and I went back to the dump and picked up as many of the old toys as we could carry. When we got home, we found Dad working in the machinery shed. Gordon was helping him.

"Dad," I said excitedly, "look what we found in the rubbish dump."

"They're my old toys," said Gordon, picking them up to look at them.

"What were you kids doing rooting around in the dump?" asked Dad. "There could be snakes in there."

"We were careful," I said. "But look at these toys. I've never seen anything like them. Where did they come from?"

"I told them they came from Japan before the war," said Gloria.

"That's right," said Dad. "Before the war Australia used to bring in a lot of stuff from Japan. It was very cheap, and not well made, but you could buy it, because it didn't cost much. Gordon was lucky to get a lot of these cheap toys as presents from his grandparents and friends, as well as from me and your mother. But they soon broke, and once the war started there was no more trading with Japan, so we took the whole lot of them to the dump. The toys you younger kids had mostly came from England, but there weren't as many, because of the war, and because they were expensive, so you didn't have as many."

We all thought about this for a bit, then I said, "But why did we go to war with Japan? If they could make all these things, and we could afford to buy them, why would we want to fight them?"

"It's a long story," said Dad, "but the truth of the matter is that we didn't start the war. Japan did. They wanted to take over the world, and they came pretty close to invading Australia. Our Prime Minister was called a fool, because we sold them iron ore before the war, which they used to make guns and ships to attack us with. People called him 'Pig Iron Bob.' They also attacked the Americans, and sunk a lot of their ships without warning at Pearl Harbour."

"The Americans dropped that big bomb on them and killed all the people and children," I said sadly.

Dad sat down on his haunches, and put his hands on my shoulders, and looked right into my eyes.

"Yeah, it was a bad business all round," he said. "But it's over now, and you kids can have a good life once Australia gets back on its feet. Now, I see you've been picking mushrooms. Let me have a look at them."

"We filled the two billies, as well as this can from the dump," said Gloria.

Dad looked at the paint can full of beautiful round mushrooms. Then he looked at us.

"I'm sorry," he said, "there's a problem here. The paint that was in that can was full of lead. It's deadly poisonous. We can't take a risk. You'll have to dump all the mushrooms in that can. The ones in the billies are all right. You can take them down to your mother. I'll get rid of the others."

We picked up the billies and the toys, and walked down to the house.

We were all pretty quiet.

"You know," I said to Jim, "there's a lot of things that don't make sense to me."

"You mean like fighting in the war, and not being able to buy the toys any more?" Jim said.

"Yeah, and making paint full of lead, so kids like us can get poisoned. What if Dad wasn't there to tell us?"

"Yeah, don't make much sense," said Jim.

"You're right. We'll have to do better when we grow up."

"Too right," said Jim.

"Yeah, too right," I said.

Then we all went inside to show Mum the mushrooms and the toys we had found in the dump.

The Fancy Dress Ball

Later in the year Mum told us there was going to be a fancy dress ball at the Athol Hall.

"You mean like when people get dressed up like in the comics?" I asked.

"Yes," said Mum, "it will be a lot of fun. What would you like to go as?"

I had just been reading a comic book about cowboys and Indians, so I said, "I'd like to be an Indian with a great big headdress made of feathers and mocky skins on my feet."

"You mean moccasins," said Gloria, who was listening.

"That's what I said, 'mocky skins,'" I replied. "Could you make me a costume, Mum? I can show you a picture from the comic book."

I ran and got it. Mum looked at the picture of the great big red man on the cover who was leaping over a log waving a tomahawk in one hand, and holding a bow up above his head in the other. She thought about it for a bit.

"I don't know what Indians wear," she said. "Probably skins. We can't do that, but I think we can make the jacket and pants out of sugar bags."

Gloria burst out laughing. "You better put on a lot of itchy powder, or you'll spend the whole night scratching yourself like a monkey. That would be a better costume for you."

"Very funny," I said. "What will you go as? I know, the witch, with a long beak and a big hat like in Snow White."

"No, I'll be a princess with a beautiful dress and a tiara," she said and put her nose in the air and walked out of the room.

"Don't worry about the itch," Mum said. "I can put a lining inside the bag material." Then she had another idea. "I know what I'll do. I'll write to your Aunty Evelyn and Aunty Carrie in Brisbane, and ask them to make the costume. That's what they do for a living."

I thought about the baggy short pants they always gave me for Christmas, and wasn't too sure. "Tell them not to make the pants too baggy," I said. "You can send them the picture from the comic. Now, what will I do for the bow and arrows?"

"Herbie could make you a bow," Mum said. "He's really good at that. That can be your birthday present, because the ball comes just after your birthday."

Herbie didn't live with us on the farm anymore, because he was doing what you call his apprenticeship to be a carpenter in Toowoomba. We could ask him next week when we went to town. I already had a tomahawk in the woodheap that I used to split chips for the kitchen stove, so that was no problem. It was great how everything was decided all at once. I took off for Jim's place right away to tell him about it.

"If I go as an Indian, you could be a cowboy," I said.

"You bet," he said. "I've already got two pearl handled revolvers and a bullet belt. All I need is a fancy shirt and cowboy hat. I'm sure Mum and Dad will get them for me."

"What about those things they tie on their legs like flaps?" I said.

"Yeah, I think you call them chaps," said Jim. "Maybe Dad could cut them out of some old leather we've got in the barn."

"Boy, this is going to be terrific," I said. "I can hardly wait. Oh gosh, I almost forgot."

"What?" asked Jim.

"I need a headdress," I said, "with lots of feathers all round my head and down my back."

"That shouldn't be too hard," said Jim. "There's plenty of feathers in the chook house. Let's go and have a look."

We went out to the chook house, and sure enough found a lot of feathers. They were pretty ordinary, though, and not very big.

"We could dip them in red ink and blue from school," said Jim. "That should brighten them up."

"Good idea," I said. "But I still need a few longer ones for the front. Where can we get them?"

We looked around, and then spotted the rooster strutting around with his long tail feathers.

"What d' you think?" said Jim. "We could run him down and pull out a couple of feathers. He won't miss them, and besides they grow again, don't they?"

"I think so," I said.

The rooster was pecking around in the dirt with a few hens. Jim and I circled around, like a couple of Indians stalking their prey. It was a bit tricky, but we managed to shoo off the hens, and get the rooster on his own. I think he got wind of what we were up to, and he tried to make a dash for it, but Jim cut him off, and I chased him into the hen house. Now we had him cornered, and after a few short bursts of dodging this way and that, we grabbed him. I held his head trying to keep clear of his beak, while Jim ripped out a couple of tail feathers. They were beauties. We let the rooster go, and he took off like a rocket. He looked a bit lopsided at the back, but not too bad.

"If Mum notices, I'll tell her he probably got chased by a fox," said Jim, "and was lucky that he got away alive. Now we need to go to your place, and do the same thing with your rooster to get a couple more."

"Yeah, but not today. I've had enough excitement for now," I said.

As it turned out, we didn't need to chase our rooster, because when I told Mum what I needed, she came out with an old hat that had a couple of perfect feathers in it. I put them with the others, and she asked where I got the two long ones from.

"Oh, from Jim's place," I said. I was glad she didn't ask anything else, because I don't think I could have gotten away with telling her the story about the fox. I'm not sure if Jim's mother ever asked him.

The colouring also worked out fine. It was Barbara and Dawn's turn at school to mix the ink powder for the ink wells that the older kids used. We told them what we wanted to do, and they mixed a bit extra of the blue ink and put it in a jar. They even mixed up a bit of red ink that was mostly used by Mr. Fisher for marking. They gave us the ink and a brush, and we set to work painting the feathers under the school, when none of the other kids were around. It was a bit messy, but we cleaned everything up with water from the water tank. It didn't take long for the feathers to dry, and I wrapped them up carefully, and took them home in my school bag.

The hard part in making the headdress was to fix the feathers on to a head band. Dad helped with that with some strips of leather and glue to hold the feathers in place. By the time it was done, it looked pretty smart, and I carefully put it away until the rest of my costume arrived.

At my birthday party Jim was there as well as Margaret and Phyllis. The big moment came when Herbie arrived from Toowoomba with my present of a bow and a quiver full of arrows. He had driven out especially to give it to me. The bow was a beauty, almost as tall as me, and made in a curve of polished wood with a thicker part in the middle as a hand grip. The string was made of cat gut, like the strings in a tennis racquet, pulled really tight. The quiver was made of leather stretched on a wood frame, with a long strap to sling over your shoulder. Inside the quiver were five long arrows, each with a copper pointed tip at one end, and four feathers around the string notch at the other end to guide it. It was the most terrific present you could ever want to have.

"Oh, Herbie, thank you, thank you," I said. "It's just terrific."

"Yeah, well, you'll have to learn to shoot it," Herbie said. "I tried it out, and it seemed to work all right, but I'm no Robin Hood. You'll need to practice, and no shooting at animals or other kids. This is a real weapon. They used to kill each other with these things in the olden days."

"Let's go right now and give it a shot," said Jim. So he and I took off, followed by the girls, who were curious to see what we would do.

"You have to have a target with a bullseye," I said. We found a big sheet of cardboard and some paint, and we made a pretty good target, and propped it up against the orchard fence. I put the quiver full of arrows on my back, then whipped one out and fitted it on the bow string. But when I tried to pull it back, I could hardly do it.

"It's a bit stiff," said Herbie. "Needs to be broken in. Here, I'll give you a hand."

Herbie knelt down behind me, and helped me pull back the string. The whole thing was wobbling under the strain and I forgot to sight the arrow on the target, and when I let it go with a thwang, it just went up in the air and flopped on the ground. I heard the girls giggling behind me.

"Don't worry," said Herbie. "Let's try again. We'll go in a bit closer to the target." This time he held the bow and put his hand over mine to pull the arrow back. "Now sight it up," he said, and I squinted along the arrow at the target. "Ready?" asked Herbie. I grunted. "Let 'er go."

This time the arrow took off straight to the target. It didn't hit the bull, but went right through the cardboard and knocked it off the fence. The girls clapped, and I felt pretty good.

"Crickey!" said Jim. "Let me have a go."

Herbie repeated the trick with Jim, who also hit the target, and we all cheered. Then Herbie had a shot on his own and put the arrow right through the bullseye.

"Good on you, Herbie," we all shouted. It was such fun.

Jim and I played around with the bow on our own for a while. We didn't get much better at shooting, and the girls got bored, so we all went back to the house to cut my birthday cake. Eight years old and I had my own bow and arrows. It didn't matter about those cheap Japanese toys Gordon used to have. Nothing could be better than this.

But, I still didn't have the main part of my costume, which was being made by Aunty Evelyn and Aunty Carrie in Brisbane. It was just two weeks to the day of the fancy dress ball and I was getting worried that the costume might not come. Then one night I had a bad asthma attack, and I was too sick to go to school. I was sitting in the sun room in the front of the house, feeling pretty sorry for myself. I had the door open because it was getting hot, and I could see right down to the front gate. Suddenly I saw the mail truck from Westbrook come up to the gate, but instead of dropping the mail off at the gate as he usually did, he drove in over the cattle grid, and came up the drive and around to the back of the house.

"Hey, Mum," I called as best as I could through my wheezing and sore chest, "the mailman is coming up to the house."

I heard the back door bang as Mum went out, then after a bit she came back in, and the mailman was with her. He was a short cheerful looking man like Uncle Henry with a red face, and the bottoms of his trousers rolled up above his shoes.

"Well look at you," he said to me. "Not feelin' too good, eh, cobber?"

"No, I'm a bit sick," I said.

"Well, this will cheer you up," he said, whipping out a big parcel wrapped up in brown paper from behind his back. "It's addressed to Master Desmond Berghofer. Would that be you by any chance?"

"It must be my costume from Aunty Evelyn and Aunty Carrie," I said, jumping up out of the chair to take it.

"Look, missus," the mailman said to Mum, "he's feelin' better already."

I started struggling with the string to open the parcel, and Mum brought a knife to cut it. I unwrapped the paper, and there was my wonderful Indian costume. Just like Mum had said, the jacket and pants were made out of sugar bags, but the ends of the sleeves and around the shoulders had this bright red fringe, and the same thing ran down the pant legs.

"Oh boy," I said. "I'm gonna try it on." I tore off my clothes, and pulled the Indian pants on, and felt right away that they had some soft lining inside so they wouldn't be itchy. The same with the jacket. As groggy as I was from the asthma and the medicine I took for it, I ran down the hall to my room, and got the headdress and bow and arrows out of my wardrobe. I came whooping back down the hall to show Mum and the mailman.

"Gawd struth, missus," the mailman shouted, "it's a red Indian savage. Look out, he's gonna scalp us!"

"No I'm not," I laughed, "but I scared you didn't I?"

"Right out of me boots, boy," the mailman said. "But you look a bit pale to be a redskin. You'll have to ask your mother for some rouge."

And that was the way I did it on the night of the fancy dress ball. Mum patted her rouge all over my face and hands and used black boot polish to make lines down my face and around my eyes. When I was all dressed up and had my headdress on, I looked in the mirror and I thought I was terrific. I had the bow and quiver of arrows across my back, as well as the tomahawk and a hunting knife in a leather pouch that Dad had made for me on my belt. I wore my slippers for moccasins (I had finally learned to say it right), and I ran around the house whooping it up, while everyone else was getting ready.

When we climbed into the back of the ute to go to the ball, we must have been quite a sight. Gordon was dressed as a sheik with a great white cape (actually a bedsheet) tied around his head and flowing down his back. Gloria went as she had said she would as a princess in a sparkling blue dress, with a shiny tiara made out of cardboard and bits of shiny glass on her head. Val was a fairy with tiny wings that Mum had made for her, and a little wand.

Just as we arrived at the ball Jim and his family drove up, too. It was too dark to see his costume at first, but when we got inside I could see that he looked the part, in his white cowboy hat, red shirt, fancy leather chaps down his legs to his big cowboy boots, and around his waist a big broad bullet belt with a holster on each side, and two pearl handled cap gun revolvers sticking out.

We swaggered around the hall together with Jim saying "Howdy pardner" to everyone, and me doing my best imitation of a war whoop. All the kids from school were there, and they all had terrific costumes. When it came time for the parade we all marched around the hall with the parents clapping and Aunty Milly and Uncle Ralph playing some marching music on the piano accordion and drums. We were all given a prize ribbon for our costumes, and then the dancing began, and we all danced as best we could in our costumes in a great swirl of princesses, fairies, cowboys, Indians, sheiks, goblins, clowns, soldiers, nurses, witches, pirates, and what have you. I danced with Margaret, who looked lovely as a ballerina, and she said I had the best costume of all. It was a wonderful night, and a great end to all the hard work everyone had done in putting our costumes together. It was my first fancy dress ball, and I knew I would remember it forever.

Jim and I Go Shooting

For Christmas 1946 I got Gordon's air rifle. This was the same one I had tried out a couple of years earlier, when I was just a little kid. I had learned a lot about shooting since then, so Dad thought it was time for me to have a gun of my own. This was no ordinary air rifle. It had been made in Germany before the war, and passed on down to us from our older cousins, Herbie and Kenny. It had a break-the-barrel loading mechanism, and you put the lead slug in the chamber while the barrel was open, then closed it up, and the gun was loaded and ready to fire. There was a safety catch on the trigger, so it wouldn't go off by mistake. The stock was made of beautiful polished wood, and though the gun must have been more than ten years old, it looked like new. Gordon had kept it well oiled and cleaned, and there was no question that I would do the same.

Jim also had an air rifle, but his was a cheaper English kind that you loaded by pushing the barrel against something hard to compress the spring. Then you loaded it with a piece of round lead shot by rolling it down the barrel. It had a flimsy wood stock that looked more like a toy than the real thing. It was still a good enough gun, I suppose, but we were lucky to have my German one as a proper rifle.

They were called air rifles, because they worked by compressing a spring that had a tightly fitting leather washer on the end of it, so that when you pulled the trigger the spring let go, and the washer sent the air in the tube with a thwack against the slug, and shot it out the barrel. You might not think that would work very well, but I can tell you that slug came out really fast, and it would put a hole in a tin can at 20 yards. My rifle had good open sights and fired pretty true, so that if you were a good shot, you could hit your mark every time up to 20 or 30 yards.

On Boxing Day, the day after Christmas, Jim came down to my place and brought his air gun with him. We were going to go on our first hunting expedition together. I was dressed up in my khaki shirt and shorts and helmet, and carried my army issue water bottle in my school bag on my back. Jim wore his gun belt with the two pearl handled cap-gun revolvers to make him look the part.

"So where are you two tiger hunters off to?" asked Gordon, as we were about to set off.

"Oh, just out and about," I said.

Dad was working on the tractor as we went by the machinery shed.

"Now remember everything I've told you about shooting," he said. "You don't shoot at anything without a good reason, and you make sure you know everything that's around you, so there won't be any accidents."

"Yes, Dad, we'll be careful," I said, and we set off.

I knew exactly where I wanted to go first—to that sign on the tree in the bush up above our top paddock that said "Trespassers Will Be Prosecuted," which Gloria had thought meant "executed." I wanted to put a couple of more bullet holes in it for scaring me that day I rode to Uncle Henry's place with Gloria.

We went up our lane to the top paddock, then trudged along the headland till we came to the bush beyond it. At first the bush wasn't too thick, but as we went further in, it changed to thick scrub that you had to push aside to make your way through. The yellow dry grass was up to our knees, and what with dead logs and rocks everywhere, you had to keep a good lookout for snakes. We were working our way down a bit of a gully, when I began to wonder if I knew where we were going. Jim wondered the same thing.

"Are you sure you know where we're going?" he asked.

"Yeah, we're just taking a short cut across to the road," I said.

"Well, if this is a short cut, I'd hate to see a long one," he replied.

"Don't complain," I said, "we'll be there in a bit." I wished I was sure about that, but I wasn't going to let Jim know I was lost. I had never been this far into the bush before, and everything looked pretty much the same in all directions. However, I knew that if we kept going we'd have to hit the road or some cultivated paddock eventually. It was funny how quiet it was in there, except for an old butcher bird I could hear yodelling off in the distance.

Just then, right in front of us, there was a mighty eruption, and something went crashing off through the bush.

"Holy smoke!" Jim yelled. "What was that?"

I thought I caught a glimpse of the red rump of a cow disappearing through the trees.

"Looks like a cow," I said. "Why would she be out here on her own?"

We went a bit further and found out. She had a newborn calf hidden in the bushes. It looked pretty groggy, and it still had some of the slime from the birth sticking to it.

"Hello, little fella," I said, patting its head. "Don't worry, your Mum will come back."

"You're bloody right," Jim yelled again. "Here she comes!"

I looked up just in time to see this wild eyed big red cow with long horns coming at us. We had no time to move before she was on us, bellowing like she'd been stuck with a red hot branding iron. Luckily the calf was between her and us, and as we leapt back she stopped short, head down sniffing the calf, but still glaring at us out of red-rimmed eyes.

"It's all right old girl," I said. "We're not gonna hurt him. Back up, Jim, slowly. Let's just get out of here. She's probably not interested in us." I added the last bit hopefully, before I heard Jim cry out.

"Oh damn!" he yelled. He had tripped over a log as he backed up through the bush.

"Come on," I said. "This is no time for fooling around."

I helped him to his feet, and we took off as fast as we could away from the cow. Fortunately, she had lost interest in us, so after a bit we eased up, while I tried to figure out where we were. The trees had thinned out, so I could see the sun, which I knew should be in the west. I also knew the road was to the north of us, which meant we were going in exactly the opposite direction to what we should.

"We're going the wrong way," I said. "We have to go back."

"Not towards that mad cow," said Jim.

"We can circle around," I said, "but we have to go north to hit the road."

I must admit that after we had been crashing through the bush for what seemed like forever, I was beginning to have my doubts. Then suddenly there it was, the road—but where exactly on the road were we? There was bush on both sides, so you couldn't really tell, but I thought we had probably gone too far west, so we turned east to go back.

"We've been walking all this time and haven't seen a thing to shoot," Jim said.

Just as he said it, a couple of top notch pigeons came sweeping down across the road and landed in a tree somewhere in the bush paddock we had just come out of. The thing about top notch pigeons is that you can hear them before you see them, because of the tinkling sound their wings make when they fly. Jim was keen to chase them, so we crashed back into the bush to look for them. Of course they were nowhere to be seen, but then all of a sudden we heard them flying again, and this time saw them land in an old dead tree about 50 yards away. Keeping our eyes fixed on the birds, we crept along as quiet as we could to get close enough to have a shot.

"You've got the best gun," said Jim. "See if you can bag one."

I loaded my rifle and crept round behind a tree, so I could see the pigeons quite clearly against the blue sky. I took careful aim at one, but before I could pull the trigger, I suddenly had a queer feeling inside. It was a perfect shot, and I knew I could hit the pigeon, but I was no longer sure I wanted to. We didn't really need to kill the bird, and because they were a pair, what would the other one do if I killed its mate. These were the thoughts that flashed through my mind while I was taking aim. I must have waited too long, for Jim gave me a nudge and whispered, "What are you waiting for?"

I didn't answer, but moved the sights off to one side of the pigeon and fired. Of course, I missed, and the birds took off again.

"Aw, too bad," said Jim. "Let's keep after them."

"No, I don't think so," I said. "We should just let them be."

Jim gave me a queer look, but didn't argue, and we went back to the road. We walked along in silence for a bit, and then I saw the sign nailed to the tree.

"There it is," I said, and I suddenly wanted to blow that sign to smithereens. I dropped down on one knee, took aim and fired. Ping! The slug hit the sign and bounced off somewhere into the bush. I reloaded and fired again, and again, and again. Ping! Ping! Ping!

"Crikey, what's got into you?" asked Jim. "Here, let me have a go."

He fired his gun and missed, then took a second shot and hit it. "Here, try mine," I said. I gave him my gun and let him bang away. I suddenly had lost interest in the shooting and the sign and everything else that a while ago had seemed so important. I wasn't quite sure what it was. I knew I was a good shot, and I loved my air rifle, but seeing that pigeon in my sights and knowing I could kill him—but for what reason? Dad said you had to have a reason for shooting something. I needed more time to think about that. I waited for Jim to finish firing at the sign, and sat down, and took a long drink out of my army water bottle. Then we headed for home.

We Go to Caloundra

Ever since our holiday at Redcliffe last year we had wanted to go to the seaside again, so Dad arranged another trip in the school summer holidays. This time he said we were going to the ocean at a place called Caloundra. Redcliffe had been good, but this would be even better, because we would be staying at a real ocean beach.

There was another added surprise this time, too. Herbie had just married a really pretty lady named Dorothy. She had long dark hair and a jolly laugh. She was a school teacher, I think, from a place called Burton, where Mum used to go to school. So she was not only very pretty, but also smart, and I was pleased that Herbie had found such a lovely lady to marry. The surprise was that Herbie was going to drive our ute to Caloundra with Mum and us kids and Dorothy, while Dad stayed home to milk the cows and look after the farm. Then after a week, Herbie and Dorothy would come back to the farm, and Dad would drive to Caloundra to spend the rest of the holiday with us.

To get to Caloundra it was another long drive back to Brisbane, and then about another hour or so further north, and over to the ocean. This time we must have gone a different way through Brisbane, because we didn't get mixed up in all the traffic. Herbie was a really good driver, so we made good time, though it was still a very long way from Athol to Caloundra. The four of us kids rode in the back of the ute with Mum in the front, and Dorothy in the middle sitting next to

Herbie, like she should, because she was his beautiful bride, and they were going on their second honeymoon.

It was getting dark as we came along the last part of the road towards Caloundra. We had been driving through a lot of bush and some forest, where the trees were planted in rows by the government forestry department. They were straight tall pine trees, not like the ironbark and gum trees you find in the bush. I thought they looked like soldiers standing tall at attention.

We could see the lights of Caloundra as we came in. Herbie stopped at a petrol station to ask directions. We were staying at a place called Golden Beach, which I thought sounded pretty good.

"Are the waves really big at Golden Beach?" I asked the man who was filling our petrol tank.

He laughed and said, "They are if you're a midget."

I wondered what he meant by that, but he just kept laughing as he walked away. Herbie came back and said to Mum, "This is a bit strange. They say we have to turn off the main ocean road to get to Golden Beach."

We set off again, and soon came to what looked like the sea in the dark, but I couldn't hear any waves like I remembered at Moreton Island last year. I could see some small boats in the water, but they were just sitting there and not even bobbing up and down.

"Doesn't look much like the ocean," said Gordon.

We finally found the place where we were staying. It looked pretty old and a bit run down. There was a lady there to let us in.

"We were told that Golden Beach is on the ocean," Mum said to her.

"Yes, that's right, dear," the lady said. "You just catch a bus and in five minutes you're at the beach."

"Catch a bus?" Mum repeated. "No one told us anything about catching a bus."

"Well, you can go swimming here, too, dear. It's a lot safer anyway for these little ones. You wouldn't want them being swept out to sea in a rip tide now, would you? And there's plenty of row boats here, so you can go fishing if you want to."

"But where exactly are we?" Herbie asked. "We thought Caloundra was on the ocean."

"Well, part of it is, dear," the woman said. "But at Golden Beach you've got the best of both worlds. We're on the passage and, like I said, you can go swimming and fishing where it's safe. And you can row across to Bribie Island, which is just over there, and walk to the beach through the bush, which is really something to see, miles and miles of ocean beach and no one else around. Or, like I said, you can catch a bus right from here, and that will take you to the main surfing beaches here in town. Now, here are the keys to the house. You'll find everything's ready for you. Have a lovely holiday." And with that she walked off.

"There's something funny going on here," said Herbie. "We'll have to sort it out in the morning. For now, we'll get you settled in here, then me and Dorothy will go and find our hotel."

"Why aren't Herbie and Dorothy staying with us?" I asked Gloria.

"Because they've just got married," she said, "and they want to be alone."

I wondered about that, but I didn't ask any more questions. There were some things about growing up that I didn't understand. Herbie had always been like a big brother to us, and I hoped that wasn't going to change. Anyway, I really liked Dorothy, so that meant we now had a big sister as well, so everything should be fine.

The next morning Gordon and I were up early, and we went down to the beach. Now that we could see properly in the daylight, we could tell that we certainly weren't at an ocean beach. We were looking out over a patch of water to some more land on the other side.

"That must be what the old girl last night called Bribie Island," said Gordon.

There was a man down on the beach pulling his boat up onto the sand. He had just come in from fishing, and overheard what Gordon said.

"Yeah, that's the north end of Bribie Island," he said. "Are you boys here on holidays?"

"Yeah, we just got in last night," Gordon said.

"We're looking for the ocean," I said. "We thought Golden Beach was on the ocean."

"Yeah a lot of people make that mistake," said the man. "Bribie blocks off the ocean. This here is called Pumicestone Passage. The water here is as flat as me old woman's chest, but go on down there a bit and you'll find a current ripping out to the ocean. You don't wanta get caught in that. All the surfing beaches are down there. You boys must like fish, don't cha?"

"You bet," we said together.

"Thought as much. I just caught a heap of whiting. Here, take some home for breakfast."

He tipped a pile of small fish out of a bucket into a cardboard box and gave it us.

"Gee thanks," we said.

"No worries, boys. If your Dad wants to take you out fishing or over to Bribie, you can borrow me boat. The oars are in it. I won't need it again today."

"That was real nice of him," said Gordon, as we headed back to the house with our box full of fish. Mum cooked them up for breakfast, just as Herbie and Dorothy arrived to join us. There was plenty of food for everyone.

After breakfast we all got in the ute, and drove down to the main part of Caloundra. Herbie already knew where to go, and soon we were at the main ocean beach called King's Beach. It was a good name, because it was wide and golden, with the big waves rolling in from the ocean, as wide and blue as the sky. Just the place for a king.

We had a great time on the beach all morning. Mum kept an eye on us to make sure we didn't get sunburnt. Though we all had brown arms and legs from living on the farm, we could easily get sunburnt in our swim suits. We had fun splashing on the edge of the surf and playing with Herbie and Dorothy on the beach. They were really good sports.

We went back to the house at Golden Beach for lunch, and Mum decided she was going to look for another place to stay. We would have to stay here for a week, because we had paid a week's rent, but after that we could move. Mum also wanted to try out the bus, so she said that she and Dorothy and the girls would take the bus downtown, while Herbie, Gordon and I could try out the rowing boat that the man had told us we could borrow.

When we went down to the beach we found the boat was there, and the man who owned it was sitting in a chair by an old shack where he lived.

"The boys told me you said we could borrow the boat," said Herbie.

"Yeah, that's right mate," said the man. "But you're a bit young to be their Dad, aren't you."

"I'm their cousin," said Herbie. "Their Dad's back on the farm, but he's coming down later."

"All in the family, eh?" the man said. "That's good. Yeah, take the boat. You know how to row?"

"Good enough," said Herbie. "I thought we might row over to Bribie."

"Good idea. If you go straight across you'll find a good place to pull the boat up on the shore, then you can walk through the bush on a track over to the ocean. That's a sight to see. Miles and miles of beach all to yourself. You should take some water though. Here, take this water bag. The young one can carry it."

He handed me a canvas water bag that was wet and cold on the bottom. I knew the water inside would be nice and cool to drink. He gave us a hand to push the boat into the water. I got in the front. Herbie worked the oars in the middle, and Gordon sat in the back. Out on the water it was calm and quiet, with just a few sea birds swooping around and occasionally dive bombing into the water to catch a fish. I sat in the front with the cool breeze in my face, and listened to the creaking of the oars. Herbie was really good at rowing, and it didn't take long to get over to Bribie. Just as the man said, we found a place to pull up the boat, then walked along a track through the low bush. We could hear the pounding of the ocean long before we saw it. There were no big sand dunes here like I remembered from Moreton Island, but when we came over a bit of a hill and out of the bush it was like an amazing new world.

There in front of us for as far as you could see was the golden beach—the real golden beach—with the waves rolling in and surging up on the sand and the white foam flying in the bright sunlight. I dashed down to the water's edge, and ran along the sand where there were no other footprints, only mine behind me, and none in front, just wide open golden sand forever and forever. Finally, I stopped running, out of breath, but wanting to go on and on, until Herbie and Gordon caught up to me, and the three of us walked side by side along the wide empty beach. It was such a super sight that none of us could talk, because there just wasn't anything to say. The ocean was saying it all in its big rolling voice, as it crashed down onto the sand and swirled around our feet.

Then Gordon spotted something ahead on the edge of the beach, a kind of a building. But what could it be away out here where no one lived? As we came closer, Herbie figured it out.

"I think it's part of the Bribie Island war fortifications," he said.

"What's that mean?" I asked.

"During the war," Herbie said, "Australia was worried about attack from the sea by the Japanese, so they set up gun emplacements and other things to protect us. I don't think it would have done much good, but lucky for us the Japs never got this far."

We came up closer to the building. It was made of concrete and looked like a shoe box standing on its end, and with a big open hole on the top looking out to sea. There was no one around, so we went inside. It was just an empty room with some rubbish lying around. We climbed up some steps to the upper level, and it was like looking out on the ocean from a house with a big window.

"Did they have a gun in here?" I asked.

"No, I don't think so," said Herbie. "The gun emplacement was probably somewhere else. This looks more like a lookout for a searchlight."

Standing there looking out at the beautiful blue ocean, I thought about the big bomb that I remembered had been dropped on Japan, and about all the great toys Gordon had from Japan before the war. It seemed like things were all mixed up, and I wondered why they had to be like that.

"Why does there have to be war and fighting?" I asked Herbie. "Why can't people just get along in the world?"

"Yeah, good questions, Des," he replied. "We didn't pick the fight with Japan, but once it started we had to do the best we could to defend ourselves. Thanks to the Americans, the Japs ended up getting the worst end of the stick."

"Will there be another war?" I asked.

"Let's hope not," Herbie said. "Now, we better get going, because I'm not sure we're allowed to be here."

We walked back along the beach. It was still a beautiful day, and the sand and the ocean and the sky were as wonderful as before, but seeing that ugly old building and remembering the war and the bomb and all the children who were killed made me feel sad. I might be only a kid, but it seemed to me there should be a better way of doing things than going to war.

Adventures by the Ocean

At the end of the week Herbie and Dorothy drove back to the farm, but before they left they moved us into a new house that Mum had rented at Moffat Beach in Caloundra. This meant no more riding in the rickety old bus from Golden Beach. We were now close to our own beautiful ocean beach, and we could hardly wait to show it to Dad when he arrived. We had loved our time with Herbie and Dorothy, who were real good sports, but it would be good to have Dad join us to share the holiday.

He arrived late on the next day after Herbie and Dorothy left. He was very tired from his long drive all by himself, but we couldn't wait to tell him all about what we had been doing.

"Oh Dad, this is such a beaut place for a holiday," I told him.

"The first place we stayed at on Golden Beach was a bit crummy," said Gloria, "but this is much nicer."

"There's a terrific channel where the water rips out between the end of Bribie Island and the mainland," Gordon added. "They say it's great for fishing. We should go there tomorrow."

"Herbie took us over to Bribie in a row boat," I said. "You should see the beach over there. It goes on forever. And we saw this ugly old gun building that the soldiers built to look for the Japs in the War. I didn't like that very much."

Dad listened to us and laughed, and said he could hardly wait to see it all. So next morning we were all up early, and we went down to the beach after breakfast as a family. Moffat Beach was a nice wide beach, maybe not as grand as King's Beach, but really good for us kids, not many people around and the waves rolling in as a gentle surf. We bobbed around in the waves, and sometimes they were big enough to go right over my head, and I would splutter and gasp as the salt water got up my nose and stung my eyes.

The undertow was pretty strong too, so we had to be careful not to go in too far, or we could be swept off our feet. But Dad kept good watch over us in the water, while Mum sat on the beach under a big umbrella from the house.

After our swim we walked along the sand to the next beach, and there we saw this most amazing sight. At first it looked a bit like a great big whale washed up on the sand, with all of its bones sticking out. But as we got closer, we saw that it was the remains of a rusty old ship. There weren't any of the main parts left, just what you might call the skeleton, half buried in the sand and half sticking up. The front end was still all there, and when you stood beside it, it was sticking way up above your head. It must have been a really big ship before it got wrecked here on the beach.

"Gosh, Dad," I said. "Where did it come from and how did it get here?"

"Search me," said Dad. "But it's sure been here for a long time."

Just then a man came walking along the beach with his big Collie dog. We played with the dog, but I listened in while Dad talked to the man.

"Do you know the story about this old wreck?" Dad asked.

"Yeah, more or less," said the man. "It's called the Dickey. That was the name of the ship the 'S.S. Dickey.' Funny name for a ship, don't you think. It gives the kids something to joke about."

He looked at us, and Gordon giggled, but I didn't see the joke. I would have asked him, but the man went on talking.

"The story is she was caught in a bad storm over fifty years ago. The captain was probably trying to make a run for it to get into Moreton Bay, but he got in too close to shore. You can get really big seas here, when there's a cyclone blowing, and what with the waves and the wind, she came right up onto the beach and got stuck. I don't think there was anyone drowned. She was a cargo ship, so there was only the crew on board. After the storm they took one look at her and decided she was a goner. Her back was broken, and she'd never sail again. So they stripped everything off her, and left the shell here to rot. Later on the beach was named after her, so this is Dickey Beach."

We all listened to this story open mouthed, and I tried to imagine what it must have been like on the ocean when the ship got wrecked. It was all so calm and peaceful now that it was hard to think it could be so wild and rough. The man continued on his way, and we poked around the wreck with the water swirling around our knees. You had to be careful or you could cut yourself on the rusty old steel.

"Why did the man say that Dickey is a funny name for a ship?" I asked Gordon.

He laughed at me and said, "Your little dickie is too small, or otherwise you'd see the joke."

And then I got it, but I still didn't think it was very funny. Maybe older boys and men thought about their dickies like that, but it just seemed silly to me.

After lunch Dad asked us to show him where this fishing channel was that Gordon talked about. We still had the old fishing gear from Redcliffe last year, so we threw it in the ute and headed back towards Golden Beach. We pulled up along the shore where the tip of Brisbie Island comes in really close. It was only about 50 yards across, but like Gordon said, the current was running really fast. We walked back a bit along Pumicestone Passage where the current wasn't running quite so fast and decided to try fishing. We had a few worms in a can that we got from the garden, and Gordon threaded one onto his hook, and twirled the line around his head, and threw it out into the water as far as he could. We didn't have any rods, so the line was just wound up around a small stick. It seemed to work pretty good, so I walked a bit further along the shore towards the ocean, and decided I would give it a go. Dad came with me to help.

Just as I was threading on my worm, I heard Gordon cry out, and I looked up to see him running along the beach towards us.

"It's in the water!" he yelled. "It's getting away!"

Dad and I looked in the rushing water, and saw what Gordon was pointing at. It was his fishing line heading out to sea. He must have made another cast and let go the end of the line, and the whole thing ended up in the water.

Quick as a flash, Dad grabbed my line, and twirled it around his head, and threw it out towards Gordon's line. He was trying to hook it, and pull it back in. But he missed. He pulled my line back in to try again, but by now Gordon's line was getting away in the fast current. So the three of us set off running along the shore with Dad twirling my line over his head, and throwing it out to catch Gordon's. But he missed again, and the further Gordon's line went the faster the current was going, until we were all running flat out, while Dad kept trying to haul it in. He never did, and the last we saw of Gordon's line it was heading full steam ahead out into the Pacific Ocean.

We were all jiggered from running so hard, and while we were trying to catch our breath, we heard a great belly laugh from behind us. We looked around to see this fellow with a big stomach hanging over the belt of his shorts laughing his head off.

"Watcha tryin' to do, boys?" he laughed. "Tryin' to hook a shark? Look out! He's gonna jump out of the water and grab ya. Har! Har! Har!"

I looked around, but there was no shark there.

"Yeah, well you betta look out for that mad dog that's about to bite your bum," Dad called back.

The man didn't stop laughing, but he looked around all the same, then turned back, and we all started laughing as hard as we could.

"Come on, boys," the man said, when he could finally speak. "I'll buy you an ice-cream. The show was worth it ten times over."

That was the start of the second part of our holiday at Caloundra with Dad and Mum. It was a wonderful two weeks, most of it spent on the beach, until all of us were as brown as berries. I got a bit better at riding the waves, but because I couldn't swim I had to be careful not to go out too far. We went on some drives into the country around Caloundra, and while it was nice we never saw anything as rich as our farm up on the Darling Downs. At the end of the time we were all ready to leave and go home. For me it meant the start of a new school year in Grade 2 and the chance to do new things. I could hardly wait to get back to tell Jim about our holidays. As we rode home in the back of the ute, I kept reliving all of the things we had done, storing them away in my memory as special treasures forever.

A String of Problems

At the start of the new school year and the end of January in 1947 some new little ones arrived in school. They were all girls, and all sisters of kids already attending. My youngest cousin, Joan, sister of Johnny and Jimmy, was one of them, along with Kathleen, Margaret's sister, and Margaret, sister of my best friend, Jim. It was good to see these girls coming to school for the first time, but it was also a sad time for our family, because now we knew that my youngest sister, Val, would not be able to go to school at Athol.

We had known for a few years that Val was not the same as the rest of us. Mum and Dad had been doing the best they could to help her, but she had not learned how to speak, and though she was now five years old, just like our cousin, Joan, she was not ready to go to school. The doctors told Mum and Dad that Val was born deaf, and that it was because Mum had been sick with German measles while Val was still in her tummy. I didn't understand too much about what all that meant, but I would hear Mum and Dad talking about how there was a bad outbreak of German measles in Australia in 1941, just before Val was born, and that many of the children her age were born deaf because of it. I suppose Joan and Kathleen and Margaret were lucky that their Mums didn't get sick with the measles. But Val was the unlucky one. She wasn't completely deaf, because you could make her hear if you made a really loud noise. The doctors had told Mum and Dad about a new invention called a hearing aid that would help Val hear better, but we didn't have one yet.

We tried bringing Val to school with us for a few days, so she could be in the class with the other girls her age, but that didn't work out very well. She liked to ride behind Gloria on Patsy, but in school she didn't know what was going on, and she would make loud noises and disturb the other kids. Mr. Fisher did his best, and Mum came along a few times to help, but we all could see that it wasn't going to work, so Val had to continue to stay at home, while the rest of us went to school.

Mum and Dad had heard about a school in Brisbane for the deaf, and they were told that Val could go there as what you call a boarder, but they hadn't had a chance to check it out, and they thought that Val was just too young to be away from home like that. So she just stayed at home. We knew that Mum and Dad were very sad about that, but what else could they do? We all tried to help Val as best we could, and teach her some things, but we knew that this wasn't working out too well.

For me, school was getting to be a more exciting place every year. I especially liked getting a new Queensland School Reader at the start of the year. Each one was a different colour. Our Grade 1 Reader was red and our new Grade 2 Reader was brown. I could hardly wait to look through it, when Mr. Fisher handed it out, to see what the stories were. What a surprise when I saw that one of the stories was "The Tin Soldier." This was the very same story that Aunty Dora had told me about, when I lost my toy soldier in the sea, when it fell off the ferry at Redcliffe. Now here it was in my Grade 2 Reader, along with other stories I also knew something about, like "Little Red Riding Hood" and "Cinderella" and "Beauty and the Beast." There were also a lot of other stories and poems that I had never heard of before, so I knew it was going to be a real fun year reading them.

But I especially kept thinking about "The Tin Soldier" and out in the playground I told Jim about it, and how I had lost my own soldier in the sea, and I knew he would never come back like the one in the story.

"That's too bad," said Jim.

"Yeah, it sure is," I said, "but you know what else I think?"

"No, what?"

"Well, I think that maybe it was because I lost my soldier, who was one of my best friends, that you came to live at Athol and became my new friend."

"Gosh, do you think so?"

"Yes, I really do, because that's the way the world works."

"What d'y'mean, that's the way the world works?"

"Well," I said slowly, because I wasn't really sure of myself, "I think that when one thing happens, it kind of makes other things happen, like in the story of Cinderella. Because her step sisters treat her so bad, she gets to marry the Prince. The same with Snow White."

"But they're only stories," said Jim. "Life isn't like that."

"Maybe not exactly," I said, "but I still think that the things that happen in life, the good and the bad, sort of balance each other out."

We left it at that, but I kept this idea in the back of my mind. I had reason to think about it again not long afterward when something bad happened to me at school. We were playing rounders, which is a game you play with two teams. One team is batting and the other is fielding. One person on the fielding side pitches the ball to a batter, who tries to hit it and run around a circle marked by three cricket stumps. If you don't get all the way round the circle before the ball is thrown in, you can stand by one of the stumps. Gordon said it was like the

American game of baseball, but none of us knew much about that, so we just played it our own way.

We used a tennis ball as the ball and a cricket stump as the bat. One person on the fielding side had to stand behind the batter as the catcher. That was what I was doing. I was doing pretty good at it, and catching a lot of balls, because it was hard to hit the ball with the thin cricket stump, and a lot of balls came through to the catcher.

Anyway, I was catching, and one of the older girls in Gloria's class, Barbara, was batting. I forget who was pitching. Barbara missed a couple of balls, and I caught them and threw them back. Then on the next ball Barbara took a step back when she went to hit it, and as she brought the cricket stump back to swing, she hit me right in the mouth. Well, it was pretty bad, because the metal cap on the top of a cricket stump can do a nasty job on your lip if they connect. I hardly knew what had happened. All I can remember is that I was lying flat on my back with blood gushing everywhere.

The kids called Mr. Fisher, who patched me up as best he could with the school first aid box, but he said I had to go home right away, because the lip might need to be stitched. I didn't really know what that meant, and it didn't sound too good. Barbara was really upset that she had hurt me, but I knew it was an accident, so when I stopped crying I told her it was all right, but I'm sure she still felt pretty bad. Gloria caught Blackie and Patsy, and we rode home together with me holding a hanky to my lip, which was now really puffed up.

When we got home, Mum took one look and went running for Dad, who luckily was not too far away. He bundled me into the front of the ute and we took off right away for town to see the doctor. Mum didn't come because she had to stay and help Gordon with the milking.

When we got to the doctor's office, the nurse sent me in right away ahead of everyone else to see the doctor.

"Looks like you've been in the wars, mate," he said. "What happened to the other chap? I hope you gave as good as you got."

I didn't' know what he meant by that, so I said nothing.

"We're gonna have to put a few stitches in that," the doctor said. "Don't worry though, it's only the top lip, so I won't have to sew your mouth shut. You didn't lose any teeth, so that's the good part. We wouldn't be able to stitch them back in."

The doctor probably thought he was being funny, but I didn't laugh.

"Now, we're going to freeze your lip," he went on. "It will hurt a bit at first, then you won't feel anything, and we'll stitch it up."

He actually had a real needle and thread just like Mum uses when she darns my socks. I didn't fancy the idea of being stitched up like an old sock, but he worked away for a bit, then announced it was all done with three stitches. He put a big bit of plaster over my lip, and told Dad to bring me back in a week or so to get the stitches out.

The next day I was back at school, and I got a lot of special attention because of the plaster. Barbara was still feeling pretty bad about it all, but I told her not to worry. These things happen.

I was right about that, because not long afterwards I copped another blow to the head. This time it happened at home and Mum was the one who hit me.

I was sitting in the kitchen on a stool at the end of the dresser reading a comic book, while Mum was preparing some beans for lunch at the kitchen table. She put the cut up beans in a saucepan, and swung around to go over to the sink to put some water in the saucepan. The only problem was that my head somehow got in the way, and she cracked me a good one with the heavy saucepan, just above the left eye. I didn't fall off the stool, but I saw a few stars. Mum dropped the saucepan and grabbed my head in her hands.

"Oh, my God, Des, I'm sorry. Are you all right?"

I said I thought I was, and she took me into the bathroom to fix me up. I saw in the mirror that I had a gash above my eye, but it wasn't flopping open like my lip was when I got hit, so Mum didn't think I needed to go to the doctor to be stitched up again. Just as well, too, because he probably would have made some more jokes about always putting my head in the wrong place. After a while the gash healed up, though I had a black eye for a while. I now have a little scar on my eyebrow, and I think my left eye is a bit squinty, though I can still see perfectly well.

But that still wasn't the end of my troubles, because not long after that I got the measles, and the other kids in the family got them as well. We were just a bit sick for a few days, but we got these awful red spots all over our face and bodies, and Mum had to keep us home from school for three weeks until the spots went away.

But then something much worse happened, because Dad got sick with the measles, too. I mean he got really sick, and Mum was so worried that she got our neighbours to go into Westbrook to a telephone to call the ambulance. The long yellow ambulance with a big red cross on it arrived at the house, and they took Dad out on a stretcher and put him in the back, and took him off to hospital. All of us watched as quiet as mice, feeling really scared.

Mum was very worried, and she was crying, but she had to stay with us and help Gordon with the milking. Then next day Herbie and Dorothy arrived to stay with us kids, and Herbie took Mum into Toowoomba to stay with Granny and Grandfather so she could be close to Dad and visit him in the hospital. We couldn't understand why he was so sick because he only had the measles, but Dorothy told us that when a grown up gets the measles it's much worse than it is for kids. I found out later that Dad was so sick he could actually have died. We were so glad when he came home from the hospital and gradually got better, until he was his old self again.

Jim and I were talking about all this one day not long afterwards, and he said, "It doesn't look like your idea of the good and bad things in life balancing themselves out works very well. You've certainly had more bad things than good in the last while."

I thought about that carefully before I answered, and then I said, "You know, you're partly right, but the really good thing that happened was that Dad got better. He could have died, you know, and just think how terrible that would have been. And I'm no worse the wear for my thick lip and black eye and spotty face. So all in all I think my idea is still all right."

And I really meant that, because I think that's the best way to go through life, because it means that everything is going to be an adventure. The good will come with the bad, but it will all work out, as long as you're brave and do your best. That's the story of "The Tin Soldier," you know. He had some terribly scary adventures going through the sewer and being chased by a rat and eventually swallowed by a fish. But finally he came back to the boy who loved him. So that's the way I expect life will work for me.

The Story of the Bees

The next weird thing that happened on the farm was what I call "The Story of the Bees." One day Dad came in and said he had discovered a hive of bees in the hollow of a tree up in the hill paddock. We all went to take a look, and sure enough you could see the bees buzzing around and coming and going about their work. I knew a bit about bees and that there must be a queen inside, and that the worker bees were building honeycomb to feed all the bees in the hive. But, of course, you couldn't see any of that, because it was down inside the tree.

When Dad came back from the cheese factory the next morning, he said he had been talking to Mr. Rosenberger, the manager, about the bees. Mr. Rosenberger was very interested, because he kept bees as a hobby in some hives near his house, across the road from the cheese factory. He said he would like to come and see the hive that Dad had found, and maybe catch the queen and the other bees, and put them in one of his hives. That meant he would also rob the hive of its honey, and we would have plenty for ourselves.

The best time to rob the hive is late in the day, when the bees are not very active. So after milking Mr. Rosenberger arrived along with his son, Neville, who was younger than me, but a bit of a wild boy. Mr. R brought along some special stuff that you need when you're dealing with bees, like a big hat with gauze to cover your face, and especially a thing you call a bee smoker. Mr. R told us that if you blow smoke into the bee hive a lot of the bees will fly away, and the ones left inside will be too groggy to sting you. The smoker was a tin can with a kind of funnel on the top, and another part called a bellows attached to it. The way it worked was to light a smoky fire inside the tin can, then pump the bellows, like the way a frill lizard puffs up its cheeks, and that blows the smoke out of the funnel.

Because the hive was up in an old dead tree about ten feet off the ground, we needed a ladder so Mr. R could get up there to blow in the smoke. Dad brought a ladder in the ute, along with a couple of axes for cutting down the tree, and a tin tub to put the honeycomb in, when we got it out of the hive.

Mr. R leaned the ladder against the tree, and up he went, with his beekeeper's hat on his head and the smoker in his hand. He had an extra hat that he gave to Dad, who stood at the bottom holding the ladder. All of us kids stayed well out of the way, so we wouldn't get stung by the bees.

"Hey, Dad," young Neville called out to his father, "be careful you don't fall off the ladder." Then he started to run around like a wild thing, yelling, "Bzz, bzz, bzz, I'm an angry buzzing bee, and I'll sting you, but you can't sting me."

"Neville, be quiet, please," his father called down from the ladder. Mr. R always spoke softly to his children and never raised his voice, which meant that Neville just went crazier, running around like a chook with its head chopped off, until Gordon collared him, and we sat on him, so his Dad could get on with the job. I know if my Dad had been a bit closer, Neville would have got a backhand that would have sat him down in a hurry.

By now Mr. R was up the ladder and puffing smoke down into the hollow of the tree. Sure enough, after a bit the bees came buzzing out of the top, and from a lot of other holes and cracks as well. They took off in all directions, zinging over our heads like tiny rockets on Guy Fawkes night.

Mr. R came back down the ladder. "All right, Ken," he said to Dad, "the rest of them should be quiet for a while. Let's chop her down."

The two men got to work with the axes, and in no time the tree was down. They split it open, and all of us kids crept forward (with Gordon still hanging on to young Neville) to take a look. I had never seen such a thing. The inside of the tree was like a house full of chunks of golden brown stuff peppered with tiny holes. There were still a lot of bees, but they all seemed rather groggy, and were just crawling around.

"The ones left inside gorge themselves with honey," explained Mr. R, "as a kind of protection in case their food is stolen, which, of course, is exactly what we are going to do. But first, I want to find the queen. She should be deep inside here where all these bees are bunched up protecting her."

I couldn't believe that even with gloves on he just reached down inside and picked up this lump of bees and honeycomb.

"Ah, yes, here she is," he said, and he popped the whole bunch of crawling bees into a cardboard box.

"What are you going to do with it?" I asked, still hanging back, because I wasn't too sure about all the bees crawling around.

"I'll take them home and put them in one of my hives," Mr. R said.

"Yes everyone knows that," piped up young Neville. "Don't you know anything?"

"Neville, please don't talk like that," said his father.

"Yes, Neville, please don't talk like that," said Gordon, as he gave him a good solid tweak on the ear. "Or maybe you'd like a handful of bees down your pants."

That seemed to settle the matter. Dad and Mr. R packed all the honeycomb into the tin tub, and brushed off any remaining bees. I thought it was then safe enough to creep over and have a taste. It was just the most beautiful sweet honey in the world. We all rushed in to have a feed, and we soon had honey smeared all over our faces. Then I had another thought.

"What happens to all the bees that flew away?" I asked.

"I'm afraid they're going to die," said Mr. R. "It's too bad, but their queen and all their mates will have a nice new home."

I thought about that, and decided it was just another case of the good and the bad going along together.

Mr. R. and Neville took off to go home with the bees in the box, and the rest of us brought the tub of honeycomb down to the house in the ute. When Mum saw it, she nearly fell over backwards.

"What on earth are you going to do with that?" she asked.

"I'm not too sure," Dad said, "but we have to get the honey out. Why don't we put it in the bags you use to make the Christmas puddings, and hang them up outside overnight to let the honey drip out into the tub?"

No one had a better idea, so that's what we did. We scraped off a lot of honey first, and put it into jars, but we figured there was still a lot left in the honeycomb, so we strung the bags up by the tennis court overnight.

Next morning I got up early with Dad and went out first to have a look. When I opened the door, I could hardly believe my eyes. The hair stood up on the back of my neck as I slammed the door and ran back inside.

"Well, I sure know now where all the bees are that flew away from the hive," I said.

"What do you mean?" asked Dad.

"They're all out there," I said, "millions of them, hanging on the bags of honeycomb."

Dad went to have a look.

"Oh, my God," he said, "we've gotta get rid of that lot before your mother sees them."

"What are we gonna do?" I asked.

"Time for another smoke session," Dad said. By now Gordon had got up, and came outside rubbing the sleep out of his eyes. He sure woke up in a hurry when he saw the bees—and not just the sight of them, but all the buzzing like a motor car stuck in a bog with its engine revving—and right outside our back door.

Dad got an old kerosene bucket, and lit a fire in the bottom of it, then threw in some wet hessian to make it smoke, and he marched out to the bees. I thought for sure they would be wise to him this time, and get into formation and zoom in for the attack—just like I had seen in one of my comics. And he didn't even have the beekeeper's hat any more. I backed up behind cover.

But, you know what? He got away with it. Once those bees got a dose of the smoke, they just took off again. Dad took down the sticky bags, and Gordon and I dragged the tub, which was now half full of honey, and we put everything in the laundry, and closed the door and windows.

We were all sitting down in the kitchen having a cup of tea with thick slices of toast and honey when Mum came in.

"What are you three smiling at?" she asked.

"It's all right, Mum," said Dad. "Des can tell you. Gordon and me are off to milk the cows –it's a lot easier than robbing bee hives."

We Go Crayfishing and Mum Gets a Refrigerator

The good thing about living on the farm was that there was always something new happening. After the experience with the bees the next adventure was going crayfishing in the creek down at Rose and Harold's place. One thing we didn't have on our farm was a creek. It was nice to have the dam up in the top paddock, but I didn't go up there very often, and there weren't any fish in it—a few frogs, sure enough, and it was interesting to see them grow up from being tadpoles—but that wasn't the same thing as having fish to catch.

After our holidays at Redcliffe and Caloundra, where we had got a taste of fishing, we were interested in doing it again. That was when Harold said one day in school that they had fish in the creek on his place.

"No kidding?" I said. "Like real fish that swim?"

"Well, not exactly swimming fish," said Harold. "They're crayfish or yabbies that crawl along the creek bottom. They have claws like a crab and can nip you if you're not careful. But they're good to eat."

Gloria was in on this conversation, and she said she'd like to see them. "Sure thing," said Harold. "Come on down on Saturday."

We told Gordon about it, and he said he already knew about crayfish, but that he would like to come, too. We worked it out with Mum and Dad that we could get a few hours off from our jobs on the farm, and the four of us set off on our horses with Val riding behind Gloria on Patsy. This was the first time I had been to that part of Athol, though it wasn't far away—maybe as far as the school, but in the opposite direction—down past the Catholic Church into the hollow where the creek ran through. It wasn't much of a creek—more like a string of waterholes—but at Harold's place there was a good sized waterhole, and that's where the crayfish were.

When we got there, Harold's older sister, Rose, and his younger sister, Dawn, were there, too. Rose was kind of in charge. She showed us how you tie a lump of meat on a line and drop it in the water. Pretty soon you feel a tug on the line, and you pull it in slowly, and as it comes to the top you see this ugly looking creature with a long body inside a shell and two big claws hanging onto the meat, and you pull it right onto the bank.

"What d'ya do now?" I asked, looking at the wriggling scaly thing about twice the size of my hand.

"If he's a good one, pick him up and put him in the bucket of water," said Rose. "If he's too small, toss him back in."

"You've got to be kidding," I said. "Pick that thing up! He'll bite your fingers off."

"Not if you're careful," said Rose. "Just pick him up back of his claws where he can't get at you, like this." She picked the crayfish off my line and dropped him in the bucket of water.

Gloria was watching, and Harold showed her again how to do it, and after a few tries, she got one off the line. The first time I tried I got such a fright when I felt him wriggling, that I dropped him on the grass. Everyone laughed, and Rose picked him up and put him in the bucket. Gordon was pretty good at it right off the bat, and soon we had quite a few in the bucket. Val and Dawn didn't try, but just sat on the bank watching the rest of us.

"All right, now it's time to cook them," said Rose. She grabbed the bucket and took it up to the house. She emptied the water out, and the crayfish were all tumbled up on top of each other in the bottom. There was a pot of water on the stove and Rose just picked up the first crayfish and dropped him in.

"He's still alive!" Gloria cried out. "You're cooking him alive!"

"Of course," said Rose, dropping in another and another. "You start with cold water, and gradually heat it up. The crayfish don't know the difference. That way you cook them when they're fresh and nice and tender."

"Oh, yuck!" said Gloria, and I felt much the same way.

After a while all the crayfish were cooked, and Rose took them out of the pot, and piled them up on a big plate. I was half expecting to see them wiggle on the plate, but they didn't.

"All right, everyone tuck in," said Rose. "There's plenty of salt and butter and slices of bread and some sauce if you like."

We sat around the table staring at this pile of scraggy looking things, which certainly didn't look like anything you'd want to eat. Rose showed the way, by tearing off a leg and cracking open the shell with a knife and pulling out the thin white flesh inside. She gave a piece to me, and when I tasted it with a bit of salt and butter, I found it was absolutely delicious. Needless to say we all tucked in. I wouldn't say we got all that much crayfish to eat, because it was mostly shells, but what with the fresh bread and butter, it was one of the most fun meals I have ever had.

When I told Jim about it next day, he was really impressed. "You mean there are live things like that in the creek," he said. "You wouldn't want to go swimming in there, or they might bite you on the bum."

"Yeah, that's what I told Harold," I said, "but I'm sure glad we had the chance to see them."

"Too bad there's nothing interesting like that around here," said Jim. He had come down to my place, and we were mooching around trying to think of something different to do. We had a few shots at tin cans with our air rifles up behind the machinery shed, but we were getting bored with that. Suddenly I had an idea. Dad had a couple of old sawn off steel vats behind the shed filled with all kinds of spare parts and bolts and things off different kinds of machinery.

"Let's build something out of all this junk," I said.

Jim took a look and his face lit up. "That's a great idea," he said. "I bet there's enough pieces in there to build a motor car."

We started pulling pieces out of the vats, spreading them all over the ground. The problem was that try as we might, we couldn't get anything to fit together, at least, nothing that might make a motor car.

"What about an airplane?" said Jim.

"That's even harder," I complained.

"But there's still a lot of pieces left," said Jim.

So we dug further into the vats and spread more stuff all over the ground. We managed to put a few pieces together that looked a bit like the tail of an airplane, but it still wasn't going too good. However, there were still plenty of pieces left in the vats. Jim found a long pipe that looked like the barrel of a gun.

"Let's make a cannon," Jim said.

"That's the best idea, yet," I said.

"Look, we can mount it on these wheels and move it around."

"And this big spring will fire the cannon ball."

We were so busy diving into the vats and pulling pieces out, that we didn't hear Dad come around the back of the machinery shed.

"What the bloody hell are you two up to?" he roared.

"We're building stuff," I said lamely. I didn't like the look in his eye. Jim kept very quiet.

"Yeah, well all I can see is a big mess," Dad said. "Those are all spare parts. I might need them one day."

"But you'd never find anything in here." I knew I was taking a risk, but I thought I would try to talk myself out of it. "We've been looking for ages and we can hardly find anything that fits."

Dad stood back with his hands on his hips, looking from the mess on the ground, to us, to the vats and back again. Jim had crawled down a bit further into one of the vats, and his head was just poking over the top. I stood my ground, holding on to the barrel of our cannon. Then Dad actually smiled and laughed a little.

"Well, you know, you've got a point," he said. "And that gives me an idea. Now you've got all this stuff out on the ground, you can put it back in better order. I'll show you how to do it."

Jim crawled out of the vat, and we set to work with Dad directing. There seemed to be a lot more pieces to put back than we took out.

"What were you trying to make?" Dad asked after we had worked for a while.

"Well, we started on a motor car," I said.

"Then switched to an airplane," Jim added.

"And we were working on a cannon," I concluded.

"Hmmmm, well I can't fault you for trying," Dad said. "But it's too bad you were working so hard up here that you're missing out on the action down at the house. That's why I came to get you."

"Missing out on what?" I asked.

"I bought a refrigerator," Dad said. "The fellas brought it out on a truck from town. They're setting it up right now. I came to tell you."

"A refrigerator?" Jim was amazed. "You mean like they have in the shops to keep things cold?"

"That's right," said Dad. "It runs off a kerosene burner. It's the latest thing."

"Will it make ice-cream?" I asked.

"I suppose so," said Dad. "But that's your mother's job. She'll have to find a recipe."

Needless to say, we didn't need any more encouragement to fire Dad's junk back into the vats as fast as we could. He seemed satisfied enough, and let us take off flat out for the house. There was a big truck parked outside that said "Fair

Dinkum Deliveries" on the side of it. We rushed inside and saw these two big fellas just putting the finishing touches to setting up the refrigerator in the end of the breakfast room near the kitchen, where the meat safe used to hang. Gordon, Gloria, Val and Mum were all standing around watching. The refrigerator was kind of like a big white tin cupboard standing on four steel legs, with a long kind of tank underneath with a wick at one end with a flame burning on it, and a long rod with a knob on the end, so you could make the flame burn higher or lower.

"You'll have to play around with it a bit, missus," one of the men said. "The height of the flame adjusts the temperature inside. If you turn it up too high it's likely to smoke."

I couldn't see how a flame burning on the outside could make it cold on the inside, but that was the magic of it. After the men left, we all sat around the breakfast room table staring at our new refrigerator. Mum had a book of instructions she was looking at.

"Does it tell you how to make ice-cream?" I asked.

"Yes, there is one recipe here," said Mum. "It's made out of condensed milk. You have to beat the mixture up with the egg-beater to get it as fluffy as you can, and pour it into these ice-cream trays that go in the freezer part at the top of the refrigerator."

She had no shortage of offers to beat up the mixture in one of the bowls she used for making cakes. We all took turns with the hand beater, mixing it up until it was as frothy as we could get it. Then Mum poured it into the tray and put it in the freezer. There was another tray that had a piece you could put inside it to cut it up into squares. We mixed up some lime cordial and poured it in to make ice blocks.

"How long does it take to freeze?" Gloria asked.

"I don't know. I've never done this before," said Mum. "Probably a few hours."

Jim had to go home, but I promised him he could have some ice-cream on his way home from school tomorrow. That night after tea we were ready to have ice-cream for dessert. Mum pulled out the tray.

"I don't know," she said. "It doesn't look too good."

She served some up. It didn't look like any ice-cream I had ever seen. It was kind of lumpy and runny at the same time. It tasted all right, but you wouldn't call it ice-cream. More like cold lumpy milk pudding.

Mum kept experimenting with different recipes, and after a few tries she got one that was pretty close to the real thing. She bought some ice-cream cones in town, so when we came home from school on a hot day we could sit outside under the peperina tree eating ice-cream. Life had suddenly become a whole lot more enjoyable on the farm. Now we could have ice-cream and ice blocks whenever we wanted them. We could keep our meat in the refrigerator, so it didn't go rotten with maggots from the heat. And the milk and cream could be kept longer without going sour. The refrigerator was a wonderful invention. The thought did cross my mind that maybe Jim and I could build our own out of Dad's spare parts in the vats up behind the machinery shed, but we never did try to do that.

Things Begin to Change

The next year at school, beginning in January 1948, brought some very big changes for me. I lost all of my class mates. Phyllis's family moved away, Margaret left to go to a convent, I think, and Jim transferred to another school, though he was still living with his parents at the same place. So now I was all alone in starting Grade 3.

"Well, it looks like you're going to be top of your class this year, Des," Mr. Fisher said to me on the first day of school. I knew he meant it as a joke, but I was feeling too lonely to smile.

"You know what," Mr. Fisher continued. "I think you're smart enough to do two grades in one year. We'll start you off in Grade 3 today, and work through everything quickly, so that before the August holidays you can start Grade 4. By the end of the year you will finish Grade 4, so you can start Grade 5 this time next year. Then if you're still on your own, we can move you through Grade 5 and 6 next year so you will be caught up to the other Grade Sixes by the end of next year. That way you can all do Grade 7 together, and you will finish school two years earlier. Would you like that?"

"I think so, sir," I said. "I wouldn't like to be on my own in school forever."

"That's the spirit. I'll talk to your Mum and Dad about it, but I'm sure it would be best for you. So let's get started. Here's your Grade 3 Reader."

Mr. Fisher handed me my green Grade 3 Reader. It was a little thicker and heavier than the Grade 2 one. I started to look through it, and saw that there were some longer stories like "Jack and the Beanstalk" and "The Adventure with Wolves" and a lot of poems as well. Because I was on my own, Mr. Fisher let me pick and choose which stories I would like to read, so that over the next few weeks I started to build up what he said was a good vocabulary. At the back of the Reader there were notes to explain the meaning of difficult words like "astonishment" and "contrivance" and "cock of the whole walk." The last two came from the story of "The Tar Baby," which was written with this man Uncle Remus speaking in a kind of voice I had never heard before that Mr. Fisher said was the way American slaves used to speak. It was all about how Brer Fox tricked Brer Rabbit into getting stuck on "a contrivance" that looked like a baby made of sticky tar. Then Brer Rabbit tricked Brer Fox into slinging him and the tar baby into the briar patch, and because that was where Brer Rabbit was born, he knew how to use the thorny bushes to get free from the sticky baby. I had never heard a story like that before, and it made me want to know more about America and other parts of the world.

There were so many good stories in that Grade 3 Reader, and I loved exploring them on my own, then getting Mr. Fisher to explain the parts I didn't quite understand. I read about King Midas, who wanted the gift to turn everything he touched into gold, then found out that he couldn't eat or drink, because as soon as his lips touched the food or water they turned to gold. This taught you not to be greedy and to be satisfied with what you have. And there was also the story about the slave who pulled a thorn out of a lion's paw, then later when the slave was put into this big place called a circus with people looking on to see slaves torn to pieces by wild lions, the same lion was there, and recognized the slave who had been kind to him, and just lay down at his feet, and the slave took him by the mane, and led him back to his den. There were just so many stories that taught good lessons about being kind, telling the truth, being brave, and so on.

I also liked to read aloud, especially the poems like "My Shadow" by a famous writer called Robert Louis Stevenson.

> "I have a little shadow that goes in and out with me,
> And what can be the use of him is more than I can see.
> He is very, very like me from the heels up to the head;
> And I see him jump before me when I jump into my bed."

I liked this poem because it reminded me of my own shadow that I saw all the time when I was out in the sun, and like in the poem would grow shorter and taller "like an India-rubber-ball." My shadow usually had a very big head, because I would be wearing my helmet to protect me from the hot sun.

The most interesting story in the book was called "Uncle Jim's Story" about how the strange Australian animal called the platypus came to be a mixture of other kinds of animals. It went around looking at all the other creatures, and asked the fairy who was putting things together to give him a bit of this and a bit of that: webbed feet like a duck and also a duck's bill, but no feathers, rather a seal's skin instead. In the end the platypus thought he was very smart, because he could swim and lay eggs like a duck, and he could walk on land and live in the water like a frog. Then the fairy gave him a long strange name, and the trick at the end of the story was to be able to spell his name: o-r-n-i-t-h-o-r-n-y-n-c-h-u-s. After I learned this I went around all day spelling it out loud, and I found that all of the older kids could spell it too, because once you learn how to do it, you never forget it.

All the time I was reading these stories and poems, I was also beginning to learn my multiplication tables and getting good at doing sums in arithmetic and learning about Australian history and geography. I was also starting to get pretty good at playing tennis for my age. I played against Gordon and the older boys, and though they could always beat me, that was the way I learned to get better and better. At home on our own tennis court, Dad would teach me how to improve my shots, and he told me I was going to be a good player.

The other big thing that was going on in our family at this time was that Mum and Dad had decided to put Val in the School for the Deaf in Brisbane. They had been down with her to look at the school and talk to the teachers, and they decided they would put her in as a boarder. This was very hard for everyone, to send her away from home, when she was so young, but there didn't seem to be any other way for her to go to a school where she would be able to learn how to talk better, and how to read and write.

So Mum got all of her clothes together and sewed her name onto them, so they wouldn't get lost in the laundry. Then they put everything into a port, and one day Mum and Dad left with Val to drive to Brisbane. We were all crying as we said good-bye to Val. I don't think she really understood what was going on, and she was half laughing and half crying as she said good-bye. This was the first time the family had ever been split up, and we all felt very sad about it.

Aunty Holly came out to stay with us while Mum was gone and Uncle Ralph helped Gordon and me with the milking. Everyone was pitching in to help with our family problem. After a couple of days Mum and Dad came back without Val. They didn't want to talk about it very much, but they said Val had cried a lot when they left. However, they said there was a nice matron at the school who said she would look after Val.

We all then went on with our ordinary lives, but we continued to feel something was missing, and we wondered how Val was doing so far away in Brisbane. This went on for about a week, then we got a terrible telephone message from the lady in the Post Office at Westbrook that Val was in hospital. Apparently she had terrible pains in the tummy, and the nurse called the ambulance to take her to the hospital, where the doctors found that her appendix had burst, and they had to operate immediately. Of course, Mum and Dad rushed off to Brisbane again right away. After a couple of days Dad came back and said that Val was recovering in hospital, but that Mum was staying in Brisbane with Aunty Evelyn and Aunty Carrie so she could visit Val every day. A week later Dad went back to Brisbane, and after a couple of days he and Mum came home again and brought Val with them. She looked so thin and sad. We all cried and cried, and Val wouldn't let Mum out of her sight. Finally, Dad said that he would never again send her away to go to that school, and we had to find another solution.

Dad Cuts Down the Peperina Tree

I didn't know what the other solution for Val was going to be, but I had a feeling it was going to change our lives some more. In the meantime, however, Dad made another big change. He said he was going to cut down our great big peperina tree, which had been our friend for all these years, where we had all grown up climbing in its branches, and swinging in the swing hanging from its biggest branch.

"You can't cut down the peperina tree," I said. "It's our oldest friend."

"It's full of our memories," said Gloria.

Even Gordon agreed with us that the peperina tree was a special part of our lives.

"I know all that," said Dad, "and I'm sorry to have to do it, but I need to build a garage for the truck near the house, because I need the space in the machinery shed."

"There's plenty of places you can build a garage without cutting down the peperina tree," I said.

"That's the best place," Dad said, "but there's another reason why the peperina tree has to go. Its roots are everywhere in the garden and under the lawn, and nothing will ever grow properly while it soaks up all the moisture from the rain, and takes the goodness out of the soil."

"We don't care about the lawn and the garden, do we, Gloria?" I said. "We want to keep our tree."

"Please, Dad," said Gloria, "don't cut it down."

"I'm sorry," said Dad, "I've thought a lot about this. It's got to go, and that's the end of it."

"It's the end of the tree, you mean," I said angrily, as I felt the tears coming to my eyes. I stormed out of the house, and went straight to the tree and climbed up as high as I could into the top branches. I stayed there for hours. Nobody bothered me for a long time, but when it started to get dark Mum came out of the house and called up to me.

"Des, it's getting dark, you'll have to come down."

"I'm not coming down," I called out. "I'm going to stay here all night."

"Don't be silly, you can't do that. Dad is already upset. If he has to come up and get you, he'll give you a hiding."

"I don't care. I'm not coming down, ever."

Mum went away, and after a while Gloria came out and climbed part way up the tree.

"I know how you feel, Eddo," she said. "But Dad has made up his mind, and nothing you can do will change it."

"But why does he have to cut down the tree? He could build his old garage over by the wood heap or beside the clothes line."

"You're right. But I think there's another reason." Then Gloria said something very wise that I would not have thought of. "I think he's angry about Val, and he's going to take it out on something else that's bothering him. If we complain too much, it will only make matters worse. We'll just have to say good-bye to our tree."

I suddenly knew she was right, and I felt a great rush of sadness come over me, and I burst into tears. I came down from the tree and put my arms around it and said good-bye, then rushed into the house without talking to anyone and went straight to bed.

A few days later, Dad started cutting down the tree. We never talked any more about it. He used a ladder to cut down the high branches first. Then he and Gordon sawed through the trunk with a cross-cut saw. Dad never asked me to help, and I kept right out of the way. Finally, he hooked the tractor up to the stump with a big chain and pulled it out. There was a great big gaping hole in the ground, and an empty space in the sky where the tree used to be. And suddenly I knew that our lives were changing, and things would never quite be the same again.

My World Begins to Fall Apart

A few weeks later I found out that the change in our lives would be bigger than anything I could have imagined. I was getting on well at school, just sailing through Grade 3 very fast, and Mr. Fisher said I was on track to start Grade 4 in July.

We had just finished reading one of the most beautiful though sad stories I had ever read. It was called "The Little Match Girl" by a famous writer named Hans Christian Anderson. The little girl in the story was very poor, and had been trying to sell bundles of matches to get some money. But no one bought any from her, and she was afraid to go home, because her cruel father would beat her. It was winter time in this far away country, where the winters are very cold. She crawled into a corner between two houses on the street to find some shelter. Desperately cold, she took one of her precious matches, and drew it along the wall of the house to light it. In the tiny flame she imagined she saw a warm wood stove. The match went out, so she lit another one, and this time she saw a big goose cooking on the stove. Again the match went out, so she struck one more, and now she was in a warm room with a Christmas tree, just like in the houses of the wealthy people where she was curled up outside. She struck match after match, and in the wonderful light her Grandmother came and took the little girl in her arms up to Heaven to be with God. In the morning the people of the town found the little girl frozen to death, with a bundle of burnt out matches in her lap. They thought she had been trying to warm herself, and felt sorry that she had died like that, but they didn't know about the beautiful visions she had seen, and how she had been carried away by her Grandmother to a place of peace and joy, where she would never be cold again.

I was very touched by this story, and went home and told Mum about it. I thought I saw a tear in her eye. Val was there, and Mum put her arms around her, and I suddenly understood that Mum was thinking about how Val had been left without her family, and had got very sick, and might have died. It was not really anything like the little match girl's situation, but I could see how because Val was just a little girl, Mum would think like that. Then she told me what she and Dad had been talking about.

"Val has to go back to the Deaf School," she said. "There's no other place for her to go. But we can't send her back as a boarder. That means we are going to have to buy a house in Brisbane, and some of us will have to go there to live."

This news hit me like a rock.

"What do you mean some of us will have to go there?" I asked. "Who will look after the farm?"

"Nothing is decided yet," Mum said, "but I will have to go with Val, and you will have to come, too, because you're too young to stay here without me."

In a flash I saw my world was coming to an end.

"But I don't want to go to live in Brisbane," I cried. "I hate it there. It's noisy, and full of cars, and there's that awful gas smell like at Aunty Carrie and Aunty Evelyn's. I don't want to go there."

"I know, I know, dear," Mum said, as she put her arms around me. "But we will have to do it for Val."

It seemed like everything was being done for Val. But what about me? I didn't want to leave the farm. I had no friends in Brisbane. Where would I go to school? I was sure they had big schools there. I didn't want to go to a big school. I just wanted to ride Blackie to Athol School every day. This was a disaster. It was the worst possible thing that could happen to me.

On Saturday I went up to Jim's place to tell him about it. Though he was going to another school, we still got together most weekends.

"That doesn't sound too good," Jim said, when I told him I would be going to live in dirty, smelly Brisbane.

"No, it's bloody crook," I said.

"Where will you live?" he asked.

"I dunno, somewhere near Val's school, Mum said."

"Where will you go to school?"

"I dunno that either. Probably in some horrible place where the city kids will pick on me and the teachers have big canes and beat you."

"Struth, that sounds real bad. Why can't you just stay here on the farm?"

"Mum says I'm too young."

"You could come and live with us."

"Now, that's an idea. I'll ask Mum."

Suddenly, I had some new hope. But I wasn't sure if it would work. On the way home from Jim's place, I walked by the rubbish dump where we had found Gordon's old toys made in Japan before the war. Now I could see for the first time that I was a real misfit in the family. As the oldest boy, Gordon was special, and had got everything he wanted. Dad taught him to do things and be useful on the farm, but I was always second best. Gloria was the oldest girl, so she was special, too. And Val was the youngest, and because she couldn't hear properly and couldn't talk, she was getting all Mum's attention. So that left me, just stuck in the middle, no one special, and sick half the time with asthma, so I was more trouble than I was worth, and now I would be just dragged along with Val to Brisbane, without any thought about what I wanted to do.

I was pretty quiet and sulky all through tea time, and Dad told me I should smarten up, and not be such a dope. After tea I told Mum about Jim's idea that I could stay with them. She said that was nice of Jim to offer, but she didn't think it would work out. Besides, she said, she would need me to help her in Brisbane, because I would be the only man around the house. That made me think that maybe I could be useful after all. But I really wanted to stay on the farm, and learn to be more useful there. Then that night I got a bad asthma attack, and Mum had to sit up with me for hours, and I was too sick to go to school the next day. After that I knew in my heart that I really wanted to be with Mum, and if she had to go to Brisbane with Val, then I would have to go, too.

My School Days at Athol Are Over

Not much more was said about going to Brisbane for a while. Dad got his new garage built, where the old peperina tree used to be. Herbie and his brother Kenny worked on that. They were very good carpenters, so the garage with room for two cars looked great when it was finished, and maybe our old ute felt happy about having such a nice new house to live in. Dad also worked at putting a terrace at the end of the tennis court and behind the garage. The old dunny was now gone, and replaced with a new chemical toilet that Dad built beside the tank stand closer to the house. There were a lot of new improvements, and I sometimes wondered why Dad was going to all this trouble, when some of us would be going to Brisbane to live. The good thing was that it showed he still put the farm first, so I knew that even though I might have to go to school in Brisbane, I could come home for the holidays, and eventually come back here to live when I was older.

I knew that whatever happened with this Brisbane business with me and Val, Gordon and Gloria would also have a tough time of it. Gordon had just started on a new time in his life. He had finished his scholarship year at Athol School last year, and he was now going as what you call a day student to a special boarding school that had been set up a couple of years ago in the homestead of the old Westbrook Station, a few miles from where we lived, down in the direction of Harold's place.

I had never been there, but I knew it was a special place. Gordon had to get dressed in the school uniform every day, and ride off on Larry early in the morning. The school was called the Couper Memorial School, and there were a lot of older boys there as boarders, and Gordon said they had cricket and rugby teams that played against other big schools in Toowoomba. It had been very exciting when Gordon started there at the beginning of the year and came home and told us these stories. I couldn't wait to grow up and go there, too. But now this business with Val had come up, and everything was changing. Gordon said there was also a problem at his school. The Head Master had left, and many students as well, and there was talk that the school would have to close. It seemed that you couldn't count on anything any more.

Gloria was in Grade 6, and she was worried if Mum went to Brisbane with Val and me what would become of her. Would she have to stay on the farm with Dad and Gordon and do all the cooking and housework? How could she manage that and still go to school every day? It was a big problem, and we talked about it a lot, but there was never a solution.

The next thing that happened was that Dad went off to Brisbane to look for a house near Val's school. He came back a few days later and said that he had found one. My last hope for being able to stay at Athol was now gone. Mum and Dad said that after the August school holidays, Mum, Val and I would be going to Brisbane. Gloria would stay on the farm to finish her Grade 6 at Athol School. Aunty Jane was going to come out from Toowoomba to help look after the house, at least for some of the time, so Gloria wouldn't be on her own, and things would be a bit easier for Dad and Gordon. So that was the plan, as near as I understood it. It was going to be a big upheaval in our lives, and though I tried not to think about it too much, I was really scared about what was going to happen to me. It would be good for Val, of course, and we all had to keep thinking about that, but that didn't really make it any easier.

By now I had begun my Grade 4 work at school. When he heard that I would be leaving at the start of the August holidays to go to Brisbane, Mr. Fisher said he would push me ahead as fast as he could so that I wouldn't be too far behind the other kids when I transferred into Grade 4 in a new school. I hadn't even thought about that problem. Not only would I be going to a new school where I didn't know anybody, all the kids in my class would be ahead of me, because they had been in Grade 4 since the beginning of the year. There seemed to be no end to my problems.

Mr. Fisher spent most of the time on arithmetic, because he said that was where I was likely to have the most trouble. I was learning how to multiply and divide and memorize Tables of Measurement. It didn't seem too hard, but Mr. Fisher warned me that there were some tricky things coming up that he knew we would not have time to cover before I left. This worried me a bit, but I worked hard on everything he gave me.

I loved my new Grade 4 Reader. I read quickly ahead on my own, and enjoyed stories like how Horatius defended the bridge in the old city of Rome, and how Black Beauty saved his master from being swept away in the river by refusing to cross the broken bridge. My favourite poem was "The Teams" by Henry Lawson, which I learned off by heart, and was surprised to find out that Dad knew as well. We recited it together at home one night:

> "A cloud of dust on the long, white road,
> And the teams go creeping on
> Inch by inch with the weary load;
> And by the power of the green-hide goad
> The distant goal is won."

And so on, to the end of the poem, with hardly any mistakes.

But all too soon I came to my last day at Athol School. It was the start of the August holidays, and all of the kids were excited about that, but nevertheless they also seemed a little sad to see me go. Mr. Fisher asked me to stand up in front of everyone and he made a nice speech.

"We're sorry to see you go, Des," he said. "You're a good student, and you will do well in your new school in Brisbane. It will be a lot different, and will seem strange at first, but just remember that all your old friends here at Athol will be cheering for you."

At that everyone clapped, and someone said, "Good on ya, Des," and I just stood there, feeling the tears coming to my eyes. I couldn't say a word. It was hard to think I would never be inside this school again, but that was the way it was going to be. My school days at Athol were over.

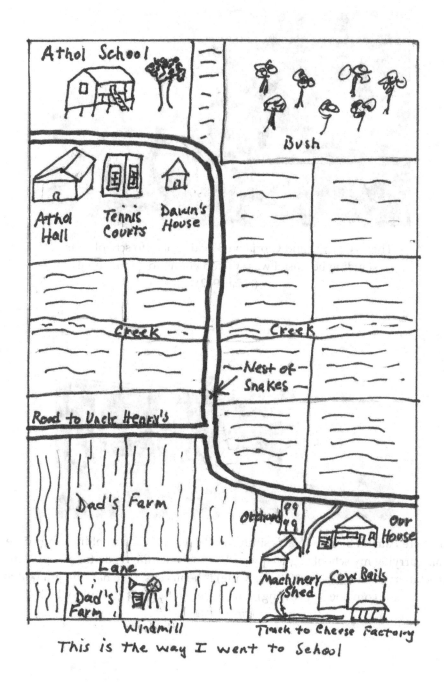

This is the way I went to School

This is Gordon and Gloria on Blackie going to school. I am
standing because I was still too young to go to school.
(*circa* 1942)

Now here I am on Blackie. Val is sitting on Patsy with Gloria holding the bridle. I
am carrying my school bag on my back because we are ready for school. The
machinery shed (with the 1936 Chev ute) is behind us. The hay and grain barn
with the combine (for sowing) can be seen in the background to the left.
(*circa* 1946)

Athol Hall
1921-69

Athol School
1887-1962

This is a sketch of Athol School with the
Athol Hall and tennis courts in the background.
(*circa* 1940s reprinted with permission from Harold Newton)

Here is Gordon all grown up wearing his cadet uniform and holding
Blackie while Val sits in the saddle and I am peeping out from behind.
(circa 1948)

This is our beautiful new house on the farm at Athol
looking its best with garage and tennis court.
(*circa* 1950)

Here I am with Gloria walking on
Ruthven Street in Toowoomba at Show time.
(*circa* 1948)

Part 3

City School Years

The heights by great men reached and kept
　Were not attained by sudden flight,
But they, while their companions slept,
　Were toiling upward in the night.

Longfellow

Revenge, at first though sweet,
Bitter ere long back on itself recoils.

Milton

We Arrive in Brisbane

My new life began on a cold August morning on the platform of the railway station in Toowoomba. Mum, Val and I were taking the train to Brisbane. Dad and Mum had gone down earlier in the ute, taking a lot of the stuff we would need for our new home and to make sure the house was ready for us. Now Val and I were going with Mum on the train, because Dad could not get away from the farm again. Gloria and Gordon had come into town with the rest of us to say good-bye. Now we were all standing on the railway platform feeling miserable.

I remembered the first time I had been here, when Gloria and I were going with Aunty Holly to spend our August holidays at Aunty Joy's place at Karara. That had been a wonderful exciting adventure. This was a scary trip to a place where we didn't know anyone, and where we would have to stay and not be able to come back to Athol—at least not until the summer holidays.

Dad put our ports up on the luggage rack. Then he gave Mum a big kiss and hugged Val and me. He told me to be a brave boy and look after Mum. That made me feel important, but no less scared. Then the train was moving, and we were waving good-bye to Dad and Gordon and Gloria, and watching them grow smaller and smaller as the train pulled away.

At first the trip was interesting enough, as the train wound slowly down the mountain range. Again I remembered doing this with the whole family, when we drove down in the ute to Helidon Spa on New Year's Day a few years ago, and when we were going on our holidays to Redcliffe and Caloundra. The thought of that, and the memory of how noisy and busy Brisbane was, with all of its cars and trains, was suddenly more than I could bear, and I burst out in a tearful rage at Mum.

"I don't want to go to Brisbane," I sobbed and yelled. "I don't want to go to a big city school. I don't want to live in a horrible house in Brisbane, and not have my own bed, and not be able to ride Blackie and play with the cats and go out with my air rifle with Jim." I was working myself up into a real frenzy. I was absolutely terrified of what was coming. "I don't want to go! I don't want to go!" I wailed over and over, even though I knew it was useless to cry and bad of me and hard on Mum. It just wasn't fair. I was trapped, and there just wasn't anything I could do about it, except yell and scream and cry—and that's exactly what I did.

Somehow Mum got me settled down. I don't remember much more about the trip, except that it was long and boring. I think I was asleep when Mum said we were pulling into Roma Street Station in Brisbane, and it was time to get out. It was late afternoon, and just as I expected, there were people everywhere pushing and shoving. I trudged along beside Mum and Val on the platform, carrying my port as we tried to find our way out onto the street. The train station was like a big brick cavern, with a big clock and signs everywhere pointing this way and that, and people lining up to buy tickets at cubby holes with bars on the windows that looked like gaol cells. Brisbane was just one big prison, and now I was trapped inside.

Finally, we got out to the street, and Mum found a big black car called a taxi. The driver wore a cap pulled down over his bushy eyebrows. He put our ports in the boot, and we all climbed into the back seat.

"You can sit up here with me, cobber, if you like," the driver said to me. I wasn't too sure, but Mum said, "Go on," so I climbed into the front seat beside him.

"Where to, missus?" he asked Mum.

"We want to go to 24 Carl Street in South Brisbane," Mum said.

"Never heard of it," he replied. "Any more clues than that?"

"I think the suburb is called Thompson Estate," said Mum.

"Yeah, well that helps a bit. Let's see if we can find it." He set the car off with a big jerk, and soon we were whizzing along in all the traffic.

"Ever been to Brisbane before, mate?" the driver asked me.

"Yes and I don't like it," I said.

"So that's the reason for the long face, eh? Ah well, it's not so bad when you get used to it. Are you here for the holidays?"

"No, we have to stay. My sister is going to the Deaf School."

"Is that so? That's at Dutton Park. It's not far from where you're going. We can swing by there on the way if you like, missus."

"That would be nice," Mum said. "Then Val can see how far she has to go to school."

We went careening on through traffic for quite a while. Then the driver pointed out an ugly looking place, with a high brick wall and barbed wire on the top, and a little hut with a man standing inside it with what looked like a rifle.

"Is that the Deaf School?" I asked, suddenly worried that Val would be going to such a place.

"No, no," the driver laughed. "That's Boggo Road Gaol, where they put all the crooks away." Oh fine, I thought to myself. Just where I wanted to live, near a gaol. A bit further on we slowed down in front of a brick building with big tall trees outside. Val recognized it immediately as the School for the Deaf, and she started to make loud noises and cry. This was not going well, but Mum managed to settle her down.

"This, here's Cornwall Street," the driver said, as we came down a long hill, "and that busy road up ahead is Ipswich Road. We cross here at the tram sheds, where they park the trams overnight, and I think Carl Street is just up behind that ... Yes, here it is. Number 24 you said, did you, missus?"

We pulled up in front of an old house. It was built on high posts, and it had steep rickety looking steps going straight up to a verandah, with blinds that ran across the front and down one side of the house. The roof was made of rusty corrugated iron, and the whole house looked as if it could use a good coat of paint. It was nothing like our beautiful tiled roof home at Athol.

The taxi driver helped us with our ports through the squeaky gate in a rickety wood fence, and up the steep steps.

"Good luck, missus," he said to Mum, then added to me, "Cheer up, son, you'll soon get to like it here in the big smoke."

Yeah, for sure, I thought, sarcastically. Then, with a cheery wave he was off, and we were left at the top of the steps, with Mum fumbling for her key. Inside, the house looked just as old as it did on the outside. There were only two bedrooms, so I would have a bed on the front verandah, where there were cracks in the floor boards, and I could hear the wind whistling through. There was a big room in the middle of the house, with a dinner table and chairs and a big couch. The kitchen was at the back. It was quite big, and it had a corrugated iron recess for an old wood stove. A table and chairs stood in the middle of the room, along with an old cupboard, and a smaller wooden one against the wall, with a door on the front and a hinged top.

"What's that?" I asked Mum.

"It's an ice chest," she said. "The ice man brings a block of ice, and you put it in the top to keep things cool inside the cupboard." We had a nice new fridge on the farm, but this old-fashioned ice chest in the city. Still, I didn't mind too much. It would be fun to see how all this worked.

Another verandah ran across the back of the house. A small bathroom was set off to one side, with an old tub and wash basin. The back steps ran down into a big yard, where there was a large bushy tree at the back, which turned out to be a mulberry tree. Underneath the house (I was exploring it all within the first ten minutes) was a set of laundry tubs, and the lavatory that you flushed by pulling a chain, like Grandfather's in Toowoomba. The rest of it was bare ground, which I could see right away would make a good racetrack, with the posts serving as obstacles. The posts were almost twice as high as me, so there was plenty of scope for rigging up ropes for swinging on. I could see right away that the house had possibilities after all.

Another special thing in the back yard was a huge bird cage big enough to stand up and walk around in, with wire netting on three sides. I went over to have a look, and I saw a dozen or so small birds that I think you call finches, flitting around among different perches. This would be something new, looking after birds. I didn't know much about that, but thought it wouldn't be too hard.

The yard was fenced on both sides and at the back with big rough wood slabs. It was really solid on one side, but on the other side there were a few boards missing, and when I looked I saw three figures staring at me through the fence. One was a boy who looked like he might be a bit older than me. Another was an older boy about Gordon's age. The third was an older girl, who I thought must be their sister. Though it was a cold day, the boys were dressed in shorts and old jumpers. The youngest boy was in the front peering at me through the hole in the fence, with a bare foot perched on the lower rail.

"Hello," he said. "My name's Fred. Who are you?"

"I'm Des," I said.

"Are you going to live here?"

"Yes, with my Mum and sister."

"How old are you?"

"Nine. What about you?"

"I'm eleven. This is my brother, Rob, and sister, Norma. We've been looking after the birds, but I s'pose you'll do that now."

"I s'pose so, but I'm not sure what to do. We have hens on the farm, but no birds, at least not in cages."

"That's all right. I'll show you how. Did you used to live on a farm? Where?"

"A long way from here, near Toowoomba. My Dad and older brother and sister still live there."

"I'd like to come and see your farm. My Dad makes pies."

"What? You mean real meat pies like you buy in the shop?"

The older brother, Rob, now spoke up for the first time. "Yeah, they're the best in town. But we don't sell them in shops—just off the pie carts. I get to drive the horse on Saturday, when I'm not at school."

"You mean you have pie carts and horses?" My eyes must have been getting as wide as saucers. "Where do you make the pies?"

"Right here in our pie shed," said Fred. "Do you want to see it?"

"Too right," I said. "Pies are my favourite food."

I climbed through the fence and for the first time got a look at their house. If I thought ours was a bit old and broken down, theirs was a disaster. It was on high stumps like ours, with bits falling off everywhere. It looked like a good wind would blow it away. But I wasn't really interested in the house. I wanted to see the pie shed.

It was a big white building made of fibro, right up against our fence. They took me inside through a screen door. There were a lot of counters, and endless trays stacked on racks, with at least two dozen tin pie-sized cups on each tray. At one end was a big brick oven, and long sticks with flat boards on the end for shoving the pie trays into the oven and pulling them out. I had never seen such a thing. It was marvellous.

"We always have some pies left over at the end of the day," said Rob. He pointed to a tray on the counter, with at least a dozen beautiful brown meat pies on it. "Do you want to have some for tea?"

"Boy, would I ever," I said, "but I don't have any money."

"That's all right," Rob said. "These are free." He put half a dozen pies into a brown paper bag, and gave them to me. I could hardly believe it. I had six meat pies in a bag all for nothing. Wait till Mum sees this.

"Take them home to your mother," said Norma, speaking for the first time. "We have to go in for our tea now. We'll see you later."

I took off back through the fence and up the steps into our house.

"Mum, Mum," I shouted, "Look what I've got. Six meat pies for tea. There's a pie place right next door, and the kids gave me some. You should see it. They make hundreds and hundreds of pies every day. Isn't that terrific?"

"Well, you certainly get around," said Mum. "I'll get the stove going and warm them up in the oven."

"I'll help," I said. "Maybe things aren't going to be so bad with a pie place next door."

"That was very nice of them to give you the pies," Mum said. "We have good neighbours."

"And one of them is a boy named Fred, who is just a bit older than me. He's going to show me how to feed the birds." Then I had another thought. "I wonder who lives in the little house on the other side."

"It's an older couple and their son," said Mum. "I met them when I was down here before with Dad."

We had hardly sat down in the kitchen to eat, when there was a knock on the back door. It was our other neighbour, an old lady with a sweet face. Her name was Mrs. Calder.

"I've brought you some scones," she said. "We saw you arrive and thought you might like some for tea." She stayed for quite a while talking to Mum. It was nice that our next door neighbours were so friendly and kind.

Rob was right about the pies. They were the best I ever tasted, and full of thick brown gravy. I polished off two, and would have eaten a third, but Mum told me to ease off or I might get sick. After tea, we sat on the couch together in the big room, and listened to our serials on the wireless, and read some books together. We were all a bit sad about being away from Dad and Gordon and Gloria. Mum made up the beds and I helped. Val followed us around, never letting Mum out of her sight. Mum tucked me up in my new bed on the verandah with lots of blankets. So here I was in my new home in Brisbane. It was all so different, but there were good bits, too, like the kids next door and the pies, especially the pies. I went to sleep wondering about what would turn up tomorrow.

Checking Out the Neighbourhood

Next day was Sunday, and I was up early poking around in the back yard. Pretty soon I met old Mr. Calder next door. I saw him over the fence, sitting on his back steps in the sun.

"G'day young fella," he said. "Wot d'you know?"

"Not much," I said.

"Yeah, well I wouldn't tell anybody if I was you," he said. "Come here and take a look at this."

I looked over the fence and saw a magpie hopping around on the ground. I wondered why it didn't fly away, like all the wild magpies on our farm would do if you got too close.

"He's a pet," said Mr. Calder. "Our son, Les, found him when he was small. Must have fallen out of his nest. We clipped his wings, and now he's part of the family."

Just then a man about Herbie's age appeared from further down the yard.

"Ow yer goin?" he said to me. "Wanta take a closer look?" He bent down, stuck out his arm, and the magpie jumped on it, and crawled up onto his shoulder. He came over to the fence to show me. I stuck out my hand to touch the bird, but it let out a god awful screech, and took a few jabs at me with its sharp, pointy beak.

"He's a bit mean till you get to know him," said the man. I reckoned that this must be the son, Les.

"I don't think magpies make good pets," I said.

"Yeah, you're probably right, but he gets along all right with Trixie."

"Who's Trixie?" I asked.

"Mum's fox terrier." Les gave a whistle, and a small black and white dog dashed up from the back yard. Les put the magpie on the ground, and the dog ran circles around it barking, while the bird danced around squawking its head off.

"Regular bloody circus," yelled Mr. Calder above the noise. "But Trixie's great with the rats."

"Rats?" I asked. "Have you got pet rats, too?"

"Not bloody likely, mate," said Mr. Calder. "You've gotta draw the line somewhere. These are wild buggers, half as big as the dog, but she grabs 'em by the tail, gives 'em a flick, and breaks their back. Keeps them away from the chook feed."

"Chooks? Have you got chooks, too?" I was beginning to wonder what else was going to turn up in that small yard.

"Just a few to give us fresh eggs," said Les. "Not like your neighbours on the other side. They've got horses for their pie carts. Look, there's Fred now."

I turned and looked across our yard to the other side, and I saw Fred waving at me from over the fence. I went over.

"Did you like the pies?" he asked.

"Too right," I said.

"Yeah, well jump over the fence, and I'll show you the horses."

I crawled over the fence, and across a whole pile of rubbish behind their pie shed, and was amazed to see that the rest of their back yard was filled with a couple of old sheds, and a fenced off area full of horse manure.

"These are the stables," said Fred. I picked my way through the horse dung and looked inside the sheds, and saw a couple of ponies and some harness.

"Where are the pie carts?" I asked.

"Under the house," said Fred. "Come on, I'll show you." Sure enough, parked under the house were two pie carts, with little tin ovens on them, with chimneys on the top, and a sign on the side of the carts saying "Newton's Hot Pies." It was amazing. All of this in one city house yard no bigger than ours. I began to wonder what I might be able to put in our place.

Just then Mum called out looking for me, so I went home to tell her about what I had found on both sides of our house. The next thing to explore was the street, so after breakfast Mum, Val and I set off. Most of the houses on Carl Street were pretty old like ours, some on high stumps and others on low. We were about in the middle, so we explored in both directions. At one end was an old church called St. Philip's Church of England. It was actually on Cornwall Street, right across from the tram sheds, which I decided I would have to explore better another day. At the other end Carl Street ran into O'Keefe Street, which went down a big hill to a shopping area on Logan Road called Stone's Corner. Because it was Sunday not many shops were open, but there were a lot of them, and I even saw a picture show called the Alhambra Theatre. A creek ran right through Stone's Corner, and on the other side of the creek up a bit of a hill was Buranda School. That was where Mum was going to take me tomorrow to begin my new life at school. Just seeing it set off all my fears again about what was going to be waiting for me there. We went home, and I spent the rest of the day and night worrying about it.

I Arrive at Buranda Boys' State School

Next morning I got dressed in my khaki shirt and shorts, and put on my helmet. I was ready for school. If I'd known how much that outfit would make me stick out like a sore thumb, I would have worn something else. But I was just a boy from the bush, scared silly, who didn't know any different. Neither did Mum. She cut me a nice lunch, packed it in my school bag, and off we went to enroll me in my new school. Val came, too, and afterwards Mum would take her in the opposite direction to the Deaf School.

As we walked down the hill on O'Keefe Street towards Stone's Corner, I could feel my heart beating faster and faster. We crossed Logan Road at the school crossing, dodging the cars and the trams that rattled by, and went up the quiet street that led to Buranda Boys' School. I noticed the tennis courts near the entrance, and I thought that at least was a good sign of something where I knew I could hold my own.

The school was huge, but there was no one in sight as we entered through the front gate, because everyone was in class. The school was built on high stumps, and you had to walk underneath it to get to the steps, which ran up to the long verandah from a large gravelly playground. There were actually several sets of steps because the school stretched out like a long snake, twisting and turning from one end of the playground to the other. The playground actually looked like a gravel pit, which it probably was once upon a time, because along the side opposite the school was a high rock cliff. On top of the cliff I could see what looked like another school. I later found out it was the girls' school.

Mum wasn't sure where to go, but she took a guess, and we went up the nearest set of steps. As we got to the top and onto the verandah, I could see a classroom full of boys. The teacher was a gruff looking man in a brown suit, with his leather belt sort of knotted below his stomach. He was standing near the door of the classroom, and he saw us as we came up the steps.

"If you're looking for the office," he said to Mum, "it's right there," pointing to a room beside the steps. His voice croaked like a rusty hinge, and his yellow tobacco-stained teeth showed in a sly smile, as his hooded eyes swept over us, like a hawk sizing up its prey. He then turned back to the classroom and tweaked the ear of the nearest boy, who was staring out at us. Crikey, I thought, it's worse than I imagined.

The door to the office was open, and Mum knocked gently. I was peeping out from behind her, and I could see into the room, where a man with a head like a large black spider sat behind a big wooden desk. When he saw Mum he stood up, and I saw the rest of the spider, with its long gangly limbs and thin body in a black suit and white shirt and tie and shiny vest.

"Good morning," he said in a croaking voice.

"Good morning," Mum replied. "I've come to register my son, Des, for school." The spider gave me a long cold stare from behind his steel rimmed spectacles. I thought he was going to say "Welcome to my web," but instead he gave us a crooked smile and waved us to some chairs and said pleasantly enough, "Please sit down."

He pulled out a big black leather bound book, which I knew was the school register, and I remembered when Mr. Fisher had put me in the one at Athol School, when I first went there in Prep 1.

"We've got a transfer," said Mum, as she fished the piece of paper out of her purse that Mr. Fisher had given me on my last day at Athol. The spider studied it for a bit, then looked at me again.

"Berghofer. Sounds German. From the country. Your father's a farmer, eh, son?"

"Yes, sir," I said.

As he wrote things in the register, Mum told him the story of how we came to be in Brisbane. When she got to the bit about my grade, Mum explained that I had only just started Grade 4, but she wanted me to continue in that grade, even though I might be a bit behind the others.

"Do you think you're smart enough to do that, Berghofer?" he asked. I jumped a bit because no one had ever called me by my surname like that before. But I managed to nod and say, "Yes, I think so."

"Well, we'll soon find out," he said. "I'm going to put you in Miss MacNish's Grade 4A. She'll try you out for a week to see what you can do. If she thinks you can handle it, you can stay in her class. Otherwise, we'll drop you back to Grade 3. Now, come along, I'll take you to your classroom." To Mum he said, "Leave him with us, Mrs. Berghofer, we'll sort him out. By the way, my name's Merrell. I'm the Acting Head."

Mum gave me a hug, and I thought I could see a tear in her eye. "I'll be back to pick you up after school," she said, and she took Val and went back down the verandah to the steps where we had come up. As she disappeared from sight, I felt my stomach hit the floor.

"Come along, follow me," Mr. Merrell said, and he headed off along the verandah in the opposite direction. Now that I could see him in full stride, I thought he looked more like a praying mantis than a spider, as he was hunched over, and his suit coat flapped open behind him, and his shiny vest gleamed around his tight thin body. I trotted along a step behind, as we hurried along the wide verandah, past two or three other classrooms, until he stopped and called to the teacher inside.

"Miss MacNish, can you come here for a minute."

When I saw Miss MacNish, light suddenly flooded into the gloom that had settled over my soul since I first set foot in the school. I thought she was the most beautiful lady I had ever seen. Lovely blonde hair, blue eyes, and a smile as wide and bright as a rainbow. She took me in with one sweet glance as Mr. Merrell disposed of me.

"I've brought you a new boy, a farm boy from outside Toowoomba on the Darling Downs. His name's Berghofer. Here are the details for your class roll."

He gave her a slip of paper. "He went to a one-teacher school and only started Grade 4 in July. See what he can do, and let me know if you want to keep him." Mr. Merrell strode off back the way we had come. Miss MacNish bent down to look at me and came close so I could smell the sweetness of her.

"Hello, my name's Miss MacNish," her voice tinkled like a silver bell. I was already in love with her. "What's your first name?"

"Des," I mumbled.

"Hello, Des. I won't call you by your first name in class. We don't do that in this boys' school. Come on in and meet your new class mates. You can take off your hat and bag."

For the first time I realized how silly I must have looked in my helmet with my old school bag on my back. Miss MacNish put her hand on my shoulder and gently turned me to face the sea of curious boy faces looking at me.

"Boys, this is Des Berghofer. He comes from Athol School in the country. He's going to join our class."

This announcement of the most terrible thing that had ever happened to me didn't seem to stir any excitement in the class, as the faces continued to stare blankly at me. There were eight long desks in the room, more than we had in the whole school at Athol, four on each side of an aisle down the middle with four boys at each desk. A long blackboard stretched across the front of the room, where I stood shuffling my feet. Maps and charts and pictures hung everywhere on the walls at the back and on one side. The other side was all windows.

Miss MacNish told me to sit at an empty spot right in the front next to a boy who stared at me with a surly look, and a kind of twisted smile. The teacher gave me an exercise book and a pencil.

I Survive My First Challenges

"Now, let's get back to the lesson," said Miss MacNish. "We were just revising our weights and measures tables. Now I want you to do this sum."

I looked at the blackboard, and I realized right away that I was in trouble. Miss MacNish pointed to what she had written on the board and read it aloud to the class.

"We have two loaded trucks. In one there are 2 tons, 15 hundredweight, 3 quarters and 16 pounds. In the other there are 3 tons, 12 hundredweight, 2 quarters and 20 pounds. How much do we have all together?"

My whole body froze. I didn't have the slightest idea what she was talking about. I had heard about tons and pounds, but what were hundredweights and quarters, and how could you add them together?

"Copy down the sum from the blackboard in your exercise books and do the addition," said the teacher.

Well, at least I could copy it down, so I did that. I then looked at what the boy next to me had written, but all he had was unreadable squiggles across the page. I sat staring at the impossible task in front of me, and I felt tears welling up in my eyes. But then Miss MacNish was standing beside me.

"Have you done this before?" she asked.

"No, Miss," I mumbled. "I don't know what to do."

"Do you know your tables? How many pounds in a quarter? How many quarters in a hundredweight? How many hundredweight in a ton?"

She might as well have been speaking to me in Chinese.

"I don't know, Miss. I've never heard of this." My voice was little more than a whisper. Miss MacNish turned to the class and said, "Our new boy hasn't done this before, so let's help him. How many pounds in a quarter?"

"Twenty-eight," everyone chimed out.

"How many quarters in a hundredweight?"

"Four."

"How many hundredweight in a ton?"

"Twenty."

"So now let's add them up starting with the pounds. If we had 16 and 20 pounds, how many pounds is that?"

"Thirty-six."

Now Miss MacNish looked at me. "How many pounds in a quarter, Berghofer."

"Twenty-eight," I said, hopefully.

"So if we've got 36 pounds, that's one quarter plus how many pounds?"

"Eight," I said.

"Very good. So we write down the eight pounds and carry the one quarter over to the next column, and add it to the 2 and 3 already there. Now how many quarters do we have?"

"Six," I said. I was beginning to get it. Miss MacNish was smiling at me, and I could see in her eyes that she wanted me to continue.

"That makes one hundredweight and two quarters left over," I said.

"Is he right, boys?" Miss MacNish asked the class.

"Yes, Miss MacNish," they shouted.

"Good on ya, Berghofer," someone said from up the back.

Miss MacNish laughed, and so did everyone else, except the boy next to me, who I could see out of the corner of my eye was scowling.

"All right everyone, finish the sum on your own, and then do the next one," said Miss MacNish.

I now turned back to the task. I ended up with the answer of 6 tons 8 hundredweight 2 quarters and 8 pounds. I put up my hand and showed it to the teacher. She put a big check mark on it with a red pencil and whispered, "Good boy. I knew you could do it." I think it was at that moment that I thought no matter how bad things might be in this new life for me, I would be able to get by, using my brains, and with the help of nice people like Miss MacNish.

When we went out onto the playground for the 11 o'clock break, I was standing around on my own, feeling a bit lost, when a boy came up to me.

"Hello, Berghofer," he said. "What's your first name again?"

"Des," I said.

"I'm Don, but the kids call me Macker, because my surname's McLaren. I'm in your class, and I'd like to be your friend."

"I'd like that, Don—Macker," I smiled, and we both laughed.

Just then the boy who had been sitting next to me in class came up to us. He shoved his face right in front of mine.

"How many quarters in a hundredweight, Grasshopper?" he leered at me, and before I could say anything he gave me four quick raps with his bare knuckles on the muscle in my upper arm. It hurt like hell. "One, two, three, four," he chortled.

I was so surprised I didn't know what to do, and the pain of it almost brought tears to my eyes. But my new friend, Macker, pushed the other boy away, and a few other boys who had been standing around also pulled him off.

"Lay off, McCallum, you prawn," someone said. I was rubbing my arm furiously, trying to ease the pain.

"Don't mind him," said Macker. "He's a bully and a drongo. Just stand up to him, and he'll back off."

I was certainly getting introduced into school life at Buranda in a hurry.

"Why did he call me Grasshopper?" I asked.

"Oh, he was just trying to be smart," said Macker. "Berghofer-Grasshopper. Actually, that's pretty good. Soon everyone will be calling you that. You'll get used to it—just like they call me Macker." And he was right. From that day on Grasshopper was my nickname.

The Singing Lesson

During the lunch hour, I found out that the playground at Buranda was a lot bigger than I thought. There was a lower level field, like a big oval bordered on the far side by mangroves growing on the edge of the creek. Across the creek was Stone's Corner, but the kids told me we weren't allowed to go there without a note from our parents, and there were school monitors on the gate to check up on you.

The oval had a cricket pitch in the middle of it, and goal posts at both ends. It was the football season, so the cricket pitch was covered over with a tarpaulin, and a lot of the boys were running around in football jerseys and spiked boots. I learned that they played three kinds of football—soccer, rugby league, and another game I had never heard of called Aussie Rules.

"Do you play football, Grasshopper?" one of the boys asked.

"No," I said, "but I play tennis."

"Ar, that's a sissy's game," said someone else.

"Not if you play it hard," said Macker. "I'm a good tennis player. Bring your racquet to school one day and we'll have a game."

Just then we met up with Fred and Rob, the two boys from the pie place next door to me. Rob was dressed in football togs.

"How's it goin?" he asked. "Is everyone treating you all right?"

"Yeah, pretty good," I said.

"Glad to hear it. Just let me know if you have any problems," Rob said, and he ran off to the football field.

"Gosh, do you know Rob Newton?" Macker asked, obviously impressed. "He's a champion soccer player."

"Yeah, we live next door," said Fred. "He's gonna help us with the pies."

Now Macker was really impressed. "Gosh, are you ever lucky," he said. "Can I come round to your house soon?"

"Yeah, sure," I said. "That would be fun." All things considered, I thought to myself, I'm off to a pretty good start.

That afternoon in class brought on another weird challenge in my struggle to fit in at this new school. It was the last half hour of the day, when another lady teacher turned up in our classroom. Everyone except me knew who she was. She was an older lady in a grey suit. She wore her hair in a bun, and she looked at us through horn rimmed glasses.

"All right, boys," said Miss MacNish, "clear everything off your desks and sit up straight. Miss Grimes is here for your music class."

Music class? I had never heard of such a thing. Apparently some of the boys weren't too keen, for I heard a few low groans go round the room. Miss Grimes hung a chart over the blackboard, displaying what you call a music staff of five lines with a lot of notes with curly tails sprinkled across it.

"Good afternoon, boys," Miss Grimes said in a crisp friendly voice. "Let's begin with the scales."

What followed next was the strangest thing. Miss Grimes went through the doh-ray-me scale using all kinds of weird hand signs for the different notes, beginning with a clenched fist down low for bottom doh, and ending with a clenched fist up high for top doh, with all kinds of gyrations in between. Then it was our turn. Miss MacNish joined in up front, and to my amazement all the boys in the class followed along, doing the hand signs and singing in piping boy soprano voices. Completely bewildered, I did the best I could, trying to follow Miss Grimes and Miss MacNish with the hand signs, and keep in tune with the notes. After we finished the warm up on the simple scale, Miss Grimes then went to her chart, where she had all the notes mixed up. Pointing to the notes with one hand, and making the signs with the other, she led us through this maze of vocal gymnastics. I stole a look around at the boys behind me, and saw they were all following along, hands opening and closing and reaching this way and that, as they sang out with great gusto. I turned back to the front, and I saw Miss MacNish smiling at me, so I put my whole heart into it, and did the very best I could to join the strange performance.

Eventually, Miss Grimes was satisfied with the scales, and she flipped over the chart to a song. It was some kind of sea shanty. The boys apparently knew it, and they had no trouble in belting it out. We didn't have to do hand signs for this part, but sat up straight with hands folded on the desk, so no one could prod anyone else during the singing. After that, Miss Grimes taught us a new song that we sang in parts to a lively marching rhythm, which got all of our feet tapping, until Miss MacNish had to call a halt, because she said we would be disturbing the classes next door. When the class was over, Miss MacNish thanked Miss Grimes for coming, and then she said something that I'm sure made me turn beet red with embarrassment.

"I want to congratulate our new boy, Berghofer, who had never seen anything like this before, but nevertheless did his very best to join in. That's really good spirit, and I think we should recognize it."

This was greeted with a bit of clapping, some half-hearted cheers, and a few low groans of something that sounded like "teacher's pet." As I recalled the muscle bruising I had already received earlier in the day, I wasn't too sure that it was a good thing to be singled out like that, though I knew that Miss MacNish did it with a good heart.

That was the end of the day. Boys began pouring out of classrooms from one end of school to the other. Macker grabbed me and said he would walk part way home with me. We also bumped into Fred and Rob, who, of course, were also going in my direction. It wasn't until we crossed Logan Road at the school crossing that I remembered Mum had said she would come and pick me up after school. I couldn't see any other mothers around, at least not for boys my age, so I felt too embarrassed to say anything. I hoped we might meet Mum along the way, and sure enough we did. She still had Val with her, who was going to start school tomorrow, so it was good that I had settled in so well on my first day at my school, and she wouldn't have to worry about me any more. I introduced her to Macker and Fred and Rob, and we all set off together. Macker peeled off at the bottom of the hill to go to his place, and the rest of us continued up O'Keefe Street. All in all, I thought the day had gone pretty well.

Getting the Cuts

When we sat down for tea that night Mum asked me to tell her about my day at school. "My teacher is Miss MacNish," I said. "She is really lovely. Just like Dorothy, only with blonde hair, not black." (I was remembering the holiday we had at Caloundra with Herbie and Dorothy, when they were just married). "I'm really lucky to have her as a teacher. She helped me with a sum I had never seen before. Do you know what a hundredweight is?"

"No, I don't think so."

"Well, there are 20 of them in a ton, and if you get more than 20 you carry it over and add it to the tons. There are 4 quarters in a hundredweight, and that makes 112 pounds, which is a bit strange, don't you think, because if it's a hundredweight it should be 100 pounds. That would make everything a bit easier, don't you think?"

"I suppose it would."

"At morning break this bully punched me in the arm, and called me Grasshopper, but the other kids chased him off. There's a great big oval and most of the kids play football. Rob Newton is a champion soccer player. Macker said he would like to play tennis with me. But do you want to know what the weirdest thing of all is?"

"Yes, tell me."

"We have music classes with Miss Grimes, who makes all these funny hand signs for the notes. I did my best to follow, but I wasn't very good at it. Miss MacNish said I was good for trying. But do you know the other thing I learned?"

"No, what?"

"If you get sent to the office, Mr. Merrell pulls out this great big cane and gives you the cuts, sometimes three on each hand."

"He cuts your hands?" Mum sounded worried.

"No, there's no blood, but they say it hurts just as bad."

"Well, I hope you won't get sent to the office."

"Me too. I don't want to get the cuts."

Next morning during school parade, I became even more sure about that. I had walked to school with Fred and Rob, and not long afterwards one of the sixth graders, who was a bell ringer, rang a loud bell that was hanging on the corner of the verandah just outside the seventh grade classrooms. That was the warning to get ready, and all the kids started to line up in their classes on the gravel playground. The other kids showed me what to do. Then there was another bell, and that was the signal to stand up straight and shut up. We were all lined up in two lines for each class, the whole school, probably three hundred boys, more than I had ever seen in one place before. A lot of them were wearing a kind of school uniform of grey and maroon shirt, grey shorts, and a grey and maroon cap. Hardly any of them wore shoes, just bare feet, which I thought was amazing, because the parade ground was rough and pebbly. I was glad to have my shoes.

A couple of older boys stood up front with drums slung over their shoulders. The teachers stood with their classes, and Mr. Merrell was up on the verandah, looking out over us with his steely eyes. In a big voice he called "Attention!" and we all stamped our right foot, and stood up straight like soldiers. The boys with the drums gave a long rat-a-tat-tat roll with their drum sticks, and we all sang "God Save the King."

Mr. Merrell made some announcements, then he said he had some boys he wanted to see up on the verandah. He called out their names, and four boys slowly moved out of their lines, and went up the steps.

"Come on, smarten up, step lively," shouted Mr. Merrell. He lined them up on the verandah, where we all could see them. "You boys have all been reported to me for bad behaviour, swearing, and back answering a teacher." Mr. Merrell glared down at the rest of us. "You all know what the punishment for that is." He picked up a long cane, which he had been hiding out of sight, and he waved it around for us to see. He told the first boy to step forward and hold out his right hand. Up went the cane, and down it came on the boy's hand with a thwack that rang out across the parade ground. Then he gave him another one. "Now, hold out your left hand," and thwack, thwack, he gave him two more on that hand. "Back to your class. Next!" And so on. Each boy got four cuts. They tried not to cry, but one of them was a fifth grader close to us, and I could see the tears in his eyes as he came by me and went back into line. All the rest of us were standing as still as death.

"That's the first lesson for the day," shouted Mr. Merrell. "Now into school. Quick march!"

The boys on the drums gave us a marching beat, and the teachers led their classes off to the steps closest to their rooms. Miss MacNish stood at the door as we all marched right into our places. I looked at her face, and I thought she seemed very sad and pale.

I Show My Skill at Tennis

That evening I told Mum about the boys who got the cuts. I could see she didn't like it, but I told her the rest of the day went well in class, because I didn't want to worry her to think that she might have to send me to another school where they weren't so strict. She was already worried enough about getting Val settled into her school.

"I think I should get a school uniform," I said. "It's not a strict rule, but I wouldn't want Mr. Merrell to pick on me because I don't have one. You can get them at a shop at Stone's Corner."

"All right, we'll do that on Saturday," Mum said.

"I think I'll take my tennis racquet to school tomorrow," I said. "Macker wants to have a game to show me how good he is."

"That's a good idea," Mum said. "You're a good player so you should do all right."

I wasn't so sure, because I had only played at our small country school at Athol. Who knows how good these city kids might be. We went out onto the courts during lunch time. Macker got some balls from the teacher in charge of tennis. There were two courts. Two boys were hitting up on the other court. I recognized one of them from our class, but I didn't know him. The other one was an older boy. I could see right away they were good players.

"Come on Grasshopper," Macker called to me from the other end of our court. "Let's get started."

He lobbed a soft ball down to me, and I whacked it back really hard, low across the net. I think Macker was surprised, because he just stood there without making an effort to hit it back.

"Good shot," he said and lobbed another ball, a bit harder this time, onto my backhand. Again I whacked it back hard, right at Macker's feet, and he jumped to get out of the way.

"You've got some good strokes," Macker said. I was beginning to think that maybe he wasn't as good a player as he thought he was. I hit one down to him, not too hard, and he lobbed it back. We had a bit of a rally, but I could already tell that Macker wasn't a strong player.

"Let's have a serve," he called. He had a funny wind up motion, and he served a really soft one onto my forehand, which I belted back down the sideline, leaving him flatfooted and gaping at it open mouthed.

"I'll serve one," I called out. Following the style I had learned from Gordon and my cousin Jimmy, I served a hard one swinging wide on Macker's forehand. He just watched it go by—a clean ace. When I turned round to pick up another ball, I found the older boy from the other court staring at me.

"That was a hell of a serve," he said. "You're pretty good. What's your name?"

"Des Berghofer," I said.

"He's a new boy in our class," said the other boy, coming over towards us. I found out his name was Neil.

"I'm Brad," said the older boy. "Where did you learn to play like that?"

"We all play like that at Athol," I said.

"Where's Athol?" Brad asked.

"Out in the country," I said.

"He's my friend," said Macker, who had now come over to join us. "He's pretty good, isn't he?"

"Yeah, I reckon," said Brad. "Would you like to play for the school?"

"What's that mean?" I asked.

"We play other schools on Friday afternoons during the tennis season," said Brad. "I think you should try out for the team. Come on, let's have a game of doubles, and we'll see how good you are."

Brad played with Macker, and I teamed up with Neil. Brad served a rocket at me that I could barely touch. He did the same to Neil, but when it was my turn again, I managed to whip it down the sideline past Macker at the net. Brad smiled and called "Good shot!" We had time to play four games before the bell rang to go back into school. We each won our serve, even Macker, but only because Brad was so quick at the net that neither I nor Neil could get anything past him.

"Thanks for the game," Brad said, as we walked off the courts. "I'll talk to you later about joining the team."

"Well, you sure made a hit with Brad," said Macker. "He's the captain of the tennis team, you know. I'm sorry I couldn't give you a better game. I didn't know you were so good."

"That's all right, Macker," I said. "You're a good friend, and that's the main thing."

I Get a Tennis Coach

I saw Brad again the next day, and he said that he had talked to Mr. Hennesy, the teacher who looked after the tennis team, about me. Mr. Hennesy said it was fine for me to join the team, but the tennis season was over for the year, and we wouldn't be playing other schools until next year. In the meantime, however, a special opportunity was coming our way, because a tennis coach had said he could come to the school to coach us one day a week, if enough kids signed up. I certainly wanted to do it, but I had to make a choice between that and joining a mouth organ club, because the lessons were going to be on the same day. I would have liked to learn to play the mouth organ, but I was more interested in tennis, so that was my choice. I never did learn how to play the mouth organ.

I told Mum about the tennis coach, and because it was only going to cost a few shillings for each lesson, she said I could do it. Next Thursday afternoon after school about a dozen kids turned up to meet the tennis coach. Brad and Neil were there, but Macker didn't come. The coach's name was Tom Whitworth, and he was dressed in his white tennis shirt and shorts.

"Now I know some of you are already good players," he said, "and some of you are beginners. But no matter how good you are, you can always be better. If you asked Frank Sedgman, he would tell you the same thing."

Frank Sedgman was my tennis hero. He had just won the Wimbledon doubles final with John Bromwich (who was much older) and everyone knew that he was going to play for Australia in the Davis Cup. If I could learn to play like him, there would be nothing better.

"First, you've got to learn how to hold the racquet," the coach continued. "For your forehand you say hello to the racquet, and shake hands with it." He came around and checked our grips. Mine was pretty good, but just a bit off. Then he showed us how to swing, keeping the head of the racquet up and following through. We practised swinging for a long time without hitting any balls, while he came around and checked us. Then he lined us up in groups on the back line. He hit balls onto our forehands from the other side of the net. He kept this up for the whole lesson, because he said that was enough to learn for one day.

The next week he taught us backhand and showed us how to change our grip. I wasn't too sure about that, because I preferred to use the same grip for forehand and backhand, like Frank Sedgman. Mr. Whitworth said I should try both for a while, then decide what I was going to do. He had already noticed that I was a pretty good player, and he said I should practice hard to become better.

Over the next couple of weeks he taught us how to serve properly, by throwing the ball up just right, and getting the full weight of your body behind it. I could see how this made a big difference, and I tried hard to do it correctly. Between lessons I would practice on the courts with the other boys, and we all became better players, even Brad, who had been so good to begin with.

After a few weeks, Mr. Whitworth took some of us aside. He said he would like us to come out to his courts on Saturday mornings for extra lessons. He wouldn't charge much, because he thought we had what he called potential, and he just wanted to help us become good players. The problem was that his courts were way out on the other side of Brisbane, at a place called Virginia, and I had no idea how you would get there from where I lived. Brad said not to worry because he would go with me. So I asked Mum and she said it was all right as long as someone older was looking after me.

The first Saturday I met Brad at the tram stop near the school on Logan Road. It seemed like we had to travel for ages on the tram across town, then catch a bus to get out to Virginia. This was a real adventure for me, because I remembered only too well how I had been afraid of the trams and buses when I first saw them. But Brad was an old hand at this kind of thing, and we found our way there without any problem.

There were half a dozen tennis courts, and Mr. Whitworth was there along with another coach, and quite a few boys from various schools where he coached. He gave us extra lessons, then matched us up for games. I thought this was the most terrific thing that had happened for me. Coming to Brisbane to live had been a big problem, but now that I had found something to do that I could never have done at Athol, it wasn't so bad. School, too, was continuing to be all right, even if I did get picked on and bullied a bit. Mostly I could hold my own, and I had made some good new friends. Miss MacNish was always kind and helpful to me and encouraged me, so that I was gradually catching up with the top boys in the class. All in all, I could say as spring turned into summer, and I was coming up to my tenth birthday, things were going all right for me in Brisbane.

Introduction to Marbles

One morning when I arrived at school with Fred and Rob I saw right away that something different was going on. The gravel playground where we lined up to go into school was covered with kids down on their hands and knees, rooting around in the dirt.

"What's going on?" I asked.

"Marbles," said Fred. "Come on, I'll show you."

He hung up his school bag on the nearest peg, and pulled what looked like a dilly bag out of it, and dashed out onto the playground. I ran along behind. We joined a group of boys, who were standing around a big ring that someone had drawn in the dirt. In the middle of the ring were a few brightly coloured marbles. One boy was down on his haunches, with a marble crooked between his finger and thumb in his right hand, with his knuckles on the ground. He had the finger of his left hand on the ground to steady him, and he seemed to be taking sight.

"What's he doing?" I asked Fred.

"Haven't you ever seen this before?" he asked.

"No," I said, "never."

Just then the boy fired the marble out of his hand and knocked another one out of the ring. He picked the marble up and put it in his pocket. The marble he shot with was still in the ring, and he lined up to have another shot.

"He's knuckling down," said Fred, "and shooting his taw to see how many dibs he can get."

You could have fooled me, I thought to myself. The truth was I didn't understand a word he had said. The boy fired again and knocked another marble out of the ring and pocketed it also. The next time he missed, and another boy took over, and in a couple of shots collected the remaining marbles.

"We've got time for one more game before the bell," one boy said. "Two in, who wants to play?"

Fred joined four other boys. They each put two marbles out of their bags in the middle of the ring. Then they stood behind a line and tossed their shooting marble, what Fred had called a taw, at the edge of the ring to see who could get closest. Fred won, so he went first and promptly won two marbles. He was pretty good. By the time the bell went he won two more, so he was two up on the game.

"Will you teach me how to play?" I asked him.

"Sure thing," he said. "I'll lend you some marbles, then you can get your own."

I noticed that a lot of kids from my class had marble bags, and Miss MacNish told them to put them away before coming into class. However, we weren't more than a few minutes into the first lesson, when suddenly from somewhere up the back of the room there was a plop, plop, plop on the wooden floor. I turned around to see a boy on his hands and knees in the aisle trying to gather up some marbles rolling down towards me. Miss MacNish came over and just stood there. She didn't say a word, just held out her hand, and the boy sheepishly got to his feet, and handed over a fistful of marbles.

"Anyone else?" asked the teacher.

Silence. Not a word. Miss MacNish walked back to her desk, pulled out the drawer, and plunk, plunk, plunk, in went the marbles. She then went straight on with the lesson. There were no more marble droppings after that.

Throughout the day at every break the kids were playing marbles. Hardly anyone was down on the main oval. It seemed that football was over and cricket hadn't started, so everyone was shooting marbles. I walked around watching the action. The main game they played was with the big ring that they called Ring Tawr. But there were other games, where they were dropping marbles and shooting them along the ground into holes. I couldn't really tell what the rules were. There were all kinds of marbles, some as big as a golf ball, and even some steel ones, which were really ball bearings. I heard kids talking about alleys, cats' eyes, and corkscrews and tigers and bumblebees and swirls—and all of them were called aggies. Each kid had a special marble to use as his taw.

After school Fred came over to our house with his marbles to teach me how to play. The best place was under the house in the dirt, where we drew as big a ring as we could between the house stumps. Fred showed me how to shoot, but try as hard as I might, I couldn't get the same force as he did, and if I hit another marble, which I usually didn't, it wasn't hard enough to knock it out of the ring. Obviously, there was a skill to playing this game, and I didn't have it. Nevertheless, I asked Mum to give me a shilling, and on the way to school next morning I bought some marbles at the comic shop on the corner of O'Keefe Street and Logan Road. Mum had given me a dilly bag to carry them in. When I tried playing my first game, most of the kids laughed at how clumsy I was, and before long I had lost most of the marbles I had bought. A few of the kids took pity on me, and gave me some of their own, the plain ones that they didn't like. No one wanted to part with their cats' eyes or bumblebees, with their beautiful swirling green and brown colours. I kept practising at home and gradually got a bit better, but I never became a good player. I think you have to start playing really young to do that.

At the Swimming Pool

Another thing you need to start young if you want to be good at it is swimming. Growing up on the farm, I had never learned how to swim. Now that it was summer I soon found out that I was as far behind the other kids in my class on this score as I was at shooting marbles.

The school had its own swimming pool. Imagine that. I'm not talking about the dirty smelly creek that ran around the boundary of the school on one side, but rather a real swimming pool filled with fresh clean water. At Athol we didn't even have a horse trough let alone a swimming pool. So I was impressed, but also a bit scared because I knew only too well that I didn't know how to swim, and at one end of the pool the water was 6 feet deep, way over my head, and even at the other end at 3 feet it was still deep enough to drown in. I well remembered the day we went to Helidon Spa and that bad man held me under the water in the shallow part of the big pool.

The pool at Buranda was not all that big—25 yards long by 5 yards across. It was tucked into a spot surrounded by trees and shrubs on the opposite side of the school from the parade ground. Now that it was summer we were to have our turn at going there as a class once or twice a week for a half hour or so during school time. Special instructors would be there to teach us, though sometimes Miss MacNish put on her blue swim suit to help, and she looked really smashing.

We would change into our swim togs in the change rooms and go to the pool by stepping through a tub of pink water called Condy's Crystals, then sit on the benches to wait our turn to get in the water. The first day I was really scared, and I told Miss MacNish that I didn't know how to swim. She said not to worry, that the instructors were there to teach me, and she would take special care to see that I was safe.

The instructors divided us up into different groups according to how good we were at swimming. Some of the boys were already good at freestyle, so they would be learning breaststroke or backstroke at the deep end. Others, not so good, would be practising freestyle by swimming across the pool half way down, and a few beginners like me were splashing around in the shallow end. They taught me how to kick by holding onto the side of the pool, then how to do a dead man's float with my face down in the water. I didn't like that very much, because the chlorine in the water stung my eyes and water got in my ears. Learning to dog paddle was better, because I could keep my head up out of the water. After a few lessons I was able to dog paddle all the way across the pool and felt pretty good about it.

One day as we were finishing the class I was walking along the edge of the pool up towards the deep end to get my towel, when a boy came flying past me from behind and knocked me into the water. I sank like a stone and all of my fears of drowning came flooding back. My mouth was open, and I took a couple of big mouthfuls before I had sense enough to shut it. My eyes were open, and I could see the side of the pool and the blue sky up above the surface even as I sank, and I could feel the cement bottom under my feet. I gave a push up with my legs all the while thrashing with my arms and kicking furiously. Just as I broke the surface I felt a pair of strong arms around me. One of the instructors had jumped in and had me out of the water and on the edge of the pool in no time at all. I sat there spluttering and coughing for a bit, and when I looked around I saw the class bully standing with another instructor looking very scared. Miss MacNish was kneeling beside me and she put her arms around me.

"It's all right, Des," she said. "Just sit here for a while until you feel better."

I heard the instructor tell the other boy that he was taking him to get dressed, and then he was going to the office for pushing me in the water.

"But I didn't mean to push him," the boy wailed, almost crying. I looked at the boy and could see he was really scared. Then I said as best as I could through my coughing and wheezing, "It wasn't his fault. It was an accident." The instructor looked at me and at the boy and seemed a bit uncertain. "Yeah, well you shouldn't have been running along the edge of the pool," he said to the boy. "There are rules about that." Then Miss MacNish helped me up and said to the instructor, "It's all right. I'll take both boys and look after it." The other boy didn't get sent to the office, and I had no trouble with bullying from him after that.

I Turn Ten and Get a Biro

About a week before my birthday in late October Dad came down from the farm in the ute. It was great to have him stay with us for a while. I told him all about what was going on with me at school, especially about how well I was doing at tennis. He was interested in everything, but said that life couldn't be all school and play, because I would need to look after the yard for Mum. I knew that things were a bit of a mess—the grass was growing long and the few flower beds were all covered in weeds. Dad had brought some tools with him, especially a reaping hook for cutting the long grass, and a lawn mower for keeping it short and under control.

Mr. Calder from next door had a scythe, so he came over, and the three of us hacked away at the long grass and stacked it up in a pile in the middle of the backyard. Fred was watching us from next door. He said the pile of grass would make a good start for a bonfire on Guy Fawkes Night.

"We'll all come over to your place with our crackers and stuff a guy with the grass and throw on some wood," he said. "It should be a beauty."

"Yeah, real bonzer," I said.

"You'll have to be careful of fire," said Dad. "All the more reason to get this grass cut short. You don't want any crackers setting off a fire."

On the farm we didn't have to worry about that so much, because we used to have our bonfire and crackers on the tennis court, and there was no worry about anything getting away, except perhaps for a skyrocket, but we always pointed them toward the lawn and they usually didn't go far anyway. I hadn't thought much about Guy Fawkes Night until Fred brought it up. It was still a couple of weeks away on the 5th of November, so we had plenty of time to get the yard cleaned up.

Dad had the first go at mowing with the lawn mower, because the grass was still pretty long and tough, and it was hard pushing the mower through that. It took Dad a couple of hours to go over the whole thing, and rake up all the long grass, and put it on the pile. Once the grass was short, I had a go with the mower. I could handle it all right, though it was still hard work.

Dad said we should also have a vegetable garden at the bottom of the yard, so he got to work with a long garden fork and dug up a few beds.

"This Brisbane soil is just terrible," he complained. "Hard as an old maid's heart, and full of clay." We got some horse manure from Newton's (they certainly had plenty) and dug it in, then planted some beans, peas, lettuce, potatoes and tomatoes.

"You're going to have to look after this," Dad said to me. "Keep it watered and pull out the weeds. Be careful you don't pull out the vegetables when they come up." I said I would. I hoped I would be able to tell the difference between the weeds and the vegetables.

The other thing Dad had brought with him was a pile of meat. He had killed a pig and butchered it up. I was sorry I hadn't been there for that. I remembered once before when he had killed a pig. He had scraped off all the hair on the skin with boiling water and a scraper, then strung the pig up by its front legs in the shower room under the high tank stand down at the house. Gloria had invited the girls from our closest neighbours, Thelma and Bonnie, to come and watch, and they had a couple of other girls from the city with them, who turned green when Dad slit open the pig's stomach and all the guts fell out.

I think Dad might have forgotten that we didn't have a big refrigerator like he did on the farm, just an ice box. That was another job I had if I was around when the iceman came. The men came along the street in a van with blocks of ice in the back of it. They were always going flat out, because the ice would be melting as they carried it into the houses with big ice tongs. Each block of ice was a pretty fair size, and they dumped it in a tin dish we left on the steps, and I would have to struggle to get the dish and the ice up the steps and into the kitchen where the ice box was, and then Mum and I would lift this big slippery cold block of ice into the top of the ice box.

But there wasn't that much room in the lower part of the ice box, so when Dad arrived with all this meat wrapped up in white butcher's paper, we couldn't fit it all in. We gave some away to Newton's and Calder's next door, and Newton's gave us a dozen pies in return, so that was a pretty good deal, and Dad got his first chance to try out the pies. He agreed with me that they were the best he ever tasted.

Dad stayed until my birthday on the 28th of October. I was ten years old. I had just a small party. I invited Fred and Rob from next door and Macker from school. Aunty Carrie and Aunty Evelyn also came, and they gave me the most interesting present of all. I wasn't quite sure what it was when I unwrapped it. It was in a small box and looked like a pencil.

"It's the latest thing," said Aunty Carrie.

"They say it will change the way we write," said Aunty Evelyn.

"It's a ball point pen."

"It's called a Biro."

"Try it out on a piece of paper."

"Write your name."

Through this patter from Aunty Evelyn and Aunty Carrie I figured out that I was the new owner of the latest thing in writing. I looked at it closely, and sure enough there was a tiny ball bearing on the end. I tried writing my name, and the pen flowed smoothly over the paper without digging in like a nib.

"It's like a fountain pen without a nib," said Mum.

"How do you fill it up with ink?" I asked. I was familiar with Mum's fountain pen, which had a little lever on the side that pressed against a bladder inside the pen that sucked up the ink. But this was just a smooth cylinder.

"You don't fill it," said Aunty Carrie. "When it runs out you throw away the inside part and buy a refill."

"Let me try," said Macker. He wrote his name. "Wow!" he said, "but I betcha Miss MacNish won't let you use it in school."

"Why not?" I asked.

"Because it's not a real pen, and it wobbles as you write," he said. "She won't even let you use a fountain pen."

"Well, it's a lot better than those scratchy old nibs," I said, "and you don't even need any blotting paper."

But he was right about Miss MacNish, because when I brought it in to show her she said, "Oh yes, I've heard about these things. But you can't use it in school. It will ruin your handwriting. You're just starting to write with ink, and you have to learn to do it properly. You can play with that at home. It's only a toy. People will never use those pens to write with."

Miss MacNish was usually right, but I wasn't sure about it this time. In any event I thought it was a really beaut present, and I put it with my special things at home.

Guy Fawkes Day

On the afternoon of Guy Fawkes Day, Fred and Rob came over to my place to help build up the bonfire and make a Guy. I had never done that before, and I didn't really know too much about it.

"Why do they call it Guy Fawkes Day?" I asked Fred.

"It's named after a cove called Guy Fawkes, who tried to blow up the Houses of Parliament in London in England a long time ago," he said. "It was called the gunpowder plot. That's why we set off firecrackers, because they're made with gunpowder. We stuff a Guy and burn him on top of the bonfire."

"Is that what happened to the real Guy Fawkes?" I asked.

"Nah, they probably hanged him in gaol. That's what they did in those days to people who tried to blow up the Houses of Parliament."

"I saw Boggo Road Gaol the day we arrived in Brisbane," I said. "Do they hang people in there?"

"Yeah, every morning before breakfast," said Fred.

"Really?" I asked.

"No, he's just pulling your leg," said Rob. "Come on, let's make the Guy."

We stuffed a sugar bag full of grass for the body, and a couple of Mum's old stockings for the legs, and two old long socks for the arms that we stitched onto the body. The head was another smaller bag, and Fred had an old hat to finish him off. We stuck a long stick up his bum and put him on top of the bonfire.

Dad had already gone back to the farm, but before he left he took me to a shop at Stone's Corner to buy crackers. There were all kinds: little ones in a string that would go off rat-a-tat-tat like a machine gun; big bungers that went off with a loud bang (you could put them under a tin can and blow it sky high); Catherine reels that you stuck on a post so they could spin round and round; Jumping Jacks that would go jumping all over the place with every bang; Roman candles that gushed out like a water fall; and sky rockets on sticks that you stuck in a bottle and lit for blast off. Dad bought a few of each kind, and warned me again to be careful.

It was a nice night, not too hot, and after tea we set up a few chairs in the backyard, and waited for it to get dark. Fred and Rob came over, and we pooled our crackers so we had a good pile. Mrs. Calder came over to sit with Mum, and Mr. Calder and Les watched from over their fence. Norma came over with Fred and Rob to keep an eye on her brothers. Mr. and Mrs. Newton watched from their back verandah.

We had the water hose hooked up and on the ready in case we needed it, and a few wet bags like we used on the farm to control a burn.

"It's really silly to be playing with crackers and lighting fires at this time of year in Brisbane," Mrs. Calder said. "Every year the fire brigade has to rush around putting out fires."

"Those silly buggers on Council are too stupid to ban it," said Mr. Calder from across the fence. "They shoulda put a stop to it years ago."

"Well, we're going to be very careful, aren't we, boys," said Mum.

"Yeah, no worries," said Rob. "You've got a good big yard and no long grass. This'll be the best cracker night we've had in years."

It was getting dark and already we could hear crackers going off from houses all around, and every now and then a rocket would streak across the sky. We started off with the small stuff. We lit a few small crackers and threw them up in the air. I helped Val light some Catherine reels that we had hooked up to the clothes line so they would go spinning across the yard. Everyone clapped at that. We had a line of tin cans with big bungers on the ready. You had to do it just right, because if you lit the fuse and plonked the can over the cracker too soon the fuse would go out and nothing would happen. On the other hand, if you left it too late, the cracker could go off just as you were putting the can over it, and that would give you one hell of a fright. After a while we got smart and punched a hole in the bottom of the can, so it couldn't snuff out the fuse. We had the sky rockets all pointing straight up in beer bottles that Fred's Dad had given us. That way they fell back to the ground in our yard, so we didn't have to worry about upsetting the neighbours.

Finally, it came time to light the bonfire. Once it got going we tossed our remaining crackers into it, so they were going off bang, bang, bang as the flames reached up higher to the Guy sitting on his pole at the top. We had stuffed him with bungers and Catherine reels and Roman candles, so as the flames set them off there was quite a show of whiz banging explosions. The glow from the fire lit up the whole yard so it was almost as light as day. Our Guy was at the top, dancing around on the end of his pole. Just as it reached its brightest we heard fire engines roaring along the street not far away, and we thought for sure they were coming to us, but they just kept on going as we sat there watching the bonfire burn down, our crackers all gone, and feeling pretty pleased with ourselves about the show we had put on. Mum served up some cold cordial and passed around a few ice-cream buckets, and after that we called it a night.

Next morning there were all kinds of reports in the paper and on the radio about fires that got out of control, and boys who got burned by holding the fire crackers in their hands as they went off.

"Every bloody year it's the same," said Mr. Calder when I saw him over the fence. "When will those silly yobs on Council get their heads out of their bums and do somethin' about it?"

I suppose he was right, but I think he enjoyed our Guy Fawkes show all the same. I thought we had done pretty good. It was certainly the best Guy Fawkes Night I could remember.

Books, Comics and Films

One of the things that pleased and surprised me about Buranda School was the library. Coming from Athol School, I had no idea what a school library was like. We had our Queensland School Readers, but apart from that just a few books on a shelf on the back wall. At Buranda they had a whole classroom full of bookshelves filled from top to bottom with books of all kinds. The library was on the lower level at the far end of the school next to Miss MacCallum's Grade 2 classroom. You didn't want to make too much noise going to the library or Miss MacCallum would straighten you out.

You could go down to the library at lunch time and borrow a book to take out. Each book had a card in it, which you would take to get stamped with the date you had to bring it back, and the card would be put under your name in your class box of cards. Different teachers took turns in looking after the library, and there were Grade 7 monitors to help. Miss MacNish was always talking about how important it was to read books and go to the library, so I went down one day when she was there, and she showed me around. I had never seen so many books in one place before.

I borrowed a few books, but I didn't really get into serious reading until Fred told me about the William books and the Biggles books. The William books were about this eleven-year old English boy called William Brown, who lived in a village in the English countryside. He was always getting into and out of trouble with his friends, who were called the Outlaws. He had an older brother and sister, like me, but they were a lot older. Ethel, the sister, was a good looker, and she always had boys chasing after her, which didn't make much sense to William, because she was always mean to him. Robert, the brother, was always trying to get a new girl friend, but William usually got in the way and messed things up.

There were a lot of different William books, and as soon as I read one I would take it back and get another. Each book was made up of different stories about what William and his friends would get up to. Some of them were set in war time in England, and usually involved some kind of a mix up or misunderstanding, like putting up wrong road signs or changing home names to confuse the Germans if they were to come to the village, but, of course, that caused a lot of problems for the people who lived there. William got into scrapes, but always managed to come out all right in the end, and often got some kind of reward. They were really good stories.

Biggles was a fighter pilot in the war against Germany, but with his friends Algy, Ginger and Bertie he also had adventures all over the world. He got shot down behind enemy lines, but always managed to escape, often by pretending to be a German searching for this pest Bigglesworth, who was really himself. The stories were full of adventure and suspense, and, like the William books, I would read one and right away take out another one. They were written by Capt. W.E. Johns, who knew a lot about war and flying because he was a fighter pilot himself.

As well as books from the school library, I loved to read comics. My favourite comic shop was on the corner of O'Keefe Street and Logan Road on the way to school. Most comics would cost sixpence, so I could get one a week and, of course, we shared our comics at school, so there were always a lot to read. My favourite comic heroes were the Phantom and the Lone Avenger. The Phantom always wore a mask over his eyes and had a skull ring so he could leave his mark. You could send away to get a skull ring of your own, so I did that, and no one would want to mix with me when I was wearing my skull ring. The Lone

Avenger was a cowboy who rounded up outlaws. He also wore a mask like a hanky over his mouth and nose so no one knew who he was.

My other favourite comic was "Classics Illustrated." This was a good way to read some of the world's great stories without having to read the book, which usually was a bit hard for me. There were stories like *Gulliver's Travels*, *Huckleberry Finn*, *Robinson Crusoe*, *The Three Musketeers*, *Robin Hood*, *A Tale of Two Cities*, and on and on. After reading the comic I would sometimes look for the real book in the library, like *Kidnapped* by Robert Louis Stevenson.

We were also lucky to have a new school theatre, which was a room downstairs at the opposite end of the school from the library under one of the Grade 7 classrooms. The windows had dark curtains over them, so you could make it really dark in there. There was a small screen and a projector with big reels on each end. I think it was 16 mm, not like the big 35 mm that you saw in real theatres, but it was still pretty good. When the Grade Fours went down there to watch a film, the other Grade 4 teacher, Mr. Hennessy, would work the projector. He had to thread the film around all these rollers, and he was pretty good at it, but sometimes the film would break, and he had to fix it, and all the kids would groan until Miss MacNish turned the lights on. Then we would shut up, because no one wanted to get sent up to the office to get the cuts.

We saw a lot of interesting films about subjects we were studying in class, and sometimes on a Friday afternoon we would get a special treat and see a story film like "Treasure Island" or something like that.

But much more fun than the school film was to go to the Saturday afternoon matinees at the real theatres. We were lucky where we lived that we had two theatres we could walk to. One was the Boomerang Theatre on Ipswich Road. It was called the Boomerang because it had a big boomerang sign across the top of the entrance. You came in at the front where the screen was and walked up a rise to the seats. The best ones were the canvas chairs down the middle, right in front of the screen. You would sit two to a chair, which is why going to the pictures was so popular with the older boys, who would take their girlfriends into the canvas seats to smooch while the film was on. They were pretty strict at the Boomerang and didn't let anything get out of hand, because the ushers would prowl around with their torches, and shine them right on you. The Alhambra Theatre at Stone's Corner was not so strict, and all kinds of things would go on in the canvas seats there.

But us younger kids were not interested in smooching. We went for the show, which always had a cartoon, a newsreel and a serial, as well as the main film. Serials like "Tarzan the Ape Man" and "Flash Gordon" were terrific because they would always end with the hero in big trouble with no possible way of escape, until you would come back the next week and find out how he did it. The best cartoons were "Tom and Jerry" and "Donald Duck" and the best cowboy heroes were Hopalong Cassidy, Tom Mix and Roy Rogers. Other good pictures were "The Adventures of Robin Hood" with Errol Flynn and any Abbot and Costello film.

Compared to the things I could do on the farm, I had to admit that moving to the city gave me a chance to do a lot of things I had never done before. I still missed the farm life and my old friend, Jim, and riding around on Blackie, but certainly I was finding a lot of other things to do and learn, so I suppose, all in all, the move to the city was not so bad. It would still be good, though, when the school holidays came and we could all go home to the farm for Christmas.

Cricket and Boxing Gloves

Now that the cricket season had come at school, I thought I should have a crack at that. But it wasn't like walking onto the tennis court and showing what I could do. We never played cricket at Athol the way these boys played it at Buranda. First of all, they had a cement wicket pitch, and they used a real cricket ball that was hard as a rock, so if you got hit with it, you really knew it. The batters wore leg pads that came up above their knees to protect their shins. Another boy would stand behind the stumps as wicket keeper. As well as pads he wore big gloves to catch the ball if the batter missed. They even had small pieces of wood called bails, which sat on top of the three stumps, and the rule was that if the bails came off the batter was out. There were various ways the bails could come off: the bowler could get one past the batter and hit the stumps; the wicket keeper could grab a loose ball and whip the bails off with it, and if the batter was out of his crease he was out; a fielder could throw the ball and hit the stumps if the batter was out of his crease; or the batter, if he was stupid enough, could back up and knock the bails off himself with his bat.

Then there were the bowlers—two kinds, fast and slow. Some of the taller boys were really fast bowlers. They would take a long run-up going flat out, then let the ball fly over-arm aiming at the stumps at the other end of the pitch. They could make the ball bounce so the batter had to duck or it would take his head off, or they could skid the ball along the ground right under the batter's feet. Of course, the batter was trying to hit the ball to get a run, but that wasn't so easy to do when the ball was coming at you faster than a train. The other kind of bowler was the slow one, who took only a short run-up, but he could put a spin on the ball, so the batter couldn't be sure what it was going to do when it came off the pitch at his feet.

I watched all this for many days during lunch hour and had various kids explain to me what was going on. They laughed when I told them we used to play cricket with a tennis ball at Athol and bowl from both ends of the pitch. They said that the same bowler had to bowl eight balls from the same end and that was called an "over." They also told me about positions in the field, like slips, square leg, and silly mid off.

There wasn't time to play a game during the lunch hour, because it takes a long time to play a game of cricket, like four days in a test match between Australia and England or the West Indies. So kids were just practising at batting or bowling, and others were out in the field. The older kids mainly got to run things, and we younger ones kind of looked on. Because there was only one pitch we had to share the time among the different grades on different days.

I finally got my chance to try one day when the Grade Fours had the pitch. I first tried my hand at bowling. I couldn't bowl fast, and I wasn't much good at slow bowling either at first, and the batter just belted my short lobs way out to the boundary. However, after a while I got the hang of it, and I managed to bowl a few good length balls. One got past the batter and took out the stumps. All the fielders yelled "Ow zat?"(which is what you yell to the umpire, who tells the batter if he's out). We didn't have umpires for these practice games, because it was always pretty clear if the batter was out or not.

When I got my turn to bat, I needed some help to put on the pads, and I felt a bit like a duck as I waddled out to bat. No one really showed me how to bat properly, so I copied what I had seen the other kids doing, but I really had no idea what that ball was going to do as it came whizzing down at me. I took a swing and, of course, missed, and the ball went past, but didn't hit the stumps. After a couple of balls like that I heard someone yell, "What's up, Grasshopper? Did you forget to wear your glasses?"

The wicket keeper behind me said, "Keep your bat straight and see if you can block it." So I tried that and caught an edge so that the ball flew off through slips and everyone yelled, "Run!" So I ran up to the other end of the pitch, and the other batter came down to my end. He hit a run, which brought me back to face the bowler again, and this time he bowled me clean out. I walked back to the edge of the field. As I took off the pads I thought to myself that I should best stick to tennis.

I was certainly having my share of new experiences at Buranda. Another one was seeing how they handled a fight. I don't remember anyone ever fighting at Athol, but at Buranda there were small fights going on all the time. Many of them were started by bullies trying to throw their weight around, but there were also arguments of all kinds about everything, which would lead to pushing and shoving and remarks like, "Who says so, Dickhead?" and "Who are you calling a Dickhead?" and "Do you see anyone else around here, Dickhead?" and "Take that back or I'll knock your block off!" and "You couldn't knock a fly off your own nose!" and "I'll knock one off yours!", "Yeah?", "Yeah!", "Well just you try it."

This would usually lead to a few swings, and then other boys would break it up. But every now and then a real ding-dong fight would break out, and the two boys would go at each other full bore. The other kids would gather round in a circle and yell things like "Sock it to him!", "Put in the boot!", "Give him one in the knackers!", and such like. After a bit the teacher on playground duty would come over and force his way through the crowd and grab the two fighters by the scruff of the neck. Sometimes that might be the end of it, but sometimes the teacher would say, "You want to fight? Then bring out the gloves." That was the signal for someone to rush off to the office to get the boxing gloves. Back he would come with these real boxing gloves, and the teacher would tell the boys to "Put 'em on," and then they would pound away at each other, with the teacher acting as referee. By now with the whole school would be crowding around, trying to get a look, everyone yelling at the top of their lungs. After a few minutes the teacher would step in, grab each boy by the wrists, and hold up their hands with the gloves on, and declare it a draw, and tell everyone to get out of there, and that was the end of it.

The first time I saw this I thought it was a pretty good way of settling a fight. I also thought it was probably a good idea to know how to box, so I decided to ask Mum to get me a pair of boxing gloves for Christmas. She wasn't too keen about it, but I hoped she understood that I needed to know how to defend myself in a school of boys.

I Finish Grade 4 in Good Shape

It was December and we were coming to the end of the school year, and the last days of my time in Grade 4 at Buranda. We had an end of year exam in all subjects to see who was going on to Grade 5 and if anyone was going to be held back to repeat Grade 4. The exam would also determine where we sat at the start of Grade 5 according to how well we did. The boys with the highest marks would sit in order in the back row, and you would work your way down from there to the front, until you got to the bottom of the class.

I had been sitting in the front row all the time I was in Grade 4, because that was where Miss MacNish had put me when I first arrived. I didn't mind it at first, because I knew I had a lot to catch up, but after a while when I began to figure out how things worked, I was determined to do well in the exam, so that I would not be in the front row in Grade 5.

By the end of the year I had pretty well caught up in geography and history, so I could answer those questions all right. Arithmetic still gave me some trouble, because I had missed some steps along the way, but I still did well enough. My favourite subject was English, especially reading the stories and poems in the Grade 4 Reader and answering questions about them.

One question asked us to pick the story you liked best and retell it in your own words. I wrote about "The Drover's Wife" by Henry Lawson, which told about a mother and her four "ragged, dried-up looking children," who were left alone in a bark hut in the bush, because her husband had gone off droving. A snake got under the floor boards, and the mother had to sit up all night watching in case it came out and bit one of the children. They had "a big black yellow-eyed dog" called Alligator, who broke his chain trying to grab the snake before it got under the floorboards. All night the mother and the dog sat watching by the fire, until just before dawn the hair on the back of Alligator's neck began to bristle. "An evil pair of small, bead-like eyes" glistened at a hole near the wall and the black snake came inching out. Slowly he crawled out as the mother and the dog watched, then Alligator sprang, and his jaws came together with a snap. He missed, and the snake was getting away, down another hole, but the dog lunged again, and got the snake by the tail and dragged it out. The mother thumped it with her stick, thud, thud. Alligator pulled the snake all the way out. He was five feet long. The dog grabbed the snake by the back of the neck. Tommy, the oldest boy woke up, grabbed his stick and tried to whack the snake, but his mother forced him back as she clubbed the snake thud, thud with her own stick, while Alligator tossed him around. The snake was dead, and the mother picked up the mangled mess on the end of her stick and threw it in the fire. She was sobbing with tears filling her eyes, and Tommy threw his arms around her and said: "Mother, I never will go droving; no, I never will." He was young, probably about my own age, but he knew how hard it was for his mother to be there alone without his father, just as I knew Mum must feel lonely without Dad, though luckily we didn't have any snakes crawling around our house.

Miss MacNish liked what I wrote about this great story and gave me a high mark. When all the marks were added up, would you believe, I came sixth in the whole class with 80%. I could hardly believe it. Miss MacNish said she was very proud of me, and she gave me a good report card to take home to Mum.

I felt very pleased with myself. It had been a hard few months for me trying to settle in at school and helping Mum at home. But I had shown everyone I was a good tennis player, and now I had come near the top of the class in the final Grade 4 exam. Now we could all go home for the holidays to the farm.

Fred Comes Home to the Farm for the Holidays

Dad came down in the ute to take us home. We packed everything we needed into the back and closed up the house. Mr. Calder and Les said they would look after the yard and the garden while we were away. I told them to take whatever vegetables they wanted from the garden. They hadn't done very well, even though I had tried my best to look after them. There were too many bugs and grubs, and I didn't know what to do to control them. Dad said not to worry, because he had a good garden on the farm, and there was always Grandfather's great garden in Toowoomba.

Val was really excited to be going back to the farm for the holidays. She had settled in all right at her school and seemed to be learning some things. One thing that worried Mum was that she was learning sign language, because most of the other kids couldn't speak at all, and this was the way they talked to each other. This meant that Val wasn't getting enough practice at speaking, even though she now had a good hearing aid. We all said we would try to give her a lot of practice over the holidays.

Fred said he wanted to go to the farm for part of the holidays, so his mother said he could come with us until after Christmas, and then return to Brisbane on the train. So we all piled into the ute, Fred and me in the back and Val up front with Mum and Dad.

"This is terrific," said Fred as we rattled out along Ipswich Road.

"Yeah and we've only just started," I said.

"How long does it take?" he asked for the umpteenth time.

"Oh, hours and hours," I said.

"Yaay!" Fred yelled as we passed a broken down old jalopy with two kids and a big black dog in the back. The kids gave us the finger, but I just waved back. There was no need to be rude when life was so good.

We stopped at our usual place half way to Toowoomba for hot pies and a pee. Fred said the pies were all right, but not as good as his Dad's.

"Yeah, your Dad makes the best pies in the world," I said.

"Will we be there soon?" Fred asked.

"I told you it takes hours," I said. "When we start going up the Range, then we're getting close."

"What's the Range?"

"It's the mountains. We have to get to the top of the mountains to get to the farm." I thought to myself that Fred might be a smart city boy, but he didn't know much about anything outside Brisbane. When we did start to wind our way up the Range, his eyes were fairly bulging out of his head as he saw the big drop off over the side.

We stopped at Granny and Grandfather's place in Toowoomba. They were really pleased to see us after such a long time. Fred was amazed at Grandfather's garden, and we loaded up with vegetables to take with us. Finally, we came along the last stretch of gravel road to the farm.

"There it is!" I yelled excitedly to Fred. The house with its beautiful red tile roof was clearly in view. "That's our place and Dad owns all the land as far as you can see." Fred said nothing, but his mouth was wide open with astonishment. He had never seen anything like this, and I was pleased and proud to show it to him.

It was really great to be home. Gloria rushed out to greet us, and we all laughed and hugged. She was surprised to see Fred, but I could tell she liked him right away. Gordon was there, looking very grown up in his big rubber boots, ready to go up to the bails to do the milking. We quickly unloaded, and Dad got changed into his work clothes to help Gordon with the milking. I took Fred up a bit later on to see the cows and how the milking was done. He didn't want to get too close to any of the animals. He said he wasn't afraid, but I think he was scared stiff. For me, it was like I had never been away, and I just soaked up the smell of the cows and the milk, and the steady beat of the milking engine, and the sight of everything neatly ordered from the house and tennis court to the machinery shed and all the paddocks, with their ploughed ground and green cultivation on both sides of the long lane stretching away into the distance as far as you could see.

"Come on," I said to Fred. "Let's find the horses."

We didn't have far to go. The ponies were all together in the grass paddock next to the house—Blackie, Patsy and Larry.

"Oh, my God," I cried, when I saw how fat Blackie was.

"Is she going to have a baby?" Fred asked, who thought he knew something about such things.

"Not likely," I said. "It's a he. He's my horse, Blackie. He's just fat because he's been mooching around here eating with no one to ride him and give him proper exercise." I went towards the horses with Fred hanging back behind.

"Hello, Blackie," I called. "Look, it's me. I've come back for the holidays."

Blackie lifted his head from feeding, pricked his ears, and stared at me. I held out my hand, walking towards him. He snorted, tossed his head, stamped his foot and backed off a few paces.

"Come on, old boy," I said. "You know who I am." He then stayed his ground and let me come up and put my arms around his neck. I looked around for Fred. He was lagging back a bit, but he came up and rubbed Blackie's nose. He wasn't so scared of horses because he knew about them from the pie carts.

"Tomorrow we'll catch them and go for a ride," I said. I patted Blackie on the rump and he trotted off.

"Wow, look at that big codger!" Fred exclaimed. I looked to see where he was pointing and saw Plum, our big draught horse, coming out from behind some trees.

"That's Plum," I said. "He's a draught horse. We put him in the cart or dray to pull heavy loads. Dad has a horse, too, the big stallion. He's probably over in the horse yard by the barn." We went to take a look, and sure enough there he was. Fred was clearly impressed.

"Wow, he looks like a race horse," he said.

"Yeah, he's really fast and strong," I said. "Dad is the only one who can ride him."

After that we took a look at the chooks, but they were already up on their perches ready for sleep. Jim, the cattle dog, joined us, and he jumped all over me, and went with us while I took Fred to show him the pigs.

It was so good to be back on the farm again, and to be able to show it all to my new friend from the city. Of course, I could hardly wait to see my old friend, Jim, to find out what he was up to, and to tell him my story of life in Brisbane. But all of that would have to keep until tomorrow. Tonight, we were going to have what you call a big family reunion, and we would all be around the big table again. It was good to be home.

I Learn the Facts of Life in an Unusual Way

Next day I took Fred with me to go up to Jim's place. We were just coming out of the trees in our hill paddock when I saw Jim near his house across the road.

"Jim! Jim!" I yelled. "I'm home for the holidays."

Jim started running toward us. I climbed through the fence and sprinted across the road to meet him at his gate. We stopped dead in our tracks, just staring at each other.

"Ow yer goin?" Jim said.

"Not bad," I said. "How about you?"

"Not bad," he said, then added, looking at Fred, "who's your mate?" Fred had come across the road slowly behind me.

"This is Fred," I said. "He lives next door to us in Brisbane. His Dad makes pies. Fred, this is Jim."

"G'day, Jim," said Fred.

"Pies?" Jim asked. "Real meat pies?"

"Too right," I said. "Best in the world. They've got horses and pie carts."

Jim thought about that for a bit, then asked, "So what's it like living in the city?"

"It's all right," I said. "I get to play a lot of tennis and go to the pictures every week."

"Really?" said Jim. "What about school?"

"It's a bit tough," I said. "They give you the cuts for just about everything."

"What's the cuts?" asked Jim.

"Whacks with a big cane," said Fred, "three feet long and thick as a sausage. Hurts like hell."

"That don't sound too good," said Jim.

"No, but I haven't got them yet," I said. "I had a nice teacher. She never sent me to the office. I came sixth in the class in exams."

"Out of how many?" Jim asked.

"Oh, about thirty."

"Crikey. Thirty in one class?"

"Yeah, and there's two classes in each grade."

I could see Jim couldn't understand how a school could be so big, so we dropped the subject, and Jim took us to show Fred around their farm. Because Fred was there, Jim and I couldn't play the way we used to, but Jim seemed to enjoy showing Fred around. I told him I would come back after Christmas, and we could go shooting.

We arrived back at my place just as the cows were coming into the yard for milking. Fred took a special interest in Dad's big stud bull. He had a ring in his nose for leading him around if you took him to a show for judging. But that wasn't what attracted Fred. He saw that the bull was paying special attention to one cow that was making low mooing noises and turning her rear end towards the bull. All of the cows, and the bull, too, went into the yard, and Gordon shut the gate. All of a sudden the great big bull reared up on his hind legs and kind of half climbed onto the back of the cow he was favouring. I had seen this many times, but Fred never had. The bull's great long red cock came out, and he shoved it into the cow's hole, and humped her around the yard, while the other cows scattered to get out of their way.

"Wowee! Will you look at that!" Fred yelled. "He's fucking her."

I knew that was what you called it, but we didn't use that word much around the farm. Mum had told me it was a rude word, but I knew some kids used it a lot at school. I think this was the first time Fred had ever seen what it really meant. He was absolutely fascinated, so we climbed up on the rails to get a better look. When the bull was finished he got down, and the cow kind of nuzzled up against him licking his shoulder. Fred just hung onto the rails staring like he never wanted it to end. Finally, we slid down off the rails and sat on the ground at the bottom.

"Did you see what he was doing?" Fred asked.

"Course," I said. "That's what bulls do."

"Not just bulls," Fred said.

"Yeah, I know, horses and dogs, too. I've seen them."

"I didn't mean that."

"What are you talking about?"

"People."

"What d'ya mean, people?"

"People—men and women. They do that, too."

I was dumbfounded.

"No? You're pulling my leg."

Fred looked right in my eyes. He was two years older than me in Grade 6. Maybe he knew something I didn't.

"Why d'ya think animals do it?" Fred asked.

"Dad says it's the way they make babies," I said. "I've seen the way a baby calf comes out of its mother."

"You have?" Now Fred was impressed, but then he dropped a bombshell. "It's the same with people babies."

I stared at him. "Go on," I said. "Now you're pulling both legs."

"It's true," said Fred. "I've seen pictures in books."

"Did your Mum tell you that?"

"No. She won't talk about it. But Rob knows it's true."

We stared at each other in silence. Then I had a thought that blew Fred's idea to smithereens.

"Can you imagine your Mum and Dad doing—that?" I asked. Fred's mother was a really big woman, and his Dad was short and skinny. Fred screwed up his face. I had got him with that one.

"Yeah, well I've thought about that," he mumbled. "I can't picture it, but it must be true. Your Mum and Dad, too."

That was enough. I didn't want to talk about it any more. I got up and started to run toward the house.

"Come on," I yelled back at Fred. "We have to feed the chooks."

And that was the last time we talked about that.

Another Christmas on the Farm

It was great to be home on the farm for Christmas. It was going to be like old times. Granny, Grandfather and Aunty Holly were coming out from Toowoomba. Dad drove in the day before to bring them out to stay. Fred and I went in with him, and rode home with Aunty Holly in the back of the ute. I told her I hoped to get boxing gloves for Christmas. She must have told Granny, because later on Granny took me aside and said she wanted to talk to me.

"Why do you want boxing gloves for Christmas?" she asked.

"Because some kids at school like to pick fights," I said, "and when they bring out the boxing gloves I want to be able to knock any bully's block off."

"That's no way to talk," said Granny. "I don't want you fighting."

"I don't start it," I protested.

"If someone else starts it, you should turn the other cheek," said Granny.

"What's that mean?" I asked.

"It means you should turn away and not fight back. Jesus said that."

"Yeah, well he never went to Buranda."

"Don't try to be funny."

"I'm not. But you just don't know what it's like in a boys' school."

That was the end of that conversation. Next morning on Christmas Day when I looked in the pillow case at the end of my bed, there were the gloves. They were beauties—big, black bruisers that felt so good when I put them on. Fred was sharing the bedroom with me, sleeping in Gordon's bed, and he looked drowsily out from under the sheet.

"Lookit, Fred," I said, "I got my gloves."

"Beauty," he said, "but who you gonna box with? You've only got one pair."

"No problem," I said. "There's an instruction book. I can shadow box and practice my footwork."

We checked Fred's pillow case. He got a 500 piece jigsaw puzzle. Mum had given us great presents—just as good as when I was a little kid and believed in Father Christmas. The girls did all right, too—dolls and dresses and that kind of girl stuff. Gordon got some nice clothes, but I think I did best of all with my boxing gloves.

Uncle Ralph, Aunty Milly and Dawn came over for Christmas dinner as well as Uncle Henry and Aunty Eileen. It was the usual great blowout—roast chook, thick slabs of ham, roast potatoes and pumpkin, and all kinds of other vegetables, followed by Mum's great Christmas pudding with white sauce and home made ice-cream. Fred said he had never seen such a feast. I told him this was what we did every Christmas, and we hadn't even got to the watermelon yet.

Before dinner Fred had helped me water and roll the tennis court. We hit a few balls around, but Fred wasn't much of a player. The serious tennis didn't start until about an hour after we finished dinner, so that the food had a chance to settle. We played mostly doubles: first me and Gordon against Dad and Uncle Ralph. They made us work hard for it, but in the end we won 6-4. Dad and Uncle Ralph were surprised to see how much my game had improved since I went to the city. The ladies played a game of doubles, then we played mixed doubles. It was a pretty hot day, so we were all happy enough after that to sit on the lawn in the shade of the house and eat thick slices of juicy red watermelon from Dad's garden. I was glad that some things never change.

When the visitors had gone home and Dad and Gordon were doing the milking, I finally got my chance to practise properly with my boxing gloves. Fred helped me by reading the instruction book aloud, while I got into the proper stance and pranced about doing my footwork.

"Lead with yer left," Fred shouted, as I danced around on the lawn, shadow boxing. "Keep yer guard up. Bob and weave. Now sock him with your right."

I soon worked up quite a sweat. At one point Granny and Grandfather came out to take a look.

"See, Granny," I said, as I danced around her, but kept my distance, "boxing is just a sport like tennis."

Grandfather put up his fists and shuffled towards me. He pretended to spar with me.

"Look out for my right cross," he shouted, as he swung his right fist.

"Aagh," I groaned and fell flat on my back, pretending to be knocked out.

"Ted! Don't you encourage him!" Granny complained at Grandfather.

"Aar, it's all right, Mum," he replied. "A boy's gotta learn to take care of himself."

Granny walked off in disgust, but Grandfather stuck around.

"Let me have a go," Fred asked, so I gave him the gloves, and I took over as the instructor with Grandfather adding his bit from time to time. Finally, Fred had had his fill.

"That's enough boxing," he said. "Let's wrestle."

I knew what was coming now. Fred liked to wrestle. He had shown me that more than a few times in our backyard in Brisbane. He was older and stronger than me, so he always managed to pin me. I didn't like wrestling all that much, but he had been a good sport in helping me with my boxing, so now I had to return the favour.

"Grandfather, you can be the referee," I said. "You have to check if one of us has both shoulders on the ground for a count of three, and that's a fall."

"Righto," he said. "Go to it."

The trouble with wrestling is getting started. Fred and I danced around each other until one of us made a grab and tried to get a hold. On the lawn, twisting and turning, he got me in a headlock, but I slipped out and tried to flip him, but no such luck, as he slithered free and somehow landed on top of me.

"One, two, three, Fall One," Grandfather shouted, kneeling to check that my shoulders were down, and pounding the ground on each count. We went at it again, over and over. Fred was winning two falls to one, and we locked into a full embrace, with neither of us willing to give an inch, and Grandfather growing tired and cranky from squatting on the ground. Suddenly, I heard Dad's voice.

"What are you two twerps up to?"

But we didn't reply, still locked in our holds.

"They've been like that for ten minutes," Grandfather said. "Both too stubborn to give in."

Out of the corner of my eye I saw Gordon circling around us.

"Maybe a bucket of cold water would sort them out," he said.

"Don't you dare," I yelled.

Fred let go his hold a bit, and I pinned him.

"I think we'll call it a draw," said Grandfather.

Fred and I got up rubbing our stiff arms and legs.

"Good match," said Grandfather. "You boys have got good spirit."

"Yeah," said Dad. "I like to see you're ready to have a go. Maybe tomorrow you can put some of that energy to good use pulling weeds out of the garden."

That's the way it was on the farm. Compliments on the one hand, then a backhand shot to keep you in your place. All in all, though, it was a pretty good Christmas Day.

Challenging the Crows

After Christmas Fred went back to Brisbane on the train, and I took out my air rifle and headed off for Jim's place. Soon we were out in the bush searching for prey. There were plenty of mickey birds and peewees around, but we didn't want to shoot them for no reason. We saw a flock of quarions and the bright splash of two rosella parrots high up in the trees, but we didn't bother them either. Two pair of top notch pigeons came whizzing in with the crisp tinkling sound of their wings giving them away. But the truth of the matter was that we didn't want to bag one of them either. We had our sights set on the five black crows we saw hanging out in the old dead tree on the edge of the bush down by one of Dad's cultivation paddocks.

The thing about crows is that they are crafty, mean beggars. They would steal eggs, attack chickens or kittens, and rip open a bag of grain and spill seed all over the place. And they always worked in small groups, where one or two would keep an eye out for danger, and the others would go in and do their mischief. I reckoned that the ones we saw in that old dead tree were the same ones that were always hanging around our house making a nuisance of themselves. Maybe if we could nail one of them they would get the message and keep away.

The problem is that it's almost impossible to shoot a crow with an air rifle. They can always tell if you're carrying a gun, and they'll never let you get close enough to have a shot. Still, we thought it might be worth a try.

"The thing you've got to do," I said to Jim, "is outsmart them."

"Yeah," he said, "think like a crow, distract them, then kapow!"

"That's right. They're perched up in that dead tree out in the open so they can see everything for a hundred yards in all directions. But they've made one mistake."

"What?"

"See that clump of bushes down by the fence. If one of us could sneak down there, then we'd have a pretty good chance of lining them up for a shot."

"Yeah, but they'd see you long before you got there."

"That's where we outsmart them. One of us has got to distract them, while the other sneaks up into position."

Jim thought for a moment. "Might work," he said. "You've got the best gun. Why don't you sneak up while I distract them."

We were still well back in the bush, so we were pretty sure the crows hadn't seen us yet. We split up. Jim took a wide swing so he would come out of the bush about 50 yards from the dead tree. I crept cautiously forward as far as I could but still be hidden by the trees. I lost sight of Jim, but then I heard him doing his decoy act.

"Well, well, what d'y'know?" he yelled. "Five dumb crows sitting in a tree. Lookit me, you black boneheads. You think you're so smart, dontcha? You think you can count. How many of me do you see? One. Yeah, well that's where you've got yer bird brains stuffed up each other's rear end. There's two of us, and the other one is sneaking up on you right now, and he'll blow yer head off. So you just keep lookin' at me. I'm such a pretty fellow. Kootchy, kootchy, coo! Wanna see me dance? One step, two step, three step, four. Five dumb crows, soon there'll be four."

Jim was putting on a great show, but I wished he wouldn't tell them about me. I wasn't sure they couldn't understand English. By now I was crawling on my stomach through some long grass along the fence and was almost up to the bushes. I didn't lift my head so I couldn't see either the crows or Jim, but I could clearly hear his wild caterwauling. Finally, I was in the bushes, and I parted them ever so slightly to take a look.

Jim was about 50 yards away. He had thrown his hat down on the ground, and was doing a wild dance around it like a deranged demon at a Corroboree. He was waving his arms and yodelling like a banshee from hell. I looked at the crows. They hadn't moved an inch and were just sitting there staring at Jim. It's working, I said to myself, as I gently parted the bushes and brought my rifle up. Good on ya, Jim. Just keep it up a bit longer. It was a long shot, but I might just do it. I brought the rifle sights onto one of the crows and held my breath for a shot. But I wasn't expecting what happened next.

Just as I was about to pull the trigger, the bushes in front of me erupted, and a hare leapt out, and took off through the grass. It scared the living daylights out of me.

"Holy smoke!" I cried as I jerked upwards and pulled the trigger. The gun went off with a bang, and the crows let out five raucous screams and took off as fast as I've ever seen crows fly.

"What the hell happened?" Jim yelled.

"Bloody hare," I yelled back. "Leapt right out of the bushes, just as I was about to fire."

"Damn!" said Jim. "I really had those buggers fooled, too."

"Yeah, you did a great job. You'd get a job in the circus any day."

"Yeah, and you're a pretty good clown, yourself."

And with that we both began to laugh, until the tears were streaming down our faces. It was probably the best outcome all round, because I'm sure we would never have laughed like that if I had actually shot a crow. I don't know if crows laugh, but I'm inclined to think they probably had a good story to tell their mates, about the day they escaped from two crazy kids and one mad hare.

I Say Good-Bye to Jim

After walking around in the bush for a couple of hours, Jim and I decided it was time for lunch. Jim's mother had packed us some Vegemite and peanut butter sandwiches, and I had brought my army issue water bottle that I had strung on my belt. It was pretty hot, so we sat down in the shade of a big old gum tree with its bluish grey bark peeling off in strips. I watched a green caterpillar crawling slowly up the tree, making his way carefully along a groove left by the peeling bark.

"Look at this fellow," I said to Jim. "D'ya think he'll ever reach the top?"

Jim squinted up towards the midday sun through the branches and the long thin leaves of the gum tree. He scratched the back of his head and picked a long blade of yellow grass to chew on.

"Depends," he said.

"On what?" I asked.

"On whether he gets picked off by a bird, or some kid carrying an air rifle."

"I wouldn't do that," I protested.

"Then that improves his chances a lot," said Jim. "At least for now. But if he was smart he'd hide under the bark till dark, so the birds don't see him."

"I think we're all like that caterpillar," I said. "Just mooching along through life until something comes along to pick you off."

"What is that supposed to mean?" asked Jim as he bit into a Vegemite sandwich.

"Well look at me," I said. "A year ago I was happily going along through life in Athol, then I got picked off and taken to Brisbane." I took a mouthful of my peanut butter sandwich.

"It's not the same thing," said Jim. "Nobody gobbled you up, and from what you tell me you don't seem to be doing too bad."

"Yeah, I s'pose it's all right," I said, handing Jim the water bottle, "but it makes you wonder what's gonna happen next to change things."

"Yeah, I know," Jim replied. He handed the water bottle back to me. "We might be movin' soon, too."

"What? You can't." I suddenly felt upset. "What for?"

"Dad's looking for another farm. So we might have to move."

"Then you won't be here when I come home for holidays?"

"Maybe not."

I think we both suddenly understood that this holiday might be the last time we'd have together. We sat silently for a while watching a procession of red ants going along a track towards their nest. I thought to myself that their life was probably pretty good, unless some kid poked at them with a stick. But I wasn't about to do that.

"Do you want to buy my bike?" Jim suddenly asked. "You could use a bike in the city, and I probably won't be needing it."

"Gosh, I never thought of that," I said, remembering the day I had learnt to ride his bike at his place. "But, you're right, I do need a bike. I'll have to ask Dad. It's a great idea. I might not be able to see you, but I'll have your bike to remember you."

Jim looked at me and nodded. "Yeah, that's right," he said.

I suddenly had another thought. "You should have something to remember me, and especially the day we had together. I'd give you my gun, but I've decided to take it to Brisbane to shoot sparrows. You know you can get threepence a head from the Council for them because they're such pests."

"Crikey, that sounds like a good deal. What d'ya do with the heads?"

"You put 'em in a jar with vinegar."

"Boy, pickled sparrow heads."

"Yeah, and I could make enough money to put a bell on your bike."

We both laughed at that, and I took a swig of water. Then I suddenly knew what to give Jim to remember me.

"Here, take my water bottle. Every time you swallow you can think of me." I handed him the bottle.

"Gee, thanks, mate," Jim said. "It'll be a good memory."

We finished eating our sandwiches, and it was time to go. Before we left, I checked to see how the caterpillar was doing. I couldn't see him at first, because he had taken Jim's advice and crawled into the shade under a strip of bark. I thought he would probably be all right, and maybe that was a good sign for me and Jim in our lives ahead.

I Set the Birds Free

When we went back to Brisbane at the end of the summer holidays in January 1949, there were two extra passengers in the back of Dad's ute: my sister, Gloria, and Jim's old bike, now my new bike. Gloria was coming to join Mum, Val and me and take her Grade 7 Scholarship Year at Buranda Girls' School. Gordon was finished with school. Couper Memorial School, where he had started high school last year, had closed down, so he would now be working full time with Dad on the farm. The two of them would be batching while Mum looked after the three of us kids and the home in Brisbane. I felt sorry for Gordon, because he was only 14, and though he was very grown up it would be hard for him to be on the farm without Mum to cook and look after the house. Of course, I also missed Dad, but this was the way it had to be so Val could go to her school.

As soon as we arrived at Carl Street Mrs. Calder was looking over the back fence wanting to talk. I don't think she got much conversation from Mr. Calder and Les, so she had saved it all up for us. She was very nice, but it was hard to get the ute unloaded and talk to her at the same time. We introduced her to Gloria, and that helped solve the problem as they could talk while the rest of us worked. Les had done a good job in looking after the main part of the yard, though the back end where the garden was had gone a bit wild. Dad said he and I would have to get to work on that tomorrow. But first things first. I unloaded my bike and yelled over the back fence for Fred to come and see.

He was there in a flash, with Rob coming along behind.

"Lookit what I got," I said. "Dad bought Jim's bike for me. I'll be able to ride it to school."

Fred and Rob climbed over the fence to take a look. Fred tried it out, riding around the yard a couple of times.

"Not bad," he said, "but it's only got one speed. You'll have to work hard on the hills."

"I didn't know there was any other kind," I said.

"It looks great," said Rob, but he wasn't looking at the bike. He had his eyes on Gloria.

"This is my sister, Gloria," I said. "She's gonna go to the girls' school. Gloria, this is Rob, Fred's brother." She, of course, knew Fred from his holiday on the farm.

"Ow yer goin'?" said Rob to Gloria.

"Pretty good," she said back.

Then they both went kind of quiet, until Mum called Gloria to come and help in the house.

"Gotta go, now," she said. "See ya later."

"Yeah, see ya later," said Rob, watching her go up the back steps.

"I brought my air rifle back from the farm," I said. "I'm gonna shoot some sparrows and take their heads into the Council."

"That's a good idea," said Fred. "But talking about birds, a couple of your finches kicked the bucket while you were away."

I went over to the big bird cage to take a look. I actually hadn't done a very good job at looking after the birds since we arrived last year and a few of them had died before Christmas. Now with two more gone, we were down to just four.

"I just don't think birds are meant to live in cages, no matter how big," I said. "These last few will probably die, too. Maybe I should just leave the door open and let them fly away."

"The cats will probably get them," said Rob.

"Yeah, there's a couple of big buggers that come prowlin' around," said Fred. "I think that's what killed the others. They panicked, even though they were safe in the cage, and just dropped dead."

That clinched it for me. "Well, if they're gonna drop dead inside the cage," I replied, "I might as well let them go, so they can at least fly away. I'll leave the door open in case they want to come back."

"Yeah, and the cats will get in and lie in wait," said Fred.

"I never thought of that," I said.

At that moment Gloria came back, so I asked her what she thought.

"Of course you should let them go," she said. "No one should live in a cage. Anyway, Mum says you've got to come in for tea now."

"Would you like some pies?" Rob asked Gloria.

"Too right," I said.

"He wasn't asking you," Gloria said to me, then to Rob she added with a smile, "That would be nice."

Rob vaulted over the back fence like an Olympic Champion and was back in a flash with a bag of pies. He handed them to Gloria.

"Thank you," she said and peeked inside the bag. "They smell delicious." Then to me she said, "Come on, Eddo. We're all waiting for you."

"See ya later," I said to Rob and Fred. "I'll ask Dad about the birds." When I did so while munching through a hot pie, he said, "Free is free. If you let them go, you can't worry about the cats. The birds are on their own. Anyway, you can't let them go at night. They're roosting now. Check it out in the morning, and if you still think it's the right thing to do, let them go. That old cage is an eyesore anyway. We can tear it down."

I got up early next morning, which was Sunday, the day before school started. I immediately checked on the birds. I saw right away that they were agitated, chirping at the top of their lungs and zipping from one end of the big cage to the other, back and forth, round and round, like a cat on an ants' nest. I went over to check it out, and a great big black tom cat leapt out from the small space under the cage. He must have been lying there peering up through a hole in the floor boards, and it was driving the birds nuts. I picked up a rock and threw it at him, as he took a flying leap over the back fence.

"Get outa here, you black bugger," I yelled at him. Then I opened the door of the bird cage. "All right, boys and girls, it's time to go." I stepped back to watch. After a bit one of the birds saw that the door was open and flew out. Right away the others followed. They circled round a bit then landed on the clothes line watching me.

"It's all right," I said to them. "You can take off to wherever you want to. Look, I'll put a dish of bird seed up here on the fence post and you can come back and have a feed whenever you want to."

Then I went inside the bird cage and carefully gathered up their nests. They were still sitting on the clothes line watching me. "Look, I'll put your nests in the mulberry tree," I said. "I know it's not too good, but it's the best I can do. You'll probably want to build some new ones when it's time for you to lay eggs and have babies."

They probably didn't have a clue what I was talking about, but at least I tried. After a bit they took off again and disappeared. When I came back to the house I saw Mr. Calder watching me from his back steps.

"What are you up to, young fella?" he asked.

"I just let my birds go," I said. "I set them free. Do you think they'll be all right?"

"Better than bein' cooped up in a cage," he said. "Now, no one can ever tell them what they have to do. They're better off than an old bugger like me who's stuck here with nowhere to go."

Free is free, as Dad said. Even Mr. Calder in his own weird way seemed to agree. I thought that might as well be the last word on the subject.

My New Friend Willy

The first day of school Mum and Val went with Gloria to get her enrolled at the girls' school on the hill above the boys' school. Dad decided he would come with me to have a look at Buranda Boys. We all walked together along with Fred and Rob. Rob actually wasn't going to school, because he finished last year. He was going to work on the pie carts for his Dad. I think he came with us just to walk with Gloria. I noticed that they hung back having a great conversation. I was glad they seemed to have already become good friends. When we crossed Logan Road at the school crossing, the girls and Mum went one way, and us boys and Dad the other.

I already knew which Grade 5 class I was going to be in. My teacher was Mr. Kimlin. He was a big man with a nice face and from what I had heard he was a good teacher, so I hoped for the best. On the way up to my new classroom, which was around the corner of the long verandah from the Grade Fours, we bumped into Miss MacNish. She looked as lovely as ever in her pretty summer dress.

"Hello, Des," she said with a big smile. "Ready for Grade 5? I hope you had a good holiday. Is this your Dad? I'm Miss MacNish."

"Ken Berghofer. Pleased to meet you," said Dad. "I thought I would drop in to see where Des went to school."

"That's nice of you," said Miss MacNish. "He's a good pupil. He'll do well in Grade 5. Who's your teacher, Des?"

"Mr. Kimlin," I said.

"Oh, you'll like him," she said.

"I wish you were still my teacher," I said.

"Why, that's sweet of you," she flashed her big smile and ruffled my curly hair with her soft hand. I was still hopelessly in love with her. "I must go now. Nice to meet you, Mr. Berghofer. Good-bye, Des," and she was off down the verandah, high heels tap-tap-tapping and hips swaying.

"Quite a dish," said Dad.

"You bet," I said.

By now we were at my new room. Boys were coming and going. Dad just stood in the doorway while I found my new place in the back row. Just as I was coming back out Mr. Kimlin arrived. He saw Dad and extended his hand.

"Kimlin," he said.

"Ken Berghofer," said Dad, shaking his hand. "I'm Des's Dad."

"Ah, yes," said Mr. Kimlin, giving me a friendly look. "We haven't met yet. You come from the country, don't you?"

"Yes," said Dad. "Just outside Toowoomba."

"My niece used to teach up that way," said Mr. Kimlin. "Dorothy Kimlin. Do you know her by any chance?"

"Well, what a small world," said Dad. "She married my nephew, Herbie Mauer. They've helped me on the farm quite a lot."

"Herbie's my favourite grown up cousin," I said, "and Dorothy is terrific."

We all had a bit of a laugh at that. Then the bell rang to line up for parade. Mr. Kimlin shook Dad's hand again and we went down the steps. I said good-bye to Dad who stood under the school for a bit watching us all line up, then when I looked again he was gone. I was still thinking about the coincidence of Mr. Kimlin being Dorothy's uncle. That must be a sign for a good year.

On parade, Mr. Merrell gave us the usual razz-ma-tazz about needing to smarten up and work hard and keep out of trouble. At least nobody got the cuts on the first day back. When we marched inside we all stood at attention in our new places, until Mr. Kimlin told us to sit down. Things looked a bit different from the back row, and I decided I liked it there and would work hard to keep my place, and even move up if I could. The first thing Mr. Kimlin did was call the roll, and he told each of us to stand so he could get to know us. Because my surname started with B I was one of the first to be called. I heard someone snicker "Grasshopper" from the front of the class, but Mr. Kimlin shut him up with a withering look. He nodded at me and told me to sit down and called the next name.

The first day of school went off all right. We got our Grade 5 Readers, which I was ready to read right away all the way through. We also got our Grade 5 copy books that we would be filling out in ink to improve our handwriting. We had to work with the scratchy old pens and nibs dipped into inkwells on our desks, and we each had a piece of blotting paper. I would have preferred to use my Biro pen that Aunty Evelyn and Aunty Carrie had given me for my birthday last year, but there was no chance of that. Mr. Kimlin said we would need to buy a special exercise book because we would soon be doing a page of writing called an "exercise" for homework once a week on different topics from geography and history. The idea was to do a perfect page of writing, no spelling mistakes, no crossing out, and no blots. I thought I was up for that.

The next day I rode my bike to school for the first time. Fred had a bike, but he didn't ride it to school, so I took off on my own. Fred walked in with Gloria. Rob couldn't go, because he was working in the pie shed. Gloria hadn't said much about her first day at school. I think she was a bit overwhelmed by how different it was from Athol, just as I had been on my first day. Mum said Val had settled in at her school all right, so we were all off to a good start.

It was fun going down the hill on O'Keefe Street on my bike, but I knew it would be tough coming back up. When I got to school, I parked my bike in the stands under the school. My friend Macker saw me arrive.

"Nice pair of wheels," he said.

"Yeah, I bought them from a friend in the country," I said.

"I didn't think you had bikes in the country," he said, "only horses."

"That's why he sold it to me. Now I have a bike in the city and a horse in the country."

Just then another boy from our class arrived. His name was Grant Williams, so we called him Willy. He had the flashiest bike you could imagine—mudguards, foot brakes, a soft leather seat, a rack on the back for carrying stuff, and even a headlight with a generator. His father was a dentist so he could afford all these gizmos.

"Glad to see you've joined the two-wheeled world," he said. "That's a nice bike."

"Thanks, but it's not as flash as yours," I replied.

"Looks pretty good to me," he said. "We should go for a ride."

"Yeah, sounds good."

I didn't know Willy very well. He didn't sit near me in class, and we hadn't talked much outside, but with the bikes we now had a common interest, so next day when we were leaving school he said to me, "Why don't we ride home together. Where do you live?"

"On Carl Street."

"That's just down the road from me. I live on Cornwall. Tell you what. Why dontcha come round to my place and afterwards I'll ride home with you. That way we don't have to go up O'Keefe Street. That hill's a killer."

We rode along Junction Street to Cornwall, then up the hill a bit to his home on the corner of Duke. It was a nice looking place with a white fence and neat garden out the front. We wheeled into the back off Duke Street and right in under the house. It was all cement, not dirt like ours, with an empty space for a car. There was a lot of other stuff under the house, but two things caught my eye: a ping pong table and what looked like a racing car made out of a wooden box with cast iron wheels and a cord tied to each end of the front axle to steer it. It was painted green and white with its name "Atom Gal" in black letters on the side and some kind of symbol like a spinning top. It was a beauty.

Willy also had a little black dog called Rex, who was barking like crazy and jumping all over us ever since we came in. He jumped in and out of another smaller box with straps and his name, Rex, printed on the side of it.

"Yeah, I know you wanta go for a ride," said Willy, "I'll take you in a bit, but not right now."

"You take him for a ride on your bike in that box?" I asked, trying to imagine what that would look like.

"Yeah, he loves it," said Willy. "Down, Rex, down! Come on up and meet Mum."

We went up the back steps and found his mother, Mrs. Williams, sitting round a table with a few of her lady friends playing cards. She was all dolled up with lots of makeup and red fingernails and a cigarette hanging out the side of her mouth as she shuffled the cards. Her friends all looked much the same, and each one had a glass of something I was sure wasn't soft drink sitting beside them.

"Hey, Mum," said Willy. "This is my new friend, Des. He comes from a farm."

"How nice," said Mrs. Williams, giving me a big smile and waving a hand full of cards at me. "There's chocolate cake and milk in the kitchen. Help yourselves. Now girls, let's get back to business."

Willy led me into the kitchen, opened up a big cake tin, and took out half a chocolate cake. It was made of two thick dark slabs with half an inch of chocolate icing joining them, and smothered with the same icing over the sides and on the top. Willie cut off two thick slices.

"See that?" he said. "I made that."

"You made the chocolate cake?" I gasped. I was really surprised.

"Yeah." He dropped his voice to a whisper. "Mum's not much of a cook. I always make the cake." He gave me a big glass of milk out of the fridge. Then I saw a photograph of a really pretty older girl.

"Who's that?" I asked.

"That's my sister, Judith. She's even more useless in the kitchen than Mum."

"She's a knockout," I said.

"Yeah, I s'pose so. All the boys think so, but she can't do anything useful."

After we finished the cake and milk I said I should be getting home or Mum would be worried about me.

"Why don't you phone her?" asked Willy.

"We don't have a phone," I said.

"Oh well, that takes care of that," he said. "All right, let's go. I'll come with you and give Rex a ride." He called to his mother as we went out the door. "I'm going round to Des's place for a bit."

"That's nice, dear," she said without looking up from her card game.

Rex went absolutely nuts as Willy strapped his box on the back of the bike. Then away we went with Rex sitting up like the little king he was, while the two of us pushed and grunted our way to the top of the hill, then zipped down along Carl Street to our place.

"Looks a bit the worse for wear," said Willy, as we came into the yard and he surveyed our old house.

"Yeah, but we've got a nice place on the farm," I said.

"Who lives there?" Willy asked, looking at the Newtons' tumbledown place next door. "You wouldn't want to drop a match in that lot."

"That's Newtons, you know, the pie people."

"You live next to the Newton boys and all those pies! Humdinger!" Now it was Willy's turn to be impressed.

We let Rex run loose in the yard, while I took Willy up the back steps to meet Mum. Gloria and Val were there, too. Dad had already gone back to the farm.

"G'day, Mrs. Bergh and Glor and Val," he said cheerily after I had introduced him. "Watcha got cookin'?" We could smell the delicious aroma coming from Mum's wood stove.

"Lamb stew," said Mum. "Would you like to stay for tea?"

"Boy, would I ever," said Willy.

"But your mother's probably expecting you home," Mum said.

"No worries about that," replied Willy. "She's in the middle of a card game. We'll have to look after ourselves. Can I help with the vegetables?"

"Yes," Gloria piped up, wanting to get out of a job. "You two can shell peas and peel potatoes on the verandah."

And that's what we did—at least, we started to do it. Willy looked out over our backyard and Newtons' horse stables. "You've got a regular jungle and zoo here," he said. "Look at Rex. I'll bet he's got a rat cornered under that pile of boards." Sure enough Rex was barking and digging like crazy, with his nose under a stack of boards by the fence and his bum up in the air.

"I've got an air rifle," I said. "Maybe we can bag the rat."

"You beauty," said Willy. "Let's go."

Peas and potatoes were forgotten as I grabbed my air rifle out of my room and we dashed down the steps to help Rex. Willy took an admiring look at my air rifle. "That's a beauty," he said. "Are you a good shot?"

"Yeah, just call me Deadeye Des," I said.

"All right, you stand ready to shoot," said Willy. "Me and Rex will flush him out."

Willy started pulling boards out of the pile. Rex got increasingly frantic as he sensed he was getting closer to his quarry. I stood back, gun ready to fire.

"Get ready," shouted Willy. "He'll probably come out like a rocket." He pulled another board aside. Rex leapt into the air with all four feet off the ground, then dived into an open space under the boards. All at once a furry black blob half the size of a cat came streaking out from under the boards, heading along the foot of the fence.

"There he is, the bugger!" shouted Willy. "Blow his brains out."

I only had one second before the rat could get away or Rex would be after him, and get in my line of sight. I pulled the trigger. The rat lurched to one side, and in a flash Rex was on him shaking the living daylights out of him.

"You got him! Great shot," shouted Willy. "Good boy, Rex. That's enough now, give him to me." But Rex was having none of it, as he tore off around the yard with the rat in his mouth, with me and Willy after him. The commotion had stirred up Calder's dog next door, who was running up and down on their side of the fence, yapping its head off. Mr. and Mrs. Calder and Les were lined up looking over the fence, and Rob and Fred piled over the fence on the other side, and joined Willy and me chasing after Rex. We finally cornered him along the side of the house, and Willy extracted one sorry looking lump of half chewed rat from Rex's jaws, and held it up by the tail.

"Poor bugger," he said. "He never knew what hit him."

By now Mum, Gloria and Val were on the back verandah looking down on the fracas.

"Oh yuk!" Gloria shouted. "Put that filthy thing in the rubbish bin."

"No, put him in a can," said Les. "You'll probably get a coupla bob from the Council for him."

Fred right away produced a big empty pea can from the pie shed, and we dropped the rat in. I grabbed a bottle of methylated spirits from the kitchen and poured it all over him. Then we stuck the can up on top of a stump cap under the house where Rex couldn't get at him. The show was over. Fred and Rob went home. Mum stood over me and Willy while we scrubbed our hands, then we went back to shelling peas and peeling potatoes. You can guess what the conversation was over tea, until Mum finally put her foot down and told us to drop it. Willy had made quite an impression on our household.

At Willy's Place

Willy and I right away became best friends. Sometimes I called him Grant, but mostly Willy, and he was always Willy around our house. I learned a lot of new things from him. One of the first was how to ride Atom Gal down the hill on Cornwall Street. We pulled her up to the top of the hill and, of course, Rex came along, too. Willy put Rex in the box and climbed in behind him. His feet stuck out the front to help steer, and he held the ends of the steering cord in each hand. My job was to give Atom Gal a push to get her started.

"All set. Let 'er rip!" Willy shouted, and I gave them one almighty shove and kept it up, running along behind.

"Holy cow, not so hard!" Willy yelled, struggling to keep control. Part of the challenge was that the bitumen on the road didn't go all the way to the gutter, and there was a two inch drop off onto gravel and small rocks. Some of the gravel was kicked up onto the bitumen, so if the wheel hit a large enough rock it could knock it off course, and you were only a split second from flipping over. However, Willy was up for it, and he and Rex went zig-zagging down the road leaving me in their dust. When they finally ran out of hill about a hundred yards away, I was able to catch up to them.

"Bloody beauty!" Willy shouted. "But you nearly sent us arse over tit back there."

"Sorry," I said, "but you said to push."

"Yeah, well not so hard next time. Now it's your turn."

We trudged back up to the top of the hill, pulling Atom Gal along behind. There was the odd car on the road, so we had to keep an eye out. At the top of the hill I got in the box. Rex was ready for another ride, but Willy wouldn't let him. "I don't want you to kill him," he laughed. He gave me a shove, and off I went flat out down the hill.

The cart drifted a bit to the right. I saw a car coming up the hill towards me, so I tried to correct in the other direction, but then I saw the drop off to the gravel getting too close, and I had to turn again the other way, just as the car went roaring past, its horn blaring. I got such a fright that this time I did go into the gravel, and I felt the whole thing starting to go sideways. I closed my eyes as she began to tip, and I could already see myself spread out over the road like a squashed banana. But at the last moment I heard Rex yapping, and suddenly Willy was there with his hand on the cart steadying it. We came to a slithering stop in a shower of gravel.

"Holy cow! Next time use the bloody brake," he blurted out, gasping for breath.

"I forgot it had one," I said. Indeed, the cart did have a brake. It was a wooden lever with a piece of car tire on the end of it, which you could jam onto the back wheel, that is, if you remembered it, and could grab it and steer at the same time.

We were just recovering from this episode when a car came up from behind and pulled up beside us.

"Oh cripes," I heard Willy groan. "It's the cops."

A policeman got out and stood looking at us as we shuffled our feet. He stood there with his feet wide apart, and his big thumbs hooked in the leather belt of his dark blue uniform.

"And what the hell do you two nincompoops think yer up to?" he asked, though I don't think he really wanted an answer. "Tryin' to kill yourselves and cause an accident at the same time?"

Neither of us said a word.

"Where do you live?" the policemen asked.

"Just over there," said Willy, pointing to his house, which was just across the road from us.

"Is yer father home?"

"No, he's at work," Willy said. "He's a dentist."

"Well it's too bad he hasn't drilled a bit of sense into you," said the policemen. "Now, you know what I want you to do? I want you to pick up that piece of junk, and get into your yard so fast you'll be there before you've left here. And if I ever catch you out on the road again with that thing, I'll stick both of you in Bogga Road Gaol and throw away the key. Now, get movin'!"

Needless to say we were gone in a flash and breathed a sigh of relief when we heard his car drive off.

"He called Atom Gal a piece of junk," Willy complained.

"He couldn't really put us in Bogga Road, could he?" I asked.

"Course not, he was just tryin' to scare the shit out of us."

"Well, it sure worked for me," I said.

"Yeah, I can see it running down your leg," Willy laughed, but I think he was just as scared as me, or maybe he wasn't, I'm not sure. You see, even though we were in the same grade at school, Willy was two years older than me. He said he came from Cunnamulla out west, and somewhere along the way they had put him back a year in school, while I had been pushed a year ahead. The upshot was that he knew a lot more about life than I did, and that probably included run-ins with policemen.

Not long after, while we were still hanging around under the house, his father came home. Mr. Williams drove a great big brown Pontiac with a Red Indian mascot on the front and chrome strips down the back over the boot. I'm not sure what year it was, probably about 1938 or 1940. He was just coming home from work and was dressed in a suit. I hadn't met him yet, so I wondered what Willy's father would be like. I had never met a dentist before, except when I went to have a tooth fixed, and it always hurt like hell. I wondered if they did it deliberately. However, Mr. Williams seemed pleasant enough, as he looked at me and smiled.

"Hello, who are you?" he asked.

"This is Des," Willy answered before I could. "He comes from a farm." It seemed that coming from a farm was some kind of important distinction in the Williams' household.

"Good for you," said Mr. W. He didn't seem to want to know anything about the farm. "What are you two up to?" he asked.

"Not much," said Willy. I hoped he wasn't going to say anything about the policeman, and he didn't.

"Well, have fun doing it," said Mr. W. "It's been a long day. I'm going to put my feet up." He headed off up the back steps.

"He's gonna hit the rum," Willy whispered, when his father was out of sight. "He'll be flying high by tea time."

"Do both your Mum and Dad like the grog?" I asked.

"Yeah, it's like mother's milk to them," he replied.

"Well they seem nice enough," I said. "I like them."

"Yeah, they're good sports. They mostly let me do whatever I want," said Willy. Then he asked, "Do you want a game of ping pong?"

"I've never really played," I said, "but it must be like tennis, so I should be able to do it."

Once we got started I soon found out it wasn't really much like tennis, except for the bat and ball. Willy was pretty good, and he knew how to hold the bat to make quick forehand and backhand shots. I tried to stand back and drive the ball, and most of the time it went off the end of the table. However, after a while I started to get the hang of it, and I was able to give him a pretty good game, though he won easily enough.

"We should have a game of tennis some time," I said.

"I know you're pretty good at that. Macker says you whipped the pants off him."

"I learnt to play on the farm. We have our own tennis court."

"I'd like to see that."

"You'll have to come up for the holidays."

"Yeah, that'd be beaut."

We finished playing ping pong and went out to the front of the house to sit on the steps, and see what different cars went by. Cornwall Street was fairly busy at this time of day with people coming home from work. Willy was a champ at naming the cars. I think he knew every make and model there ever was, and he usually had a comment about how good they were, from the Ford Prefect "piece of junk" to the "bloody beautiful" big black Bentley that cruised by.

He was still watching the Bentley lovingly when I saw something even more beautiful coming in the front gate. She was gorgeous with her short brown bobbed hair and white blouse and swishing green skirt. I thought she was probably about fifteen or sixteen years old, and I knew right away from the photo I had seen inside that this was Willy's sister, Judith.

Willy hardly paid any attention to her, but she looked right at me as she came up the steps. She gave me a great big smile and spoke in a lovely soft voice.

"Hello, I'm Grant's sister, Judith."

I opened my mouth to speak, but no words came out.

"This is Des," Willy said. I swear to God I could have strangled him if he said I came from a farm, but he didn't. He just added, "We're watching the cars."

"That's nice," said Judith. "See you later." And she swished past up into the house.

"She's gorgeous," I said, finally finding my voice.

"What that old thing?" said Willy, thinking I meant the green Hudson going by.

"Not the car," I said. "Your sister."

"Oh, yeah, I s'pose so."

"Was she coming home from work?"

"Yeah. Boy, they oughta take that bucket of bolts off the road."

"Where does she work?"

"Who, Judith? I dunno. She's a secretary somewhere. Boy, look at that MG. What a beauty!"

She sure was, I thought. I had lost all interest in the cars. I liked Willy's Mum and Dad, but his sister was something else. It's too bad I was just a kid. I could have gone for her in a big way.

My Great Composition

In school I was doing all right in Grade 5, or at least I thought I was, until one morning Mr. Merrell came in to give us a test in mental arithmetic. I liked Mr. Kimlin as a teacher. He was stern but fair, and whenever he occasionally gave a kid the cuts it was always for a good reason. Not so with Mr. Merrell.

On this particular morning he breezed into our class and told Mr. Kimlin he was going to give us a test in mental. Now, I never liked this subject, but for some reason the school thought it was important that you could do mental gymnastics in your head. "There were 10 men working in a field, 4 went home for lunch, and half of the remainder lay down for a rest. The ones who were left working were joined by twice as many as had gone home for lunch. How many men are now working?" Now, I ask you, what kind of a stupid question is that? But Mr. Merrell had ten of them. We had to write our answers in our exercise books, and then change books with the kid sitting next to you for marking. Mr. Merrell said 7 out of 10 was a pass, and anyone who got less than that would get a cut for each one wrong to make it up to 8. Somewhere in the middle of the test I panicked, and I ended up with 6 out of 10. That meant two cuts. There were only ten kids who got 8 or more right, so the rest of us were paraded out along the verandah outside the office. Mr. Merrell went in and got his cane, and for the next ten minutes it was like a thrashing machine, as he gave each of us who got more than one wrong a cut on each hand. Some kids got almost none right, but he settled for two cuts each, or he would have been there all day. He started with those of us at the top end of the class, who he said should have done better. It hurt like hell and stung for ages. I don't know how he thought that would improve us in mental. It just made me hate the whole thing more.

However, most of the school work was a lot better than that. I especially liked the reading and comprehension from the Grade 5 Queensland Reader. We were now also doing compositions, where you would try to write like the authors in the book. One story I especially liked was "Don Quixote and the Windmills," which Mr. Kimlin said came from a longer book written a long time ago by a man named Cervantes. In this story Don Quixote, an old nobleman who is a bit crazy, thinks he's a knight, and he attacks some windmills that he thinks are evil giants. His companion, Sancho Panza, whom Don Quixote calls his squire, tries to tell him that they are only windmills, but Don Quixote won't listen and charges at them full tilt. The sails of a windmill sweep down, snap his lance in half, and knock the silly old man off his horse. When Sancho Panza picks him up, Don Quixote can't walk straight, but he says he will never complain of his wounds, because knights don't do that.

I decided to write a story like that for my composition. I also noted how the author was using words like "sweep these wicked monsters off the face of the earth" and "his wicked arts will not always prevail." I thought I would try to write like that. Here is my story.

"Don Merrello snapped awake from dozing in his office chair. He opened the door in the bottom of a bookcase and took out the tin helmet he always wore when he was about to sally forth and do battle with evil doers. With the helmet strapped on tight, he grabbed his long wicked cane and marched out the door.

"Don Merrello was a small man, lean, always scowling, and he walked with a stoop. Outside his office door on the verandah he spotted a small boy, rather scruffy looking, covered in freckles, with eyes wide open and frightened.

"'You, boy,' snapped Don Merrello, 'what's your name?'

"'Sammy Poncho,' replied the boy, quivering at the sight of this strange helmeted figure waving a cane. But instead of telling the boy to hold out his hand for the cuts, Don Merrello wheeled on his heels and headed for the steps, shouting to the boy, 'Follow me, Sammy Poncho, we are off to do battle.'

"At the bottom of the steps, Don Merrello stopped short. 'Where's my horse?' he shouted. 'I need my horse. Every soldier must ride a horse into battle.'

"'Please sir,' mumbled Sammy Poncho, 'we don't have any horses, only bikes.'

"'Then bikes it will be,' said Don Merrello. 'Get me a beauty.'

"Sammy Poncho disappeared under the school and came back wheeling two bikes. One was bright yellow with smart looking mud guards and a big headlight. The other was small and plain. Don Merrello grabbed the yellow one, got on, wobbled a bit, then set off, weaving an erratic path towards the school gate. Sammy Poncho followed along behind as fast as he could on the small bike.

"'Fortune will favour us,' shouted Don Merrello. 'We will do battle with evil monsters.'

"At the end of the street they came to the tram tracks, just as a lumbering old tram rattled to a halt at the stop.

"'There's an evil monster now,' cried Don Merrello. 'Come, Sammy Poncho, attack. We will sweep this beast off the face of the earth.'

"'But, sir,' protested Sammy Poncho, 'that's not a monster. It's a tram.'

"'It's easy to see,' Don Merrello replied, 'that you are not used to adventures. That is a monster. If you are afraid, go home to your mother, while I wage a fierce war against it.'

"The valiant warrior charged off after the tram, completely unaware of the cars on the road that swerved with honking horns to avoid him. Sammy Poncho shouted after him to stop and followed along behind, keeping to the footpath, where, fortunately, there were no people.

"The tram started off again from the stop. 'Do not run away, you giant coward,' shouted Don Merrello, 'for only a single warrior is attacking you.'

"With coat tails flying in the breeze, Don Merrello wheeled up behind the tram, and started banging on it with his cane. A startled conductor looked out and caught a swift whack across the side of his head.

"'What the hell are you doing, you idiot?' he yelled, trying to fend off a barrage of blows from the undaunted Don. He finally grabbed the cane, and gave it such a mighty yank that it sent Don Merrello and his bike swerving off into the gutter, where they crashed in a pile of flailing arms and legs, spinning wheels, and a dented helmet. The tram rattled away with the conductor still shaking his fist at the demented Don.

"Sammy Poncho hurried to the assistance of the fallen warrior, who lay for a time unable to move a limb.

"'Alas, sir,' Sammy Poncho said, 'didn't I tell you it was a tram, not a monster?'

"'Hush, Sammy Poncho,' answered the Don, 'the fortunes of war are always changing. I am certain that some magician turned that monster into a tram so as to rob me of the glory of conquering the beast. But his wicked arts will not always prevail, and I shall win fame with my good sword.'

"Sammy Poncho was going to mention that the broken stick Don Merrello was holding in his hand was a cane, and not a sword, but he thought better of it.

"'I hope you may,' said Sammy Poncho, as he helped the Don get on his bike and wobble off back towards the school. When they got to the office, Don Merrello flopped down in his chair and fell into a deep swoon. Sammy Poncho scuttled away. Shortly afterwards Don Merrello woke up with a start and exclaimed, 'Good grief, what an awful dream!' But he wondered why his precious cane lay on his desk broken in several pieces."

I copied the story into my composition book and showed it to several boys, who laughed and laughed when they read it.

"You better not show that to Mr. Kimlin, or you will be in deep shit," said one of them.

"What is it you better not show me, Berghofer?" Mr. Kimlin had come into the room unnoticed. He picked up the composition, took it to his desk and sat down to read it. The room went deathly quiet. I stared at Mr. Kimlin's face, and thought I saw a faint smile flicker across his lips. But he showed no sign of it when he looked up and beckoned me to come up to his desk. He closed the composition book and handed it to me. He took a new composition book out of his drawer.

"You better take that other one home," he said, "and never bring it back to school. It was a good story. You may have a future as a writer, but a word of advice. Don't get too big for your boots."

I knew what he meant, and I was lucky he was such a good sport about it. I suppose I could have been thrashed for writing a story like that, but I still thought it was pretty good, and I was glad I had written it.

Anzac Day

One of the many things I found strange when I first went to Buranda School was something they called the School Houses. The idea was to divide all of the pupils into four houses, so that we could earn points at sports or in class, and at the end of the year the house with the most points would be the winner. We had never had anything like that at Athol, where we were just one small school family.

Just as strange to me as this idea of houses were the names they gave to them. They were named after leaders in the war against Germany and Japan. I knew the name Churchill as the Prime Minister of England, and Roosevelt as the President of the United States. I wasn't too sure about Curtin, though I should have known he was the Prime Minister of Australia during most of the war. The fourth name was completely new to me. It was Stalin, and I was told that he was the leader of Russia. But now that the war was over, I also knew that we weren't too sure about whether Russia was our friend or enemy, so I wondered about why his name would be used for one of our school houses.

Anyway, there they were: Churchill, Roosevelt, Curtin and Stalin. The names were printed on different coloured pennants and were put up on the back wall in the classrooms. Having these names of war leaders always in front of us also kept reminding me of the war, which had now been over for almost four years, but which I was learning more about as I got older. I learned that Australia was very close to being invaded by the Japanese, and that they even dropped bombs on Darwin and sent a mini submarine into Sydney Harbour. Australians were therefore very thankful to our soldiers for having saved us from a terrible invasion, and I knew we couldn't have done it without the help of the Americans, so we were very thankful to them, too.

Most of the time we young kids didn't think too much about all of this, though, as I say, it was always in the background. We had one day that was special for remembering what our soldiers had done for us. This was called Anzac Day, and it was held on the 25th of April every year as a very special holiday. I knew about the Anzac Day holiday before I came to live in Brisbane, but I really didn't understand it very well until the first Anzac Day I was at Buranda on the 25th of April, 1949.

Because it was on a Monday, we had our special school ceremony on the Friday before. In class Mr. Kimlin told us about the meaning of Anzac Day. The word Anzac stands for Australian and New Zealand Army Corps, and it commemorates, in particular, the landing of the Australian and New Zealand soldiers on the shores of Gallipoli in Turkey on the 25th of April, 1915 in the First World War. We learned that it was a terrible battle, in which many of the soldiers were killed because the Turks were expecting them, and cut them down with machine gun fire as they landed on the beach. I don't know the exact history, but I think the Australian and New Zealand soldiers were successful at first in gaining some high ground, but were eventually forced back to the beaches, and after many weeks had to be withdrawn. Though the campaign was considered a military failure, it nevertheless was regarded as a great tribute to the courage and fighting ability of the Anzacs, and that is why we continue to honour them on Anzac Day.

The ceremony at school was very solemn. We all lined up in our classes on the parade ground, saluted the flag, sang "God Save the King" and listened to speeches from some military officers, who came to the school especially for the occasion. A bugler came and played the "Last Post," and we all bowed our heads in silence. I had never seen anything like that before, and it made me sad and puzzled about why there had to be war in the first place.

When I went home I talked to Mum about it, and she said I might want to go to the Anzac Day parade, which would be held on Monday the 25th in the heart of the city, where the Anzac Memorial had been built many years ago. She said there was a service at the memorial at dawn to remember the time of the landing of the Anzacs at Gallipoli, and that would be followed later in the morning by a parade through the city streets. We decided to go to the parade as a family.

On Monday morning we caught a tram up on Ipswich Road to go into town. I noticed that all of the streets were quiet with only a few cars out. All of the shops were closed, because this was a very solemn holiday. When we got off the tram in the city, there were already hundreds of people around lining up for the parade. We were pretty early, so Mum thought we ought to try to get a spot on Adelaide Street near the Memorial in Anzac Square just beside City Hall. It was a bit of a squeeze, but we managed to find a place near the Memorial, and people let us kids move to the front, where we could sit on the edge of the gutter. Mum was able to stand behind us.

I could just see the Memorial at the back of the square behind some trees and the statue of a soldier from the Boer War mounted on a horse. The Boer War was an even older war than the one the Anzacs fought in, when some Australians went to South Africa to help with the fight against people called the Boers, about fifty years ago. When I thought about it, there seemed to be an awful lot of wars being remembered here today.

We hadn't been there long when a few big black cars came down the street, and pulled up in front of a wooden platform that had been built on the side of the street in front of the Memorial. I couldn't see very well, but I was able to make out some important looking people getting out of the cars. Mum said it was the Governor and the Premier, and other what you call dignitaries. The Governor would be saluting the soldiers as they marched by.

Then the parade began. We could hear it coming long before we saw anything, as it was led by a bagpipe band, who marched right by us. Then we saw the soldiers. The first group were the "diggers" from the First World War, the original Anzacs, some still wearing their uniforms from over thirty years ago, others in civilian clothes, all proudly sporting medals on their chests as they marched by, looking straight in front with their heads held high. A few of us kids had small Australian flags that we waved, and people in the crowd applauded, but not too loud, because this was a solemn parade, when people were also remembering all the soldiers who had been killed in the war.

But that was only the beginning. I couldn't believe how lucky I was to be here to see all this—and so proud, not because I liked war, because I didn't, but to know that all of us were now safe and free because of how hard the men, and some women, too, marching today had fought for us, and how sad it was that so many of their mates had been killed in the fighting.

Wave after wave of soldiers, sailors and air force men and women from the Second World War came marching by to the music of many bands. All of us watching knew that just a few short years ago these men and women had helped save Australia from a terrible invasion. We waved our flags and clapped and cheered as they marched by. Then came today's fighting men and women, all in uniform, telling us that they were there to keep us safe. And the cadets were marching, too, kids just a bit older than me, and I thought that one day I would be marching, too, when I was in High School.

When it was over, we mingled with the crowds and went over to take a closer look at the Memorial. It was solid and tall, built in a circle with tall pillars out of whitish-brown sandstone. Inside was the eternal flame packed around with wreaths today from the dawn ceremony. On the wall below were the names of soldiers from Brisbane who had died in the wars. Hundreds and hundreds of names, men I would never know, who had died so I could grow up and go to school in a free country.

On the way home we caught one of the old trams with an open air section in the middle, and two closed-in cabin areas in the front and back. I got separated from Mum and the girls, who went inside, while I sat on one of the long benches that ran across the tram in the open section. It was pretty crowded, and I squeezed in among a group of men wearing medals. I guessed they had been marching in the parade. I looked in their lined and weather beaten faces, and I wondered what awful things they must have seen in the war.

"Been to the parade, have you, mate?" I heard this raspy voice, and looked up into the eyes of a man across from me. He wasn't in uniform, but like the others he had his medals and ribbons pinned to his chest. He wore the soldier's slouch hat with the shiny polished Australian army badge pinned to the turned up brim, and the chin strap was pulled tight across his square jaw. He was wearing a light coat against the cool air in the rattling tram, and I saw that the right sleeve hung loose blowing in the breeze with no arm in it. His wide blue eyes looked deep into mine.

"Yeah," I said, "I had never been before."

"First time, eh?" he replied. "So what d'you think?"

"I dunno what to think," I said. "They teach us in school about the war, but seeing all of you marching makes me think I don't know anything about it."

"Just as well you don't, mate. It's a bloody bad business is war. Never let anyone tell you it isn't."

"Ar, come on, Fred, don't go all solemn on us." One of the other men sitting in the group had spoken. I felt all their eyes on me. "He's only a kid," said another. "He doesn't want to hear old dogs like us cryin' the blues."

The tram rattled on and lurched around a bend in the tracks. I could feel some kind of strong energy around us.

"Is that what you think, son?" said the first man. "That we're just washed up old buggers, out for a day to show off our medals, then go home and mope?"

"No, no," I found my voice catching in my chest. "I don't think that at all. I just feel I want to say thank you. I never thought much about it before, but now I know how lucky I am that all of you went off to war to protect kids like me."

"Thank you, son," said one of the men.

"No," I said. "I'm the one who thanks you."

They all went quiet at that, but just for a bit, then one of them with a really good voice started to sing, and the others joined in, and then a lot more people on the tram, singing old war songs like "It's a Long Way to Tipperary," and "Roll Out the Barrel." They were all singing "Waltzing Matilda" when we came to my stop, and I got off with Mum and the girls to cries of "Good on yer, mate", "See ya next year," and "Keep yer chin up."

"What was that all about?" asked Mum as we walked away from the tram stop. But I couldn't answer her. I didn't have the words. I wasn't sure what, but I knew that something had happened to me today that I would remember for the rest of my life, something too deep and mixed up for words, but all the more powerful for that. I had been touched by the spirit of Anzac.

Willy, Me and Our Dogs

Willy and I were now best friends, and we would spend so much time together after school and on the weekend that Mum and Gloria were always wondering what we got up to. The truth of the matter was, not much. Mostly fooling around, pulling our bikes to pieces and putting them back together again, reading comics, looking at pictures of nude women in old magazines that Willy had stashed away in a box. I wasn't too interested in the pictures at first, but Willy explained the finer points to me, so I started to pay a bit more attention.

But mostly we just enjoyed riding our bikes around all the city streets, ranging out a bit further every time, until I had a pretty good map in my head of everything for miles around. Willy usually brought Rex, who would sit up in his box on the back of the bike, sniffing the breeze with a kind of silly grin on his face. That was most of the time, but every now and then we would run across a stray dog in the street, and as soon as he saw Rex he had to attack, and Willy would have this vicious dog barking and snapping at his rear wheel, while Rex bounced around in his box barking and snapping back. Of course, one barking dog was a magnet for every other dog that could get loose and join in the fray, until Willy would have a pack of dogs after him, as he pedalled faster and faster to try to get away. I was usually bringing up the rear, so that I found myself weaving and dodging around this frenzied barking mass of canine stupidity, yelling and trying to land a few good kicks without falling off my bike. We always managed to escape, because no pack of dogs is a match for two determined kids pedalling flat out to get away. When it was over, we would pull up to catch our breath, and laugh and laugh at how we outstripped them.

"You should get yourself a dog," Willy said. "Then we'd have twice as much fun with the dogs chasing both of us."

"Good idea," I said. "I'll ask Mum." And I did, but she said, "I'll have to ask your father." Of course he wasn't around, so that put the kibosh on that idea for a while, but then, wouldn't you know, Dad turned up on one of his visits from the farm not long after, and he had a little black pup with him that had a white spot on his head and long floppy ears.

"I heard you wanted a dog," he said. "I picked this fella up from a chap who had a bitch with six pups. This one was the runt of the litter. His mother is a Border Collie, so he's probably pretty smart. God knows who his father was."

"You beaut," I cried. "I'm gonna call him Jim." That wasn't too original, but our farm dog, Jim, was the only dog I had ever had, and he wasn't really mine. Now I had a Jim of my own.

I shoved Jim inside my shirt, and took off on my bike for Willy's place.

"Look what I got," I shouted when I saw him. "I've got my own dog, Jim."

Willy burst out laughing. "Struth, he's a bit on the small side, mate," he said.

"Yeah, but he'll grow. Dad said in six months he'll be twice as big as he is now."

Willy took Jim and showed him to Rex. "What d'you think, Rex?" he said. "Will he do?" We put Jim on the ground, and within a minute the two of them were bounding around the yard together.

"Well, that clinches it," said Willy. "Rex approves, so he must be all right. Let's build him a box."

We got to work right away and cut down an old wooden box to one about the same size as Rex's and painted it green and gold with his name JIM in big letters in black on both sides. We cut up an old blanket, and put it inside for a soft lining. When I put Jim in the box, he almost disappeared, with only the top of his head and his floppy ears sticking out above the sides.

"Well, you've gotta leave room for him to grow," Willy said. "We can just add more padding for now."

"You know, we've got another problem," I said. "I don't have a bike rack."

"No problem," said Willy. "I'm sure I've got an old one around here somewhere." And sure enough we found a rack, and put it on the back of my bike. Willy sneaked upstairs and pinched one of his father's old leather belts to tie the box onto the rack.

"There you are, Sir Jim," said Willy. "Your carriage awaits you. Now you've gotta teach him not to jump out while you're riding along, or he'll break his neck."

We put Jim in the box, and I got on the bike and rode it around the yard while Willy ran along behind, holding Jim down in the box. After a few yelps the little fellow seemed to get the hang of it, and I did a few turns around the yard solo while Willy watched.

"Not bad," said Willy. "He's a smart pup. It's time to hit the street." Rex knew right away what was coming. He leapt up in the air and Willy caught him and put him in his own box.

"You go first," said Willy. "I'll keep an eye on Jim."

We set off slowly along Duke Street, where there weren't any cars. Jim seemed to be doing all right. Of course, I couldn't see him, because he was behind my back, but Willy said he was sitting up nicely. We went up and down the street a couple of times, and we thought everything was going to be all right, but wouldn't you know it, a big German Shepherd came trotting along the footpath, and when he saw Jim in his box he went nuts.

He was almost as big as the bike, and he let out this great deep bark. I pedalled like mad, and though I couldn't see him I knew the brute was right behind me, with his head almost up level with Jim in his box. Willy was right behind trying to nudge the big dog with his front wheel, and yelling at him to get away. We were coming back down the street towards Willy's yard, and I flew straight in through the gate, almost becoming airborne as I ripped up and over the dip in the gutter. The German Shepherd and Willy were right behind, but once we got inside the yard, the big dog thought better of it, and turned around and headed for the gate. Rex flew out of his box determined to protect his territory against this burly invader. Willy dumped his bike and fortunately was able to collar Rex and bring him back, before he was eaten alive.

I got off my bike and turned to look at Jim. He was just sitting there in his box with what I swore was a big grin across his face.

"Gawd, talk about a trial by fire," said Willy, as he came back into the yard carrying Rex under his arm. "If your little fella can survive that, he should be up for anything."

"Dad said he was smart," I said, "but I reckon he's pretty brave too."

We knew then that we were going to have a lot of fun with Rex and Jim on our bikes, though we both agreed that we'd had enough excitement for one day.

I Play Tennis for Buranda

Playing tennis on the Buranda Boys team against other schools was one of the highlights of my Grade 5 year. I was still keeping up my coaching practice with Tom Whitworth at school and on most Saturday mornings, but playing in competition against other schools would be an exciting new achievement for me.

The thing about tennis is that you are one-on-one against the other player, or two-on-two if you're playing doubles. It's different from being on a football team, or even on a cricket team, where so much depends on everyone else on the team, and on how well you play together. In tennis in singles it's just you against the other player, and when this is someone you don't know, whom you've never seen play before, you always have the anticipation that you will have a good day and beat this unknown opponent, but you also know that maybe he will be a humdinger and will wipe you off the court. Because I was the youngest player on our team, I was always coming up against older boys, so I never knew how well I would do.

We played on Friday afternoons, and Mr. Hennessy was the teacher in charge. We would alternate playing at home on our courts and travelling to the other school, which was always exciting, especially when you went to a school for the first time, because you would never know what the courts might be like, or who might be around to watch. We played against schools that were mostly on the tram line, so they were easy to get to, at places like Coorparoo and Camp Hill, and even way out at Belmont at the end of the tram line.

The first time we played was at Camp Hill. There were four of us on the team, and each of us played a game of singles and doubles. Brad was our captain and always played first. He was such a good player that he always won and got us off to a good start. We were playing on two courts and I followed Brad. Our second player had lost badly on the other court, and it looked like our third player was already in trouble on the same court, when it was my turn to come on. My opponent was a tall chunky kid, who looked like he was at least thirteen years old. When we started to hit up before the game, I could tell he was strong, because his shots were deep and coming off the court very fast. The court was a bit gravelly, so the bounce was not always good, and because he was used to playing on this surface he had the advantage. Of course, what he didn't know is that I came from Athol, where our courts were anything but perfect, so a few bad bounces weren't going to worry me.

Brad was watching us warm up, and he came over to have a word with me before we started.

"This kid's not bad, Des, but he's slow, and his backhand isn't worth a pinch of shit, so if you run him around, and keep pressing his backhand, you should be able to do him in."

Of course, that was easier said than done, especially when he won the toss to serve first, and he sent these big boomers down at me that came off the court so fast that I was lucky to get them back over the net, let alone do anything serious with my returns. He had me at 40 love before I knew what had happened, and he took the game at love.

However, my serve was also working well, though not nearly as hard as his, and by following Brad's advice of concentrating on his backhand I was able to take the game. With his next service game I was able to get more control, and though he kept his serve I made him work for it. We kept on going like this, each of us winning our serves, until it was 5 each, and he was going to serve for the last game to decide the set.

By now the match on the other court was over, and we had lost, so we were now down 2 to 1. If I lost my match, we would be down 3 to 1 before the doubles started, and that would not be good. Also, by now school was out, and a lot of the Camp Hill kids had gathered around the courts to cheer their side on. This included a lot of girls, because it was a mixed school. I felt like the whole world was watching me.

I had followed Brad's advice and tried to run the other kid around as much as I could, so by now he was pretty tired and his serve had lost a lot of its oomph. I whacked my returns hard and deep onto his backhand, and I had him at 15-40 with two match points to me.

"You've got him by the tits now, Des," Brad whispered to me from the sidelines, where he was standing at my end of the court. "Just give him the knockout punch."

But the other kid was not ready to give in, and he sent down two blistering serves to level the score at deuce. Needless to say all the kids in the crowd were cheering madly for their man.

"Not to worry, mate," Brad said to me again. "Just keep the pressure on, and you'll cook him."

His next serve came to my forehand, and he thought I would return it up the line to his backhand, but I saw my chance and whipped it across court, and left him flatfooted for a clear winner. A big groan went up from the crowd. It was advantage to me. I heard a few kids yelling at me to drop dead, but the umpire and a couple of teachers quieted them down. I caught a glimpse of a cute looking girl outside the wire smiling at me, and that gave me a lift.

His next serve was a bullet to my backhand, and I think I surprised him by getting it back pretty deep to his forehand, because he hit his return short to my forehand, and I ran in and hit that ball with everything I had right down the line on his backhand. He was nowhere near it, and I had won the match. There were a few groans and boos from the crowd, but mostly they were good sports and cheered my hard fought win. My team mates were, of course, pleased, because we were now back in the overall match with two wins each.

I played with my friend, Neil, from my class in the doubles. We were the youngest players, and we lost one set, but won the other. Brad and his partner won both their matches, so at the end of the day Buranda was the winner by 5 sets to 3. We felt pretty good about that, but I felt especially pleased, because I knew my singles win had saved the day for us.

On the way home in the tram Brad asked me when my birthday was. I told him it was the 28th of October.

"And you're only ten now, aren't you?" he asked again. I nodded. "That means that next year when the Queensland Age Championships are on at Milton you'll still be under 12. We're going to have to make sure you're registered for that, because I think you have a good chance to be the Queensland under 12 Champion." I had never thought of anything like that. I wasn't even sure where Milton was, but I knew it was the centre for tennis in Brisbane. It was certainly something for a boy from the bush to think about.

The Brisbane Ekka

One good thing about living in Brisbane was the Brisbane Exhibition. That was a fancy name for a show, like the Toowoomba Show, where I had gone with Dad and Gordon to see Tex Morton a few years ago. I had heard from Aunty Carrie and Aunty Evelyn that the Brisbane Exhibition was the show to end all shows, the biggest in Queensland, and maybe in Australia, except for the one in Sydney, but that was almost at the end of the world, and I could never go there. But here I was living in Brisbane, so this was my chance.

The only problem was that it was held during the August school holidays. I suppose that was deliberate so that all the kids could go with their parents, but for us it wasn't so good, because we needed to go back to the farm for the holidays. In the end, we struck what you call a compromise, and came back early from the farm so we could catch the last day of the Ekka, which was what everyone called the Exhibition.

The other good thing about this was that Dad could go, too, and see all of the terrific livestock and agricultural exhibits that he knew were there. Unfortunately, Gordon couldn't come, because he had to stay and look after the farm.

We decided to make a day of it with Aunty Evelyn and Aunty Carrie joining us, and Gloria and Val inviting some of their friends to come along as well. Willy was away so I couldn't ask him, but Fred from next door said he would like to go.

The Exhibition grounds are on the other side of the city from where we lived. Dad said he didn't want to take the ute out in all that traffic, so we caught a tram across town to the Valley, then changed trams and took another one up the hill to the Exhibition grounds. It was really crowded, like I mean *really* crowded. You almost needed to have a rope tying everyone together so you wouldn't get separated. Because different people were coming from different places we had arranged that we would all meet together near the Tasmanian Potato place, where they made buckets and buckets of delicious long thin chips out of what I suppose must have been potatoes from Tasmania, though what they were doing in Queensland I don't know.

After we got our tickets and went inside we found the meeting place, and there we found Aunty Evelyn and Aunty Carrie looking like they were ready for a good time in their warm jumpers and skirts and big sun hats. Everyone dressed up in their best to go to the Ekka, and they were no exception.

"Lor, Evie," said Aunty Carrie, as she swept over all of us with her expansive gaze and warm kisses, "will you look at these kids, growing like weeds."

"Yes," replied Aunty Evelyn, "and ready for a fun day, I warrant. Here's two shillings each to have a good time."

"Gee thanks, Aunty Evelyn," we all chortled. "You're a good sport," I added.

"Evie likes to shout with money," said Aunty Carrie. "I just shout out loud. Hellooo!" And she laughed at her own joke.

There's so much to do at the Ekka that it's hard to know where to start. Mum said we should begin with the pavillions. This is where women can see the latest gizmos for the house, like egg beaters, and electric toasters, and carpet beaters, and what have you. For kids the best things were the cheap showbags you could get from different booths, with small Cadbury's chocolate bars and lollies and Jellex jelly crystals and ETA peanut butter and small toy planes and cars that you could wind up with a rubber band. Dad liked the big agricultural displays, which were twice the size of anything you saw at the Toowoomba Show. The women's industries of cooking and sewing were another hit with Mum and Aunty Evelyn and Aunty Carrie, and I swear they could have stayed there for hours. Fred and I got bored and took off to buy some fairyfloss. Gloria, Val and their friends came along, too. The girls looked like tricks decked out in their best dresses and berets, while tucking into the huge bunches of sweet, thin, wispy sugar strands, which soon coated their faces from ear to ear.

When we finally came out of the pavillions it was time to take a look at the Show Ring, but there wasn't much going on there, except for some sheep dog trials, which, though the dogs are very smart the way they move the sheep around, is still a lot like watching treacle run down hill. Dad said he wanted to go and see the farm machinery, and the women said they wanted to find a place that served a good cup of tea with nice china and lace tablecloths. That left the coast clear for Fred, me and the girls to head off for Sideshow Alley, with promises to be back at the Ring for the Grand Parade later in the afternoon.

Fred and I didn't particularly want to hang out with the girls all the time, so on a ride on the great big Ferris wheel we rocked the swinging seats so much that Val started to feel sick, and when we reached the ground Gloria told us to buzz off, which is really what we wanted to do in the first place.

If I thought the sideshows at the Toowoomba Show were terrific, I can't begin to describe Sideshow Alley at the Brisbane Ekka. You twisted and turned this way and that, through row on row of tents with open fronts featuring every kind of shootem, knockem, hitem, bangem, drownem game you can imagine, and a lot more besides. I saw a shooting gallery where tin ducks and rabbits and wallabies would pop up out of nowhere, and you had to blast them with an air rifle. There wasn't any prize for hitting anything, and the guns were god awful apologies for a rifle, but I had fun blasting away at the targets. Fred tried his luck at trying to throw a cricket ball into the mouth of a wooden clown, but I told him he had Buckley's chance of winning a prize, because the clown's mouth was too small for the ball. Further along was a chocolate wheel that the showman spun, and if you had the winning number where the leather tongue stopped, you got a box of chocolates. I had a few tries at that, and on the third time I got lucky and won a box of chocolates—so now we were set for lunch.

Further along were the freak shows, where they had the tiniest, biggest, fattest, thinnest, tallest, shortest, strongest, weakest specimens that ever there was. If you believed the mumbo jumbo they were shouting at you, you could go inside and be confronted by a tarantula the size of a dinner plate, crawling through a jungle filled with venomous snakes, and a boa constrictor that could strangle a cow and swallow it whole. However, what really caught our eyes was this one tent labelled "Girls of Paradise," where on a platform out front were these beautiful dark-skinned women in leopard cloths, doing a voluptuous dance in time to a drum beaten by this muscle-bound coot in a Tarzan outfit. I remembered the Jimmy Sharman Boxing Troupe from the Toowoomba Show, but I tell you they had nothing on this crowd for appeal to two young boys diving into their pockets to see if they could come up with the one bob admission price.

We had just about figured out we could do it and still have enough left over for a hot dog and Tristam's soft drink, when this spoil sport at the ticket booth looked at us and said, "Sorry boys, can't you read?" and he pointed with a long stick at a sign that said "No Minors Allowed." To top it off we saw a policeman standing at the entrance to the tent.

"I bet he gets in for free just for keeping kids like us out," Fred complained.

"Yeah, I wonder what they do in there," I said.

There was certainly no shortage of men filing into the tent to find out. Fred gave me a nudge and beckoned me to follow him around the side of the tent. We stepped over guy wires and pegs and managed to get round the back.

"I bet you could squeeze under the flaps," said Fred.

"What if you get caught?" I asked.

"The only thing they can do is throw you out," said Fred.

"And maybe put you in Boggo Road Gaol," I said.

"Don't be stupid, that's only for crooks. We're kids."

While we were debating like this, we saw a couple of other boys come round the tent from the other direction. They kind of leered at us, then immediately ducked under the flaps and disappeared inside the tent.

"See what I mean," said Fred. "If they can do it, so can we."

He moved towards the spot where they had gone under, but before he had taken two steps the side of the tent ripped open, and the two boys were marched out by another big burly Tarzan, with a hand screwed tightly on each boy's ear. He gave them a final heave-ho that sent them flying, then turned to glare at us.

"If you know what's good for you, you'll piss off, quick," he growled. We knew what was good for us, and pissed off very quick.

"Well, look on the bright side," said Fred, when we stopped running. "We saved ourselves two bob."

"Yeah, and from being mangled by a monster," I said.

It was then we spotted the Dodgem Cars that you could drive around and bash into each other. We spent some of our money on a couple of tickets, and had great fun taking our frustration out by crashing into everything. Then we sauntered off and came to the wood chopping place where big muscle men in Jackie Howes were racing against each other to get to the top of a wooden pole and cut the top off. I had never seen chips flying as fast as those fellows made them go, as their polished axe heads swung and danced in the sunlight.

We strolled around a bit more, and eventually found the girls having a nice quiet ride on the miniature railway, where a real steam engine chugged along blowing clouds of smoke in the air.

"What have you two been up to?" Gloria said, "or shouldn't I ask?"

"Yeah, you shouldn't ask," I said, "but look I won a box of chocolates. You can each have one."

That kind of settled the peace, and we all went off to find the adults. When we were all together again, we found a picnic table to have a feed of hot dogs, hot pies, Tasmanian Potato Chips, and Tristram's soft drinks. After that, Dad took me and Fred to the livestock barn, while the women and girls headed up into the grandstand to have a good view of the Grand Parade, and to save us some seats.

It's one thing to see the animals in the barns, but to see them all come out and walk in concentric circles around the show ring is really something else. Prize bulls, pedigree ponies, dancing thoroughbreds, sheep dogs, and everything in between came out for the Grand Parade. When they were all out in the middle, I swear it was the grandest sight you ever saw. The crowd cheered and clapped like they never wanted it to end. I was certainly glad I hadn't missed this.

When the Parade was over, we stayed up in the stands to watch some trots and other Ring events. By then it was getting dark, so they turned the floodlights on. The whole place took on a new kind of magic at night in the flickering lights. We walked around some more, just enjoying the place and the crowds, but we were all getting tired, so it was time to go. We said good-bye to Aunty Carrie and Aunty Evelyn at the tram stop, then rattled our way home through the night lights of Brisbane. In all, I reckoned it had been a pretty special day, even if I didn't get to see the "Girls of Paradise."

The School Bottle Drive and Fete

It may not have been the Brisbane Ekka, but we had our own show of sorts at Buranda Boys. This was what you call the School Fete, which is a fancy name for a show put on by the parents, teachers and pupils to raise money for the school. It was one of several ways the school used to get extra money for things it needed to do, like buy sports gear, improve the tennis courts and playgrounds, buy library books, and things like that. And there was another fun way to raise money, too. It was to have a bottle drive.

I had never been on a bottle drive before, so I asked Willy how it worked.

"We get together in teams and go out and scrounge empty bottles from wherever we can," he said," then you bring 'em back to school and sort 'em and count 'em, then the bottleo comes along, pays the school, carts them away and Bob's your uncle. The best part is that we get to do this on a school day, so we don't have to put up with old Kimo yakking away at us in class."

I didn't share Willy's dislike of school, but nevertheless the idea of having a day off to go out and scrounge bottles sounded like fun. When the day for the bottle drive arrived, all the kids came to school with a whole mess of different ways to carry the bottles: trolleys, wagons, sugar bags, carts you could hook on behind your bike, wheelbarrows—anything you could roll along, or carry on your back. Willy brought Atom Gal, and I had a trolley cart of my own that wasn't so fancy. We all got a head start by loading up with whatever bottles we had at home, or could pick up from next door.

We went out in house teams, so you could get points for your house for the bottles you collected. Willy, Macker and I went out together, down along Logan Road, and then out into the side streets. I soon learned that you never know what to expect when you start poking around in back yards and under houses looking for bottles.

Usually it was the old woman at home with a couple of scruffy looking kids holding onto her dress, or trying to hide behind her back. Sometimes the old man was at home, too, lounging around in his Jackie Howe and drinking a bottle of beer.

"Any empty bottles?" we would ask.

"Jeez, mates," he might say, "I got hundreds of 'em lyin' around if you can find 'em. But you can't have this one, because I haven't finished it yet. Har! Har! Har!"

So off we would go, rooting around under piles of rubbish looking for bottles. It would curl your hair to know some of the other things we found. I kept wondering if we would turn up a dead body, but thank God it never came to that, though it got pretty close.

I was poking around down the side of this one house that seemed to have some kind of extra room built under the front steps. I noticed a window at just about my eye level, but I didn't give it too much attention at first as I passed by looking for bottles. I found a few down the side, then as I came back I took a closer look at this window, and I swear to God I saw bars on it, and this shrivelled up old woman's face was peering out at me through the bars, with two long thin bony hands and long dirty fingernails hanging onto the bars.

I was out of there like a streak of greased lightning and grabbed Willy, who was out on the street loading a bag of bottles into Atom Gal. I tried to talk, but no words came out.

"What the hell's the matter with you?" he asked. "You look like you've seen a ghost."

"W-worse than that," I stammered. "They've got an old hag locked up in prison in there."

"Go on," he said. "Where? Show me?"

"Not on your life," I said. "I'm not going back in there." And I took off down the street. He told me afterwards that he went back to have a look, but didn't see anything, but all I know is what I saw, and I'm not making it up.

The other thing you had to be on the lookout for were redback spiders. The necks of old bottles make pretty good nesting places for those little devils. If we saw any, we raked them out with a stick and stomped on them as they tried to scurry away. We didn't want to waste a good bottle just because a redback made his home in it.

But not all of the places were like that. Sometimes we hit the jackpot, when the lady of the house would give us a big smile and say she'd been collecting bottles all year for us, and there they would be all washed and clean and lined up like soldiers. Macker was the smooth one, and he would thank her very politely and make a note of the address, so we would remember it for next year.

So it went on all day like this. When we had a full load we would haul it back to the school, then go out again. Other kids were working under the supervision of the teachers, sorting and counting. By the end of the day we had thousands of bottles all ready to be picked up. I'm not sure how much the school made out of all that, but I bet it was a few hundred quid.

So much for the bottle drive. Now back to the School Fete. This was a pretty big deal as a way to raise money. All the schools had them, but of course Buranda's was the best. It was held on a sunny Saturday afternoon.

We had been preparing for it for weeks, and all the kids brought in stuff from home, like old books, comics, clothes and toys for sale at different stores. Different teachers took responsibility for different things and us kids worked with them to help.

On the day of the fete everything was set up under tents down on the oval. There were plenty of parents along to help. Mum made a big batch of pikelets and lamingtons and came along to work in the cake stall. Brad told me his Dad was going to be in charge of the hot dog stand and that he would introduce me.

"This is Des, Dad," said Brad. "He's only in Grade 5, but he's one of our best tennis players."

"In that case," said his Dad, "you can have a hot dog on the house." He gave me this great big saveloy on a bun with lashings of fried onions and tomato sauce. I swear it was the best hot dog I ever tasted.

Now, as I said before, the Fete may not have been the Ekka, but it was a pretty fair imitation. We had a dozen different stores selling all kinds of stuff. One of the biggest was the second hand book and comic store. Anything with food was also pretty popular. I worked on an "odds and ends" store. We didn't have a clue what to charge for anything, so I would name a price, and if I saw a twitch of disgust I knew I was probably too high, and would lower it. If people were nice, I would practically give things away, but if they started to argue, I would jack up the price even higher.

We had a chocolate wheel run by one of the dads, which did very well, though most of the prizes weren't chocolates, because we didn't have a lot of them. There were also a few merry-go-round rides for the smaller kids and some "knock 'em down" stalls for the older ones. All in all it was a pretty good show.

But the best part came with the official opening around 3 o'clock. This was held on a bit of a stage that had been set up for performances, like kid's choirs and pipe bands and the like. These were pretty good, but, as I say, the highlight came with the official opening. Mr. Merrell was there looking pretty spiffy in his best suit, along with another man looking very important in his suit. We kind of closed the stores down, so everyone could gather round for the ceremony.

Mr. Merrell introduced the other man as the Director of Public Instruction for the whole of Queensland. Now that had to be important. The man gave a speech about how good it was to see everyone out supporting the school and so on. Then he said that Mr. Merrell had told him how hard all of us kids had been working on the Fete, and how we were giving up a Saturday to come out and help the school. He said that Mr. Merrell had suggested that such good work should be rewarded, and therefore he was proclaiming (I thought that was a very important sounding word, proclaiming)—he was proclaiming that next Monday would be a school holiday for Buranda. Now I knew he was important; anyone who could proclaim a school holiday had to be someone special. We all clapped and cheered like mad. And that also made me think that Mr. Merrell (my Don Merrello) maybe wasn't such a bad chap after all. True, he was very strict, and he didn't hold back in swinging the cane, but here he was out making our school look important and getting us a holiday into the bargain. That was a really good thing for him to do, and I respected him for it.

The School Fete and the bottle drive showed us another side of school life and the teachers, who were all there helping to make things work, and to raise money so we could have the things we needed in the school. That's what you call school spirit, and I felt proud to be a pupil at Buranda.

It was also a pretty good deal that I could go back to Brad's father on the hot dog stand at the end of the day, and eat my fill of the hot dogs that were left over.

The End of Grade 5

At the end of my Grade 5 school year in December I was feeling pretty pleased with myself. I had done well in the final exam, and I was near the top of the class going into Grade 6. We didn't know which Grade 6 teacher we were going to have, but I knew the one I didn't want—Mr. Starke. He was the teacher I had met first when I came to Buranda with Mum over a year ago. He had scared the wits out of me then, and nothing I had seen or heard since then had changed my mind. He was generally regarded as a tyrant with an evil eye, and he was sloppily dressed in a perpetual brown suit. I don't think I had heard any of these opinions from anyone who had actually been in his class, but I knew for sure I didn't want to be one of them. In any event, I wouldn't know until after the school holidays, so I had to tuck that fear away in the back of my mind.

One of my great joys in every class I had been in was being introduced to wonderful stories and poems in each grade's Queensland School Reader. In Grade 5 I have already mentioned the story of Don Quixote, but that was only one of many. Here I also met Christian in the story of "Pilgrim's Progress," which was a special kind of book called an allegory, where the names of the characters and places revealed the kind of people or places they were, like Timorous and Mistrust and the Hill of Difficulty and the City of Death. Here I also learned by heart John Masefield's poem, "Sea Fever," and met Hiawatha as told by Henry Longfellow. I also learned a lot of history and geography—about the Roundheads and the Cavaliers in the English Civil War, about the rebels in the American Civil War, about the British army in India, and much more, all told in stories about bravery, and reward for sticking to the job, and belief in yourself, and never giving up, and about fairness and justice. I knew enough about life to know that things didn't always work out so well in the real world, but I loved these stories in my Reader, and thought that if ever I wrote stories they would be like them.

But now school was over until next year, and it was time to go back to the farm for Christmas. I had been telling Willy about the farm for so long that he really wanted to come and see it. Mum got together with his mother, and they agreed that he could come up to the farm for the holidays after Christmas, so I was very pleased about that. Gloria was sure she had done well in her Scholarship exams, so next year she would be off to High School. Val was doing all right, too, I suppose, learning to read and write a little bit, but not nearly as well as she should be able to. I wished I could help her more, but I was only a kid and her brother to boot, so there was no way she was going to listen to me.

So that's where we all were in our school lives, as we packed things up in Carl Street, and headed home with Dad to the farm for the holidays.

My Long Ride on Blackie

It was good to be back on the farm again, especially to see Blackie and go for a ride. As usual he was pretty frisky and fat from not having anything to do except hang around and eat. However, once I caught him and rode him for a bit he settled down. If the truth be known, he probably enjoyed having something to do. As it happened, it wasn't long before I gave him, and myself, an extra workout.

Mum had a parcel she wanted to get away so that it could be delivered before Christmas. Dad was too busy to take it into the post office at Westbrook, about eight miles away, and because we only got a mail delivery three times a week, Mum didn't want to wait an extra couple of days to send it with the mailman. So I said I would take it for her on Blackie.

Now, eight miles is a lot further than I had ever ridden before, and, of course, it was eight miles back, so that was sixteen altogether. This was going to be quite a workout, particularly for Blackie. He started off happily enough, but when he figured out I was riding him a lot further along unfamiliar roads, I could tell by the way he was twisting his head and balking at every little object, like a fallen tree or a bit of a gully, that he was not altogether happy about this expedition. It was also pretty hot, and I could feel myself getting a bit of a sunburn on parts of my thighs exposed by the way I was riding in the saddle just wearing shorts.

Anyway, after almost two hours we made it to the post office. When I got off, I could tell right away that I was going to suffer for this. When you haven't been riding a horse for a while, and you get on and ride a distance like this, the muscles in your thighs tell you they don't like it. Add to that the fact that you're riding a fat horse so your legs have to spread a bit further, and add in a touch of sunburn in a sensitive place, and you've got a recipe for a dose of pain.

I tied Blackie up to the fence and hobbled into the post office. The man behind the counter took one look at me and said, "G'day mate. You feelin' a bit sorry for yourself?"

"Yeah, I haven't ridden for a while," I said.

When he saw Mum's name on the return address on the parcel he said, "Struth, you've ridden all the way from Athol. You wait till tomorrow. The way you feel right now isn't a patch on what's coming."

I felt like saying thanks for nothing, but bit my tongue. I paid for the parcel and bought a bottle of cold lemonade with the change. The man gave me our mail to take home, and I hobbled back out the door.

"Happy returns," he called after me. "It's only eight miles back."

Smart Alec, I said to myself. Poor Blackie was looking just as bad as I felt, so I found a water trough to let him have a good drink and feed on the green grass around the trough, while I had a sandwich and finished my lemonade. Then, gritting my teeth, I swung myself back into the saddle and turned Blackie's head for home. As soon as he realized where we were going, his stride picked up right away, and we started to make good time. The pain in my legs subsided as they settled in for the long haul.

Though I had been along this road many times with Dad in the ute, you have a different experience when you ride it on horseback. There was a well worn track over by the fence clear of the traffic on the road, and in places we could canter and move right along. In other places we had to pick our way more carefully through trees and around logs. I saw the occasional hare and, of course, plenty of birds whose medley of songs filled the air, and kept us company along the way.

When we turned off the main road and headed down the last stretch towards home, Blackie got his second wind, and it was all I could do to hold him as we galloped along full tilt towards the house. Again, when I got off it was a repeat of the pain I had felt at the post office, only quite a bit worse. I could still hear the mailman smirking at me. I let Blackie go to join the other horses, and hobbled down to the house.

Mum took one look at me and realized I was not in good shape. She told me to strip off, and she bathed me down with cool water in the laundry, then rubbed some soft lotion into my aching sunburned thighs. I flaked out on the sofa in the dining room, and must have fallen asleep right away. When I went to get up a couple of hours later, I found I had no legs at all. I crawled to the kitchen and pulled myself up using the table. Gloria and Val were there helping Mum make cakes. When I stood up, all the agonies of hell went shooting down my legs. I had never felt such pain. I didn't have to wait until tomorrow, as the man in the post office had said. Tomorrow was already here for me, and I was suffering so much that the girls didn't even make fun of me. I hobbled into the breakfast room and sat down in my place on the stool. It wasn't time to eat, but I didn't care. I wasn't moving again, no matter what.

Thinking about it, I felt that I had had a good day out with Blackie, but I now knew that you can have too much of a good thing. I had learned a hard lesson about pacing myself and not going overboard. If there was any consolation, I had got this experience out of the way before Willy arrived. I would have hated for him to see me, the experienced farm boy, hobbling around half crippled from overdoing it riding a horse. Fortunately, I was well recovered before he arrived.

Willy Comes to the Farm

We picked Willy up at the bus depot in Toowoomba a few days after Christmas. He was looking a bit unsure of himself after the long bus ride and arriving alone in a strange place. However, as soon as he saw me he brightened up. We slung his port into the back of the ute and climbed in after it. First stop was Granny and Grandfather's for afternoon tea before we set off for the farm.

"You two could be brothers, you're so much alike," Granny said handing Willy a big slab of chocolate cake.

"Your grandparents are terrific," Willy said to me later as we whistled along in the back of the ute heading for home. "They made me feel like part of the family."

"You are," I said. "You'll find that out soon enough when Dad puts you to work."

"Gee, this is terrific riding along in the back of the ute," Willy said after a bit. "You can hear the pop, pop, pop of the exhaust and look at everything around."

"Yeah, it's beaut," I said. "See that place over there? You know what it is?"

"Looks like some kind of a school."

"More like a prison. That's the Westbrook Farm Home for boys. See there's a few of them working in the paddock with guards watching them."

"Gosh, what did they do to get put in there?"

"I dunno. Bad stuff, like stealing or bashing someone up, I suppose."

Willy looked a bit worried when he heard that. "Do they ever escape?" he asked.

"No, I don't think so. But don't worry, if they did, they wouldn't head in our direction. Dad had a couple working for us a few years ago, and they ran away. Couldn't get back to the city fast enough."

"You don't have any working for you now, do you?"

I felt like teasing him that we had one of the worst, but I could see he was worried, so I told him there were none on our farm or anywhere around. Soon after that we pulled up at our house. Willy's eyes were fairly bulging out of his head.

"Wow, this sure beats your dump on Carl Street," he said. "And look, there's Jim boy."

"Yeah, I brought him home for the holidays. I couldn't leave him in Brisbane. He's learning to be a farm dog, but he's not very good at it. There's the real Jim, our cattle dog."

The farm Jim had come bounding down from the cow bails. No sooner was Dad out of the ute than he sent him off to fetch the cows. Willy's eyes bulged out of his head again.

"Crikey, can he do that all by himself?" he asked as Jim streaked off.

"Yeah, he'll bring the cows in in no time. Come on, let's put your port in the house and we'll go up to the cow bails to help with the milking. My brother, Gordon, is already up there fixing up."

"What's fixing up?"

"Getting things ready for milking. Come on, I'll show you."

Not long after we were up at the cow bails, and I introduced Willy to Gordon.

"G'day," said Gordon, "you gonna get your hands dirty?"

"What d'ya mean?" asked Willy.

"Farm's a working place," said Gordon. "No room around here for loafers."

"I told him that already," I said, "but he needs to learn what to do."

"Yeah, I was only teasing," Gordon said. "Come and have a look around, but keep out of the way when the cows start coming in."

Willy was full of questions about how everything worked, and Gordon seemed to be enjoying himself showing him. By now Dad had changed into his work clothes and come up to the bails. The first of the cows were just arriving, with Jim working the herd carefully from behind. Dad started up the engine, and the lead cows went into the bails.

"Gawd, everything's happening at once," said Willy, shouting over the noise of the engine.

"Yeah, I have to go and help," I said. "You just stand here and watch."

For the next hour I was busy putting cows into the bails, washing tits, and keeping an eye on the tit cups to make sure they didn't fall off. Every now and then Willy would venture in to see what we were doing, then dive for cover as a cow starting kicking or shitting all over the place. When it was all over and Dad shut the engine off and everything was suddenly quiet, Willy just stood there shaking his head.

"Gawd, doc," he said to Dad. "Do you do this every day?"

"Twice a day," said Gordon. "We'll see you here again at 5 o'clock in the morning."

"Not likely," said Willy, "that's the middle of the night."

"Best time of the day," said Dad. "Here, try your hand at washing this vat."

So Willy was what you call inaugurated into our family on the farm. At tea time he sat beside me on the stool at the breakfast table as Mum served up the usual big meal of chops and veggies, followed by steam pudding and custard, and Dad teased Willy with all kinds of tall stories. But for the most part, Willy gave as good as he got, and I could see that everyone liked him.

Gordon gave up his bed so Willy and I could sleep together in the same room. We talked late into the night before we finally turned off the light and went to sleep. At 5 o'clock Gordon came in and shook us out of bed.

"My God, he really meant it," groaned Willy, as he rubbed the sleep out of his eyes. By the time we got to the kitchen Dad already had a pot of tea and a tin of Mum's oatmeal biscuits on the table. Then we were off to the cow bails for a repeat performance. This time Willy pitched in and helped Dad in his two bails, while I helped Gordon in his. After milking, Willy and I went with Dad when he took the milk to the cheese factory. Willy marvelled at everything he saw there and wanted to know chapter and verse on how the cheese was made. When we got back to the farm I introduced him to the pigs.

"Crikey, look at that big bugger," he said when he saw the boar. "You could play cricket with those balls."

"I wouldn't advise you to try it," I said, "or you might lose yours."

Then we went down for breakfast, where Mum had a huge pile of sausages and fried eggs waiting for us.

"I'm so hungry I could eat a horse," Willy said.

"You're in luck," said Gordon, "that's what the sausages are made out of."

We all laughed as Willy's face turned a light shade of green, but Mum said not to tease, and told him they were really pork sausages.

And so it went, day after day, as Willy was introduced to everything on the farm. He was particularly interested in the tractor, so one day we went with Dad up to the machinery shed as he got the tractor out to do some scarifying. After he filled the tank with kerosene and gunned the motor a bit, he showed Willy how to get the tractor started by pulling the hand clutch. Willy wanted to have a go. Now, I knew what was coming because that clutch was so stiff that there was no way that either he or I could pull it to get it engaged. But Willy gave it everything he could, and tugged and pulled until he was blue in the face, but he couldn't do it. Then Dad reached over and pulled it and the tractor took off with a lurch that nearly sent the two of us off the back into the dirt. But we hung on and rode with Dad up the bumpy lane.

He hooked up the scarifier, and off we went on the first round of the paddock. For me it was just like old times, when I had first done this with Dad, when I was a little kid. For Willy it was a whole new experience. After a while he yelled at Dad over the noise of the engine to ask if he could have a go at steering. Dad showed him how to keep the front wheel in the furrow and let him take over for half the length of the paddock. As we came to the corner, Dad stopped the tractor.

"How'd I do?" asked Willy.

"Pretty good," said Dad, "why don't you turn around and take a look."

We all turned around. The furrow that was supposed to be as straight as an arrow wandered all over the place, like a drunk at a christening.

"Jeez, I thought I was holding it straight," Willy groaned.

"You were, one second out of every ten," said Dad. "Now I'll take it round the corner, and you can have another crack at it to see if you can do any better."

I knew that Dad didn't like anyone messing up his furrows, so he must have really liked Willy to let him do it. At the next go he did better, and by the time we got all the way round, he was keeping the tractor pretty straight.

Another thing Willy wanted to do was ride a horse, so one day we went out to the horse paddock and caught Blackie and Patsy. We brought them to the harness room and saddled them up. I wasn't sure how good a rider Willy was, so I watched as he mounted Patsy. He seemed to know what he was doing, but just to be sure I rode on Blackie with him and Patsy around the house yard before going out on the road. Willy wasn't too keen on getting up any speed, so I thought we might just walk the horses up to the corner and back.

We went out the gate and headed up towards the turn in the road. We hadn't gone more than fifty yards, when suddenly a ground thrush flew out of some long grass just in front of us. Well, of course, both horses shied, and I instinctively gripped Blackie tight with my legs as I felt him start to leap sideways. Willy wasn't so swift. He lost one of his stirrups and flopped forward over Patsy's neck, as she leapt to the side. He probably jabbed her with his heel, because right away she took off, leapt over a little gully that ran across the road at that point, and headed up the road at a fast canter. Willy's straw hat sailed off his head, as he hung on for dear life, trying to get his foot back in the stirrup, and get a hold of the reins. I kicked Blackie into a gallop to catch up with them.

"Pull her head up," I yelled as we came abreast.

I didn't hear any reply, but I could see Willy was doing his best to stay on. Fortunately Patsy wasn't a very energetic horse at the best of times, so after her initial burst she was quite happy to slow down as Blackie and I pushed her over towards the fence. Just as suddenly as it began, the excitement was all over, and we turned the horses around to go back and retrieve Willy's hat.

"She scared the bloody daylights out of me," Willy said. "I wasn't ready for that."

"You did good to stay on," I said. "I've had my share of busters when a horse shies."

We took it easy after that, just letting the horses pick their way along, but I could see Willy was keeping a sharp eye out for anything that might set Patsy off again. We didn't go anywhere in particular or too far, because I didn't want Willy to get a dose of the same leg cramps that half crippled me before Christmas.

Another thing that fascinated Willy were the ants' nests we had all over the place on the farm. They were mostly big red meat ants. Quiet often they built good sized mounds, as they brought the dirt up from out of their underground tunnels. Willy was fascinated at how furiously they would attack if you poked their nest with a stick. They would pour up out of their tunnels in the thousands, and run every which way and back looking to attack the intruder.

"I know what we could do to drive them crazy," Willy said. "We could light a fire on the nest and cook them."

"Why would you want to do that?" I asked.

"Well, there's too many of them to start with, and they're no good for anything." I wasn't too sure about Willy's arguments, but it was a new idea, so I went along with it. We picked a nest that was well out in the open on clear ground, so there would be no danger of starting a grass fire. I got a couple of wet bags as an added precaution, and we piled the nest high with sticks and grass and lit it. The flames leapt up in quite a show.

"Bloody beauty," chortled Willy, dancing around. "That'll cook the little red devils."

The flames were still going pretty strong when Dad arrived on the scene.

"What the bloody hell do you two think you're up to?" he roared. I knew that tone of voice, and feared we were in for it. I should have known better than to get talked into this fool idea.

"G'day, doc," Willy said, not realizing that he was close to getting his block knocked off. "We're cooking the ants."

"I got some wet bags to make sure the fire wouldn't get away," I said, hopefully.

"That's the only smart thing I see around here," said Dad, a bit more quietly. I hoped that I may have saved both of us from getting a hiding. He turned to Willy. "And just what do you think the ants are doing while you're dancing around the fire?" he asked.

"They can't do anything," said Willy. "They can't escape. They're cooked."

Dad grabbed the wet bags and beat out the rest of the flames. He raked the burnt sticks aside to expose the top of the ash strewn nest.

"And just how do you think ants have survived bush fires for millions of years?" he asked Willy, as he picked up a long stick and prodded the top of the nest. Immediately thousands of ants came pouring out of their holes just as they had done before the fire. Willy couldn't believe his eyes.

"Where'd they come from?" he gasped.

"Out of their tunnels, you dope, which is where they went as soon as you lit the fire. Now I want the pair of you to get out of here and go and grab a couple of hoes and clean up all the weeds around the tennis court. I'll be down in an hour to see how much you've got done."

"Looks like that wasn't such a good idea," Willy mumbled as we set off at a sprint.

"You're bloody right it wasn't," I said. "We're lucky he didn't give us both a backhander."

We did a good job on cleaning up the weeds so that by the time Dad came to check it was all done. He had calmed down by then, so he told us we could take off. We decided we would prepare the tennis court and have a game. This meant watering and rolling the surface, putting up the net, and marking the lines. I was used to doing this on my own, but with Willy helping, it was much easier, especially with the two of us pulling the roller. It was soon done, and we went inside and got our racquets.

Willy was not a strong tennis player, but he was game and determined, so that although I could beat him he usually made me work for it. It was a pretty hot afternoon, so after a couple of sets we decided to take a break and sit in the shade of the house.

"You know what I would like right now," Willy said, "some of your Mum's beaut cakes."

So we went inside into the kitchen where Mum was cutting up some sponge cakes into squares to make lamingtons. She already had a huge plate of pikelets sitting on the counter, and a fresh batch of ginger biscuits cooling on a rack. Willy's mouth was watering as we came in the door and he spied the goodies.

"Mrs. Bergh, you're the most fabulous cook that ever was," he said to Mum, as he edged closer to the biscuits.

"I was just going to call you," she said, "to see if you wanted something to eat."

"Do we ever," Willy replied for both of us. We buttered a few pikelets, spread them with raspberry jam, put them on a plate with some biscuits, and poured a couple of big glasses of cold fresh milk out of the fridge. By then Mum had finished icing the first two lamingtons with thick dark chocolate icing on all sides. She rolled them in coconut and added them to our plate.

Outside, sitting on the lawn, his mouth stuffed with a lamington and pikelet, Willy made one of his what you call philosophical statements. "If I'd known your Mum was such a good cook and life could be as good as this," he said, "I would have made friends with you the first day you walked into the classroom last year." I suppose that was a backhanded compliment, which was about as good as his backhand on the tennis court. But that's the way it was with Willy. He was a good mate, and I don't think either of us had ever had as much fun as we did on that holiday together on the farm.

Grade 6 and a Lesson on Living

Back at school after the holidays my worst fear was realized—I was in Mr. Starke's Grade 6 class.

"I remember you, Berghofer," he growled as he was going through the class list with each one of us quivering as to what he might say about us. "You came up the steps with your mother looking like a little bird about to be kicked out of the nest." Everyone giggled nervously. "But I hear you've done all right despite that. Near the top of the class and a good tennis player, too. What do you intend to do this year?"

"My best, sir," I said, hoping that was what he wanted to hear.

"Your best, eh? In this class I expect everyone to do better than their best. You've probably heard that I'm a mean old coot, haven't you?"

"No, sir."

"No what – that you haven't heard, or that I'm a mean old coot?" He came up the aisle to where I was sitting on the end of the back row, his hooded eyes boring a hole into my head. I completely lost my voice.

"Well, boy," he growled, "cat got your tongue?"

I squirmed nervously, and it didn't help to see some of the other boys smiling. Then Mr. Starke spun around and caught one of them half out of his seat with his tongue sticking out. In one slow, deliberate move Mr. Starke reached out, grabbed the boy by the scruff of the neck and bent him over the end of the nearest desk.

"Well, I'll tell you, I *am* a mean old coot," Mr. Starke said as he brought his big knarled open hand down hard across the bum of the offending boy. "But only because I expect everyone in my class to do better than he has ever done before." He brought his hand down hard for a second time. "And that doesn't leave much room for comedians." He brought his hand down hard once again, then stood the boy up, and held him facing the class. "You see, boys," Mr. Starke continued, "I make it my business to know a lot about each one of you so that I know when you are trying really hard. If I think you're not, I will give you a hand to help you." He gave the boy something a little harder than a pat, but less than a blow, across the seat of his pants, and propelled him back into his place.

Needless to say you could hear a pin drop in that room for the rest of the morning. After he finished questioning everyone the way he had quizzed me, he told us to turn to page 86 of our new Grade 6 Queensland Reader. There we found the poem "Play the Game" by Henry Newbolt. We read it aloud, line by line as Mr. Starke pointed to a different boy for each new line.

> "There's a breathless hush in the Close tonight—
> Ten to make and a match to win,
> . . .
> But his Captain's hand on his shoulder smote
> 'Play up! Play up! And play the game.'
> . . .
> The sand of the desert is sodden red—
> Red with the wreck of a square that broke:
> . . .
> But the voice of a school boy rallies the ranks,
> 'Play up! Play up! And play the game!'
> . . .
> This they all with a joyful mind
> Bear through life like a torch in flame
> And falling fling to the host behind—
> 'Play up! Play up! And play the game!'"

By the time Mr. Starke finished drumming into our heads what that poem really meant, there wasn't one of us who didn't stand a little taller and step a little bolder, as we came out of the room at the morning break. I think we all realized by then that Starkie, the mean old coot, the tyrant with the evil eye, was one of the best teachers in the school.

My Long Distance Swim

On the sports side, as well as on the learning side, my Grade 6 year moved along quite nicely. I have said before that I was no great swimmer. My early memory of being half drowned at Helidon Spa had set the pattern for my dislike of swimming pools. However, because we had our own school pool at Buranda, and because we regularly went for swimming lessons in class time, I gradually learned to swim and do all of the usual strokes, not well, but enough to get me back and forth across the pool a couple of times.

One day the coach announced that next week we were going to try out for our long distance swimming certificate. For me that meant swimming 100 yards or four lengths of the pool. I had never done more than two lengths before and I doubted that I could do four. But the coach said I should have a go. I spent all week worrying about it.

However, on the day I showed up and put on a brave front. We could choose any stroke we liked, but the only one I had any chance of using to swim that distance was freestyle or the Australian crawl. I knew how to do this properly by turning my head to breathe in, and blowing out with my face in the water. But I hated that, and preferred to keep my head up and turn it from side to side.

"Remember, Berghofer," the coach said, as I stood on the edge of the pool ready for my turn, "keep your face in the water." 'Yeah, easy for you to say,' I thought to myself, but then I realized that other kids around me were swimming twice as far as I had to. Surely, for once I ought to be able to do this.

"Go," said the coach, and I was off on the longest swim of my life. The first length was easy enough, and the second one not too bad, but I was starting to feel winded. Halfway down the third I swallowed a gulp of water when I didn't get my mouth properly out of the water to breathe. When I got to the end of that length I was almost done for, but I wasn't going to give in. I looked up to the heavens, took one big gulp of air, and turned to go. I no longer knew whether I was breathing into the water or out of the water. I could see the bottom of the pool through eyes stinging from the chlorine. My arms felt like lumps of lead as I brought them over. I could no longer feel my legs, but I hoped they were still kicking. Half way down I looked up to see where I was. There was no one else in the pool. They had all finished except me. Then I saw some of my mates on the edge of the pool, and I could hear their voices cheering me on.

"Come on Grasshopper. You can do it."

I plunged on. I think the coach had deliberately started me at the deep end so I was out of my depth on this final lap. It was either swim the last ten yards or sink to the bottom, and die a miserable death. Somehow I found a new burst of energy. In my mind I could see the end of the pool, but I had no idea where it really was.

"Straighten up. You're going crooked." Somehow, the faint voices got through to my dulled brain, and I looked up long enough to see I was going crosswise towards the side. With a superhuman effort, for me, I straightened up, and put on a spurt for the last few yards. And then I felt my hand touch the end, and I was done. I could gladly have slipped quietly to the bottom and stayed there forever, but I felt two pairs of hands on my shoulders, dragging me up and out of the water.

"Good on yer," I heard a few voices saying.

"Congratulations, Berghofer, you got your certificate," the coach was smiling at me and tousling my soggy hair. As I gradually recovered my breath and my wits and stood up, I heard some slow dull clapping. I looked up to see my teacher, Starkie, sitting there in his sloppy brown suit, almost smiling at me as he clapped his hands. I could almost hear him saying, "Play up! Play up! And play the game!" That was probably the best compliment of all.

I Play at the Queensland Age Tennis Championships

Swimming was certainly not my sport, but tennis was another matter. Throughout the year my coach, Tom Whitworth, had been pushing me hard, and I still went out to his courts at Virginia every Saturday morning for lessons. At school I practised with the team, and we did reasonably well against the other schools we played. I didn't win all my matches, but that was because I was playing against older, stronger boys. As Brad had mentioned to me last year, the Age Championships were coming up at Milton during the holidays. I was still only eleven years old, so I could enter the under twelve singles.

These were the championships for the whole of Queensland held by the Queensland Lawn Tennis Association, and kids would come in from all over the State to play. To enter you had to be certified by your coach that you were good enough. Mr. Whitworth said I certainly had a good chance, so he wanted me to enter. Brad was always encouraging me, and he said he was going to play in the under fourteen singles. I told Mum about it, and she said I should go. So Mr. Whitworth entered me.

Milton was the main centre for tennis in Brisbane. It was where the champions came to play. I had never been there, but I thought it would be great if one day I could go and watch my hero Frank Sedgman play, but I don't think he had ever come to Queensland. In any event, it was exciting to think that I would be playing where the champions play. I wasn't too sure where to go, so I arranged to meet Brad at his tram stop, and we went out together. I was dressed in my whites, but had to wear a coat and sleeveless pullover, because the weather was quite chilly.

It was very busy when we got there early in the morning. I had never seen so many tennis courts. There must have been at least twenty, and some of them were grass. I had never played on grass, but that was what the champions played on. There were stands around the main courts where people could come and watch the big matches, but all of the activity today was on the hard courts, where kids of all ages were lining up to play.

The whole thing was organized by what you call a draw. We had to find Mr. Whitworth, who took us over to the building where the different matches were set up. We found the draw for the under twelve singles. I think there were 32 names on the draw, and we soon found mine. It showed who you were playing against, on which court, and at what time. We found Brad's draw and he was playing later than me, so he said he would come over to watch my match. Mr. Whitworth had a few boys playing in the tournament of different ages, so he said he would come to watch me when he could.

I was playing at 11 o'clock, so we went to my court in good time. There was another match finishing, so we had to wait for a bit. I saw another boy there about my age with his father. I guessed he was my opponent. I wished Dad could have been here to watch me play against other boys from all over Queensland, but I knew he was too busy on the farm. When the other game had finished, an older boy turned up with an official score card. He said he was the umpire for my match. It was all very official compared to the way we played at Athol, or even in our school matches.

As soon as we started to hit up, I knew that I was feeling good, and I could see that the other boy was at least no better than me. We started to play, and right away I won my serve. We were even for a few games, but then I found his weakness and I won the match 6-2. I was through into the second round, and I was finished for the day. Mr. Whitworth had arrived in time to see the last two games, and he said I was playing very well. A bit later on I watched Brad play, and he won his match, too, so that meant both of us would be back tomorrow for our next matches.

Mum and Gloria were excited to hear about my win. "This means I am already one of the sixteen best players for my age in Queensland," I said. "I know Dad would be pleased about that."

The next day Brad and I went back again. Things were just as busy as ever, because they were starting to play doubles. We found our courts and times. Brad was playing before me, so I went to watch him. He won easily, then came to cheer me on in my game. This boy was better than the first, and I had to work harder to beat him, but I won 6-4. So now I was into the third round, the quarter finals, because there were only four matches to play.

Mr. Whitworth had watched my match, and he said I was doing well, and had a good chance to win again. He warned me, though, that if I got through the next round, I was probably going to meet a really tough player in the semifinals. His name was Tony Moss, and he already had a reputation for being a good player.

The next day I made a point of going to see Tony play his match, because it was on before mine. I saw what Mr. Whitworth meant. He was very strong, and he won his quarter final match 6-0.

Now it was my turn, and I really had to work hard for it, but I won 6-3. No matter what happened after this, I had proved to myself that I was a good player, because I had won three matches, and I was through to the final four players. Unfortunately, Brad lost his match, so he was out of his competition, but he said he would come back tomorrow to watch me play. Brad was not only a very good player, he was also a good friend to a younger kid like me.

It was a chilly morning when Tony and I went out on the court to play. I kept my pullover on against the cold wind. Brad and Mr. Whitworth were my supporters, and Tony had a few people along to cheer for him. We were playing on a grass court. This was the first time I had ever played on grass. It took a while to get used to it, but I liked the way the ball kept low and allowed you to make your shots. However, it didn't take long for me to find out that I had my hands full with Tony. His serve boomed down, and his ground shots were hard and accurate. Before I knew what had happened I was down love 3. But I fought back to make a game of it. He had me at 5-3, but I won the next game to make it 4-5. I tried everything I could to level at 5 all, but Tony could smell a victory, and he took the game set and match at 6-4.

It's hard to go so far in a competition and then lose, but that's the way it is in tennis. In any match there can be only one winner. As we walked away, Brad put his arm around my shoulder. "You did really well to come so far," he said. "Wait till they hear about this back at school. And you did it all with your pullover on." This made me wonder if I had taken my pullover off I might have won. But I don't think so. Tony was just too good. I didn't come back the next day to watch the finals, but I heard afterwards that he won, so I at least had the satisfaction of losing to the player who went on to be the Champion of Queensland. Whatever I did in the future I would have that to remember.

Jim and the Ghosts at Dutton Park Cemetery

Now that my dog, Jim, was fully grown we had a lot of fun together. One of the tricks I tried to teach him was to bring in the newspaper in the morning. The man who delivered the papers would cruise along the street in his old Morris convertible, steering with one hand, and firing papers at houses on both sides of the street with the other. He usually managed to get the paper in the yard, but it could end up anywhere—in the flower beds, under the steps, maybe stuck in the hedge. Jim's job was to lie in wait for the delivery, watch where the paper landed and bring it into the house. Once he learned how to do it, things worked well for a couple of weeks—until he found out it was a lot more fun to rip the paper to shreds than to bring it into the house. No matter what I did I couldn't get him to unlearn this trick, with the result that forever afterwards he had to be chained up until after the paper was delivered and I had found it and brought it in.

We also went on a lot of long walks together, but he was always tearing ahead and getting into trouble. I suppose I could have kept him on a chain, but that would have been pretty boring for him and me. Maybe I didn't know much about how to train a dog, but one day my technique and Jim's free spirit probably saved my life.

We were out walking in the bush on Stevens' Hill, which was a patch of rough land on a hill in a deserted area about a mile from where I lived. We had already gone past the "No Trespassing" signs, and Jim was out of sight along the track ahead, that wound up the hill over rocks and through low thick scrub. I called out to him, but as usual got no response. I quickened my pace and came out suddenly into an open area, when I saw Jim just a few paces ahead, standing perfectly still looking at something.

"You bad dog," I shouted at him. "Why don't you come when I call?" I took a few more paces to catch up to him and grab him, then stopped dead in my tracks. I was standing right on the lip of a sheer cliff, which went straight down for about a hundred feet into a quarry. That's what Jim was looking at. The track we were on stopped dead on the top of a cliff, and there was no way you could see it until you were right on top of it. If Jim hadn't been standing there when I came up, I would probably have gone clear over the edge. As it was, my feet were just inches from the drop. I sat down in sheer fright, and at that moment Jim turned around, wagging his tail and jumped all over me. Needless to say, after that Jim could do no wrong as far as I was concerned.

Though we had a lot of fun together, by far the best times were when we went out with Willy and Rex. Either Willy would come round to my place or I would go round to his, in each case with dog in box. Then we would set off, the four musketeers in search of adventure. Our territory ranged far and wide, but none was more interesting than the Dutton Park Cemetery. We got there late in the day, just around dusk. We were on our way back from a long jaunt in South Brisbane along the banks of the river. We had tried our hand at fishing with hand lines off an old jetty, and had caught a couple of miserable specimens to bring home for Mum to cook. She was pretty good about that, just like she would cook the odd pigeon we shot on the farm with our air rifles.

In any event, we came to the cemetery, which was just at the top of Dutton Park Hill not far from Val's school. I said we should go on home because it was getting late, but Willy said he wanted to explore the cemetery. We got in through a side gate that wasn't closed. It was pretty hard to ride our bikes in there because the paths were narrow and winding with a lot of ups and downs. In the end we decided to let the dogs out and push our bikes. Jim immediately took off and Rex followed him.

"That dog of yours is teaching mine bad behaviour," Willy complained.

"Don't worry, they won't go far," I said. "And you never know, they might flush out a ghost."

"That's cogswoddle about ghosts in cemeteries," said Willy. "You don't want to believe that bull."

I wasn't so sure, especially now that the sun had gone down, and it was getting dark.

"We oughta be getting home," I said. "What did you want to see in here anyway?"

"Nothing in particular, just the different kinds of tombstones. Look, there's one with an angel perched on the top of it. I expect whoever's buried there thinks the angel will protect him."

I stared at the angel against the darkening skyline, and thought it looked a bit strange, when, all of a sudden it opened its wings and flapped off low above our heads. I heard Willy gasp, and I felt the hair stand up on the back of my neck.

"Bloody big owl," I muttered.

"Yeah, scared me stiff," said Willy.

"Let's get out of here."

"Yeah, I agree. Where are those damn dogs?"

Willy whistled and yelled for Rex, and I did the same for Jim. At first there was no response, but then all of a sudden, we heard furious barking a fair way off, then coming closer very fast. We yelled some more for the dogs, and peered into the gathering gloom among the tombstones. Then we saw this figure all in white leaping up and down in the air like a banshee on an ant's nest. At first it was coming towards us, and I froze to the frame of my bike. Then it veered off and disappeared over a small hill. I was too scared to say a word, and I swear I could hear the mudguards on Willy's bike rattling beside me. At that moment the dogs arrived, looking like they were having the time of their lives. Without a word we picked them up, stuffed them in their boxes, and took off out of there, the headlight on Willy's bike weaving an eerie pattern as he twisted and turned along the narrow path in front of me. We didn't say a word until we were a hundred yards clear of the cemetery.

"What the heck do you think that was?" I finally asked.

"Probably some half-crazed metho who the dogs flushed out from sleeping among the tombstones," Willy suggested.

"Yeah, or maybe a ghost," I offered.

"No such thing as ghosts," Willy muttered, but he wasn't hanging around to check it out any further, as we headed off down Dutton Park Hill flat out for home.

The Grade 6 School Reader

Two things were happening in my life as I came to the end of my Grade 6 year. First, I was doing very well at school, and I had a new friend in class who was vying with me for top place. Second, Dad had decided to do a major renovation of our house, and he was spending more time in Brisbane working with the builders, who would do the job while we went home for the Christmas holidays.

The new friend was Bob. He lived a fair way off at Mt. Gravatt, so I had not been to his place, but he was very smart, and we enjoyed each other's company in class, talking about what we were learning. Willy was still my best friend out of school, but it was good to have a new special friend in class as well.

By now I was twelve years old, and I felt that I was learning a lot, especially about the history of Australia and the geography of the world, as well as the wonderful stories and poems in my Grade 6 Reader. I now knew that Australia was founded as what you call a penal colony with convicts coming from England in 1788, after the land had been discovered by Captain Cook in 1770 and named New South Wales. The first settlement was made at Port Jackson (now called Sydney), then later on, a place for the worst convicts to be sent was established at Moreton Bay, which eventually became Brisbane. There was still an old convict stone windmill for grinding grain (which I understand never worked very well) up on Wickham Terrace, as well as the stone foundations of some warehouses down along the river. That was all that was left of the convict days, but it was interesting to know how it all began.

Just as interesting were the authors I was meeting in my Queensland Reader, one of whom, Mr. Starke said, was writing at the same time as the terrible conditions in England were the reason why they had so many convicts to send to New South Wales. The author's name was Charles Dickens, who, Mr. Starke said, wrote many novels about these bad conditions, though the one in our book was a little different, because it was about how a poor family enjoyed Christmas in London, even though they didn't have much money. It was called "The Cratchit's Dinner Party" from a famous novel called *A Christmas Carol*. I had never read such wonderful writing or met such interesting characters, especially Tiny Tim, the poor little cripple, who rode home from church on his father's shoulder. I particularly liked the description of the Christmas pudding because it reminded me so much of Mum's Christmas pudding on the farm: "Hallo! A great deal of steam! The pudding was out of the copper. A smell like a washing day! That was the cloth. A smell like an eating-house and a pastry cook's next door to each other, with a laundress's next door to that! That was the pudding!" Now, that's good writing.

There was also a story about "How Tom Sawyer Whitewashed the Fence" by a famous American writer named Mark Twain. This was very cleverly written, telling about how Tom tricked other boys into doing all the work by pretending it was something special. Again, the writing was very good, like this sentence that summed it all up: "Tom gave up the brush with reluctance in his face, but alacrity in his heart." I was learning a lot about how good writers put words together, and I tried to copy them in my compositions. Another account in the Reader about the life of Robert Louis Stevenson said that was what he did, and so later in life he was able to write his famous novels. There was an extract from one of them in the Reader called "The Siege of the Round-House." It told of how a boy, not much older than me named David Balfour, had his first taste of fighting against cutthroat seamen, who were trying to steal the money belt off a great sword fighter named Alan Beck. This was the best adventure writing I had ever read, and right away I went to the library to get the novel from which it came called *Kidnapped*. I also found out he had written another famous novel called *Treasure Island* and I got that one, too. These were two of the best novels I had ever read, and I would recommend them to all boys.

There was also a lot of great poetry in the Reader—adventure poems, humorous poems, and great descriptive poems, the best of which was the famous Australian poem called "My Country" by Dorothea MacKellar.

> "I love a sunburnt country
> A land of sweeping plains
> Of ragged mountain ranges,
> Of drought and flooding rains.
> I love her far horizons
> I love her jewel-sea,
> Her beauty and her terror—
> The wide brown land for me."

No Aussie kid could fail to be moved by that. It went on stanza after stanza that took you right into the mind of the writer, so that you could see "the stark white ring-barked forests" and hear "the drumming of an army, the steady soaking rain." "Core of my heart, my country!" My heart filled with emotion and I learned the whole poem, so that I could recite it over and over. I was truly learning how beautiful and powerful words can be to stir deep feelings in your heart, and set your mind racing in anticipation of the next exciting adventure. I truly wanted to learn to write like that.

The Big Renovation

As I said, the other thing happening at the end of the school year was a lot of commotion around our house, as carpenters started to set things up for a major renovation, while we went home to the farm for the holidays. I had seen the plans that Dad had worked out with the builder, and I could see that our old dump of a house, as Willy called it, was going to be transformed into a really modern home.

First up, they were going to jack up the house, and replace the old wooden stumps with concrete ones, and pour concrete over the whole area under the house. That would destroy my race track, where I used to ride an old axe handle as a horse around and around in the dirt. But I didn't mind too much, because I was getting too old for that kind of thing anyway.

We had to pack all of our furniture and belongings into one big room, so they could tear down walls and work around our stuff. Best of all I was going to get my own big room out the back off the verandah. This would be great for studying for my Scholarship Year, and for building various projects. Gloria and Val would still share a bedroom, and Mum would have her own room at the front of the house to share with Dad when he came. The whole of the old open verandah would be closed in with louvres so that we would have a lot of extra space. We would also get a big new kitchen, with a modern gas stove instead of the old wood one we had now, and a brand new fridge to replace the old ice chest. The bathroom would have hot water from a water heater, and the laundry would be moved upstairs. We would even have a water softener to soften the hard Brisbane tap water, and make it more like the rain water you get from the tanks. Wow what a difference! I knew that Dad was spending a lot of money to do this, and that he was worried about how to pay for it, but it just goes to show how much he cared for us, and what he was prepared to do to make sure Val went to school, and that Gloria and I got a good education.

Gloria had just finished her first year at Commercial College, where she was studying typing and shorthand to become a secretary. She had an old typewriter at home to practise on, and I thought that maybe I could teach myself to type by using her teaching book. Val had finished another year at her school, and was doing all right. Most of all, she seemed to enjoy spending time with her deaf friends, who often came round to visit. There were a lot of deaf kids her age because of the German measles epidemic in the year when they were born. I always thought this was sad, but it was good to see them making the best of it.

It was arranged for Willy to come up to the farm again after Christmas, and I was certainly looking forward to that.

Willy, the Crows and the Guns

When Willy arrived at the farm, we just picked up from where we had left off the last holiday. Right away we got into doing all the things we did last time (except for that stupid idea of lighting a fire on the ants' nest). We rode the horses, went out on the tractor with Dad, played tennis, and tried to bag some pigeons with our air rifles. Willy had brought his Webley with him, which was a pretty nice rifle as far as air guns go.

Then one day Dad said to us, "I think you boys are probably old enough to use a 22, so I'm going to show you how, then Gordon can take you out with it." Now, this was a really big deal. Dad had a terrific pump action 22 in which you loaded 10 or 12 cartridges into the cylinder and used the pump action under the barrel, by sliding it backwards and forwards, to pump a new round into the chamber. He got it out of the cupboard where he stored all the rifles. He had quite a few: a 32 Winchester, a 44, a double barrel 12 gauge shot gun, and a smaller single barrel shot gun. And this holiday he had something else that was very special—and illegal. Our next door neighbour in Brisbane, Les, had one day called Dad and me over to the fence and said he had something to show us. He produced this thing wrapped up in a towel, and when he unwrapped it we saw that it was a shiny all metal automatic pistol. Not even Dad had seen anything like this before. Hand guns were absolutely illegal in Queensland, and you could get a big fine for having one, unless you had the proper permit.

Les said he had found it, but now he didn't know what to do with it. He didn't even know if it worked, because he was too scared to try it out. He wanted to give it to Dad, but Dad said not on your life, though he did agree to bring it home to try it out. It was a 32 Smith and Wesson, so we could use the same 32 shells as we had for the rifle without having to go to a gun shop and let on that we had an illegal weapon.

So on this day Dad brought out his 22 and the pistol and the four of us— Dad, Gordon, Willy and I—set off like a pack of schoolboys to try some target practice. We were on the way up towards the machinery shed when a flock of crows that were often sitting in an old dead tree up by the cow bails took off with a whole round of squawking. I bet they were probably the same crows that my friend, Jim, and I had tried to shoot a couple of years ago.

"Will you look at that," said Willy. "Those buggers are always sitting in that tree, but this is the first time I've ever seen them take off like that unless you get up real close."

"That's because they saw the rifle," said Dad.

"Oh, come on," said Willy. "You can't tell me that crows know when you've got a rifle."

"You bet they do," said Gordon. "You can come out carrying a stick, or even your air rifle, and they won't take any notice. But as soon as they see a 22 or anything bigger, they're off like a rocket."

"Aw, come on. Pull the other leg," Willy said. "They're over a hundred yards away. Do you mean to tell me they can tell that you're carrying a 22 from that distance?"

"That's right," said Dad. "You can try it out yourself tomorrow. Right now we need to set up some tin cans for target practice."

Still unconvinced Willy followed us over to the fence where we put some cans on a few posts. Dad showed us the action of the rifle, then warned us, "Now remember, this is not a toy. It's much more powerful than your air rifle. It can kill an animal or a person, so you always need to know what's around you when you're firing, and you need to keep the safety catch on when you're not. It's all right to shoot from here, because we're shooting down from a bit of a ridge, and the bullets will end up in the dirt of the paddock back there where there aren't any cows or horses."

Dad took aim at one of the cans and blew it off the fence from about 30 yards. He gave the rifle to Gordon, who repeated the trick. Then it was my turn. The rifle was lighter than I thought it might be. I sighted it on the can, gently squeezed the trigger, and again blew the can off the post. "Good shot," said Dad. I was surprised there was very little kick from the rifle. I reloaded it with the pump action, and the empty shell flew out onto the grass. I gave it to Willy, and he shot the last can off its post.

Dad seemed pleased. "All right," he said, "you're both good shots. Gordon will take you out hunting later. Now let's have a look at this pistol of Les's."

We set the cans back up on the fence and Dad put a round into the magazine, which was inside the handle. To load, it had a slide mechanism on the top of the barrel.

"Here goes," said Dad, aiming at the can. "Never done this before." He pulled the trigger. The pistol went off with a crack much louder than the 22, and the muzzle flew up in the air. The top of the fence post splintered, but the tin can stayed put, and we heard the bullet zing away in a ricochet.

"All right," Dad said, "That's enough. We're gonna put this bloody thing away, and give it back to Les to get rid of. It's too damn dangerous. I can see why they're illegal."

And that was the last we saw of the pistol.

Hunting the Fox

Next day we crept out of the house to see if the crows were around. Sure enough, there they were, in their favourite tree. We decided to try an experiment. First, Willy walked out in the open carrying a stick. The crows didn't move. Then I came out carrying my air rifle. Still no reaction. We both went back inside and then came out again carrying the 22. Immediately, one of the crows let out a squawk, then right away they all took off, yakking and circling and complaining at us until they finally disappeared into the trees.

"Well, I'll be damned," said Willy. "Your father was right. Those beggars can tell what's a rifle and what's not."

Later that day after milking Gordon said he had time to go out shooting with us. He carried the 22, and we took our air rifles.

"What are you looking for?" asked Willy.

"Not much around here to shoot," said Gordon. "We might see a hare or a fox."

About half an hour later we were out in the bush on a neighbour's farm on the other side of the main road to Toowoomba. Suddenly Gordon signalled to us to stop and pointed up ahead. I strained my eyes, then saw a little brown blob hopping slowly through the yellow grass. It was pretty hard to see, but then he stopped and looked around, and I could clearly see the long ears of a hare. Gordon handed me the rifle. "Here, take a shot," he said.

To tell the truth I didn't want to shoot the creature, but if I refused then either Gordon or Willy would try, and probably hit him. I brought the rifle up and took aim. It was a hard shot, and it would be no disgrace to miss, but to make sure I aimed a bit over the hare's ears and fired. A spurt of dust kicked up on the other side of the hare, and he took off right away into the bush.

"Too bad," said Willy, "but it was a long shot." I just handed the rifle back to Gordon. We didn't see any more hares or foxes, but on the way back we came by the rubbish dump in the hill paddock, and we set up a sheet of tin with some red paint on it as a target. We blasted away at it for a bit, and I certainly showed that I was a good shot. I just wasn't keen on shooting animals without a good reason.

The next day Willy and I went out on our own with the 22. Dad and Gordon were working with the big circular saw, cutting up logs for firewood on a strip of land in one of the top paddocks, where the cleared timber had been hauled and left to dry. Up beyond that near the dam was a patch of bush. We decided to go in there. Not far into the bush we saw a trail of feathers.

"What do you think that is?" asked Willy.

"I dunno," I said, "but they look like chook's feathers." There was a neighbour's house just across the road. "Maybe a fox got one of the chooks from that place over there and dragged it into the bush here to eat it."

Willy brightened up at that. "At last we're on the trail of a fox," he said. I didn't give us much chance of seeing any fox that should be much smarter than to let a couple of school kids track him down. But wouldn't you know it, not long afterwards Willy grabbed my arm and pointed. There sure enough about 20 yards away, half hidden in the bushes, was the unmistakable outline of a red fox. He hadn't noticed us. I didn't really want to shoot him, even though he was obviously raiding our neighbour's chook yard. I handed the rifle to Willy, who took careful aim and fired. The fox yelped, tottered a bit, then took off limping along the headland towards the patch of logs where Dad and Gordon were working.

"I winged him," Willy shouted, as he reloaded and pumped off another couple of rounds that missed.

"Be careful where you're shooting," I yelled. "Remember what Dad said."

Willy didn't fire any more and we took off running after the wounded fox. We were gaining on him when he reached the edge of the fallen timber and promptly disappeared into a hollow log.

"Damn," said Willy. "How'll we ever get him out?"

"He'll probably die in there," I said. "The poor thing is suffering. We have to put him out of his misery."

I took the rifle and fired a round up the hollow log. There was no sound from inside that dark prison. "Better make sure," said Willy, and he took the rifle and pumped another couple of rounds up the log.

We figured for sure that the poor creature was dead, but we didn't just want to leave him there. Willy thought that his pelt must be worth something, and if not it would make a good mat. By now we were both feeling pretty bad about the whole thing, but we had to finish the job.

"The only way we can get him out is to chop the log open," said Willy.

"Yeah," I replied, "and that won't be easy, because that's hardwood."

"Maybe your Dad will cut it open with his saw."

"Yeah and mangle the poor fox while he's at it. Besides he's too busy. This is our problem. We'll have to go and get an axe."

It was a good twenty minutes walk down to the house, and another twenty minutes back. We then set to work with the axe, but it was like pulling hen's teeth. After an hour of chopping we hadn't even got through to the hollow in the log. Dad and Gordon packed up their work to go down for the milking, and Gordon drove over in the ute to see what we were doing. When we told him he burst out laughing, and said he'd see us after dark, and drove off. He wasn't far wrong. The sun was almost setting by the time we had cut a hole large enough to feel around inside for the dead fox. Willy finally grabbed it by the brush and pulled it back, then between chopping to make the hole larger and pulling the poor fox through the jagged edges, we ended up with a pathetic mangled carcass. We both felt too sick to want to have anything more to do with it. We decided to leave it for the crows. We were sure they were hanging around somewhere laughing at us, anyway.

"You know," I said to Willy as we trudged back to the house carrying the axe and the rifle in the gathering darkness, "I don't really want to have anything more to do with hunting."

"Me neither," he said. "That experience is enough to turn anyone off for life."

We walked home the rest of the way in silence.

In Grade 7 and at the Top of the School

Back at school after the holidays I started my Grade 7 year with good news. My teacher was Mr. Howard, who was well known to be both a good teacher and a decent bloke. After he had checked the roll on the first day he told us he had something important to say.

"Well, here you are in Grade 7," he said, letting his eyes rove slowly over each one of us. He was not a big man like Mr. Kimlin, or intimidating like Mr. Starke, but a soft spoken, level headed sort of chap, who you felt wouldn't give you any bull. "You've been preparing for this all of your lives, and now here you are," he continued. "What does it mean to be in the top class of the school? I'll tell you. It means that you're the ones who set the example for all the others. When you were younger, you looked up to the Grade 7s. Now all of a sudden you're in Grade 7, and everyone is looking up to you. So you have to make sure you show them something worth looking at.

"I'm not just talking about marks, and how well you do in your Scholarship Exam at the end of the year. That's an important part of it, but all anyone expects is that you will do your best. I'm here to help you do that, and the rest is up to you. But more important than marks you get on a report, is the mark you leave at school. It shows up in how you behave on the school grounds; how helpful you are in all the little things going on around here; how you go the extra mile; how you volunteer without being asked.

"Do you understand what I'm saying to you?" And here he looked at a few of us and called us by name. We shifted in our seats and mumbled, "Yes, sir." Then he asked the whole class again, and we shouted out, "Yes, sir!"

"Good," he continued, "because, I tell you, most of you won't be famous, maybe one or two of you will be, but most of you won't. But all of you can grow up to be good citizens, dinkum Aussies, ready to see that everyone has a fair go in life. Will you promise me that, boys? Will you promise me that you're ready to do everything you can to be a decent bloke yourself and show others you expect the same of them? Will you promise me that, boys?"

"Yes, sir!" we said a little louder and stronger than before.

"Good. Then I think we understand one another. You've got a hard year of work ahead of you, and you've only got one chance to do it right. So let's get started."

With that he gave us an outline of the Grade 7 work in the different subjects and handed out our text books. As ever, I was keen to see the Queensland Reader, and Mr. Howard said we were going to read a lot of stories in there that illustrated what he had been saying. Then he spent the rest of the morning chatting to us, asking each of us what we liked, what we were proud of in ourselves, what we thought we might do a bit better. By the time it was over, all of us had a new respect for each other. We knew we weren't angels or champions, but Mr. Howard made us feel that we mattered.

And one thing we knew for sure. We had a great teacher for our last year in Primary School.

I Fall in Love

At home things were a bit chaotic. We had come back from the farm to a totally new house. It looked terrific. On the outside it had a cream weatherboard finish with louvres along the front, a concrete block and wrought iron front fence, two concrete tracks down the driveway on the side to the back yard, lattice work closing in the whole of the area under the house, which was completely concreted. Upstairs, the rooms were spacious, especially the kitchen, which had brightly coloured linoleum on the floor, and a table in the middle large enough to seat the whole family and more. It was great, but it seemed that most things weren't quite finished, and we lived for a few weeks dodging carpenters, plumbers, painters and the cheerfully irreverent Italian crew who came in to pour the terrazzo floor in the bathroom.

To add to the confusion at home and the challenges at school, another great development occurred in my life. I fell in love, or rather, I should say, both Willy and I fell in love. It certainly was no coincidence that we did this together. As a twelve year old going on fourteen, with a mate who was already two years older than me, it was a dead cert that sooner or later our fancies would turn to the fairer sex. Opportunity also had more than a little to do with it as well, because it so happened that right across the street from Willy's place on Cornwall Street lived a voluptuous young thing with long auburn hair, freckles, green eyes and budding new breasts. Her name was Marien, and she had a friend with curly blonde hair and a lively tomboy personality with the build to match it, named Val.

We met them through the dogs, that is to say, we used the dogs as a ploy to meet them. Of course, we knew the girls were there. Marien had probably lived there for years, but we'd never taken much notice, until one day we saw them both together in her front yard. We were sitting on the front steps of Willy's house across the street. We could see them giggling and making themselves obvious to us.

"Look at the blonde," said Willy. "She's a bit of all right."

"If you take her, I'll take the other one," I said. "She looks terrific."

"She lives there," said Willy. "I think her name is Marien. I've never seen the other one before."

"Why don't we go over and talk to them," I suggested.

"I've got a better idea," said Willy. "Why don't we put the dogs on the back of our bikes and ride past on the footpath. Girls go silly over dogs."

"Good idea," I said. "Let's go."

We grabbed Rex and Jim from where they were chasing each other around the yard, and stuffed them into their boxes, and off we went. We deliberately crossed over Cornwall Street, and rode right by the girls on the footpath.

"Ooo, look at Rex and Jim," we heard them coo.

"It's working," said Willy, when we got to the corner of the next street. "Let's turn around and go back, slowly."

By now the girls were out on the footpath, and as we came abreast of them they started ooing again. We stopped, and Willy manoeuvred his bike towards the blonde girl.

"Wanna pet him?" he said. "He won't bite."

"Oh, he's so sweet," she said, reaching for Rex.

By now I had edged my bike over beside Marien, who was pretending to look at Jim.

"Oh, look at his floppy ears," she said. "Can I pet him?"

"Yeah, he likes that," I said. "His name's Jim, but I expect you can tell that from his box. I'm Des."

"I'm Marien," she giggled, turning a bit sideways and arching her back so her breasts came out a bit further. "This is my friend, Val."

"I'm Grant," said Willy. He wasn't going to waste any more time. "You girls want to go for a walk?"

We dumped our bikes against the fence and set off, dogs running ahead, Willy and Val side by side, and Marien and me bringing up the rear. I don't remember what we talked about, not much I expect, but we did find out that they always went to the pictures at the Boomerang Theatre every Saturday afternoon.

"Why don't we meet you there next Saturday," I said.

"Oh yes, that would be fun," Marien agreed. Val smiled and nodded, and Willy winked at me.

Next Saturday we met them outside the picture show. Willy and I bought the tickets and some chocolates, which just about cleaned me out of pocket money for the week. We sat in the canvas chairs, Val and Willy in one and Marien and I in another next to them. The usherette gave us a hard look as we sat down, as if to say, "I've got my eye on you, and I'll be back with my torch when the lights go out." But she didn't have much to worry about from me and Marien that day. For the most part we just sat and watched the picture, though I can't remember what it was. The nearest we came to smooching was when Marien slid her hand into mine halfway through the main feature and snuggled up close to me.

The romance went on for a month or so, things getting a little steamier each week. We learnt to sit in the middle of the row where the beam from the usherette's torch was less likely to reach us. Besides, she had more than enough other kids to keep an eye on. The first time I kissed Marien in the dark of the picture show was the beginning of a whole new world. She had her head on my shoulder, and she turned her face up towards mine, and I could feel her hot breath on my cheek. The next moment I kissed her. It wasn't exactly a take your breath away experience, but it was pretty nice—a mixture of hot lips pressing with teeth touching and noses rubbing until we got the hang of it. We didn't overdo it, at least I don't think we did. I had no idea what Willy and Val were up to, except that it was so noisy I felt sure the prison guard usherette would stab us with her searchlight. The next couple of Saturdays warmed up quite a bit, and I'm not talking about the weather. When Marien moved my hand up onto her breast on the outside of her blouse, the thing took on a whole new dimension. Not that there was much there to feel, kind of like a soft little mound struggling to grow bigger under my caress, but the heavy breathing and little moans that went with it were pretty exciting, that is, until the usherette's torch beam found us out, and then the rest of the show passed with simple hand holding.

We saw the girls on and off in other places, mostly around Marien's yard or Willy's. The most memorable was one afternoon after school when Willy's mother wasn't home, and he invited the girls over to show them his prowess at making a chocolate cake. They were really impressed that he knew how to do that. Things got more interesting for me when we put some records on Willy's gramophone, and did some dancing while the cake was cooking. None of us were great dancers, but the girls showed us some fancy jive steps to the "Muskrat Ramble" and how to dance cheek to cheek to "I'm in the Mood for Love." When the cake was done the girls wanted to ice it even before it was properly cooled. We were all in the kitchen innocently tucking into four thick slices when Willy's mother came home. She said she was glad to see us enjoying ourselves. And we were, too. It was a lot of fun.

However, this first romance for the four of us eventually came to an end. We boys had other things to get on with, as did the girls, though I'm not sure what they were. It was an interesting part of growing up. For Willy and me it was our first adventure into romantic territory, and while we liked it well enough at the time, it was just another of life's experiences that we took in stride.

Several Big Projects

This was also the year for building different projects. My friend, Fred, next door had the plans for making a crystal set. He had already built his own, and when I saw how well it worked, I decided I wanted to make one, too. I didn't completely understand how it worked, but I got the jist of it. You picked up the signal from a radio station using a long wire as an antenna, which I strung up through my window to the roof of the house. The amazing thing was that you didn't need batteries, because you were using the electrical current induced by the radio waves between the antenna and the ground.

The receiving set consisted of a tuner to select a particular radio station, and a cat's whisker detector to convert the radio wave back to an audio wave that you could listen to through earphones. The fun part, and often the most frustrating, was prodding around with the tiny thin wire (the cat's whisker) on a piece of crystal, until you got the radio station coming in loud and clear. It was very easy to lose the connection, so once you got it, you didn't want to hardly breathe or create a vibration that would cause you to lose the signal. However, once I got it working, I used to listen to my crystal set for hours and hours, including listening in the early hours of the morning to the description of Don Bradman batting for Australia in England for the Ashes.

Another project was building my own projector for showing pictures on a screen. Actually the projector part was pretty crude, and it didn't really work very well, because all I had was a shoe box with a torch inside to shine through the film as I wound it through the box. The fun part was creating the film, which I made out of cellophane paper cut in strips and glued together to make a long roll. I had to draw on the cellophane with different coloured ink, and because I wasn't a good artist to begin with, and the ink didn't take too well to the cellophane, the result was not always that great. I made up comic stories about the Phantom or the Lone Avenger and the first frame on each story always said "A Berghofer Production," in the same way that the movie companies always put their names at the start of their films.

I also kept my silk worms going. I had started these last year, again with the gift of a few from Fred, who had his own farm going strong. Silk worms are long white grubs, and because their favourite food is mulberry leaves I had no shortage of supply from the mulberry tree in our backyard. Actually, I found out that you could get different coloured silk according to which leaves you fed the worms. Mulberry leaves would give you a beautiful golden thread, lettuce leaves a green thread, and beetroot leaves a red thread. I kept the worms in shoe boxes in my room. There wasn't much to do most of the time, except give them fresh leaves and a bit of water, and empty their poop out of the shoe box. Then when the magic time came they would start to spin their cocoon of silk, and turn into a chrysalis inside the cocoon. You knew the cocoon was ready to be wound when you could shake it and hear the chrysalis rattling around inside. I made a winder out of my Meccano set and would find a thread on the cocoon and start to wind it. You had to sit the cocoon in a glass of water to loosen up the thread. If you did it right the thread came off fairly easily, and if it broke, you would just moisten it and stick it together and continue. When you had wound off all the silk you would just leave the chrysalis in the box and keep an eye on it until the chrysalis turned into a moth that would lay a whole batch of eggs for the next crop of silkworms. I never did anything with all the silk, because the next stage would be to weave it into cloth and that was much too complicated for me to get into.

What with my crystal set, film projector and silk worms, I had a lot of activity going on in my bedroom. Added to that were all my school books, as well as a John Bull printing set. This consisted of rubber letters that you could take out of their places in the holding block with a pair of tweezers, and put them into a printing block backwards to make up the words you wanted to print. Then you would press the printing block onto an ink pad, and carefully press the block onto a piece of paper trying not to make any smudges. This was a pretty laborious process for printing anything of great length, but it was good for labeling, and making some of my written projects for school look a bit snazzy.

My friend, Bob, at school probably had the best hobby of all. He invited me out to his place at Mt. Gravatt to see it. He made model aeroplanes that actually had a little gasoline motor and cords for controlling the flight. We went out to a piece of open ground, and he showed me how he flew his planes. The motor was a bit temperamental, but once he got it going it would whine like a thousand blow flies. I held onto the plane while Bob backed up with the control cords, then when I let it go, he got it to run forward then take off and fly round and round in a circle, doing all kinds of manoeuvres until he brought it in for a landing. Of course, sometimes things didn't work out exactly as planned. The motor might conk out in mid air, and the plane would stall and crash. Then it was back to the repair shop for major rebuilding. I thought it was a pretty fancy hobby, but it wasn't something I wanted to get into. I already had enough on my plate.

I was still spending a lot of time playing tennis. Now that Brad had left school I was captain of the tennis team, and we did pretty good in competition against the other schools. My coach, Tom Whitworth, wanted me to enter in the Age Championships again at Milton, but things were just getting too busy in my life, so I decided not to do that. Eventually I cut back on the Saturday morning coaching as well. I knew Mr. Whitworth was disappointed, but I just didn't see myself becoming a top tennis player without putting in more time than I could afford. I was still the only man around the house, so I had a lot of responsibilities at home, as well as my school work.

I was now having to sort out priorities in my life. I had reluctantly come to the city to live a few years ago, and even though I had thought then that I would always want to go back to the land, now I wasn't so sure. Gordon would always be number one on the farm next to Dad, so I didn't really see a place there for me. We also had something called vocational guidance at school, and when I was tested they said I had aptitude to become a teacher or doctor or engineer or whatever I might want to be, if I went on to High School. So that was the course slowly taking shape in my life, and with that in mind I began to put most of my effort into making sure I did well in the Scholarship Exam at the end of the year.

I Reflect on Life

Working our way, day by day, through our Seventh Grade year at Buranda with Mr. Howard as our teacher was like being on a journey to some far off destination that you believed would be a good place to arrive at, though you weren't sure exactly what you would find there. From the pages of our texts and in the discussions we had in class came an awakening, a discovery that was also a frustration. We were learning about life through the ideas and thoughts of some of the greatest minds the world has ever known, but the life they showed us was often a pile of contradictions.

Over and over, the topic of war kept coming up. It seemed I had heard about war all my life, but at first I was too young to understand. I remembered the newsreels of soldiers fighting in the jungle and battleships firing their cannons, and the picture of the huge mushroom cloud when the atomic bomb was dropped on Japan. But I didn't really begin to understand what war was about until I went to the Anzac Day parade, when I was in Grade 5, and saw all of the old soldiers marching, and talked to some of them. They were proud of what they'd done, but none of them wanted to do it. I began to understand that war was mankind's greatest failure.

In our Grade 7 Queensland Reader there were a lot of stories and opinions about war. I could never forget the two excerpts from John Masefield's book *Gallipoli*, the first telling of the cheering of the soldiers on the transport ships as they sailed out of Madros Bay on the day before their dreadful landing at Gallipoli. The Turks were waiting for them, and in the second excerpt Masefield describes how the Australians and New Zealanders had to fight so hard while their mates were being blown to pieces all around them, and still the soldiers sang their song of "Australia will be there." But why did they have to be there in the first place, and what did it accomplish?

A poem in our Reader says:

"They shall grow not old, as we that are left grow old:

Age shall not weary them not the years condemn."

But did it make the world a safer place? Another essay called "What is War?" answers its own question: "It may be summed up to be the combination and concentration of all the horrors, atrocities, crimes and sufferings of which human nature on this globe is capable." The writer looks forward to a time when "nation shall not lift up sword against nation, neither shall they learn war any more." And, I suppose, after the First World War the nations did try to avoid future wars by forming the League of Nations. Another essay in our Reader describes the hopes held for the League: "Wars do not just happen. They are made ... We have the alternatives before us: world anarchy, or world government leading to world peace and all that makes peace worthwhile."

But it didn't work. Mr. Howard told us the League of Nations failed, and then we got the Second World War, which started just after I was born, and it was worse than the First. After that war ended, the leaders tried again, so now we have the United Nations, but already it has shown it can't stop wars because we have Australian soldiers fighting again in Korea with the Americans and others, and who knows how that is going to end, because Communist China now looks like a big enemy, helping the North Koreans against the South. Even worse, our so-called former friend, Russia, or more properly called the Soviet Union, has befriended China, and because it has already exploded its first atomic bomb, we could end up having a Third World War with America and the Soviet Union using nuclear weapons against each other. What is a kid to think growing up in the middle of all of this war mongering?

Other pieces in our Reader show that it has always been like this, and sometimes people go to war against each other in the same country, like in

America, where the North fought against the South over the right to keep slaves. The story of John Brown tells how one man and his family tried to free slaves, but he failed, and was hung for it. Then came the awful civil war, and in our Reader we have President Lincoln's famous Gettysburg address where he says, "We here highly resolve that these dead shall not have died in vain, that this nation under God shall have a new birth of freedom, and that government of the people, by the people, for the people, shall not perish from the earth." These are fine words, and right, but it seems so hard for people to live up to them. Why is that?

Our Reader has stories of great courage like the Roman soldier, Horatius, defending the bridge almost single handed against a massive Tuscan army, and like Sydney Carton in Charles Dickens' *A Tale of Two Cities*, who goes to his death on the guillotine in France to save the life of Charles Darnay. These are great stories of the nobility of the human spirit, but they are set in times of awful treachery and bloodshed. And we have the stories of great scientists like Louis Pasteur, Sir Isaac Newton and Madame Curie, all of whom helped to make the world a better place. There were many great poems, too, like "The Rime of the Ancient Mariner" by Coleridge and "The Elegy Written in a Country Churchyard" by Thomas Gray. The words and the ideas in the poems make them among the greatest in the English language. And here we met William Shakespeare in Mark Antony's oration from *Julius Caesar*. We read this out aloud in class and saw how Antony was cleverly using words to turn the people against Brutus and Cassius, who had led the murder of Julius Caesar.

So all this we were learning: about bravery in the face of treachery, sacrifice in bloody wars, victory over evil, but evil rising again. Our teachers and those who chose what we were to study were trying to tell us something, but it wasn't always clear what it was. As we came to the end of the school year, we knew that we were growing up in difficult times, but the times before us seemed to have been worse. Could we do better than our ancestors? Could we take the great words of a Lincoln and use them to build a better world? I hoped so, as I turned 13 in 1951 and came to write my Scholarship Exam. I could not be sure about the future, but it seemed to me that we had to use our minds and imaginations to see a better world, and do everything we could to create it.

The End of the Story

And so I come to the end of my story, of a little boy growing up on a farm and finishing his Primary School in the city. It took several weeks to get my marks from the Queensland Scholarship Exam, but when they came out in the "Courier Mail" there was my name. My average was well over 80 percent, and Mum and

Dad gave me a watch as a reward. So now I am on my way to High School. I will be going to Brisbane State High School into my Sub Junior year, so I will go back from being in the highest grade in the school to the lowest. I don't know what the future holds, but if I work hard maybe I can become a doctor or teacher or engineer or any of those other professions they told me about in vocational guidance.

It has been fun going back in my memory over all the years. It's like all my family and friends are here with me now, and they will always be here, just as long as I want them to be. Maybe I didn't remember things exactly as they were, and maybe I added some things in that I wished might have happened, but on the whole I think I got the story right. I know it's not the most interesting or exciting story in the world about a boy growing up, but maybe in the future if I get married and have children and grandchildren of my own, they will like to know what it was like to grow up in my time and do the things I did.

None of us chooses when or where we are born and who our parents are. I am lucky to have wonderful and loving parents, and to be part of a family where we all care a lot about each other, even though we like to poke fun and make smart Alec remarks. Mum and Dad have always taught me to do my best, and I think I have done that, though I could probably have done better at some things if I had listened a little harder and persevered a bit more.

But life is what we make it, and it's always interesting to hear what other people are doing with their lives. We probably don't talk to each other enough about that. The hardest part is trying to understand what it was like for those who came before us. Thinking about it, I don't really know much about what it was like for Mum and Dad when they were kids, and I know nothing at all about how it was for my grandparents. The only Granny I knew was Granny Grundy and she never talked to me a lot. She has just passed away, and we are all sorry about that, especially Mum. I must find time to talk to Grandfather Grundy about his life as a kid, but he is in Toowoomba, and I am here in Brisbane, so I don't know when we will get to talk. It would be good if he wrote his story down, just like I have been trying to remember my own, then I would know what it was like for Grandfather to grow up as a boy.

All grandfathers and grandmothers grow up from little boys and girls. I think it would be good to meet those little kids, don't you?

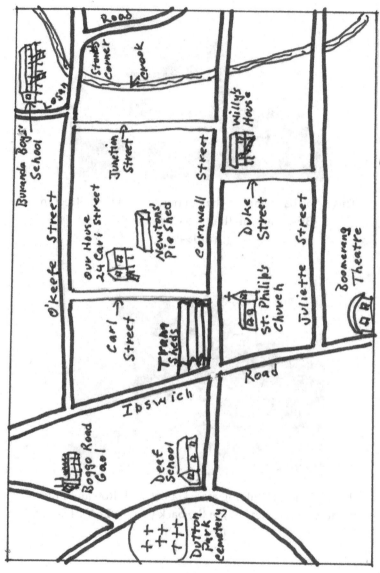

This is the back yard of the old house at 24 Carl Street in
Brisbane with the 1936 Chev ute parked.
(*circa* 1949)

I am on the left holding a cricket bat with Rob and Fred
(holding the cricket ball) in the back yard of 24 Carl Street.
(*circa* 1950)

This is our new house at 24 Carl Street in Brisbane.
(*circa* 1952)

This is Buranda School as it looks in 2010 (not much changed from Buranda Boys'
School of the 1940s) with Willy (Grant Williams) now grown up to be a Grandpa,
too, standing on what was the old parade ground and holding a copy of the school
history.

Here I am in my tennis clothes in the back yard of
24 Carl Street in Brisbane. The bird cage and
Newtons' pie shed (next door) are in the background.
(*circa* 1950)

This is the swimming pool at Buranda School as it looks in 2010,
not much changed from the pool at Buranda Boys' School in the 1940s.

That's Willy on the left with me on the farm at Athol a little older
than we were at the end of the story in the book.
(*circa* 1953)

Here I am feeding a calf on the farm at Athol.
(*circa* 1953)

The first requisite of a good citizen is that he shall be willing and able to "pull his weight"; that he shall not be a mere passenger, but shall do his share in the work that each generation finds ready to hand.

Theodore Roosevelt

O it is excellent
To have a giant's strength, but it is tyrannous
To use it like a giant.

Shakespeare

Epilogue

The Rest of the Story

No good work is ever lost; many labourers must be content to sow; others will come to reap the harvest.

Author Unknown

The avaricious man is like the barren, sandy ground of the desert, which sucks in all the rain and dews with greediness, but yields no fruitful herbs or plants for the benefit of others.

Author Unknown

In what ways does the life of the boy determine the life of the man? No one can say for sure, but I am certain the cloth is tightly woven from the first strands. The poet, William Wordsworth, wrote that we do not emerge from nothingness, or come into this world as a blank cipher, but "trailing clouds of glory do we come /from God, who is our home," bringing with us an ineffable sense of being. In this view, "the Child is father of the Man." So do I believe that whatever unconscious awareness was born into the boy in this story all those years ago, it was woven through the experiences of his early life into the garment he eventually became.

After four successful years of High School at Brisbane State High, I elected to take the teaching track among the career choices I could have followed. My health had a lot to do with it, because by the end of my Senior Year of High School my constitution was sorely beaten by recurring and severe attacks of asthma. The anxiety and pressure of study seemed to be a major contributing factor, so one year of further study at Kelvin Grove Teachers' Training College seemed a much more sensible choice than several years at University in Medicine or Engineering. As it turned out, during that one year I suffered a complete breakdown in my physical health, and for the first and only time in my life I was hospitalized with a severe asthma attack. Nevertheless, I recovered and emerged at the end of 1956 as a newly minted 18 year old Primary School teacher in the Queensland Public Service.

After two years at Upper Mt. Gravatt School in Brisbane, I was transferred to a one-teacher school at Wivenhoe on the road to Esk, about 60 miles from Brisbane. Here the country boy in me met the young teacher from the city, as I saw in the fresh young faces before me the same children I knew from my early life at Athol School more than ten years earlier. But they weren't calling me to return to the land. I knew that part of my life was gone for good. The year was 1959, I had my first car (a 1955 green four door Ford Zephyr) and I was driving 60 miles to Brisbane every Friday afternoon after school to take the dreaded French 1 at the University of Queensland every Friday evening from 6 p.m. to 9 p.m. The only reason I was doing this was because a foreign language was a required course in the Bachelor of Arts degree I had begun as an evening student two years earlier.

By the end of that year I turned 21, which was then the age of majority, and I took the time to reflect on where my life was taking me. A career in the Queensland Public Service as a teacher held out the prospect of transfer after transfer to remote locations guided by some invisible bureaucratic hand in the Department of Public Instruction. It was not an enticing proposition, so I turned away and took a position as a young High School teacher at a private boys' school in Brisbane, the Church of England Grammar School, affectionately known as

"Churchie," and not so affectionately remembered as one of the great sporting rivals from my days as a student at Brisbane State High.

Four years at Churchie saw me work my way up to the level of teaching a Senior English class. By then I was finishing up my BA at the University, after three years of English literature, and seven long years of part-time study to get the degree. It was the end of 1963. I was 25 years old. It was time for a change and a break from endless study. In January 1964 I sailed for England.

The voyage included a memorable fiasco in Naples, when I and my shipboard friend, Earle Cross, missed our ship's departure, and we were marooned on shore in the clothes we stood up in and with less than 100 Australian pounds between us. We threw ourselves on the mercy of the Sitmar Line and the British Embassy, and after a few days of enforced and mostly enjoyable holiday in Naples we made our way by train to London. A week later we went down to Southampton to meet our ship. As it came slowly into the dock, a great roar of, "There they are!" went up from the passengers lining the rails as they saw our suntanned faces among the pallid pink complexions on the dock. Needless to say, this experience cemented a strong bond of friendship between Earle and me, though our paths did not often cross after that, as he pursued his acting career, and I tried my hand in the travel business, partnered by an old friend, Bob Campbell, from Brisbane, who had travelled to London a couple of years ahead of me.

I am reminded here of the great role played in my life by friends. I have told of my early friendship with Jim in my farm days at Athol, which was replaced with my great friendship with Willy in my Primary School days at Buranda. Because Willy went to Churchie and I went to State High for High School, we did not see each other as often after that, though our friendship has endured throughout life. I should add that I eventually did begin to call him by his first name, Grant. During my High School years, religion entered my life, and I became a devout though timid Christian of the Church of England variety. This led me into the St. Philip's Church Youth Club at Thompson Estate and into a wonderful circle of friends of both sexes. Most of these I lost touch with over the years, but a special reunion in 2005 organized for my benefit brought most of us together again, and it seemed as if the years just dropped away. Sadly, my good friend, Ronnie Unwin, from those days has since passed away, but Lesleigh and Cecil Fritz are still among those I always make a point to see when I return to Brisbane. Their daughter, Andrea, my Goddaughter, also resurfaced in my life in later years as a very special person.

My journey to England in 1964 was the beginning of separation from these early friendships, as it was also separation from my family, but the bonds have always remained strong, and they pull me back repeatedly. My friend, Bob, in London in 1964 was from those St. Philip's Youth Club days. Sadly, I have since lost touch with him, though our friendship continued for many more years and into my life in Canada.

But I am getting ahead of myself. My experience with Bob in the travel business in London in 1964, though it was a gutsy undertaking, ended in my disillusionment with the business world, as far too much concerned with making money, and greatly lacking in relationships of substance. I returned briefly to the teaching world, and from January to June in 1965 I had the most enjoyable experience of my teaching career at a boys' Grammar School at Buckhurst Hill, just outside London.

After that came a whirlwind six week tour of the Continent solo in a tiny Austin minivan I had converted into a mini caravan, which I named "Caramini." France, Spain, Italy, Austria, Germany, the Netherlands and Belgium passed under the wheels of my game right hand drive little Caramini. The boyhood sense of wonder for new places, first awoken on the beaches of Redcliffe, and the pounding surf of Caloundra, and the wild bush country of Karara, saw me through the ever changing vistas of mountains, valleys, beaches and quaint villages of these foreign lands. My undergraduate knowledge of history, literature and art held me in awe in the cities and great museums of Europe, as it did in the enduring feast of experiences in the mighty city of London, and my many sojourns into sequestered corners of the British Isles.

I was also at this time trying my hand at writing, without a lot of confidence or anyone to mentor me. I had, in fact, begun to write a historical novel of convict life in the penal colonies of New South Wales when I was still in High School. I eventually abandoned that. The writing I did in London went no further, though I still have those hand written pages, and I am immodest enough to see an early talent there. However, I was not driven to make the effort to pursue a writing career, and I decided instead to return to Australia to get on with a career in Educational Administration.

In October 1965 I set sail again on another of the lugubrious Sitmar liners bound for Sydney and loaded to the gunnels with British emigrants. I was enjoying a free passage in exchange for being a Big Brother to a dozen teenage boys emigrating to Australia. After five weeks of cruising the Mediterranean, passing through the Suez Canal, and wandering aimlessly across the vast Indian Ocean, with great relief I delivered my charges suntanned and healthy to the Big Brothers' office in Sydney.

Back in Australia the nostalgia of a returning son swept over me, noticed most profoundly as we sailed into Sydney Harbour through the Heads. Immersed again in one of the world's great cities, my early boyhood relationships returned to me once more as I was taken under wing by my dear cousin, Jan, who was married to Clarrie Gluskie, an energetic GP in a working class suburb. I stayed with Jan and Clarrie while I got a new career going as an Education Officer in the Sydney headquarters of the Commonwealth Office of Education.

I fancied now that I was on track into the field of Educational Administration, out of the classroom forever, and managing the files that handled Australia's responsibilities for its various educational agreements, particularly with countries in South East Asia and Africa. I enjoyed the work and at 27 and single I was still the young Turk and ready for adventure. So when the need to fill a vacancy in the office in Adelaide turned up, I said I would go. I bought myself a 1964 Holden station wagon, and in January 1966 packed all my belongings into it, and set off for Adelaide.

I loved the easy going orderly charm of Adelaide, and in a smaller office I had more prestige as the young Education Officer from Sydney. This soon took a romantic turn, and I fell in love with Judy, one of the girls in the office. Over the years I had enjoyed many romantic attachments with girls from Brisbane to Sydney to Melbourne to London. I am a romantic at heart, and I always believed I would one day meet the right girl. I very much enjoyed female companionship, but the strict Christian ethic I had embraced from my High School days consistently guided me away from anything more than heavy duty cuddling and kissing. I was waiting for Miss Right and I finally felt that I had found her in the Office of Education in Adelaide.

Judy and I were married in Adelaide in April 1966. No longer the single young man available for regional office fill in, I was recalled by my superiors to head office in Sydney. Judy and I spent our honeymoon travelling across country in the 1964 Holden station wagon.

Ensconced in a charming little flat in fashionable Kirribilli just across the Harbour from the city, we settled into our new life. I thought I was now on a steady career track in the Australian Public Service, when quite suddenly for no particular reason I noticed an advertisement in the "Sydney Morning Herald" to come and teach in the "Land of the Big Moose," Bonnyville, Alberta, Canada. I showed it to Judy who said I should apply, just for a lark. One thought that occurred to me if I went was that I might pursue graduate study part time in the Department of Educational Administration at the University of Alberta in Edmonton. I wasn't too sure where Bonnyville was in relation to that, but I thought it wouldn't matter if I was studying by correspondence. I had seen references to this prestigious program in the files at the office. It was one of a few founded by a grant from the Kellogg Foundation in the United States to promote the study of Educational Administration as a discipline.

Still not greatly interested, however, I sent off a letter of inquiry to Bonnyville. Within a week I received a cable offering me the position of Vice-Principal and teacher at Iron River School in north eastern Alberta. It was June and near the end of the school year in Alberta, and the Superintendent was anxious to fill his quota of teachers for the School District by the start of the new school year in September.

The salary offer was good by Australian standards, but I felt they had not taken all of my teaching experience into account. They couldn't understand how someone at the age of 27 could have 10 years of experience. So I cabled them back with a counter. Within hours I had another cable offering me twice my Australian salary, which was then about $4000. I also knew from further information in the office that under an agreement among countries of the British Commonwealth of Nations I could teach in Canada for two years without paying income tax in either Canada or Australia. It was looking like too good of an offer to pass up. But I did not decide immediately. I turned instead to my network of friends for further information.

From my High School days in Brisbane, but more particularly from my teaching years at Churchie, I had a good friend, Trevor Turnbull. He had been a year behind me at State High and Teachers' College, but when we both found ourselves at Churchie in 1961 we became very good friends. Along with another teacher friend, Ian McLaren, we took a band of Churchie boys on excursions during the August holidays in 1962 to the Snowy River, and then again in 1963 to Tasmania. Those were great times.

Trevor had left teaching in 1963 to join the Commonwealth Office of Education in Brisbane. It was his experience there that had encouraged me to join the office in Sydney when I returned from England. However, by 1966 Trevor had left the office of Education to join the Department of External Affairs in Canberra. In that capacity I thought he would be able to get me some information about life and teaching in Alberta. I gave him a call and then drove up to Canberra to see him.

Trevor arranged for us to meet a couple of chaps in the Canadian High Commission. They were nice enough, but both were from Montreal, and they knew very little about Alberta. However, they gave me a book of facts, which was quite helpful. One fact that was rather intimidating was that in winter temperatures in Alberta could go below -30 degrees Fahrenheit. I had no idea what that might be like, but I thought it was likely not good. I checked it out afterwards in the freezer in a supermarket and noted that the legs of lamb were frozen stiff and solid at -30 degrees Fahrenheit.

Intimidated but not undaunted, I returned to Sydney where Judy and I made the decision to go. I think that Judy was keener than I, because she had never travelled outside Australia. I knew that I would be going back into the classroom, which I had said I would never do, but rationalized that I would also be a vice-principal and I could pursue study part-time for a Masters of Educational Administration. It was a bit of a detour on my career path, but not altogether a departure.

So I cabled my acceptance to Bonnyville, wondering what kind of a place these cables were going to. I got the confirmation and began the immigration process to work in Canada. There was no way they were going to let you in if you had any strange diseases. The next amazing thing that happened was that I got a call from Trevor in Canberra to say that he and his wife, Joy, were coming, too. This was a complete surprise to me, because he had said nothing to me in Canberra about applying. Apparently I had stirred up his interest, so he cabled them, and when they offered him and Joy two teaching positions at a place called Grand Centre they decided, like me, that the offer was too good to turn down. So now we would be a foursome on the way to the "Land of the Big Moose."

I resigned my position in the Commonwealth Office of Education and Judy and I headed for Brisbane to say good-bye, again, to my family. Dad bought my 1964 Holden wagon from me, and we packed a couple of trunks with personal belongings and shipped them off to Alberta via Vancouver. We met up with Trevor and Joy in Sydney, and the four of us jetted off in a Boeing 707 for Vancouver with short stopovers in Fiji and Honolulu. It was a wonderful trip. When we arrived in Vancouver and were admitted as landed immigrants, it was a gorgeous summer day in late August. We had a few hours to spare before catching our flight to Edmonton, so we went downtown and found our way to spectacular Stanley Park. I thought to myself then that this was a very agreeable place and I should come back to live one day. I didn't know then that it would take me 25 years to do so.

After an overnight stay in Edmonton we caught the Greyhound Bus for the three hour ride to Bonnyville. Our trunks were still somewhere at sea, so we were travelling with just our suitcases. As the bus travelled further north we found ourselves sharing it with jovial country folk speaking in heavily accented Ukrainian English, a few native Indians who didn't say much, and a couple of chickens.

It had been raining for a few days and when we arrived in Bonnyville and were met by the Acting Superintendent of Schools, he told us that the road to Iron River was impassable, so Judy and I spent a memorable night in the Bonnyville Hotel, while the Superintendent took Trevor and Joy on up the paved highway to Grand Centre.

The next day the Superintendent came back for Judy and me, and we slipped and slithered our way along the gravel road for the 30 miles north to Iron River. We found out later that the only thing further north than Iron River was the Canadian Forces Bombing Range, where they tested missiles and other such fun things.

When we got to Iron River we saw the school, a fairly large, relatively modern facility, which had been built as a centralized school to which children were bussed every day from the farms in a radius of 30 miles or so. There was no evidence of any family homes in the immediate vicinity of the school, which had been built in a farmer's field at the edge of the road. In the school yard there were a few small houses for teachers, appropriately called teacherages, and in the yard next to the school a nice looking bungalow with a big garage. That was our place, which had been rented for us fully furnished by the School Board from a local farmer. We had arrived in Iron River, Alberta on a crisp pre-fall day in late August.

That year of teaching and administration was among the heaviest of my life. It was a Grade 1-12 school, and I was teaching English and Social Studies 35 periods out of 40 a week to seven different classes, as well as doing my administrative duties. The latter consisted mainly of counselling an ambitious and rather unorthodox young school Principal and keeping him out of trouble. The kids were good country stock, and I got on well with them. The winter was colder than anything I could have imagined. One morning at -40 degrees Fahrenheit the propane in the heating tanks for the teachers gelled and would not flow. We were still all right in the farm house, because it was heated with diesel fuel. We were less fortunate when the house's septic field froze, and the sewage backed up into the basement. For the last few months of winter the septic tank had to be pumped out regularly by the School District's maintenance crew.

During that year, I found I could not pursue graduate studies part-time as I had in Queensland. This would mean resigning as a teacher and spending two summers and a winter at the University of Alberta in Edmonton. I decided I wasn't ready to do that, so I thought about advancing my career in other ways. I considered moving to Ontario, but there was no way I could get an administrative position there as a newcomer. So I applied for the position of Principal at the Elk Point Junior-Senior High School in the neighbouring County of St. Paul. I got the position as a young 28 year old, replacing the Principal who had retired after 25 years. With that under my belt Judy and I took off in the summer holidays on a 5000 mile camping tour across Canada and the United States in our red 1965 Impala sedan, with seats converted for sleeping.

It was 1967, Centennial Year in Canada, with the much heralded "Man and His World" Exposition running in Montreal. We found our way there and included a visit to the popular Aussie Pavillion with its woolen carpets and talking sheepskin chairs that told you in warm Australian tones how marvellous a place it was down under. We were there when Charles de Gaulle shafted Canada with an international insult by shouting "Vivre Quebec libre!" from the steps of the Legislature in Quebec City. Welcome to Canadian politics and the French factor!

By the time we got back to Alberta we had been to New York, Washington DC, and many US States, coming back into Alberta along the stunning "Highway to the Rising Sun" in northern Montana. I moved quickly into my role as a High School Principal surviving the local politics and essentially having a good year. I was ready to get on with my graduate work, but decided it would not be fair to the school to leave after only one year. So I signed on for a second year, and Judy and I took off on a European holiday in the summer of 1968.

During our two years at Elk Point we became good friends of the Sanders family who farmed in the Heinsburg district nearby. They were great skiers and partnered us in founding the Elk Point Ski Club on a north facing bank of the North Saskatchewan River. We never really got enough snow or local enthusiasm to make that project work, but we had great skiing holidays with the Sanders' family in the Rockies at Banff.

In the summer of 1969 we left Elk Point for Edmonton. We were still able to transport all of our belongings in one trip in our huge 1968 Ford Country Squire Station Wagon, which we had bought new the year before. We moved into an apartment near the University, and I began work on a Master's Degree in Educational Administration. I had a good scholarship in exchange for some supervision of trainee teachers, and Judy was working at the University. From this apartment we watched the Apollo moon landing on July 20, 1969. It was exciting to be part of that moment in human history.

By the spring of 1970 we both had a dose of cabin fever, and I, in particular, was feeling the call of the country. We saw another one of those "Chance of a Lifetime" advertisements in the "Edmonton Journal," and we bought a spectacular quarter section of land with a 100 acre wooded ravine on Willow Creek about 45 miles south west of the city near Calmar for $12000. This was to become our recreational and country refuge for the next 17 years.

Towards the end of my Master's Degree I decided that the program was not what I had thought it would be, and I enrolled in the PhD program in order to feel I had accomplished something. For one who had been fed up with study five years earlier, this was a significant commitment. It was also a testament to the dry prairie air that agreed with my lungs, for I never had a day's problem with asthma in Alberta. I found out on my various return trips to Brisbane in the following years that the problem for me was in the mould that lingers everywhere there to which I obviously have an allergic reaction. This has limited my stay in Brisbane for no more than ten days before I know it is time for me to get back to Canada.

I had a generous scholarship from the Killam Foundation to support me and Judy was still working at the University, so we hunkered down for the long term. We also managed to scrape together enough money from our savings to put down a deposit on a $29000 home near the University in Windsor Park. We rented out the basement to students to help pay the mortgage.

In my research work I was breaking new ground in futures studies in Educational Administration, so I felt that I was doing something significant as well advancing my knowledge. However, I had no clear career prospects at the end of my program. As I came to the end of my research and thesis writing in the summer of 1972, I was offered a one year contract with the Alberta Colleges Commission. I took it and found myself on the ground floor of helping to build the Alberta College system under the guidance of the Commission Chairman, Henry Kolesar.

However, I still had no firm career prospects after the one year, so when I heard of a position in the college system in South Australia I applied. They considered my application seriously enough to fly me to Adelaide for an interview. However, it didn't take too long into the interview process for them and me to see that I was no longer a good fit for the Australian system. I realized then that I was destined for a career somewhere in North America.

I returned to Edmonton to find that Judy had an election sign on our front lawn in support of the "NOW" campaign of the new Alberta Progressive Conservative Party. They swept the Social Credit Party out of power, which had held a stranglehold on Alberta politics for 30 years, and Peter Lougheed became the new Premier of Alberta. One of the first things the new government did was create a Department of Advanced Education and abolish the Alberta Universities Commission and the Alberta Colleges Commission. I now had several months of a contract with an entity that would no longer exist before my contract ran out.

All of the full time officers with the Commission were grandfathered into senior positions in the new Department of Advanced Education. I found myself working with the new Assistant Deputy Minister of Program Services who, ironically, was the ex Superintendent of Schools from Bonnyville, who had sent me cables six years earlier in Sydney to come and teach in the "Land of the Big Moose." I was now helping him design his new Division, but I had no clear access to any of the positions I was helping to create. I had to apply, so I threw my hat in the ring for several positions and went off with Judy to Europe to attend the wedding of our friend George Sanders in Denmark. When I got back, my contract had expired and I still had no firm offer for one of the new jobs. Eventually we worked it out, and I became the first Director of Special Programs in the Department of Advanced Education.

Looking back, the decade of the 1970s was a tumultuous time for me and my family. Judy and I had survived the turbulent 60s unscathed, but as the new decade unwound our lives changed in significant ways. Judy had a quick trip back to Adelaide to see her mother, who had undergone an operation for cancer. I received my PhD and joined the Alberta government in a mid-level administrative position. We bought a recreational property and a home. With all of that behind us we decided to start a family. This was a big decision for me because my futures research and reading were telling me that the human experiment on the planet was facing a critical turning point, as the pressures of civilization had begun to overwhelm the earth's ecosystems. Bringing children into such a world needed to be thoughtfully considered, as it was certain that a lot of the future difficulties would play out in their lifetimes. In the end our decision was that these problems could only be addressed successfully by the new generations themselves, so we would contribute by bringing our own special children into the world.

Our first beautiful daughter, Sarah, was born on December 13, 1973. What a joy and delight she was, as, indeed, were her sisters, Katie and Charlotte, equally beautiful, who followed quickly on December 20, 1975 and November 18, 1977. They were quite a trio, who kept their proud parents fully engaged every minute of the day. We had a trip to Australia in 1974 when Sarah was just over a year old. Ross and Agnes Sanders and their daughter, Charlotte, came along. We visited Judy's family and home turf in South Australia, then Ayers Rock and my sister, Gloria, and her family in North Queensland, then on to the rest of my family in Brisbane.

Dad had earlier undergone a serious operation for stomach cancer and was only a shadow of his former self, but nevertheless, he and Mum came to visit us in Edmonton in 1977. In 1976 we had bought a historic house in Edmonton in Old Strathcona called the Sheppard House as a rather rundown rooming house; then in 1978 with our third child now with us we made another big decision to renovate and restore it and move in ourselves. This was going to be an ongoing project for the next decade. As if that were not enough change to contend with, at about the same time I was promoted to Assistant Deputy Minister of Program Services and in that capacity I went to China in 1979 as part of a Canadian delegation to negotiate an educational agreement between the two countries. That was the 1970s.

My work as Assistant Deputy Minister was quite demanding and Judy bore a lot of the responsibility for bringing up the girls, but I participated as much as I could. We had a lot of happy times in our big old home, which I hoped would form a special part of my girls' memories, just as the farm at Athol had been for me. I had several trips to Paris over the next few years as part of the Canadian delegation to UNESCO. On the last one of them in 1985 I led our delegation, and we sponsored into the conference a resolution on "The Right to Learn," which later became part of a landmark United Nations Convention on the "Rights of the Child." I learned from this the wisdom of moving ahead on something you considered to be important, even if you couldn't see where it might lead.

Dad passed away suddenly in 1981, and I had a sad trip back to Brisbane for his funeral. Judy later took the girls on a trip to Australia on her own while I was caught up in business. We had some good holidays together as a family, but not as many as we should have. On weekends we spent a lot of time on the farm, where I had established a huge garden and then later began building a substantial country cottage, working only from rough plans in a book, and assisted by a neighbour's 15 year old son.

By the mid 80s we had built up a substantial real estate portfolio as we had bought both duplexes on either side of the Sheppard House and ran them as rental properties to cover the mortgages. My idea was to one day demolish them and restore the Sheppard House to its former glory, with its original yard and gardens. This made no economic sense, but it was a grand vision. We had the Sheppard House designated as a historic site so that it would be protected into the future.

Life completed a circle for Judy and me in 1986 when we went to our second Canadian World's Fair and Exposition, this time in Vancouver, called Expo 86. I had special VIP passes and the girls had a great time visiting the pavillions while avoiding the long line ups. It was a good holiday, but it was also the beginning of an ending.

Sadly, around that time things began to unravel for Judy and me in our married life. Relationships had been strained for a couple of years previously. We tried to work them out, but could not do it, and in 1987 we separated and divorced. Judy received all of the property except for one duplex where I camped out in one of the units. Most importantly we received joint custody of the children, and I did all that I could to continue to be part of the girls' lives, who by now were 14, 12 and 10. This marriage breakdown was a great blow to me, as I did not think that could ever happen to us.

At the same time my professional life was undergoing a comparable upheaval. Henry Kolesar had retired from the post of Deputy Minister and I was appointed Acting Deputy and was in the running for the job. But times had changed from the early days of the Department when educational professionals were running things. The government wanted a finance person at the helm, so I did not get the job. For me a lot of the spark had gone out of the work, for all of my original colleagues had gone on to other things. It was time for me to go as well. The Deputy and I worked things out, and I departed with a year's salary as separation. I worked for a time out of my home as a consultant, but a much different future was beginning to take shape for me.

In November 1986 a mutual friend had arranged a meeting between me and Geraldine Schwartz, a psychologist from British Columbia, who had come to Alberta to meet people of position and influence, who might work with her to promote ideas about how prospects for the future might be enhanced by raising the quality of thinking of decision makers. Gerri was a lively, vivacious personality, and when we realized that our ways of thinking were similar, we decided to work together to create a forum for decision makers in Edmonton in 1987 called the Alberta Catalyst Forum. This resulted in a core group of people who continued to meet afterwards to discuss and implement ideas presented at the workshop.

When it became obvious that my marriage to Judy was ending, Gerri and I allowed a romantic relationship to develop. She was five years divorced with a son and daughter in Vancouver, and she was very wary of entrusting her heart in a new relationship. When my life in Edmonton ceased to have its former meaning, I saw clearly how a new life with Gerri could open up for both of us. We soon fell deeply in love and in December 1988 I moved to Vancouver to be with her. We created a new company called Creative Learning International as a learning corporation to focus on leadership and the creative management of change. Gerri was already operating her busy psychological practice called the Vancouver Learning Centre in which she was having spectacular success in changing the lives of children and youth with learning challenges.

On August 3, 1989 Gerri and I were married in a memorable Jewish-Christian-secular wedding. The ceremony was held in the Beach House (now the Fish House) restaurant in Stanley Park. It was officiated over by a Jewish Rabbi (Gerri's friend, Rabbi Nathan, from California), an Anglican Minister (my friend, Rod Adamson, from Edmonton) and a Justice of the Peace (because neither Rabbi Nathan nor Rod had jurisdiction to conduct marriages in British Columbia). At the age of 50 I was marrying a partner of the heart with whom I shared a deep and abiding mutual love. My first favourable impressions from 1966 of Stanley Park and of Vancouver as being a nice place to live had now become my new reality in a way I could never have imagined. Trevor stood beside me as my best man and Sarah and Charlotte participated with Gerri's children, Steve and Judy, in holding the Huppah under which we were married.

Since that day, now over 21 years ago, time has flown swiftly and joyously for Gerri and me. We succeeded in our early dreams by hosting two major creative thinking conferences called "A Masters Course for Creative Thinkers" in 1989 and 1990. These were successfully staged at significant financial risk and we opened up brand new offices for our two companies in the Maingate Building at the entrance to Granville Island in Vancouver.

Over the next two years we conducted smaller events as I also wrote and published my first novel, *The Visioneers: A Courage Story about Belief in the Future*. With this I had come back to my early love of writing that I had abandoned over 25 years earlier. The book created a lot of interest and subsequent spin offs, including an international newsletter called "The Visioneer" and two international workshops in Israel. We secured important teaching contracts with various organizations including the Canadian Centre for Management Development, the major training agency for senior level executives in the federal civil service. We also created a leadership forum called "The Quest for Champions." All this time Gerri was continuing to run the Vancouver Learning Centre. She had a skill and talent for this work that we felt should not be abandoned, though it restrained what we could do in the other business.

We made two trips to Australia in which I proudly showed off my new Canadian wife. Gerri was always a hit with everyone. The second trip was for

Mum's 80th birthday in 1993. Sadly before she could join us for our fifth wedding anniversary in 1994 she suffered a stroke and passed away in February 1999. I made another sad return to Brisbane to attend her funeral.

In 1997 we bought space in the brand new Galleria Building on the corner of First Avenue and Fir Street in Vancouver and moved our offices there. At this time we shifted our corporate focus in Creative Learning International to ethical leadership and created the Institute for Ethical Leadership. We operated the Institute as a non-profit arm of Creative Learning International and over the next seven years we hosted monthly meetings and several conferences around the themes of stewardship and the environment, business and sustainability, health and wellness, youth and education, and relationships and personal development. Our emphasis was reflecting our conviction that only by shifting the thinking of decision makers in the direction of ethical relationships could society hope to deal successfully with the problems facing the collective human future on the planet. We touched many lives throughout those years, which undoubtedly have had an impact in ways we cannot know.

On the personal side we saw all of our five children happily married and raising families from the early 1990s to the present day. We now have eleven grandchildren with maybe more to come. Next to our own relationship they are the greatest joy in our lives. We moved in 2001 from our sweet little penthouse condominium at 2125 York Avenue in Kitsilano, which had been Gerri's home when I first met her, and which I fondly regarded as our love nest. We moved fifteen blocks up the hill to our present lovely home at 2125 West 15th Avenue. Here Gerri has created a comfortable and peaceful space inside, and I have called on my boyhood farming skills to craft a productive vegetable garden out the back and a lovely landscaped flower garden in the front.

Back to business. In 2006 we launched a partnership with Royal Roads University in Victoria to create a permanent teaching and research centre for ethical leadership. Subsequently that initiative did not work out for us, so we brought our intellectual property back into Creative Learning International and secured a multi year contract with the real estate boards of Greater Vancouver and the Fraser Valley to enhance ethical practice in the real estate industry. This has been quite successful using a Facilitator train-the-trainer model and the work is ongoing. It is primed for delivery to other professions and organizations, but at the present our energies must be directed to another important endeavour.

We have realized that Gerri's work through the Vancouver Learning Centre is the most important legacy she can leave. To do this requires that it be transitioned into a new business model with leadership from the teaching side supported through the work of several psychologists, whom Gerri will have to train to provide the unique neuropsychological lens that has proved so effective throughout the past 30 years. Related to this is the creation of a Legacy Fund at the Vancouver Foundation in the name of the International Foundation of Learning, a non-profit organization Gerri founded in 1983. This fund will support an annual seminar to foster the research and practice that has been central to the success of the Vancouver Learning Centre. All of this is a big undertaking, which both of us are engaged in as we each enter our eighth decade.

On the literary side, I have published two other novels, *The Christmas Wish* and *Antale: An Allegory of a World Reborn,* both of which I believe stand up well as skillfully crafted works of fiction. Gerri published some of her own story and poetry as well as her uniquely reflective feminine wisdom in *Journeys of Second Adulthood: A Woman's Search for Higher Ground.* Together we published *The Ethical Leadership Scales,* which contain three instruments for measuring ethical competence and leadership in individuals and organizations along with a number of our most important essays on ethical leadership and related subjects. We use this book as an adjunct to our teaching work and it is our most financially successful publishing effort.

So the years close in around us. Sadly, they have already claimed several dear to me. My brother, Gordon, passed in 2006 when I had another sad journey back for that. Quite suddenly my old friend, Trevor, took ill in 2009 while on a return trip to Brisbane and he is now buried there. Others are battling illnesses. Fortunately, both Gerri and I are in good health. I work at keeping myself in shape, encouraged by my daughter, Sarah, who works as a Fitness Coach in North Vancouver. My elder sister, Gloria, is married to Colin McCabe and living in Dinmore near Ipswich, and my younger sister, Val, whose hearing disability led us all those years ago to live in Brisbane, has her own apartment in West End in Brisbane. In March of this year (2010) we were able once more to visit Australia and saw all of them again, as well as many others who have appeared in this story of the boy who grew up to be Grandpa in Canada. Especially pleasant was the time we were able to spend with my old friend from this story, Grant Williams (Willy) and his wife, Wendy. We had great fun reading together parts of the manuscript of the story. It seemed just like yesterday that we were riding our bikes around the streets of Brisbane with Rex and Jim on the back.

Just before we left for Australia Gerri and I enjoyed the opportunity of experiencing in our own city of Vancouver another great world class event to match Expo 67 in Montreal and Expo 86 in Vancouver, which I had enjoyed visiting in my previous life. The Winter Olympics came to Vancouver in 2010 and the city was alive with the energy of again welcoming the world. It is a good note on which to close my story.

The main reason for writing this book was the expectation that in the years to come some may read it and say, "So that's what it was like when Grandpa [or Great Grandpa or even more Greats] was a boy. So that's how he came from Australia to Canada. So that's what he did with his life." I believe that children,

GROWING UP GRANDPA

in particular, want to know these things, so I hope I have left them something to appreciate. For my own part, I find it intriguing to think of the 13 year old boy at the end of his Primary School years looking out into the future and wondering what he would become. Now the man as Grandpa can look back and tell him. Would the boy be satisfied? I hope so. Certainly not all dreams were realized and many mistakes made and opportunities lost. But who is to say the life was any the poorer for that?

There are grand themes that thread through our culture and literature about concepts of destiny and divine guidance. As I look back on my life, I am inclined to believe that such a guiding hand was, indeed, at work, and that the twists and turns in my life were meant to bring me to where I now am. The point, of course, is how to use the opportunities that life provides, not necessarily to achieve fame, fortune or prominence, but to try to do one's best and what is right in the circumstances.

One is supposed to attain wisdom in later years. I am not sure I can lay claim to such achievement, but such that I have I am content to share with those who will listen to me. Have I discovered the secret of life? Not really, though in my younger days I might have thought I had. Certainly I have shifted from the strong Christian religious convictions I held throughout my teenage years and young manhood. My life with Gerri and learning to appreciate her Jewish traditions has given me a wider perspective on the Judaic-Christian religious structure. Though I respect sincerely the beauty and integrity of those traditions, they no longer define for me the meaning of our human presence on this planet.

I don't believe the world's great religions have yet sufficiently integrated into their articles of faith the vast quantity of knowledge produced over the last few hundred years by science. An intelligent, well-read human being in the 21st century does not look at the world in the same way as those who lived their lives without this knowledge, and who relied on the revealed truth of ancient prophets for understanding the meaning of their lives. Knowledge of how the universe emerged in a great cosmic event, popularly known as the Big Bang, some 14 or so billion years ago, displaces the Biblical creation myths. Understanding the role played since then by evolution, first of the stars and galaxies, then of biological life on our own tiny planet, gives us an appreciation of the origin and interconnectedness of all things that our ancestors could never have known.

Unfortunately, our cultural traditions and individual frames of consciousness have not yet led us to an understanding of how to live well together on a finite planet. This is a work in progress. Hopefully, those who follow us will be able to make the transition in consciousness rapidly enough to ensure a viable future for life.

The period of time embraced by my lifetime, from the early awakenings to reality of that little farm boy growing up in Australia in the 1940s, to the Grandpa

351

writing this account at the end of the first decade of the 21st century—that period of time has seen some of the most prodigious changes in the history of the world. With the breakthrough into something close to intelligent technology in the last decades of the 20th century has come an ever increasing acceleration in the rate of change. Those of us alive today can have but the most flimsy awareness of what is to come, and even then we will probably be wrong.

With the world changing tragedy in New York on September 11, 2001 a cloak of fear has enveloped the globe, fear that life everywhere can be held ransom to the radical beliefs and anger of people we now call terrorists. This is an equivalent though different fear from what spread out from the mushroom clouds of Hiroshima and Nagasaki when I was a boy. The world has lived with that nuclear fear ever since, and now it is compounded by the fear that terrorists or rogue regimes may one day use that terrible power for their own ends. Added to that we now have the fear that comes with knowledge of what humanity has done and continues to do to destroy the viability of our planetary home. And all the while hanging over us is the threat of overpopulation and the knowledge that already billions of people live under privations that should not be accepted as tolerable on any measure of ethical standards. These are the realities now facing us as a global community of peoples.

In contrast to the gloom that such awareness must surely generate among those who care, there are others, and I count myself among them, who think that a shift is now occurring in the collective consciousness of humanity. The Jesuit theologian and philosopher, Teilhard de Chardin, spoke of the noosphere in which we are all psychically connected. There are prophecies from the ancient Maya civilization and from indigenous peoples that suggest the noosphere is undergoing a shift, and that we are in the end years of the old ways, and on the threshold of a breakthrough to new ways of thinking and living. The change that this suggests will not be easy as it implies breakdown as well as breakthrough, and both entail more change than anyone would probably like to see.

So what does one hold fast to in the face of all of this, of ever increasing secular knowledge and its displacement of earlier faith traditions? My own conclusion, which is the "wisdom" I now give to my children and grandchildren, is to allow oneself to be engulfed by a profound sense of awe of everything that is—from the vastness of the cosmos to the minutiae of the living cell, from the majestic splendour of mountains and oceans to the incomprehensibly intricate workings of the human brain, from the beauty of a morning sunrise or an evening sunset to the smile on a loved one's face and the warmth of the human heart. As we allow ourselves the joy of embracing these experiences, so will our minds move to a sense of wonder of how it all came to be in such exquisite precision, and how it continues to flow inexorably through time. When we allow ourselves to dwell in such contemplation, then shall we find a sense of the divine, which is all we need to know to discover meaning in life.

With that discovery we know then how we must live: to give our lives in service to others, to let go of anything that hardens our hearts, to embrace all the wisdom traditions about compassion, to seek to live in harmony with the natural world, and to find our happiness in the happiness and well-being of all of life. As the great Jewish Rabbi Hillel said 2000 years ago: "What is hateful to yourself, do not to your fellow man [he might have extended that idea to fellow creatures]. That is the whole of the Torah and the remainder is but commentary."

We have much commentary engulfing us every moment of the day. The most important thing for us to do is to cut through it to the essence of living the good life. We all need to try harder to do that, every moment of the day.

With that I close my own commentary on the life I have known so far. If you have found some parts of it enjoyable to read and even touching to know, then a large part of my purpose in writing it has been achieved. Whatever the years to come might bring for me, and I hope they will be many to enjoy the love of those who are now around me, I can say now that I am content to be where I am and to continue on the journey from here.

Desmond Berghofer
December 2010
Vancouver

What a piece of work is a man! how noble in reason! how infinite in faculties! in form and moving how express and admirable! in action how like an angel! in apprehension how like a god! the beauty of the world! the paragon of animals! and yet to me what is this quintessence of dust?

(Hamlet) Shakespeare

There is a tide in the affairs of men
Which, taken at the flood, leads on to fortune;
Omitted, all the voyage of their life
Is bound in shallows and in miseries.

Shakespeare

Five great enemies of peace inhabit with us—avarice, ambition, envy, anger, and pride; if these were to be banished, we should infallibly enjoy perpetual peace.

Petrarch

Glossary

What follows is an explanation of words, expressions, terms and names used in the text that might not be familiar to some readers removed in time and/or place from the events described. Hopefully, this will help.

Aggies   Another name for marbles, as in the game of marbles.

Alley   A china marble.

(The) Ashes   The Test cricket series played between England and Australia.

Banshee   Spirit of death, often appearing as an ugly woman.

Bashing (someone up)   Beating someone, hurting severely.

Beaut   Short for beautiful, usually means great or good.

Billy   A small can with a handle for carrying liquids like tea or milk.

Biro   Brand name for an early ballpoint pen.

(In a) Bit of a pickle   In some difficulty.

Bitumen   The surface on a paved road, asphalt.

Bloke   A man.

Bloody   A common Australian swear word used to give emphasis.

Blow fly   A large fly that "blows" meat by laying eggs that hatch into maggots.

Bob   Slang for a shilling, an amount of money equivalent to ten cents.

Bob's your uncle   And there you have it; you're all set.

Bonnet   The cover for the engine of a car; called the hood in North America.

Bonzer   Good, beautiful, great.

Boot   The luggage compartment of a car; called the trunk in North America.

Bottleo   A man who collects empty bottles for cash.

Bucket of bolts   Derogatory term for a car that is not in good condition.

Buckley's chance   No chance at all. Buckley was an escaped convict who tried to get back to England by walking across Australia.

Bugger   A swear word used derogatively to be critical of someone.

Bunger   A large fire cracker.

Buster   A fall, usually off a horse.

Caterwauling   A howling or wailing noise.

Chooks   Hens, fowls, poultry.

Cobber   A friend or mate.

Cogswoddle   A lot of nonsense.

Collar   To grab hold of.

Coot   Derogatory term for a man.

Copped   Being hit or getting into trouble.

Corroboree   A ceremonial meeting of Australian Aborigines.

Corrugated iron   A structural iron sheet, usually galvanized, and shaped in furrows for rigidity.

Cove   A man.

Crikey   Exclamation of surprise.

Crook   Slang term meaning something is bad, not good. It can also be used to mean you are not feeling well.

Cuts   Hits on the hand from a cane.

Dead cert   Absolutely guaranteed.

Decked out   Dressed up.

Dibs   Marbles (in the game of marbles).

Dickhead   A stupid, ridiculous or irritating person, particularly a man.

Digger   Australian soldier.

Dilly bag   A bag with a draw string, originally an Aboriginal bag.

Dinkum   True, the real thing.

Dipper   A container (usually enamel) with a handle used for carrying water.

Don Bradman   Famous Australian batsman in cricket.

Draught horse   A large strong horse used for pulling heavy loads in a dray or wagon.

Draw the line   Make a limit.

Drongo   A stupid or dim-witted person.

Drover   A person who goes droving.

Droving   Moving livestock over a distance by walking them.

(A) Duck (in cricket)   Zero, no runs or score.

Dunny   A lavatory, toilet.

Echidna   Spiny anteater, egg laying mammal found in Australia.

Egged on   Encouraged.

Ekka   The Brisbane Exhibition or Agricultural Show.

Fair dinkum   Absolutely true

Fair go   An equal chance or opportunity.

Fibro   Building material made of compressed fibres.

Flash   Smart looking.

Frankfurter   A seasoned sausage, a hot dog.

Frank Sedgman   Australian tennis champion of the 1950s.

Gaol   Prison (same pronunciation as "jail").

Give the glass eye   Staring with hostility or anger.

Grog   Booze or hard liquor.

Guy   Stuffed figure put on a bonfire (named for Guy Fawkes).

Hanky   Handkerchief.

Have (give it) a go   Give it a try.

Heifer in heat   A young cow exhibiting sexually receptive behaviour.

Hood (of a car)   The top of the cabin where the driver and passengers sit.

Hullabaloo   An uproar or fuss.

Humdinger   Something that is exceptionally good.

Isn't a patch   Nowhere near as good.

Jackarooo   Australian term for a stockman, roughly equivalent to a cowboy.

Jackie Howe   A navy blue singlet or sleeveless undershirt, named after legendary Australian sheep shearer.

Jiggered   Worn out, exhausted.

Knackers   A man's or boy's private parts.

Knuckling down   Shooting marbles.

Lamington   A small cake, made from joining two sponge cakes with jam, cutting into cubes, icing each one on all sides with chocolate icing and sprinkling with cocoanut.

Larrikin   Slang term for a person given to comical or outlandish behaviour.

Lashings   A lot.

Loafer   Lazy person.

Lollies   Sweets or candies.

Loony   A deranged individual.

Metho   Derogatory term for a drunk inferring he has been drinking methylated spirits, which is almost raw alcohol.

Mickey bird   Common name for noisy minor; a small, bluish grey bird that makes a lot of noise in the Australian bush.

Mincer   A device, screwed onto the edge of a table or bench used to grind meat by turning a handle.

Nincompoop   A stupid person.

'Ow yer goin'?   Literally "How are you going?" meaning "How are you ?"; a common greeting.

Pee wee   A black and white bird, similar to but smaller than the magpie.

Petrol   Gasoline.

Pickaninny   A black child (potentially offensive term, but not intended as such as used in the text).

Pikelets   Small pancakes.

Piss off   Offensive exclamation meaning to go away quickly.

Play the toff   Act superior.

Prickly pear   A type of cactus.

 (Like) Pulling hens' teeth   Very slow or impossible.

Pulling your leg   Telling you a tall story.

Put a sock in it   A slang term meaning to stop talking or singing or shouting.

Put in the boot   Slang term for fighting aggressively.

Quarrion   A cockatiel, small parrot-like bird.

Quid   Slang for former Australian pound, now worth two dollars.

(A) Relly   Slang for a relative.

Rosella parrot   A brilliant crimson coloured small parrot.

(A) run (in cricket)   A score of one, made by running from one end of the cricket pitch to the other.

Sav (Saveloy)   A seasoned sausage made mainly of pork, fatter than a frankfurter.

Scare the daylights out of   Frighten a great deal.

Scarifier   In this context, a piece of machinery pulled behind a tractor for cultivating and weeding a paddock or field.

Scrounge   To get something by foraging or borrowing.

Shandy   A mixed drink, usually beer mixed with lemonade or ginger ale.

Shanghai   A slingshot.

Shout (with money)   Buy something for others.

Silly mid off   A fielding position in cricket close to the batsman on the off side.

Skin your eyes   Keep a sharp lookout.

Skittish   Restlessly active or nervous.

Slips   A position on the cricket field just behind the batsman on the off side.

Smart Alec   Someone who makes cutting remarks.

Smoko   A break for refreshments.

Spalpeen   Slang for scamp or rascal.

Spiffy   Looking smart or dressed up.

Spoil sport   Someone who ruins things; spoils a situation.

Springer   A cow that is about to give birth to a calf.

Spruiced up   Dressed up, looking good.

Square leg   A position on the cricket field on the on side approximately at right angles to the batsman.

Strainer post   A larger, stronger post in a wire fence used for tightening the wires; taking the strain.

Streak of greased lightning   Slang for moving very quickly.

Struth   Exclamation of surprise.

Sugar bag   Small sack made of hessian (jute) for carrying raw sugar.

Take a pull   Stop what you are doing.

Taw   A shooting marble.

Torch   Flashlight with batteries.

Tucker   Food.

Tuck in   Begin to eat.

Twerp   A derogatory term meaning a silly person.

Wet behind the ears   New to a situation, inexperienced.

Whip the pants off   Defeat someone very soundly.

Winded   Exhausted.

Wireless   Radio.

Yob   An uncouth individual or thug.

Printed in the United States
By Bookmasters